The Joan Palevsky Imprint in Classical Literature

In honor of beloved Virgil—

"O degli altri poeti onore e lume . . ."

—Dante, *Inferno*

HELLENISTIC CULTURE AND SOCIETY
General Editors: Anthony W. Bulloch, Erich S. Gruen, A. A. Long, and
Andrew F. Stewart

The Argonautika

The Argonautika

*The Story of Jason
and the Quest for the Golden Fleece*

by Apollonios Rhodios

TRANSLATED, WITH
INTRODUCTION AND GLOSSARY BY

Peter Green

UNIVERSITY OF CALIFORNIA PRESS

Berkeley   Los Angeles   London

University of California Press
Berkeley and Los Angeles, California

University of California Press, Ltd.
London, England

Library of Congress Cataloging-in-Publication Data

Apollonius Rhodius.
    [Argonautica. English]
    The Argonautika : the story of Jason and the quest for the golden fleece / by Apollonios
Rhodios ; translated, with introduction and glossary, by Peter Green.
      p. cm.
    Includes bibliographical references and index.
    ISBN 0-520-07687-7 (pbk. : alk. paper)
    1. Epic poetry, Greek—Translations into English.   2. Argonauts (Greek mythology)—
Poetry. 3. Jason (Greek mythology)—Poetry. 4. Medea (Greek mythology)—Poetry.
I. Green, Peter, 1924– . II. Title.
PA3872.E5   1997b
883'01—dc20
                              96-24773
                               CIP

Printed in the United States of America
9 8 7 6 5 4 3 2 1

To C. M. C. G.
amicae, uxori, collegae

CONTENTS

MAPS

PREFACE AND ACKNOWLEDGMENTS

Like most of my books, this one has taken far too long in the making. I began the translation in 1988, in the comfortable and benignly user-friendly environment provided by the library of the American School of Classical Studies in Athens. The first draft was completed by 1991 and has undergone several major revisions since. I did not start work on the commentary until 1992, using the interim period to absorb a large amount of the remarkably prolific scholarship on Apollonios published—after a long period of drought—during the past two decades, springing up (as Virginia Knight recently observed) as thickly as Jason's Sown Men from the ploughland of Kolchis. Thus translation and commentary assumed, to a surprising extent, quite separate characters in my mind, so that the problems I explored in my notes kept modifying earlier assumptions made while turning Apollonios's difficult Greek into English. The Glossary, not begun until the original version of my commentary was complete, emerged as a far more complex and lengthy undertaking than I had ever envisaged: in addition, it too shed fresh light on aspects of the Argonaut legend, not least by forcing me to recognize the interwoven, not to say ingrown, mythical family associations of Apollonios's heroic-age characters. "Only connect" was the phrase that kept recurring to me: two generations of epic nobility in which almost everyone, Jason not least, could claim kinship (by blood or marriage) to everyone else. Thus the quest for the Fleece began to take on some of the aspects of a family affair.

This take on the genealogical side of Greek myth was given a further boost by research I was carrying out, some two years ago, for an article with the tell-tale title "'These fragments have I shored against my ruins': Apollonios Rhodios and the Social Revaluation of Myth for a New Age." I found myself tracing, inter alia, the *Rezeptionsgeschichte* of myth-as-history, or historicized myth, from Homer to the Hellenistic era, with sometimes surprising results. One fact that emerged with quite startling clarity from this was the existence of a deep-rooted and well-nigh universal faith in the *actuality* of mythic narrative. These things, the Greeks were convinced, really *happened,* and such phenomena as allegory or historicist rationalization were simply devices exploited, as knowledge grew, to justify (or, failing that, explain away) the more embarrassingly archaic and outré features of traditional legend. I found a marvelous reductio ad absurdum of the rationalizing trend in Dionysios Skytobrachion's version of the Argonaut legend, epitomized at considerable length by Diodoros Siculus. This leached out the myth's entire magical or supernatural substructure—no fire-breathing bulls, no Clashing Rocks—and turned Medeia herself from a powerful virgin sorceress into a progressive rationalist do-gooder, not unlike Shaw's Major Barbara, with useful additional expertise in herbal and homoeopathic medicine. By contrast, Apollonios began to look, for the mid third century, quite remarkably old-fashioned.

Here was something with an unexpected ripple effect. The more I studied text and context, the less Alexandrian Apollonios looked, the more a courageous (or antediluvian, according to one's attitude) throwback to the archaic worldview enshrined in literature from Homer to Pindar. Yes, he had the self-conscious irony inevitable in a highly literate scholar-poet overaware of his literary heritage; yes, he had the characteristic Alexandrian preoccupation with roots, perhaps exacerbated by that *déraciné* sense peculiar to the rootless immigrant population of a new megalopolis such as Alexandria. But it became all too easy to see how the traditional conflict between Apollonios and Kallimachos may well have had a solid basis in fact. This was something I had long suspected, but which for a generation of scholarship has been regularly dismissed with scorn as a typical piece of romantic fiction, cooked up by scholiasts and commentators to fill a gap in our biographical knowledge. Once again I found myself forced, reluctantly (no, this is not ironic), into the too familiar role of odd man out. I argue the case in detail in my Introduction and various notes; here I mention it only as a factor contributing to the piecemeal development, in separate stages, of what I still find it hard to think of as a unified text. Among other things, the completion of my article on the revaluation of myth substantially modified my earlier thinking on Apollonios's place in that tradition and made my Introduction (the last part of the book to be written) a very different statement from what it otherwise might have been.

All this, as I say, has taken a great deal of time, far longer than either I or my publishers originally envisaged. On the other hand, the delay has been immensely beneficial, not only for the radical rethinking that was, in a busy academic life, its main (though very far from its sole) cause, but also because it enabled me to take into account several admirable works that would otherwise have been denied me. I am thinking in particular of Malcolm Campbell's exhaustive commentary on the first 471 lines of book 3 of the *Argonautika,* David Braund's unique study of ancient Kolchis, and Virginia Knight's careful and sensitive analysis of Apollonios's subtler-than-Poundian echoes and exploitations of the Homeric texts, which he and his audience knew, in some cases literally, by heart. The cumulative debt that I owe to these and many other scholars in a newly resurgent area of research should be abundantly apparent from translation and commentary alike.

At the same time I should, perhaps, also signal the conscious limitations of this book (the unconscious ones will all too soon be brought home to me by critics). Since it is, as a translation, aimed primarily (though not exclusively) at those with no knowledge of Greek, it is neither, in the technical sense, a critical edition, nor indeed (since it largely omits linguistic, syntactical, and grammatical discussion) a full commentary either. But it does, quite deliberately, study the historical, cultural, geographical, and literary background in far greater detail than is usual in a translation, grappling in the notes with a considerable number of textual problems that will only be of concern to those with some experience in classical Greek. The reason for this is simple: the only available commentary *on all four books* of the *Argonautika* is the outdated text of Mooney (1912), which was fundamentally inadequate even when written. Book 3 has always received far more attention than the rest, and students now have Hunter's 1989 edition conveniently available in paperback. But for the rest, in English, there is nothing. I have tried to fill that yawning gap at least partially, conscious that in order to understand Apollonios—and, more important, although the practice is academically often regarded as frivolous, to *enjoy* him—it is essential to treat his poem as a unity, and never, amid the details of piecemeal interpretation, to forget this.

Critics will not be slow to point out that I have failed to present the reader with an overall literary interpretation of the poem, preferably in the structural or poststructural mode of analysis now current. This is not for lack of studying recent attempts in this genre, and the attentive reader combing my notes will readily discern how much I have learned, mostly on points of detail, from scholars such as Bing, Cameron, Clauss, DeForest, Dräger, Fusillo, Goldhill, Hunter, Hurst, Segal, and Zanker, even when I disagree with them. But I could not but notice how their, and other, patterns differed so markedly from one another as to call the whole method into question (I had already come to much the same conclusion about the competing theories of ring-composition in Ovid). In particular, the lack of adequate scholarly controls over such speculation must always arouse suspicion. Thus since this book was designed in the first place as a handbook to further basic understanding, I decided that such exercises of the imagination, however scholarly, had no place in it; and a healthy respect for Occam's Law kept me, wisely I feel, from venturing yet another version myself. Again, the nature of my undertaking meant that many studies that I admire greatly for their insights, and from which I have learned much, nevertheless did not find a logical place here: among these I would like to single out, *honoris causa,* Mary Williams's percipient and highly original monograph on Apollonios's use of landscape.

Working on the *Argonautika* has been for me very much a labor of love. At the age of seven I first encountered, and was fascinated by, the quest for the Golden Fleece in that brilliant volume by Andrew Lang, *Tales of Troy and Greece,* never yet surpassed as a retelling of ancient myth for young people.[1] Years later, reading Boswell's *Life of Johnson,* I came across this passage:

> "And yet, (said I) people go through the world very well, and carry on the business of life to good advantage, without learning." Johnson: "Why, Sir, that may be true in cases where learning cannot possibly be of any use; for instance, this boy rows us as well without learning, as if he could sing the song of Orpheus to the Argonauts, who were the first sailors." He then called to the boy, "What would you give, my lad, to know about the Argonauts?" "Sir, (said the boy) I would give what I have."

The boy's words, then and even today, struck an emotional chord that hit me directly and physically, just as a certain high-frequency note drawn from a violin will shatter a wineglass. In one sense I have been giving what I have in pursuit of those bright, elusive, infinitely rewarding Sirens ever since. The anecdote seems to me the best justification ever put forward for a truly humane education.

This is, I know, quite hopelessly old-fashioned and romantic. Robert Graves somewhere recalls his dismay at the reply he got from an earnest student of English literature when he asked her what she enjoyed about Shakespeare's (I think) work. "I don't read to *enjoy,*" she said, in withering reproof, "I read to *evaluate.*" The absence of genuine pleasure is what makes too much literary criticism today an aridly sterile desert. Despite this I still retain my deep instinctive responses to great art and literature, though a quarter of a century's exposure to American academic critical trends has come as near to killing such reactions in me as anything could do. In that sense the present work may count as an act of calculated defiance, as well as an invitation to relish one of the Hellenic world's oldest and most deeply resonant myths, told by a master of his craft, who loved the sea, and ships, and the complexities of human nature, and let that passion irradiate everything he wrote.

---

1. Lang, together with *The Heroes of Asgard* and several other highly formative texts, was put into my hands during the three years, from six to eight, that I spent at an English P.N.E.U. (Parents' National Educational Union) school, before being transferred to the less congenial rigors of prep and public boarding schools. Most of the serious permanent passions of my later life (including the study of classics as a profession, and the absorption of world literature and music for the sheer fun of it) had their roots in my P.N.E.U. days. I did not get any remotely comparable stimulation and excitement until I returned to Cambridge after World War II as an elderly (*I* thought: I was twenty-three) ex-service undergraduate.

Nor have I ever forgotten that the *Argonautika* is an epic *poem,* though the two other translations most commonly used, the late E. V. Rieu's Penguin and R. L.Hunter's version for World Classics, tend to make readers (as I have found) do just that, being written in flat and businesslike prose. Rieu turns the *Argonautika* (as he did just about everything else he touched, including the Four Gospels) into a kind of boys' adventure story, while Hunter, on his own account, seems to have had no higher aim than to provide an updated replacement (as trot or pony) for R. C. Seaton's Loeb. There may, then, be room for a version that, while avoiding the excesses of critical fashion, is conscious throughout that Apollonios was a poet at least as talented as Matthew Arnold or Tennyson, and endowed with an even greater mastery of language. That mastery it is impossible fully to convey in English: I can only say that I have tried my level best to create an approximation to it.[2] The epic hexameter cannot easily be reproduced in a nonquantitative language: I have used for this purpose the long, loose, 5/6-beat stress equivalent developed by Day Lewis and Lattimore (for translating Virgil and Homer respectively).

I should, perhaps, also say a word about the spelling of proper names in this volume. My original idea was to eradicate the all-pervasive Latinization of Greek names that still largely persists in modern scholarship. The task proved surprisingly difficult. Many names (Herodotos, Polybios) required only minimal adjustment, but there were others—such as Loukianos (Lucian) and Kirké (Circe)—that almost literally set my teeth on edge by their oddity. For Aristotle, Hesiod, Homer, and Pindar, I retained the familiar form, and I have stuck to Aelian (rather than making him Ailianos), since he was, after all, a Roman to the extent of bearing the first name Claudius. In some cases I compromised; in a few cases I abandoned the struggle altogether. I couldn't, for instance, face calling my main character Iason rather than Jason. Ptolemaios as a revision of Ptolemy also went against all my instincts, as did Okeanos for Ocean. Finally, I didn't do anything about the Anglicization of Roman names, with the perhaps spurious justification that these were Latin anyway: I think the truth was that I felt no less uncomfortable with Ovidius (or, a fortiori, Naso) for Ovid, or Horatius (ditto Flaccus) for Horace than I did about any of the Greek metamorphoses I had choked on. So, like many others, I have ended up inconsistent in my usage.

2. I had completed the first draft of my own translation before I came upon the one included by Barbara Fowler (bare text and little else) in her *Hellenistic Poetry: An Anthology* (Madison, 1990). Since it was clear at a glance that we were employing a very similar verse format and following essentially identical guidelines, I at once put hers away without reading further: nothing is harder to shake (*experto credite*) than the influence of a competitor with similar ideas to your own. Now that my text is submitted I have read Professor Fowler's version with considerable interest and not a little admiration. The real beneficiary is the Greekless reader. Whereas for long there was only Rieu's adventure story available, the student in particular now has not one but two verse translations, plus an update of Rieu with more scholarship and marginally better prose.

Perhaps by way of compensation, I have been fiercely obstinate in the matter of punctuation. Some of the conventions established by the *Chicago Manual of Style*—I am concerned in particular here with the positioning of commas and periods vis-à-vis reported speech—regularly violate every logical principle of discourse for the sake of one easy all-purpose rule-of-thumb. Readers will notice that my treatment of quoted matter ignores these arbitrary canons, a decision which gave serious concern to my old friend and current copy-editor Peter Dreyer, whose objections I firmly overruled. I want to make it clear that what he (and possibly others) regard as solecisms are due to my insistence, and not to mere lack of proper scrutiny on his part. Indeed, he has been both meticulous and vigilant on my behalf throughout, and I am more than grateful for all his help. I also want to express my on-going gratitude, once again, to Mary Lamprech, classics editor *extraordinaire,* for always being there when she was needed, adroitly fielding all my questions, and providing throughout that nice blend of practicality, encouragement, and friendship which all authors dream of in their publishers, and too many never find.

I am equally grateful to the librarians of the American School of Classical Studies in Athens and the Classics Library and the Perry-Castañeda (Main) Library in the University of Texas at Austin for the unfailing help they have always given me throughout the writing of this book. I must also thank the ever-resourceful staff of the Interlibrary Loan department, who, as usual, found me titles that I'd written off as unobtainable, and more often than not surprisingly fast. The students on whom, in two seminars devoted to Apollonios and his work, I tried out most of my nascent ideas cheerfully gave as good as, and often better than, they got, and in innumerable ways sharpened my thinking on this simultaneously most difficult and most rewarding of authors. My translation is based on the splendid edition, as sensitive to poetic nuance as it is solidly grounded in *Wissenschaft,* of Professor Francis Vian, made for the French Budé series, and contriving to pack a remarkable amount of informative comment, over and above text and *apparatus criticus,* into a necessarily limited format. I have not often diverged from it, and when I have, it is always with a sense of profound temerity. My understanding of Apollonios's text also owes much to the editions of Ardizzoni (for book 1 in particular), Hunter (for book 3) and, above all, that great Italian scholar Enrico Livrea (for book 4). (At the same time I should, perhaps, point out that my omission of Hermann Fränkel's Oxford Classical Text from my bibliography is not due to mere carelessness.) Other debts, to many scholars—including Fränkel in his *Noten*—are duly acknowledged in the Commentary; but the greatest debt of all remains, as always, to my wife Carin, for whose love, friendship, and intellectual stimulus over a quarter of a century the dedication to this book, as indeed the book itself, remains a sadly inadequate quid pro quo.

Peter Green

Introduction

I

The author of the *Argonautika* is a remarkably elusive character. We do not know exactly when he was born, or the date of his death. At least three cities—Alexandria, Naukratis, and, inevitably, Rhodes—were claimed in antiquity, and continue to be argued for today, as his birthplace. Our main sources for his life are not only late, but contain a number of arresting discrepancies. Did he turn to poetry early or late in life? He was royal tutor to one of the Ptolemies—but which one? He was head of the Alexandrian Library—but directly before and after whom? Why is there arguably no direct surviving evidence from his own day for the notorious literary quarrel it is claimed (by the *Souda,* s.v. Καλλίμαχος) he had with his near-contemporary Kallimachos?[1] How, chronologically speaking, is his retreat or exile to Rhodes to be related to his appointment as librarian and tutor? Under which Ptolemy was his floruit? The evidence is such that scholars have put his birth as early as 300 and as late as 265, and his death anywhere between 235 and 190.[2]

The central problem occasioning such disagreement is not so much the lack of testimony (above all of *early* testimony) as the awkward fact that our

---

1. Arguably, because the authenticity of the epigram attacking Kallimachos attributed to Ap. (*AP* 11.275) has been denied, on what seem to me inadequate grounds, by most modern scholars: see, e.g., Vian 1974, xvii, with nn. 1–2, and Green 1993, 783 nn. 3–4.

2. The problem is neatly set out by Vian 1974, vii–xiii, who lists no fewer than three basic schemata developed by modern scholars for Apollonios's life and career, none of them without serious objections. At the same time, I should point out that the schema I find most plausible does in fact correspond very nearly to his first system, as worked out by Delage 1930b—a thorough and basically sensible study, largely ignored by contemporary scholars (Hunter 1989, 3 n. 11, omits it from his list of biographical studies, and it is missing from Blum's otherwise exhaustive bibliography).

few late surviving witnesses on occasion so flatly contradict one another (though some of the disagreements, as we shall see, turn out to be more apparent than real). I therefore set them out here. The *Lives* were transmitted with the MSS of the *Argonautika;* scholarly efforts to trace them back (e.g., to a first-century B.C. critic called Theon), while praiseworthy, do not offer enlightenment or remove any difficulties. The same applies to the two entries from the *Souda,* a late-tenth-century Byzantine encyclopedia.

(i) *Life A:* "Apollonios, the author of the *Argonautika,* was by birth an Alexandrian, of the Ptolemaïs tribe, and the son of Silleus (or, according to some, Illeus). He lived during the reign of the Ptolemies, and was a student ($\mu\alpha\theta\eta\tau\dot{\eta}s$) of Kallimachos. At first he was an assistant to ($\sigma\upsilon\nu\grave{\omega}\nu$)[3] his own master, Kallimachos; but in the end ($\mathring{o}\psi\acute{\epsilon}$) he turned to the writing of poems. It is said that while still a youth ($\check{\epsilon}\phi\eta\beta o\nu$) he gave a reading of the *Argonautika* and was unfavorably received. Overcome by the opprobrium of the public and the sneers and abuse of his fellow-poets, he left his native land and took off to Rhodes. It was here that he polished and corrected his text,[4] going on to give readings of it which won him the highest renown—the reason why in his poems he calls himself 'the Rhodian', He enjoyed a brilliant teaching career there, winning Rhodian citizenship and other honors."[5]

"During the reign of the Ptolemies" is the reading of most MSS, generally dismissed as, in Hunter's words, "too obvious to need saying."[6] If so, one wonders, why was it said? In fact, when we seek a specific identity for "the Ptolemies", plural, the answer at once presents itself: they are, and can only be, Ptolemy II Philadelphos and his sister-wife Arsinoë, the first and by far

---

3. Or perhaps "lived with": see Blum, 128 and 164 n. 38, where he points out, with examples, that the verb $\sigma\upsilon\nu\epsilon\tilde{\iota}\nu\alpha\iota$ "was used for younger scholars who remained after the completion of their studies with their teachers as their assistants." (The word has other suggestive meanings: see my discussion below, together with n. 7.) He also emphasizes, what the *Lives* bear out, but has sometimes been denied, e.g., by Händel 1962, 436, that it was Kallimachos as scholar rather than poet under whom Ap. studied: this is of importance when we consider accounts of his activities on Rhodes.

4. Cameron, 217, states that "the Lives are agreed that it was in Alexandria that Apollonius wrote the *Argonautica.*" Cf. the evidence of *Life B* below.

5. Cameron, 214, argues that we have here a confusion between our Apollonios and a later Apollonios from Alabanda (c. 120 B.C.), a sophist who ran a school of rhetoric in Rhodes. This is indeed not impossible. But the argument adduced in favor of it (and used a fortiori apropos of *Life B*'s claim that Ap. "was active in public affairs and lectured on rhetoric"), i.e., that while such behavior was natural for the later sophist, it was "absurd for the poet," cannot be taken seriously. Ap. was at least as much scholar as poet (on this, see n. 3 above): no clear lines were drawn between literature and rhetoric; and since when have poets *necessarily* abstained from public affairs?

6. Hunter 1989, 1 n. 3. He, and most literary scholars, accept Wendel's emendation $\dot{\epsilon}\pi\grave{\iota}$ $\tau o\tilde{\upsilon}$ $<\tau\rho\acute{\iota}\tau o\upsilon>$ $\Pi\tau o\lambda\epsilon\mu\alpha\acute{\iota}o\upsilon$ = "in the reign of the third Ptolemy [Euergétes]," agreeing with one MS (H) and, as we shall see, with P. Oxy. 1241.

the most famous of the dynasty's incestuous royal couples, known as the "Sibling Gods" (Θεοὶ Ἀδελφοί), and regularly portrayed together on both gold and silver coinage (Green 1993, 145–46, with fig. 57). It is also often argued that the account of his youthful literary performance is inconsistent with what precedes it—that is, that he turned to poetry "late"; but such flagrant self-contradiction within the space of two sentences is unlikely even for a late scholiast. The Greek surely means no more than that he began as Kallimachos's scholarly assistant (in the Library?), afterwards branching off on his own as a poet (Delage 1930, 22–25). The ambiguity of συνών is worth noting: it can imply anything from casual acquaintanceship to cohabitation and sexual intercourse.[7]

(ii) *Life B:* "Apollonios the poet was an Alexandrian by birth, his father being Silleus or Illeus, his mother Rhodé. He studied with Kallimachos, who was then a *grammatikós* [teacher, scholar] in Alexandria, and after composing these poems [sc., the *Argonautika*] gave a public reading of them. The result, to his embarrassment, was a complete failure, as a result of which he took up residence in Rhodes. There he was active in public affairs and lectured on rhetoric [cf. nn. 3 and 5]. Hence the readiness of some to call him a Rhodian. It was there, then, that he resided while he polished his poems. Afterwards he gave a hugely successful public reading—so much so that he was adjudged worthy [ἀξιωθῆναι] of Rhodian citizenship and high honors. Some sources state that he returned to Alexandria and gave another public reading there, which brought him to the very pinnacle of success, to the point where he was found worthy [ἀξιωθῆναι] of the Museum's Libraries, and was buried alongside Kallimachos himself."[8]

We see, then, that both *Lives* are fundamentally in agreement on the facts and, equally important, the *sequence of events* in Apollonios's career, though B adds the important information concerning his return to Alexandria and his success there. To "be found worthy of" the Libraries clearly means appointment as librarian, or perhaps in the first instance as a Museum scholar, not, as has sometimes—rather fancifully—been suggested, the admission of his works to the Library's holdings, for which inclusiveness, not merit, was

---

7. The temptation to speculate on an early love affair between teacher and pupil that went disastrously wrong, thus adding fuel to literary and academic flames, is considerable, not least when one considers Kallimachos's homoerotic epigrams—which, incidentally, were one reason why Wilamowitz argued that because of his proclivities, Kallimachos could not possibly have been made a royal tutor: "Erzieher eines Knaben durfte dieser Epigrammatiker wirklich nicht werden" (*Hellenistische Dichtung* [Berlin, 1924], 1: 166). However, the relevant sentence in *Life A* makes it fairly clear that what was in question was some kind of professional or educational relationship.

8. Cameron, 215, nevertheless states flatly that "the Lives do not bring Apollonius back to Alexandria . . . he leaves Alexandria as a youth and spends the rest of his life in Rhodes" [*sic*], though he does at least concede *Life B*'s reference to Ap.'s burial beside Kallimachos.

the criterion.[9] The close relationship with Kallimachos, whose own career is firmly pegged to the decades 280–50, and with Theokritos, who seems to have written mostly before 270, would point us firmly in the direction of Ptolemy II's reign—the Golden Age of Hellenistic poetry—even without *Life A*'s reference (as I maintain) to the Sibling Gods.

(iii) P. Oxy. 1241, col. ii (Grenfell and Hunt, pt. 10: 99 ff.): "[Apollo]nios, son of Silleus, an Alexandrian, called the Rhodian, a student [or perhaps 'acquaintance': γνώριμος] of Kallimachos: he also [was? ἐ[γένετο] the [t(eacher): word almost wholly illegible, possibly δ(ιδάσκαλ)ος, but could just as easily be δ(ιάδοχ)ος] of the [fi]rst king. He was succeeded by Eratosthenes, after whom came Aristophanes of Byzantion and Aristarchos. Next was Apollonios of Alexandria, known as the Classifier [εἰδογράφος], and after him Aristarchos son of Aristarchos, an Alexandrian, but originally from Samothraké, who [was] the tutor of <Ptolemy IV> Philopator's children."

This text is an extract from some sort of chrestomathy or handbook (second century A.D.), listing, in chronological order, some of the chief librarians in Alexandria. The column immediately preceding it is lost, but must have named the first appointee, whom we know from the *Souda* (s.v. Ζηνόδοτος, 74) to have been Zenódotos, Homeric scholar, epic poet, and tutor to Ptolemy I's children. Ptolemy II was born in 308: thus if we place Zenódotos's appointment c. 295, we shall not be far out. But who succeeded him? Some scholars would like to believe it was Kallimachos,[10] presumably on the principle of academic merit reaping its just reward; but the almost unanimous silence of our ancient sources is not encouraging,[11] and it should also not be forgotten that the librarian was a crown appointment.[12] Perhaps not coincidentally, both Zenódotos and Apollonios were epic poets and Homeric scholars: this may well reflect Ptolemy II's own preferences. The likelihood of Apol-

9. The "merit of inclusion" theory (see, e.g., Blum, 128–29) is most commonly justified by a reference to Pfeiffer, 141–42 and excursus 284–85; but Pfeiffer's uncharacteristically weak argument rests on nothing better than comparative usage in Eusebius (see esp. *Hist. eccles.* 3.9.2) and carries no real weight.

10. Most recently, and in most detail, Blum, 112–13 (cf. 127, 132–33, 168 n. 73).

11. The "Latin Tzetzes" (on which see Fraser, 2a: 474 n. 107, 488 n. 189) refers to Kallimachos as *aulicus regius bibliothecarius*, but this seems to be an unintelligent guess compounded by mistranslation.

12. A modern parallel may be instructive here. In 1936, Stanley Baldwin, then prime minister of Great Britain, asked Gilbert Murray whom he would like to see as his successor as Regius Professor of Greek at Oxford—a chair in theory filled by royal fiat. Murray named E. R. Dodds, who was promptly appointed. On the resultant sustained outrage among Oxford classicists, see Dodds's autobiography, *Missing Persons* (Oxford, 1977), ch. 8, esp. 124–26. It is safe to say that, left to themselves, the Oxford faculty would never in a thousand years have elected Dodds—who nevertheless went on to prove himself one of the greatest scholars ever to grace his distinguished office.

lonios having been appointed as Zenódotos's direct successor is very great. Unfortunately, it is not certain beyond all doubt: both chronologically and based on P. Oxy. 1241, there is room for Kallimachos's tenure between the two.[13] On the other hand, Apollonios must, on chronological grounds, have been tutor to Ptolemy III rather than Ptolemy I, and scholars have therefore agreed that "first" (πρώτου) was a slip, perhaps through misreading a slovenly hand, for "third" (τρίτου). After Apollonios the sequence makes complete sense (though Aristarchos is mentioned twice: I suspect that the scribe had the Samian as well as the Samothrakian in mind) and can be accepted.

(iv) The *Souda* (s.v. Ἀπολλώνιος, no. 3419, Adler, 1: 307): "Apollonios, an Alexandrian, writer of epic poems; spent some time on Rhodes; son of Silleus; a student of Kallimachos; contemporary with Eratosthenes, Euphorion, and Timarchos, in the reign of Ptolemy known as The Benefactor [Euergétes], and Eratosthenes' successor in the Directorship [προστασία] of the Library in Alexandria."

This encyclopedia entry differs sharply in two (clearly related) aspects from our other testimonia: it dates Apollonios firmly in the reign of Ptolemy III and later (Euphorion was appointed librarian in Antioch by Antiochos the Great at some point after 223), and makes him Eratosthenes' successor, rather than predecessor, as chief librarian. The obvious explanation, provided by (iii) above, is that the author of this entry confused our Apollonios with Apollonios the Classifier. Some, however, prefer, for whatever reason,[14] to accept the *Souda*'s dating, against all our other evidence, and to place Apollonios's librarianship *after* that of Eratosthenes.[15] Such a choice cannot be sustained, and most recent scholarship rejects it.[16] Dating apart, nothing in the *Souda* entry contradicts our other sources.

The biographical notice that can be constructed on the basis of these witnesses, and reinforced with circumstantial literary and historical testimony, differs somewhat from currently accepted scholarly versions of Apollonios's

---

13. "Now that the Oxyrhynchus list has proved that he was never chief librarian . . . ," Cameron (11) briskly dogmatizes; but of course it does nothing of the sort. This is only the first of many similar firm assertions in his book that turn out to be unsupported (and often, as in this case, moonshine). Fraser, 1: 330–31, is far more circumspect.

14. A late date for Apollonios is, of course, a godsend for scholars specializing in *Quellenforschung*: set him in the 270's and, as the record makes clear, no one can agree, among Kallimachos, Theokritos, and Apollonios in particular, as to who influenced whom. Shift him down into the 230's and the problem no longer exists.

15. See Mooney 1–12; Blum 128–29.

16. E.g., Hunter 1989; and now Cameron, 218, though after rejecting its chronology, he can still argue that "it is the Suda-entry that preserves the vestiges of ancient tradition," chiefly, it would seem, on the basis of its source, assumed to be "the sixth-century biographical dictionary of Hesychius of Miletus" (216)—not a work calculated to elicit universal respect: see Blum's detailed analysis, 202–10—and the fact that it describes Ap. as an epic poet.

life.[17] The main premiss of these is that the central episode related by the *Lives*, Apollonios's youthful literary setback, and his sojourn on Rhodes as a consequence of this, as well as his quarrel with Kallimachos, must be viewed as a fiction. I see no need for such an assumption. Nor do I feel the need to refute some other claims made about him that have no basis whatsoever in the evidence—for example, that his departure to Rhodes took place late in life, or that he was exiled. Here, then, is my reconstruction of his life and career (for the four sources discussed above, I use the abbreviations L1, L2, P, and S).[18]

Apollonios, the son of Silleus and Rhodé (L1, L2, P, S), an epic poet (S) and author of the *Argonautika* (L1), was an Alexandrian by birth, of the Ptolemaïs tribe (L1), and thus the first native-born Alexandrian poet. (His family may have moved to Alexandria from Naukratis.) Since he flourished under Ptolemy II Philadelphos (L1) and was a student of Kallimachos (L1, L2, P, S), who was born c. 310, his own birth can be placed somewhere between 305 and 290. The earlier range seems much more probable, especially if his relationship with Kallimachos began when the latter, not yet Ptolemy II's protégé, was still a *grammatikós* (L2; S, s.v. Καλλίμαχος) in the Alexandrian suburb of Eleusis—that is, before 285. Thus Apollonios's early, unfortunate, public reading (L1, L2) will have taken place—if the term "youth" (ἔφηβον) be interpreted in its strict sense—when he was between eighteen and twenty: that is, at some point in the period 285–280, and (interestingly enough) while he was still attached, as student or assistant (L1), to Kallimachos. It was after this, late in the day (surely that ὀψέ, in context, has to be ironic?), that he determined to make his prime activity poetry rather than criticism (L1) and removed himself to Rhodes (L1, L2, S) in order to do so.

Why Rhodes? No one has bothered with this question, except (by implication) through the mistaken claim (Lefkowitz, 12–13) that, against all the evidence, Rhodes was in fact his birthplace. I have elsewhere (Green 1993, 203–4) suggested that the independence of that proud maritime republic perhaps offered an atmosphere more sympathetic to epic, not least an epic largely bound up with the sea, than did Ptolemaic Alexandria.[19] Since then an excellent article has been published pointing out what a deep and personal knowledge the *Argonautika* reveals of navigation, maritime life, ship-

17. See Herter 1942b, 1944–55, 1973; Eichgrün, passim, esp. 15–68, 163–71; Händel 1962; Hunter 1989, 1–12; Blum, 128–33; Cameron, 214–19. I forbear from subjecting the reader to a long, and ultimately pointless, discussion of all the theories advanced in these texts.

18. In the main this reconstruction follows that in Green 1993, 203 ff., but has been modified in some particulars as the result of valid criticism.

19. Cameron (263), in the course of dismissing my earlier account (confident dogma again) as "perhaps the most extravagant embellishment of the traditional story yet published," cites the suggestion about Rhodes as the acme of this extravagance, but without bothering to offer any explanation as to why.

building, and nautical expertise in general—expertise surely gained, in the first instance, on Rhodes.[20] How long did he remain there? To become genuinely knowledgeable about seafaring, as well as to engage in public life, pursue a distinguished teaching career, complete his revised *Argonautika*—fragments of a prior draft of book 1 survive embedded in the scholia[21]—and achieve a position of international literary eminence would all take considerable time. This indeed would seem to have been the case. The *terminus ante quem* for his return to Alexandria would have to be the inception of his tutorial duties with the young Ptolemy III Euergétes, who cannot have been more than fifteen at the time, and may have been as young as twelve. Euergétes was born at some point between 288 (the year of his father's marriage to Arsinoë I) and 275.[22] We are therefore looking at a date not earlier than 273 and possibly as late as 260. If Apollonios emigrated to Rhodes in the period 285–80, he would have spent a minimum of thirteen years there, and more probably about twenty. He could thus easily have been forty—a perfectly acceptable age for such honors—at the time of his triumphant return (L2), and appointment by Ptolemy II as royal tutor (P) and chief librarian (P; S?): I would suggest a date around 265.

There followed a long period of uneventful success and productiveness. It would have been in these years that Apollonios wrote foundation poems on the origins (κτίσεις) of Alexandria and Naukratis, and an aetiological poem entitled *Kanobos*, just as during his Rhodian residence, he had similarly composed works about Kaunos, Knidos, and Rhodes itself.[23] He was equally busy in his capacity as a Museum scholar, with critical works on Homer (including a monograph attacking his predecessor Zenódotos), Hesiod, and Archilochos.[24] It is possible that he also began a second revised edition of at

20. Joanna Rostropowicz, "The Argonautica by Apollonios of Rhodes as a Nautical Epos: Remarks on the Realities of Navigation," *Eos* 88 (1990): 107–17.

21. For further discussion of this, the so-called προέκδοσις, see below, p. 8 and n. 25. It remains quite uncertain (despite a good deal of dogmatic scholarly argument) whether the changes, which are detailed but minor, indicate Ap.'s original draft, a later MS circulated among friends (see Hunter 1989, 5–6, with nn. 21–22), or work on a late and incomplete revision of what had by then become the standard text. The six passages from the προέκδοσις referred to in the scholia to bk. 1 are at lines 285–86, 516–23, 543, 726–27 (?), 788–89, and 801–13. There is also one isolated instance in bk. 2, at lines 963–64 (not signaled as such by the scholiast), where two lines quoted differ substantially from our traditional text; but none in bks. 3 or 4.

22. This is another terminus ad quem, since by 274–73, Arsinoë II, Ptolemy's full sister, was, as we know from the Pithom stele, already regnant queen: Fraser, 2a: 367 n. 228.

23. Pfeiffer, 144; Hunter 1989, 9–12; Cameron, 215, who comments: "the series of Egyptian poems lends no support to the claim of an early departure from Alexandria." Indeed, they do not, being written after his return; and since Ap. very probably never left Alexandria again, this is hardly surprising. Cameron adds: "These were mistakes only possible in a later age that knew only the *Argonautica*." Well, yes, as things turned out, but not quite the age of which Cameron was thinking when he wrote those words.

24. Pfeiffer, 145–48.

least part of the *Argonautika,* which got no further than book 1, and that it was the existence of this revision which occasioned references to the "previous edition" (προέκδοσις) by the scholiasts.[25]

On his accession early in 246, Ptolemy III Euergétes summoned Eratosthenes from Athens to take over the office of chief librarian.[26] There was no question of his old tutor being dismissed, let alone exiled: Apollonios had served with distinction for twenty years, was now in his sixties, and had earned an honorable retirement. If there is any truth in the tradition (L2) that after he died (probably at some point in the 230's), he was buried beside Kallimachos, that suggests, not (as has been romantically inferred) a reconciliation between the two men, but rather the existence of a special burial site or private cemetery for distinguished members of the Museum community.[27]

II

When considering Apollonios's place in Hellenistic literature, it is impossible to ignore the tradition, whether true or fictional, of his alleged quarrel with Kallimachos, since this lurks at the heart of several much-debated problems: appointments and working conditions in the Library and the Museum; the nature of third-century epic, the interpretation of Kallimachean aesthetic principles, and the relationship of the *Argonautika* to both; finally, the precise meaning and scope of the tradition hostile to Kallimachos, as testified to by passages in that poet's works such as lines 105–14 of the *Hymn to Apollo,* or the partly fragmentary preface (1–38) of the *Aitia* attacking the "Telchines"— malevolent mythical dwarfs here standing in for literary opponents. This is not the place to attack such problems in detail; but anyone who wishes to read the *Argonautika* with a reasonable degree of understanding should at least be able to appreciate the social and aesthetic context in which it came to be written. Even if we regard a personal vendetta between two distinguished officers of the Alexandrian Library as unproven (though hardly, bearing modern academe in mind, intrinsically improbable), are the respective literary posi-

---

25. This kind of explanation may perhaps better satisfy those who remain convinced that the προέκδοσις and the text in our possession do not differ substantially enough for the original draft to be in question: see, e.g., Herter 1973, 22, and Cameron, 217, with further references. However, it remains a moot question whether major alterations (e.g., the general "Kallimachizing" of the text with *aitia,* etc.) would show up in such short extracts; and the revision on Rhodes would surely also include the kind of close verbal corrections we find in citations from the προέκδοσις.

26. See the *Souda* s.v. Ἐρατοσθένης (no. 2898): μετεπέμφθη δὲ ἐξ Ἀθηνῶν ὑπὸ τοῦ τρίτου Πτολεμαίου.

27. It is not impossible that Ap. returned to Rhodes after his retirement; but the evidence is lacking, and my earlier statement to this effect (Green 1993, 204) was too confidently expressed.

tions of Apollonios and Kallimachos such that hostility, even if nonexistent in fact, could easily be presumed in theory?

It is fashionable nowadays to assert "that both quarrel and controversy are entirely modern inventions."[28] Like many such assertions, this one is not true. Though the *Souda* is regularly trawled for useful (i.e., supportive) evidence, but briskly dismissed as late and untrustworthy when it records testimony at odds with the theory *du jour,* the entry on Kallimachos (its format suggesting derivation from Hesychios of Miletos) contains the following comment on one title in a list of Kallimachos's works: "*Ibis,* a poem of deliberate obscurity and abusiveness, directed against a certain Ibis, who had become Kallimachos's enemy: this person was Apollonios, the author of the *Argonautika.*"[29] The reason for the hostility is not stated, but there is at least a strong chance of its having been literary. We might have guessed that such feuds were common in the Museum, and a famous squib by Timon of Phleious confirms it: "In the polyglot land of Egypt, many now find pasturage as endowed scribblers, endlessly quarreling in the Muses' birdcage."[30] Kallimachos himself, imitating Hipponax, urged scholars not to be mutually jealous.[31] But with "free meals, high salaries, no taxes to pay, very pleasant surroundings, good lodgings and servants", there was, as Pfeiffer remarks,[32] "plenty of opportunity for quarrelling with one another." Leisure, combined with the arbitrary uncertainties of royal patronage, must have made backbiting and paranoia endemic.

Despite the enormous amount of scholarship generated by this topic—Kallimachos is, after all, just about the ideal scholar-poet to most classicists, a subtly flattering *Mirror for Academe*—direct testimony for what he actually *disliked* in Hellenistic literature is limited. There are three main items of evidence, which, taken together, offer a fairly consistent picture. Two of them—the preface to the *Aitia* and the conclusion of the *Hymn to Apollo*—have been mentioned above. The third is a six-line epigram (28 [30] Pf.) on the theme of distaste for what is "base, common, or popular." There are a few other hints (e.g., the last line of *Epigr.* 8 [10] Pf. wittily closes with a six-

28. Cameron, 264, whose own μέγα βιβλίον is a compendium of just about every piece of scholarly dogma on Kallimachos and Apollonios developed over the past two decades. To call it trendy would be meiosis.

29. The *Souda*, s.v. Καλλίμαχος (no. 227): Ἶβις (ἔστι δὲ ποίημα ἐπιτετηδευμένον εἰς ἀσάφειαν καὶ λοιδορίαν, εἴς τινα Ἶβιν, γενόμενον ἐχθρὸν τοῦ Καλλιμάχου· ἦν δὲ οὗτος Ἀπολλώνιος, ὁ γράψας τὰ Ἀργοναυτικά). The last-ditch suggestion (see, e.g., Hutchinson, 86–87) that the parenthesis can be dismissed as an interpolation and that nothing more.

30. Cited by Athen. 1.22d, with a comment confirming that Timon was indeed aiming at the Museum in these lines. Timon also seems to have had a low opinion of scholarly ingenuity (probably in this case referring to Zenódotos): when Aratos asked him where he could get a reliable text of Homer, Timon told him to go for an old-style copy, and not one of the contemporary "corrected" (διωρθωμένοις) texts: Diog. Laert. 9.113.

31. Cf. Kall. fr. 191 Pf., *dieg.* 6.2 ff.

32. Pfeiffer, 97.

syllable word, βραχυσυλλαβίη, meaning "brevity"), but these three texts form the basis for all argument.

"All that's commonplace makes me sick" (σικχαίνω πάντα τὰ δημόσια) is the central message of the epigram: this includes—fact merging into literary metaphor—indiscriminate lovers, public fountains, overpopulated highways, and, a point to which I shall return in a moment, "cyclic" poetry. Popularity, in short (a perennial academic tenet, this), is suspect. The avoidance of well-trodden roads is a theme that recurs in the preface to the *Aitia* (25–28), in the form of advice from Apollo. Also, the poet should chirp like the cicada, not bray like the ass (29–32); poems should not be measured by their length (15–18). Jealous dwarfs (1–2, cf. 17), no friends of the Muses, mutter (ἐπιτρύζουσιν) against Kallimachos because he has not written one sustained epic, many thousands of lines in length, about kings or heroes (3–5), but instead turns out short poems, like a child (5–6), and is a man of few lines (ὀλιγόστιχος, 9).[33] The cryptic postscript (105–14) to *Hymn II* has personified Envy (Φθόνος) whispering in Apollo's ear (106): "I do not admire that poet whose utterance lacks the sweep and range of the sea."[34] To which Apollo replies, with a swift contemptuous kick (ποδί τ᾽ ἤλασεν), that a river such as the Euphrates may have a vast current (μέγας ῥόος), but also carries down a mass of silt and refuse; whereas Demeter's priestesses bring her, not just any water, but only (111–12) that "thin trickle, the ultimate distillation (ἄκρον ἄωτον), pure and undefiled, that rises from the sacred spring".

The general message, despite some teasing obscurities of detail that have occasioned endless debate, is clear enough. Kallimachos is advocating three fundamental qualities in poetry: brevity, originality, and refinement, whether of style, language, or form. The criticisms against him (not so different from some still current today) are for not having produced a "major" or "substantial" work. His answer is that bulk inevitably includes dross and (the donkey's bray applies here) vulgarity of utterance. The real problem in the context of our present discussion is how far any of this could be directed against epic poetry in general and Apollonios in particular. "The cyclic poem" (τὸ ποίημα τὸ κυκλικόν) of *Epigr.* 28 [30] 1 might be thought specific enough, but it has often been pointed out that κυκλικόν, "cyclic" or "epic", also carries the secondary literary senses of "commonplace", "conventional", even "platitudinous". This, it is argued, given the context, must be the meaning

---

33. The virtues of brevity are so stressed that it comes as a surprise to find how rare ὀλιγόστιχος and ὀλιγοστιχία are. Apart from this passage, LSJ cites only Diog. Laert. 7.165 (of the philosophical prose of Herillos, an exact contemporary of Ap.'s) and *AP* 4.2.6, where it is applied generically to the younger writers in the *Garland of Philip*.

34. The Greek is straightforward and does not need correction: "οὐκ ἄγαμαι τὸν ἀοιδὸν ὃς οὐδ᾽ ὅσα πόντος ἀείδει." On the heavy weather scholars have made of it (the metaphor seems to be particularly hard for them to swallow), see, e.g., Smiley, 284–86.

here. But Kallimachos (as the same scholars are eager to remind us) had an exquisite ear for the mot juste, and it is inconceivable that he could have set up such a striking verbal ambiguity by accident. The message, conveyed with pregnant brevity, is: epic = cliché. It is also historical (kings) or mythical (heroes) epic, thousands of lines long (5,835 in the *Argonautika*), that Kallimachos is reproached by the "Telchines" for not writing (*Aitia* 3–5).

This judgment would have remained comparatively simple had it not been for the existence of the Florentine scholia.[35] To expect Kallimachos himself to have named the "Telchines" is *simpliste*; but the scholia identify several of them, including Asklepiades and Poseidippos, Samian literary and erotic epigrammatists who wrote between 290 and 270 (i.e., in the golden years of Alexandrian poetry), and Praxiphanes of Mytilene, a Peripatetic critic contemporary with them. It was these men, the scholia claim, who criticized Kallimachos for not writing longer, more substantial work; and as it happens, a couple of epigrams in the *Palatine Anthology* (*AP* 9.63, 12.168), point to a text that the first two praised and might therefore have offered as a desirable model: the *Lyde* of Antimachos (fl. c. 400), a narrative elegy lamenting the loss of the poet's mistress. The scholia also state that Kallimachos preferred the shorter poems of Mimnermos (late seventh century) and Philetas of Kos (the scholar-poet who was tutor to both Zenódotos and Ptolemy II) to those of more diffuse ($\pi o\lambda$]$v\sigma\tau\acute{\iota}\chi\omega\nu$) writers (not named, but *possibly* including Antimachos). We also know (fr. 460* Pf.) that Kallimachos was acquainted with Praxiphanes and wrote a pamphlet against him.

All this is perfectly plausible and sheds a little fitful light on the kind of critical debate (if not actual infighting) that went on between Museum scholars and the rest of the Alexandrian literary coterie. The problem of course is that nowhere in the Florentine scholia or related material is there any specific mention of Hellenistic epic, let alone of Apollonios. The genres discussed are elegy and epigram. Far more has been made of this *argumentum ex silentio* than it deserves. If Kallimachos preferred (as he clearly did) to write short rather than long poems, it was not only in the field of elegy that this preference would have applied, though he may well have picked that genre at the beginning of the *Aitia* to counter the specific charges of Asklepiades and his friends.

There is also the evidence of the *Hekalé* to consider.[36] This hexameter epyllion of perhaps between 1,000 and 1,500 lines (Hollis, app. 2, 337–40), describing Theseus's victory over the Bull of Marathon, and his entertainment en route to Marathon in the hut of the old lady who provides the poem with its title, Kallimachos wrote (we are told by a scholiast on *Hymn II*) in response

35. For the standard edition of these scholia, see R. Pfeiffer, *Callimachus* (Oxford, 1949–53), 1: 1–3, *Ait.* fr. 1.
36. See Hollis; cf. Kall. *Hek.* frs. 230–377 Pf. (1: 226–303).

to those who derided his inability to compose a lengthy work.[37] There seems no compelling reason to doubt such a statement. Hollis (3–4) dates the poem to around 270, which is plausible enough; but, as almost always with poems of this period, absolute or even close chronology is out of reach, since the criteria remain hopelessly subjective.[38] From the numerous surviving fragments,[39] it becomes apparent that to attain even this length (no more than one book of the *Argonautika*), Kallimachos resorted to a whole series of individual anecdotes and *aitia* concerning both protagonists, and indeed other mythical figures (e.g., Erichthonios and the daughters of Kekrops, fr. 70 Hollis = 260 Pf.). In several respects, then—its hexameter form, its narrative exposition and development of myth, its use of aetiological material—*Hēkalē* reads like a reluctant attempt to emulate Hellenistic epic: reluctant partly because it still falls short in the matter of length, but also, more important (it is often argued), because Kallimachos lived in an age for which the heroic ethos was dead, so that any attempt to resuscitate epic would inevitably have seemed unreal, artificial, a mere exercise in nostalgia.

External social and historical realities make this view so overwhelmingly plausible that we tend to forget one uncomfortable fact: neither Kallimachos nor his presumptive opponents say anything about it. That does not necessarily mean it was untrue. The evidence so far assembled suggests that the tradition of literary dissension was in fact genuine as between short poems (personal, aetiological) and long ones (heroic, mythical), but that the real differences were taken to be literary and stylistic rather than social. This, in turn, also does not necessarily mean that an unrecognized (and probably unconscious) social component did not play a large part in the "quarrel". We also have to consider, bearing in mind his apparent absence from the ranks of the "Telchines" as delineated by the Florentine scholia, how closely we can identify Apollonios himself with the anti-Kallimachean faction, and thus ratify or challenge the notion of a fundamental literary feud between these two eminent scholar-poets of the Museum faculty.

It is hard to escape the conclusion that if Kallimachos included epic (the "cyclic poem" in its basic sense) among the types of long poem to which he

---

37. Schol. Kall. *H.* ii 106: "In these lines [i.e., the exchange between Envy and Apollo: see above] he attacks those who mocked his inability to write a big poem—the reason why he was forced to write the *Hekalé*."

38. There is, for example, no absolutely compelling reason (certainly not the scholiast: confusing Ptolemies became a popular Graeco-Roman sport) to identify the king apostrophized at *Hymn II* line 26 as Ptolemy III Euergétes rather than Ptolemy II Philadelphos, and in historical terms Philadelphos is more likely. Similarly with the prologue to the *Aitia:* this famous passage is so regularly described as "a product of [Kallimachos's] old age" (Hollis, 4) that we forget the complete lack of solid rather than speculative testimony underpinning such a verdict.

39. Also the *Digest* (διήγησις) x. 18 (Hollis, 65), together with the narrative of the myth Ploutarchos (relying on Philochoros) retails at *Thes.* 14.

objected, then Apollonios, as by far the most distinguished living exponent of the genre, must inevitably have figured as one of the targets of his scorn. The tradition of Kallimachos having composed a derisive poem attacking Apollonios under the name *Ibis* thus makes perfectly good sense.[40] Did his victim strike back? It would seem so. We possess an epigram ascribed to Apollonios,[41] composed in the form of two mock encyclopedia entries: "KALLIMACHOS: Trash, cheap joke, blockhead. Original Sin: Writing Kallimachos's *Origins*."[42] Despite inevitable attempts to dismiss this tell-tale squib as a late effort to confirm a fiction, I am inclined to regard it as genuine. The balance thus shifts a little further still in favor of a personal feud. That the two men would have been at odds over the viability of epic poetry seems certain. It is the nature of that poetry, and its role in Hellenistic society, that we must now consider.

III

There are, not surprisingly, more papyrus fragments of Homer surviving from the Hellenistic and Graeco-Roman periods than of any other author. But the runner-up, a good deal less predictably, is Kallimachos. What are we to make of this? The statistics in fact are indicative, like much else, of a paradox, a crucial dilemma affecting the Hellenistic age, and operative in many cultural areas seldom fully correlated: social, moral, and religious, on the one hand, and critical, linguistic, and literary, on the other. From what we have seen so far of Kallimachean critical principles, it might be supposed that the *Iliad* and *Odyssey* were regarded much as modern readers and theatergoers tend to regard Shakespeare—that is, with respect and admiration for their classic achievement, but without any sense that they were works in a vital, ongoing tradition, to be imitated or developed. The personal, brief, allusive epigram or elegy was now de rigueur, and, it might be supposed, for more than literary reasons: an Alexandrian under Ptolemy Philadelphos surely found the heroic ethos of Achilles both remote and (with mercenaries now doing most of the fighting) more than a little embarrassing. To imitate archaic poetry encouraged artificial pastiche, and that was bad enough;

40. For an analysis of the various disobliging meanings behind the symbolic pseudonym of the ibis—foul feeder, scavenger, purger of filth, sacred monster, corrupting influence— see Green 1993, 201–2.

41. *AP* 11.275 = Kall. *test.* 25 Pf.; D. L. Page, *Further Greek Epigrams* (Cambridge, 1981), 53–54; cf. Pfeiffer, 143. None of the arguments against authenticity (cf. Green 1993, 783 n. 3, with further evidence) strikes me as compelling, and the suspicion grows that scholars are determined to find this epigram spurious simply because it tends to confirm the personal nature of any dissension between Apollonios and Kallimachos.

42. The pun on αἴτιος-Αἴτια is hard to reproduce in English. The complete Greek text runs: Καλλίμαχος· τὸ κάθαρμα, τὸ παίγνιον, ὁ ξύλινος νοῦς. Αἴτιος· ὁ γράψας Αἴτια Καλλιμάχου. The lemmatist specifically attributes this squib to "the Rhodian".

but on top of this, Bronze Age points of honor seemed primitive and unreal (not to mention unsophisticated), while Homer's Olympians were either morally shocking or ludicrous in their aggressive anthropomorphism, as Xenophanes had pointed out as early as the sixth century.[43]

Yet the passion for Homeric epic went on unabated: the epics were not only a fundamental staple of education, to be learned by heart, but also the supreme validating source of moral as well as battlefield conduct.[44] (That old, somewhat misleading cliché about Homer being the "Bible of the Greeks" only gained currency faute de mieux, since a Bible, in the sense of a universally accepted set of doctrinal writings, they wholly lacked—through the absence, primarily, of any prescriptive dogma liable, like laws, to need codification, but also, I can't help feeling, of the rigid temperament to match.) Indeed, myth in general fulfilled many of the functions of Holy Writ, and it was appealed to in very similar fashion. The mythic past, the heroic age, was not only unquestioningly treated as historical; it was seen as *better* than the world in which men lived. Much of the ingrained conservatism that formed so basic a feature of the Greek character was nostalgic.[45] From Homer's day to that of Plato, Aristotle, and Isokrates, this attitude never changed.[46] The mythic past was rooted in historical time, its legends treated as fact, its heroic protagonists seen as links between the "age of origins" and the mortal, everyday world that succeeded it.[47] Episodes such as the Trojan War and the voyage of the Argonauts were *datable*.[48] It is worth noting that

43. Xenophanes ap. Kirk-Raven-Schofield, frs. 166–9: he attacks Homer and Hesiod for attributing to the gods "all that is matter for shame and censure among men" (ὅσσα παρ' ἀν-θρώποισιν ὀνείδεα καὶ ψόγος ἐστίν), and for claiming that the gods not only resemble humans in dress and speech and physique, but even vary according to local traits (blue-eyed Thrakians, snub-nosed Aithiopians), so that, he argues, if oxen or horses could draw, *their* gods would be oxen and horses.

44. In what follows I draw heavily upon the essay entitled "'These fragments have I shored against my ruins': Apollonios Rhodios and the Social Revalidation of Myth for a New Age," written for the forthcoming *Festschrift* in honor of Professor Frank W. Walbank, to be published by the University of California Press. Large sections of part V below, in particular, have been drawn from this essay with only minimal changes.

45. Well surveyed by B. A. van Groningen, *In the Grip of the Past: Essay on an Aspect of Greek Thought* [*Philosophia Antiqua*, vol. 6] (Leiden, 1953), 1–12.

46. Homer's heroes: *Il.* 1.260–1, 5.302, 447; *Od.* 8.223. Plato *Phileb.* 16C, where Sokrates speaks of "the ancients" as being not only superior to modern men but also as "dwelling nearer to the gods" (ἐγγυτέρω θεῶν οἰκοῦντες). Arist. *Rhet.* 2.9.9, 1387a16, where he argues that "antiquity appears to be a near approach to what is by nature" (trans. van Groningen [cited in preceding note]).

47. C. Brillante, "Myth and History: History and the Historical Interpretation of Myth," in *Approaches to Greek Myth*, ed. L. Edmunds (Baltimore, 1991), 91–140, esp. 101–2.

48. The Trojan War is dated to 1218 by the Marmor Parium (264–263: *FGrH* 23). The voyage of the Argonauts is dated to 1264 by Eusebius (ed. A. Schoene, H. Petermann, and E. Roediger [Berlin, 1866; repr., Dublin, 1967], 2: 44–47).

the so-called "Parian Marble" (*Marmor Parium*) of 264–263, which confidently dates a whole series of mythical events, from Deukalion's Flood (1528) to the Amazons' campaign against Athens (1256), is exactly contemporary with Apollonios. Indeed, Hellenistic scholars were as committed as any other group to the recovery and reconstitution of the past and its mythic heritage: what else was the aetiologizing obsession they display but a search for roots—perhaps exacerbated by their *déraciné* existence in the brave new world of Alexandria or Pergamon?

Thus any intellectual or literary attempt to challenge the validity of the myths would, inevitably, arouse acute antagonism, confusion, and distress. There was much that it was essential to preserve.[49] First and foremost, there were the "great deeds" of the heroic past: this ideal is reflected as a dominant leitmotif not only in Homer, but also in Herodotos, Pindar, and the fourth-century orators. Next, there was the educational function of myths, their service as paradigms, "moral exemplars, cautionary tales, and formulation in gnomic utterance of moral, and indeed of technical, wisdom".[50] Slightly counter to this, and much frowned on by serious moralists, Stoics in particular,[51] there was the undoubted entertainment value of the famous *gestes*. More crucial to social stability had to be the function of myths in providing explanations, authorization, or empowerment for the present in terms of origins: this could apply, not only to foundation or charter myths and genealogical trees (thus supporting territorial or family claims), but also to personal moral choices. Lastly, of course, there was religion: myths perpetuated an archetypal stratum of irrational (and often hair-raisingly amoral) belief, not least in the arbitrary and personal whims of totally unpredictable deities, which remained disconcertingly indifferent to human progress.

Such attitudes had come under steadily increasing attack at least from the time of Xenophanes in the sixth century (see above), and probably much earlier, as evidence of expurgation in the Homeric poems suggests.[52] Geographical exploration steadily encroached on the mythic unknown: the very necessary mythical fusing of the Clashing Rocks once the Black Sea became well traveled (picked up at *Arg.* 2.604–6)[53] bears eloquent witness to this.

49. The categories here described are (except for that of religion) outlined by Buxton, ch. 9, "The Actors' Perceptions," 169–81.

50. M. Heath, *The Poetics of Greek Tragedy* (London, 1987), ch. 2, "Meaning and Emotion," 47.

51. Strabo the geographer vigorously attacks Eratosthenes' argument that a poet's aim should be to provide emotional pleasure rather than instruction: 1.2.3, C. 15, ad init., repeated at 1.12.10, C. 7, ad fin.

52. Gilbert Murray, *The Rise of the Greek Epic* (Oxford, 1907), 110–35 (unchanged in subsequent editions).

53. The Black Sea remained largely unfamiliar to Greek sailors till the eighth century at the very earliest: J. Boardman, *The Greeks Overseas*, 3d ed. (London, 1980), 240. E. H. Minns, *Scythians and Greeks* (Cambridge, 1913), 9, reminds us of the nervous trepidation with which Greeks

Skepticism also extended to the various "marvels" (θαύματα), such as Aiëtes' fire-breathing brazen bulls, that had flourished in unknown territory ("Here be dragons"), and that the cold realities of experience progressively forced further and further out towards the periphery. Herodotos firmly dismissed the symbolic concept of the stream of Ocean girdling a flat disk of earth.[54]

The growth of knowledge, *logos* at the expense of *mythos*,[55] altered more than the visible landscape: its impact on Greek social, moral, and even religious attitudes was profound. The new drive towards civilized urbanism, with written law codes, and a vision (not always attained) of equality under the law (ἰσονομία), severely undercut the ancient tradition of tribal authoritarianism, of arbitrary conduct whether in heaven or on earth. Heroic egotism found itself losing ground to the cooperative virtues, aristocratic outspokenness to middle-class euphemism; personal motivation (not to mention sexual permissiveness) of the kind regularly attributed to the Olympians came to be frowned on. Unfortunately, divine conduct, being hallowed by tradition, remained immutable, and thus got further and further out of line with socially approved human conduct. Further, myths that validated family trees and territorial claims were, inevitably, subject to interpolation and forgery, while the spread of literacy and improved communications meant that innumerable local variants of myths now became common property, and had, somehow—since all traditions commanded respect—to be reconciled with one another.

As may be imagined, this rapid expansion of rational knowledge—generated by the so-called "Greek miracle", the sixth-century intellectual breakthrough in Ionia—created severe conflict between new insights and old beliefs. Tribal lore went head-to-head with polis institutions; accumulated social and religious faith, what Gilbert Murray called the Inherited Conglomerate,[56] struggled to overcome its sheer incompatibility with innovative, and for the most part anti-Olympian, ideas about the world and man's place in it. Past belief and future reason remained in acute conflict, not just between intellectuals and the masses, but, even more disruptively, *within individuals.* The ingrained beliefs of centuries were not to be jettisoned overnight by a simple application of reason. It is sometimes assumed by intellectuals that the arrival of logos will always be welcome, that mythos is simply awaiting enlightenment. Nothing could be further from the truth. Heart long remained in stubborn resistance against head: mythos persisted against all odds.

---

long continued to contemplate a Black Sea voyage. Kolchis, at its eastern end, so prominent in the Argonaut myth, and regularly mentioned in the early literature, shows no physical evidence of Greek presence till as late as c. 550: Braund, 92–93.

54. Hdt. 2.23, 4.8, 4.36.
55. For a full (if not overpercipient) account of this process, see Nestle.
56. Gilbert Murray, *Greek Studies* (Oxford, 1947), 66–67; cf. Dodds, 179.

The archaic world it represented was dangerous, baffling, and wholly un-predictable; it stressed—perhaps more realistically than Protagorean confi-dence in man-the-measure-of-all-things—human helplessness (ἀμηχανία) against nature and divinity. As we shall see, this prominent feature of Jason's character in the *Argonautika* was no accident.

The long-enduring quality of myth, despite these intellectual inroads, should therefore come as no surprise. All the primeval "marvels" contra-dicting the normal laws of nature—winged horses, the Chimaira, three-headed dogs, guardian dragons—reappear in Pliny's *Natural History* (7.9–32). Though Herodotos correctly identified the Kaspian as an inland sea rather than an inlet of Ocean (1.203), it was not long before the old view was rein-stated, largely in order to glorify Alexander.[57] Meanwhile, historians and mythographers anxious to "save the appearances" were forced either to ex-plain away or reinterpret those elements of each mythos that seemed in-compatible with the rational demands of logos. They found two ways of do-ing this: by rationalization and allegory. Both methods justified seemingly impossible, improper, or incompatible characters and events by explaining, in different ways, that they were not what in fact they appeared to be. While rationalization sought to recover factual truth from the distortions of mis-understanding, propaganda, or poetic vision, allegory looked for abstract inner truth, the hidden verity beneath the surface of things. The first dealt with physical or historical impossibilities, the second with matters morally repugnant or embarrassing. Where allegory bowdlerized myth, rationaliza-tion made a remarkably successful job of historicizing it.

Epic poetry, it would seem clear, must have found itself at the very heart of this conflict between tradition and innovation. It sought to preserve the "great deeds of men" (κλέα ἀνδρῶν) and, as we have seen, made no clear distinction between the mythical and the historical, treating both as un-questioned fact, the cumulative legacy of the past.[58] It thus catered not only to antiquarians but also to the great mass of thinking (and now expatriate) Greeks who sought validation for their culture. Since the mythic tradition formed the prime source for that validation, not least through systematic ae-tiological enquiry, an open avenue existed by which scholars as well as po-ets in Alexandria (most, of course, fulfilled both functions) could explore and develop the genre in literary terms. Yet serious objections could be lodged against this course. To begin with, the acknowledged supremacy of Homer meant that any modern epic would be relentlessly measured against the *Iliad* and the *Odyssey*. The current taste for epigrammatic concision was

57. Romm, 34, 42–43.
58. This makes the careful distinction between the two genres in Cameron, ch. 10, "Hel-lenistic Epic" (where pp. 262–95 deal with the "historical," and pp. 295–301 with the "mythi-cal") merely academic rather than real, and in ways highly misleading.

sure to discourage would-be Homeric epigonoi. Quasi-secular rationalism could not but find the whole divine apparatus of epic, from its disconcertingly anthropomorphic Olympian deities to paranormal phenomena such as the Kyklops, the Clashing Rocks, or Aiëtes' fire-breathing bulls, both artificial and embarrassing. Even were there no evidence whatsoever for a fundamental conflict between the Kallimachean school and the author of the *Argonautika*, it would still be necessary to postulate its existence.

Apollonios has to figure as the sole representative of epic in this context, since solid evidence for the existence of other Hellenistic epic poets, let alone for their texts, is woefully inadequate. Antimachos of Kolophon (b. c. 440) is far too early, and survives only in scattered fragments,[59] though he is interesting inasmuch as a good deal of his style, language, and subject matter (glosses, neologisms, variation, obscure allusions, erotic elegy) seems to have anticipated the scholar-poets of the mid third century. He wrote a *Thebaïd*, and his two-book elegy *Lydé*, on unhappy love stories, contained in book 1 an account of Medeia and the Argonauts' expedition (Wyss frs. 56–65, Matthews frs. 67–76), including the interesting information (Wyss fr. 64 = schol. 4.1153) that she and Jason had sex (μιγῆναι), or, possibly, married, beside the Phasis River in Kolchis. Though the erotic element in fact can be traced back as early as the first quarter of the sixth century,[60] it seems likely that Antimachos contributed significantly to the portrayal of Medeia in book 3 of the *Argonautika*.[61] His fragments suggest prolixity, bombast, and Home-

---

59. See B. Wyss, *Antimachi Colophonii Reliquiae* (Berlin, 1936); later discoveries (including new fragments of the *Thebaïd* [see below]) collected in *Supplementum Hellenisticum*, ed. P. H. J. Lloyd-Jones and P. Parsons (New York, 1983), 52–79. Wyss has very recently been updated by Matthews (see Biblio.), whose work supersedes all earlier publications on Antimachos. Beside extending the fragments to include all material discovered since Wyss's day, he offers a magisterial survey of Antimachos's life and work, which, while augmenting Wyss, pays a well-deserved tribute to his excellent scholarship.

60. Pausanias (5.18.3) includes in his description of the Chest of Kypselos (c. 580–70), a Corinthian votive offering at Olympia unfortunately no longer extant, the following passage: "Jason is standing to the right of Medeia, who is seated on a throne, with Aphrodite to her left. A hexametrical inscription above them reads: 'Jason marries Medeia, as Aphrodite commands' (Μήδειαν Ἰάσων γαμέει, κέλεται δ' Ἀφροδίτα)."

61. Determined, as always, to eradicate any trace of a conflict between Kallimacheans and Apollonians, Cameron writes, with his usual firm assurance (337): "So there was no great dispute about different types of poetry; no battle between traditional epic and modern poetry; between bad, boring long poems and elegant, witty brief ones. Just a few contemporaries who disagreed about one particular poem. Epic had nothing to do with it. The debate about Antimachus centered on his elegy the *Lyde*. There is no reason to believe that even Callimachus disapproved of his epic *Thebaid*." Far more sensible, and logical, is the critic whom Cameron casually dismisses, D. W. T. W. Vessey, in "The Reputation of Antimachus of Colophon," *Hermes* 99 (1971): 1–10, arguing that if Kallimachos disliked the *Lyde*, "he is likely to have had an even lower opinion of the *Thebaïs*, which he must have regarded as an example of that hated genre τὸ ποίημα τὸ κυκλικόν" (3).

ric pastiche (evidence in Matthews, 72–74). Yet he received widespread praise, and at least till the second century (Cameron, 337, with n. 167), his *Thebaïd* was regarded as the next best epic after those of Homer. The loss of Antimachos's work is a real handicap to our understanding of the way in which classical epic developed.

This remains true for the Hellenistic period. Of works roughly contemporary with Apollonios, such as Rhianos of Kréte's *Herakleias*, or a *Thebaïd* by Antagoras of Rhodes (why the popularity of this particular mythic cycle?), we know only enough to whet our curiosity for more. Rhianos edited Homer (conservatively),[62] wrote local "tribal" epic lays (we hear of a *Thessalika*, an *Achaïika*, an *Eliaka*, and a *Messeniaka*),[63] and managed—a significant point— to combine this with the production of pederastic epigrams (frs. 66–76), perhaps one reason why Tiberius admired him (Suet. *Tib.* 70). Antagoras, a noted gourmet and intimate of Antigonos Gonatas,[64] likewise had a repertoire that included both epic and erotic verse (Cameron's claim[65] that the debate was exclusively over elegy looks less convincing in the light of such versatility). The quality of his *Thebaïd* may perhaps be judged from the fact that in Thebes itself—where he might have been expected to get an enthusiastic reception on local and patriotic grounds—his reading of it bored his audience into yawning somnolence.[66] Other poets, such as Menelaos of Aigai, author, yet again, of a *Thebaïs*, this one in eleven books (frs. 551–57 *Suppl. Hell.*), are scarcely more than names to us. The *Argonautai* of Dionysios Skytobrachion, an epitome of which is preserved by Diodoros (4.40–55), I shall return to later (see part V below).

This huge lacuna in our evidence has encouraged scholars to theorize and extrapolate on the basis of current critical trends and poetic theory (which really boils down to Aristotle and Kallimachos: see, e.g., Hunter 1989, 32–33). Academe, like nature, abhors a vacuum. The one thing on which everyone till very recently has been agreed is that epic, though now lost to us,[67] flourished nonstop from Homer's day to the time of the Roman empire, when critics like Juvenal blasted the genre (see *Sat.* 1.1–14 in particu-

---

62. Fragments collected by J. U. Powell, *Collectanea Alexandrina* (Oxford, 1925), 9–21. The longest piece (fr. 1), 21 hexameter lines on the vain follies of mankind, cannot confidently be assigned to any of the known titles.

63. The *Messeniaka* was drawn on heavily by Pausanias: 4.6.1–2.

64. Athen. 8.340 f, cf. Plut. *Mor.* 182F, 668D, and Paus. 1.2.3.

65. Particularly in ch. 10, "Fat Ladies," 303–38 (an allusion to Antimachos's *Lydê*).

66. *Gnom. Vat.* 109–11, p. 50, Sternbach (cited by Cameron, 51, with n. 182). A man of sharp temper and even sharper tongue, Antagoras is said to have rolled up his book in pique, and told his audience, in an unreproduceable pun, that as Boiotians they were well named, since they had cows' ears (Βοιωτῶν, βοῶν ὦτα).

67. The key text is Ziegler's short but packed little monograph: note the word *vergessenes* (forgotten) in the subtitle.

lar) for prolixity, cliché, and themes staled by endless repetition (including that of the *Argonautika*).[68] Ziegler argued, very convincingly,[69] that the Kallimachean movement, far from being representative of mainstream thinking (the average reader preferred epic anyway), was a mandarin aberration, which only much later, under neoteric influence, actually achieved the position of authority to which it had briefly aspired in the third century. This, of course, fits in well with the royal appointment of Apollonios rather than Kallimachos (whatever the latter's scholarly claims) as chief librarian. Ptolemy's weakness for gigantism (his notorious "Grand Procession"; the Pharos lighthouse) was hardly liable to make him choose an elegist, much less an epigrammatist, over a staunch upholder of Homeric expansiveness.[70]

Now comes Cameron, however, to assure us that the Hellenistic period had virtually no epic at all—certainly no *historical* epic (to use his own artificial distinction), though he finds it harder to argue *mythic* epic out of existence.[71] The usefulness of his iconoclastic survey consists in a systematic demolition of the scholarly edifice of strawless bricks that has slowly—but perhaps, given the shortage of solid facts, inevitably—accumulated in this area over the past half-century. On the other hand, that epic was not only flourishing in the third century but a prime object of study still seems to me an inescapable conclusion: I am less than impressed by legerdemain arguments to the effect that the well-documented obsession with Homer, from Zenódotos to Aristarchos, was due entirely to the poet's personal reputation and had nothing to do with the genre he represented. At one level, too, Cameron's thesis undermines itself. If there was, as he maintains, no real epic school under Ptolemy Philadelphos or his successor, then the *Argonautika* of Apollonios (which he can hardly claim never existed) sticks out like the proverbial sore thumb, an inexplicable anomaly—and therefore all the *more* likely to be attacked by hostile critics. What Cameron in fact has provided is an extra argument (even though a false one) *in favor of* the quarrel in which he so firmly refuses to believe.

This absence of comparanda has led to some highly speculative assessments

---

68. See esp. lines 9–13: "quid agant uenti, quas torqueat umbras / Aeacus, unde alius furtiuae deuehat aurum / pelliculae, quantas iaculetur Monychus ornos, / Frontonis platani conuulsaque marmora clamant / semper et adsiduo ruptae lectore columnae" ("what the winds are up to, which shades are being tortured / by Aecus, the place from which what's-his-name is levanting with the stolen / gold fleecelet, the number of ash-spears hurled by the Centaurs / —all this re-echoes non-stop from Fronto's plane-trees and quaking / statues, from the columns cracked by endless recitation").

69. See esp. Ziegler, 13: "Das traditionelle Urteil ist schief und falsch. Für die fast drei Jahrhunderte 'Hellenismus' ist der Stil des Kallimachos alles andere als repräsentativ."

70. On Ptolemaic gigantism, see Green 1993, 33, 95–96, 183, and elsewhere. It seems to me more than possible that Kallimachos's miniaturism was in part a conscious reaction against the overblown gigantism of the court in Alexandria. See also E. E. Rice, *The Grand Procession of Ptolemy Philadelphus* (Oxford, 1983).

71. Cameron ch. 10, "Hellenistic Epic," 263–302. See 295 ff. for "mythical" epic.

of the *Argonautika*'s position in its literary context, based for the most part on our fuller (though still regrettably patchy) knowledge of Aristotelian and Peripatetic theory. This theory will have been a fortiori familiar to the Museum's scholars, who quite certainly possessed not only the *Poetics*, but other material now lost to us. Its central principle (*Poet.* 1451a16–35, 1459a17–59b16) was that an epic poet should take, as Homer did in the *Iliad*, a single unified action (πρᾶξις), with a beginning, a middle, and an end, rather than pursue an all-inclusive episodic narrative or the adventures of some individual or group. For taking the latter course, Aristotle severely criticized the poets of the post-Homeric "epic cycle"—and the *Argonautika*, of course, could be faulted on precisely the same grounds. It is hard to believe that such criticisms were not in fact made; even harder to see Apollonios's work as an attempt to meet these unitary requirements with a poem that was εὐσύνοπτον—that is, could be viewed at a glance in its entirety. The aitia and digressions that crowd it remain, despite caveats,[72] profoundly anti-Aristotelian.[73]

Such an approach, given the nature of its inadequacies, cannot get us very far. Better results, if of a rather different kind, can be obtained by examining the *Argonautika*'s position in terms of the ongoing conflict, sketched out above, between mythos and logos. To do this, we need to trace the development, from pre-Homeric to Hellenistic times, of the Ur-myth shaping the structure of Apollonios's narrative.

IV

The legend of the Argonauts is among the earliest known to the Greeks. It certainly goes back to the early part of the Dark Ages—that is, the ninth or tenth century B.C.[74] One archaeologist has even suggested that it enshrines memories of expeditions designed to acquire the new, much-prized, and still little understood techniques of smelting and forging metal, as far back as the late fourth or third millennium.[75] To Homer, Jason's ship *Argo* was already "common knowledge" (*Od.* 12.70, πᾶσι μέλουσα). Other references in the *Iliad* and the *Odyssey* are, similarly, casual enough to presume wide-

---

72. E.g., by Hunter 1989, 33–34.

73. I used to think that by casting the *Argonautika* in four books totaling 5,835 lines, with each the length of an average Greek play (bk. 4, at 1,781 lines, rather longer than most, is nearly matched by *Agamemnon* at 1,683), Apollonios might be attempting to meet the requirement in the *Poetics* (1459b21–22) that the "mass" or "bulk" (πλῆθος) of an epic poem should equal that of a trilogy plus the satyr play (which his in fact does); but though he *may* have done this deliberately, I tend on reflection to believe rather that the parallel is merely coincidental.

74. Rhys Carpenter, "The Greek Penetration of the Black Sea," *AJA* 52 (1948): 1 ff.

75. C. Doumas, "What Did the Argonauts Seek in Colchis?" *Hermathena* 150 (1991): 31–41. The theory has not found general favor, and much of the symbolic interpretation of the myth is forced; but bronze-working does figure noticeably in the narrative (the Chalybes, the fire-breathing bulls, Hephaistos, Talos), and the motive at least is credible.

spread familiarity.[76] Some details of the narrative strongly suggest universal folktale motifs, as Beye 1982 (42) makes clear: "A young prince comes to the home of a hostile being who puts him to severe trials in which he is helped by the daughter of his host. After succeeding at the imposed task he elopes with the girl and is pursued. They elude their pursuer by throwing things in his wake which must be collected." At the same time we are reminded of the intensely self-conscious delicacy and ironic wit applied to this too-familiar ancient matter by the Hellenistic poet. Apollonios mischievously makes Jason employ an almost identical tale, that of Theseus, Minos, and Ariadné,[77] to allay Medeia's fears; and he avoids using the (clearly primitive) version of events according to which the delaying objects cast in the wake of the fleeing Argonauts' ship were the butchered fragments of Medeia's young brother Apsyrtos, cut up with zest by Medeia herself.[78] Instead, Apsyrtos for Apollonios is *older* than Medeia, her half-brother only,[79] and succumbs to a murder plot initiated and carried out by Jason. Not by coincidence, I suspect—euphemizing Hellenistic censorship, together with a new sympathy for women, seems to have been at work on Medeia's behalf—our surviving sources for this version are exclusively late.[80]

But the core of the story, as the folktale element would indicate, is very old, and remains strikingly constant.[81] As always with Greek myth, it has as background a complex genealogical web of intertwined family relationships, which the Glossary illuminates in detail. Most of the protagonists are members of the vast Aiolid clan; of particular concern are two sons of Aiolos (the eponymous founder of the Aiolid district in northwestern Asia Minor), Athamas and Kretheus, and the daughter, Tyro, of a third son, Salmoneus. Tyro was first seduced by Poseidon, and as a result bore twins, Neleus and Pelias, whom she exposed (but in good fairy-tale fashion, they both survived).

---

76. *Il.* 2.711–15, 7.467–69; *Od.* 10.135–39, 11.253–59, 12.3–4, 59–72.

77. See 3.998–1004, 1074–76, with commentary ad loc.

78. See Apollod. 1.9.24: this version apparently (schol. Ap. 4.223–30a, d) goes back to Pherekydes. By a false etymology, Ovid's city of exile, Tomis, was thought to have been thus named to commemorate the "cutting up" (τομή, τέμνω) of Apsyrtos, and the burial of his collected fragments there by Aiëtes: Apollod. ibid. and Ovid *Tr.* 3.9.21–34.

79. Son of Aiëtes by Asteródeia (3.242): see Gloss., s.v. "Apsyrtos". It is noteworthy that the source making Apsyrtos Eidyia's son, and thus Medeia's full brother, Apollodoros (1.9.23), presents a version based on the early narrative of Pherekydes, and also reports Apsyrtos's dismemberment by his sister. Sophokles had already (fr. 546 Pearson) softened the shock by similarly diluting the blood kinship between them.

80. *Arg. Orph.* 1027–32 (clearly based on Ap.); Hygin. *Fab.* 23; Val. Flacc. *Arg.* 8.369 ff. (unfinished, but the intent is clear).

81. Hunter 1989, 12–15, gives a composite precis of the myth, stressing how little it varies, despite the "wide variety of literary and artistic sources covering several centuries" that combine to transmit it. The most detailed account from antiquity is that reported at length by Apollodoros in 1.9 (see esp. 1, 8, 10–11, 16–28): in his notes Frazer lists all other important sources.

She then married her uncle, Kretheus, the king of Iolkos in southern Thessalia, who had brought her up. By him she had three sons, Aison, Amythaon, and Pheres. Amythaon became the father of Bias and Melampous. Aison married Alkimédé, who bore him two sons, one of whom was Jason. Pheres' son Admetos compounded the family connection by marrying Pelias's daughter Alkestis.

The exposed twins, grown to angry manhood, lost no time in returning to Iolkos. By what must seem a curious case of psychological displacement, far from resenting their rejection by their mother Tyro, they concentrated their wrath on Kretheus's new wife, Sidero, for treating the discarded Tyro badly. When Sidero sought refuge in Hera's sanctuary, Pelias outraged the goddess by killing his stepmother at the altar and continuing to insult Hera thereafter,[82] an act the consequences of which reverberate throughout the *Argonautika,* explaining both Hera's bitter grudge against Pelias, her support for the Argonauts, and her ruthless use of Medeia as an instrument of vengeance. Both brothers were exiled by Kretheus. Neleus went to Pylos in the western Peloponnesos, where he founded the Neleïd dynasty. Pelias, however, "continued to dwell somewhere around Thessalia,"[83] and his exact status in Iolkos at the time of the expedition to Kolchis is the subject of at least two conflicting reports.

What tradition agrees on is that Pelias was then king of Iolkos; also that he received an oracle warning him to beware of a one-sandaled man. But whether his position was legitimate or due to usurpation, and just why he had to fear this unshod visitor, are questions on which our sources differ fundamentally. What we may call the pro-Pelias version, attributed by schol. Pind. 133a to Pherekydes (probably writing c. 480),[84] and reproduced by Apollodoros (1.9.16), presents Pelias, not Aison, as successor to Kretheus, with Aison's son Jason living peacefully in the country. In this version, Jason turns up to take part in a royal sacrifice to Poseidon (this god, we should recall, being Pelias's father), having lost one sandal while fording the Anauros river. What, Pelias asked his nephew, would *he* do, supposing he had the power, if he received an oracle to the effect that he would be murdered by such-and-such a citizen? "Send him," said Jason, "on the quest for the Golden Fleece." Pherekydes comments that "Hera put this idea into Jason's head so that Medeia might come as a bane to Pelias." Apollodoros concedes the possibility, but adds "unless the idea struck him for some other reason."

Quite different is the account for which our main source is Pindar's Fourth

---

82. Apollod. 1.9.8–9: Πελίας δὲ ἐπ' αὐτῶν τῶν βωμῶν αὐτὴν κατέσφαξε, καὶ καθόλου διετέλει τὴν Ἥραν ἀτιμάζων.

83. Apollod. 1.9.10: Πελίας δὲ περὶ Θεσσαλίαν κατῴκει.

84. So Braswell, 16–18.

Pythian, where we learn (106–19) that Zeus granted the royal succession to Aiolos and his descendants, but that Pelias violently usurped power from Jason's parents, Aison and Alkiméde (Polymédé in some versions), who secretly smuggled the young boy away to be brought up by Cheiron.[85] His return to Iolkos, and his confrontation there with Pelias, is for the specific purpose of reclaiming his rightful position as king. The discussion between them (136–68) is surprisingly low-key, reasonable, and diplomatic on both sides. Jason deplores violence (147–48), and is quite ready to forgo his claim to flocks and fields (148–50) provided he recovers the royal scepter and the throne. Pelias's reply is even more interesting. He is old, he says, while Jason is young. Let Jason, therefore, first remove that divine wrath oppressing the Aiolid house by making voyage to Aiëtes' realm and bringing back, not only the Fleece, but also *the spirit of Phrixos*, as Phrixos himself would have it. Do that, Pelias concludes, and I swear by Zeus, the father of our common ancestor (ὁ γενέθλιος ἀμφοτέροις), that I will turn over to you both sovereignty and kingdom.[86] The wrath, as Ap. makes very clear (3.336–40), is that of "implacable Zeus" (ἀμείλικτος Ζεύς), and Phrixos is thought of—though dead—as sentient, angry, and unappeased (Braswell, 240–41).[87] Whether we find the story of Pelias's usurpation a likely ingredient of the Ur-myth or not (and personally I regard it as all but inevitable), we need to bear it in mind when following the Argonauts to Kolchis. Though the opening of the *Argonautika* seems to imply Pelias's legitimate rule, it also presents (1.5–17) a strong motive for usurpation, and there are hints (1.287, 411) that Aison and his wife have been removed from power.[88]

Even in antiquity it was believed that the religious motive (i.e., of placat-

85. Pind. *Pyth.* 4.109–10: πεύθομαι γάρ νιν Πελίαν ἄθεμιν λευκαῖς πιθήσαντα φρασὶν / ἀμετέρων ἀποσυλᾶσθαι βιαίως ἀρχεδικᾶν τοκέων ("For I gather that unrighteous Pelias, persuaded by his blank wits, stole it [the kingship] forcibly from the just rule of my parents").

86. The stress on Zeus in this version, both as guarantor of the succession and as ancestor (presumably the allusion is to the belief that Aiolos's father, Hellen, was the son of Zeus rather than of Deukalion [Apollod. 1.7.2; cf. Braswell, 247]) would seem to be a calculated effort to trump the claims of Pelias as Poseidon's son by appealing to Zeus's paramount authority and precedence over all other gods.

87. Critical purists will, I hope, forgive me for discussing these mythical variants as though they were elements in a historical puzzle. Let me reassure them that this is simply a matter of convenience and leaves open the question of whether or not the whole legend had any historical basis. The point, of course, is that those who retailed it would seek to make it a plausible tale (this consideration applies equally to historians and fiction writers), and some, with this end in view, would be certain to consider the possibility of usurpation.

88. Vian 1980, 123. Schol. Hom. *Od.* 12.69 and schol. Hes. *Theog.* 993 allude to yet another variant, according to which Aison died early, and Pelias became regent for Jason, but this is incompatible with the general belief that Medeia on her arrival in Iolkos rejuvenated Aison. Archaeology also contributes some interesting evidence to the problem. Some 4 kms. southwest of Iolkos, at the foot of the hills leading up to the late Stone Age site of Dhimini, a late Mykenaian royal tholos tomb and a small Mykenaian town, occupied for less than a century, have

ing Phrixos) was propounded by Pindar alone, with the clear implication that he had invented it.[89] Since one of Pindar's main aims in this poem was to reconcile the king of Kyréné, Arkesilas IV, with Damophilos, a nobleman exiled for allegedly treasonable activities, the tone of sweet reason that he bestowed upon the confrontation between Jason and Pelias was clearly de rigueur. It would hardly do to have Pelias dispatch his nephew to the ends of the earth with the deliberate intention of getting him killed there. We can believe, if we will, that Pindar's Pelias is being Machiavellian; it is true that near the end of the poem (250), there is a brief reference to Medeia being "the death of Pelias" (τὸν Πελίαο φόνον). Are we also to assume divine malevolence at work? In any case, this introduction of Phrixos brings us to the second main antecedent of the expedition, once more involving the dynastic activities of an Aiolid ruler.

Athamas, yet another brother of Kretheus and Salmoneus, and king of Orchómenos in Boiotia (Apollod. 1.9.1), had two children by Nephélé ("Cloud"), Phrixos and Hellé. Like Kretheus, he remarried; like Sidero, this new wife, Ino, having borne Athamas two sons, Learchos and Melikertés, proceeded, in true stepmotherly fashion, to plot against his children by Nephélé. Having engineered a crop failure, Ino first sent messengers to Delphi, and then bribed them to declare, not the true (unrecorded) Delphic response, but her own false assertion that the blight on the land could only be cured by sacrificing Phrixos to Zeus. Athamas, in desperation, was prepared to do even this; but Nephélé came to her children's rescue with a golden-fleeced magical ram, the gift of Hermes. This ram could both speak and fly: Phrixos and Hellé escaped on its back. Hellé, as is well known, fell off over the Hellespont ("Helle's Sea") and was drowned. Phrixos arrived safely in Kolchis, where he was kindly received by Aiëtés, who gave him his own daughter Chalkiopé in marriage. The ram Phrixos sacrificed to Zeus of the Fugitives (Διὶ φυξίῳ), and Aiëtés hung its golden fleece in the grove of Ares, where it was guarded by an ever-wakeful serpent (Apollod. 1.9.16). According to Apollonios (2.1150–53), Phrixos died of old age while still in Kolchis. No accident that when the Argonauts encounter his sons (ibid.) they are on their way to Orchómenos "to lay hands on Athamas's possessions." Property again: the history of the Aiolids may be fictional, but it nevertheless embodies some disconcerting levels of reality. Even the variants suggest, Rashomon-like, competing dynastic versions of the truth.

One highly interesting aspect of the Argonaut myth is its virtually total free-

---

been found. Vasiliki Adrimi, curator of the Volos Museum, has suggested (Severin, 63–65) that this may have been where Jason's father Aison settled after Pelias's usurpation of the throne of Iolkos, and also possibly where he was buried. The abandonment of the site would then mark Jason's recovery of Iolkos from Pelias.

89. See schol. Pind. 281a, cf. on 134–68.

dom from allegory. The allegorization of Homer began surprisingly early, with Theagenes of Rhegion, a sixth-century contemporary of Xenophanes, and it is a reasonable assumption that he was reacting to Xenophanes' moral strictures (p. 14 above and n. 43). Our main evidence comes from a Homeric scholion, citing Theagenes as the earliest critic to have used allegory as a defense against charges of impropriety,[90] and offering a detailed justification of the Battle of the Gods (*Il.* 20.55, 67–74) on just such grounds. The fighting is transmuted into a conflict of the elements: dry against moist, hot against cold, heavy against light. This image is extended to all the elements of the universe, with Apollo a manifestation of fire, Poseidon of water, and Hera of air. But such manipulation never touches the Argonauts. None of our ancient testimonia, nor indeed the most thorough modern survey, that by Félix Buffière, can produce a single example of genuine Argonautic allegory (Herakles, allegorized ad nauseam, is a special case). One might have supposed the allegorizing mind would have had a field day over the Fleece, or the Clashing Rocks, or Aiëtés' tests, but history remains silent. Was it felt that this archaic tale of theft, seduction, and murder (including fratricide) was beyond moral rescue? More probably the answer is to be found in Homer's unique popularity and preeminence as an educational tool, which meant that would-be moral whitewashers concentrated on Homeric epic to the exclusion of all else.

The Argonaut legend, on the other hand, seems primarily to have attracted the attention of rationalizing conservatives anxious to preserve—at varying levels—their suspension of disbelief. That cheerful realist Diogenes of Sinopé "used to say that Medeia was clever, but no magician."[91] Herodoros (?430–?360 B.C.), an inveterate allegorizer and rationalizer, wrote an *Argonautika* (as well as a 17-book work on Herakles);[92] yet his most interesting reference to the Argonauts is the assertion (a belief shared by both Sophokles and Euripides) that they simplified their return voyage by coming back the way they had set out—thus incidentally also saving the geographical appearances.[93] This last was always the greatest problem. The Augustan geographer Strabo wrote (1.2.10, C. 21) that Homer's contemporaries "regarded the Pontic Sea as though it were another Ocean, and thought that those who

90. Schol. B on *Il.* 20.67 = Diels-Kranz 8 T2. On Theagenes, see Buffière, 101–5; Nestle, 128–31; and Feeney 8–11, who correctly points out that the detailed allegorizing described by the scholiast is not directly ascribed to Theagenes himself, merely that "some" (οἱ μέν) explain the passage in this way, and that the practice goes back to Theagenes. But Dowden (41) is probably right in his assumption that even if not all the allegorical equations here adduced belong to Theagenes, some of them will, so that "a sort of common interpretation gradually builds up, which . . . will be dear to the hearts of Stoic philosophers in the Hellenistic Age."

91. Cited by Stobaeus, 3.29.92.

92. See *FGrH* 31 F 5–10, 38–55 (*Argonautika*), 13–37 (*Heraklesgeschichte*), and cf. Nestle 146–48.

93. Soph. fr. 547 Radt; Eur. *Med.* 432, 1263–64; Herodoros *FGrH* 31 F 10 = schol. Ap. 4.259.

sailed thither were going off the map (ἐκτοπίζειν) as surely as those who ventured beyond the Pillars [of Herakles]." Other aspects of the Heroic Age could, as we shall see, be accepted, even if not reconcilable with current realities: the heroes might indeed have walked with gods, conquered marvelous monsters now extinct, or possessed—innately or by magic (the latter, of course, *pace* Diogenes, still flourishing)—supernatural powers. But their world, the stage on which their *gestes* took place, was fixed and immutable. All that had changed was the degree of human knowledge concerning it, the proportion of known to unknown. By the sixth century B.C. at latest, most of the gaps in the Hellenes' immediate *mappa mundi* had been filled with irrefutable geographical realities very different from the quasi-symbolic and largely imaginary constructs of early saga.

This proved the mythic tradition's most vulnerable feature, and in the Argonaut legend it played a large and crucial role. Aia and Kolchis became fixed as early as Mimnermos's day (late seventh century): they formed the immutable eastern kingdom of Aiëtés, whose father was the rising Sun (Helios: frs. 11, 11a West). It was from Aia, located by Mimnermos beside the stream of Ocean, that Jason brought back "the great Fleece" (our first surviving reference to it). Thus the Argonauts' outward route was, apart from minor variations (see below, pp. 33–34), now firmly established. In consequence, Aia's original proximity to Ocean was quietly forgotten, and both Kolchis and the Clashing Rocks lost most of their original significance as part of a rite de passage into the kind of off-the-map fantasy world that Odysseus describes for the Phaiakians.[94] Pindar, indeed, is the last writer, a couple of decades before Herodotos, to use Ocean as part of the Argonauts' route, or to the regard the Pillars of Herakles as a liminal barrier.[95] Elsewhere the filling in of hitherto blank or vague areas of the Mediterranean map forced some ingenious relocations. Plausible but little-known geography became much sought after, with south Italy, Sicily, and the West in general as prime targets. Whereas for Homer, Kirké is located in the east (*Od.* 12.3–4), by Hesiod's day (*Theog.* 1011–15), she has become the mother, by Odysseus, of two sons, Agrios and Latinos, who rule over the Tyrrhenians. Aia—now Aiaia—is very soon located off the Campanian coast, midway between Rome and Naples. An ingenious—and scandalous—rationalization was thought up to explain Kirké's move: she had poisoned the king her husband, and needed to take a *very* long trip in a hurry.[96]

94. Cf. Beye 1982, 43–44, and J. Lindsay, *The Clashing Rocks* (London, 1965), 7–37.
95. See Pind. *Ol.* 3.43–45, where, discussing the Ἡρακλέος σταλᾶν (Pillars of Herakles), he writes, with extraordinary emphasis and passion, as though a cherished belief were under challenge (as indeed it was): τὸ πόρσω δ᾽ ἔστι σοφοῖς ἄβατον κἀσόφοις. οὔ νιν διώξω· κεινὸς εἴην ("What lies beyond must remain untrodden, untrodden by wise and unwise alike: I shall not pursue it, I would be a fool").
96. Vian 1980, 122; Hunter 1989, 133. The scandalous anecdote is retailed at length by Dionysios Skytobrachion, ap. Diod. Sic. 4.45.4–5.

Pindar's Fourth Pythian, composed in 462 B.C. to honor the chariot victory by Arkesilas IV, king of Kyréné, at Delphoi, thus stands at a critical point in the transmission of the Argonaut myth,[97] on the very edge of the final opening up of the whole Mediterranean world, and the triumph of rationalism associated primarily with Periklean Athens. There are several features in it of significance as regards Pindar's treatment of the myth itself. First, it has been modified politically to suit Arkesilas's requirements.[98] Euphemos and the clod of earth symbolizing the colonization of Kyréné from Thera firmly and permanently link the Argonauts to North Africa.[99] Battos I, seventeenth in line of succession from Euphemos, was the founder, and Pindar's patron Arkesilas his eighth successor. The loss of the clod described by Medeia during her prophecy (*Pyth.* 4.38–49) explains the delay in colonization.[100] Thus in affirming a specific genealogy, Pindar's use of the Argonaut myth performs a central and traditional function.[101]

In one other respect, his interpretation invites comparison with that of Apollonios, whose chief fame today, of course, lies in his modernizing psychological portrait of Medeia (book 3 of the *Argonautika* has been edited more often than the other three put together). Like the basic geographical framework of the voyage to Kolchis, Medeia's central, and crucial, position in the narrative remained undeniable. Her connections with godhead were strong, and Pindar recognized this (*Pyth.* 4.11). On the other hand, his main business was the celebration of masculine heroic or athletic renown (κλέος), and here Medeia's role constituted a distinct embarrassment, since Jason's conquest of those fire-breathing brazen bulls, not to mention the eternally vigilant serpent guarding the Fleece, depended on her magical aid. But the Jason of Pindar is a fine upstanding *kouros,* and it is the age of the great *kouroi* that Pindar is celebrating (Beye 1982, 48). To him, as to so many other Greek poets, "female sexuality appears as a mode of treacherous craft (μῆτις), deceptive ornamentation, beguiling persuasion, and quasi-magical drugs,

97. Segal (8) neatly summarizes its contents: "Pindar brings together in a tour de force epic adventure, foundation legends, love, magic, family conflict, and cosmogonic myths."

98. When Eumelos of Korinthos did the same thing earlier for his city, manufacturing a local ancestry for Aiëtes and Medeia (for a brilliant reconstruction of Eumelos's appropriative scheme, see Huxley, ch. 5, "Eumelos, the Early *Argonautika* and Related Epics," 60–84, and cf. Beye 1982, 46), the changes were not incorporated into the local tradition.

99. As early as the sixth century B.C., Euphemos had been commemorated as a charioteer on the Chest of Kypselos: Paus. 5.17.4.

100. See F. Chamoux, *Cyrène sous la monarchie des Battiades* (Paris, 1953), 115–210, cf. Braswell, 89–90 and 153. Hdt. 4.159–65 offers an account of the first six Battiad kings.

101. In order to make Arkesilas's royal pedigree form the climax of his narrative, Pindar is alone in transferring the mass impregnation of the Lemnian women to the Argonauts' *return journey,* with Medeia very much in evidence! This caused embarrassment even in antiquity: see schol. Pind. *Pyth.* 4.252. The political reason for so striking a narrative transposition was clearly perceived by Braswell, 347.

unguents, or enchantments" (Segal, 165). What is his solution? A breath-takingly simple one: he transfers to Jason the magic (φάρμακον) of heroic virtue (184–87), plus a lesson in erotic spell-binding from Aphrodite herself (213–19), so that it is he who ensnares Medeia rather than vice versa. Thus *his* need for her φάρμακα has been anticipated and eclipsed by his own su-perior powers. Blending politeness and diplomacy with heroic magnificence (Segal, 7), this Jason emerges a born leader. The contrast with Apollonios's treatment is striking and immediate.

For the two centuries between Pindar and Apollonios, evidence, as we have seen (pp. 18–19 above), is sketchy and puzzles abound. The biggest single influence on the *Argonautika* is commonly said to be Euripides' *Medeia* of 431. Yet no one could guess this from the iconographic evidence, which largely ignores Medeia as *Kindermörderin* till the Roman period.[102] What does remain consistent throughout is the persistent faith in that inner kernel of historical truth supposedly immanent in all myth. Plato will impugn an aris-tocrat's moral character but never question his pedigree (*Theait.* 174E–175B). Like Xenophanes, he will attack Homer and Hesiod, but for immorally *mis-representing* ancient mythic truths (*Rep.* 377D). Aristotle too, despite his low opinion of the particularities of history (*Poet.* 1451b5–11), and the fact that his reason refused to credit nectar or ambrosia (*Met.* 1000a12), still, like every-one else, accepted Theseus as a historical character, and seemingly the Mino-taur too (*ap.* Plout. *Thes.* 16.2). His efforts to bridge the gap between the heroic and historical periods involved a curiously class-conscious compro-mise: "Only the leaders of the ancients were heroes—the people were merely men" (*Probl.* 922b).

Aristotle lacked enthusiasm for allegory (*Met.* 1000a19), regarding it, with characteristic hardheadedness, as a mere decoration or sweetener that made uncomfortable truths less unpalatable (*Met.* 1074b1). His distaste, how-ever, was more than compensated for by the enthusiasm in this area shown by Stoics such as Chrysippos. Indeed, as Long stresses (64), "What passes un-der the name of Stoic allegorizing is the Stoic interpretation of myth." In this area, the ludicrous element was never far from the surface. Chrysippos, who dearly loved a joke, also took considerable pleasure in deeply shocking all those who, with more than Victorian fervor, opposed anything even faintly redolent of "smut" (αἰσχρολογία), a word unknown before Aristotle's day. He caused acute embarrassment by referring in public to a certain notori-ous picture in Argos of Hera fellating Zeus. This he interpreted to mean "that Matter receives and holds within itself the spermatic *logoi* of the deity des-

---

102. *LIMC*, s.v. "Medeia," 391–92, lists only three fourth-century south Italian vases (nos. 29–31) directly associated with Medeia's infanticide, plus five (35–37, 39–40) in which she is portrayed in her *Schlangenwagen*, also very probably inspired by Euripides' treatment.

tined for the ordering of the Whole."[103] Were it not that this fancy is restrained by comparison with many other Stoic allegories, I would suspect Chrysippos here of practicing a little sly subversion; indeed, mythic conservatism and moral prudery were between them in real danger, by the mid third century, of creating a literary reductio ad absurdum for rationalism and allegory alike.

V

In such a world, and a fortiori in the Ptolemaic enclave that nurtured Alexandrian scholarship, what kind of attitude to the Argonautic myth would we reasonably expect? Not, if we are to be honest, that presented by Apollonios. Intellectuals—and Apollonios was an extremely well-read specimen of the tribe—are not in the normal course of events immune to the major trends of their age. Now it so happens that for the mid third century, which witnessed the apogee of the Alexandrian literary movement, we possess, in addition to Apollonios's *Argonautika*, a lengthy and detailed summary (Diod. Sic. 4.40–56) of the *Argonautai* by Dionysios Skytobrachion, a scholar from Mytilene.[104] To judge the current attitude to myth, we also have the chronological list embodied in the Parian Marble (264–263), which, as we have seen (pp. 14–15 above), makes no distinction whatsoever between myth and history, attributing specific dates to both with equal confidence, and in fact spends more time on the Age of Heroes than on recent, equally famous and indubitably actual events.

When we compare these three very different texts, what instantly strikes us, significantly enough, is the one central feature they have in common: an unquestioning belief in the *historicity* of mythic tradition. Where they differ, as might be expected, is in the means chosen to "save the appearances" in a new, cosmopolitan, skeptical, rootless world. Here, interestingly enough, it is Skytobrachion who most nearly conforms to all the developments analyzed above. The Parian Marble uses chronological specificity as a guarantee of truth; Apollonios, as we shall see, relies on aetiologizing traditionalism; but Skytobrachion shows himself a compendium of just about every intellectual trend current in his day.

---

103. Cf. H. von Arnim, *Stoicorum Veterum Fragmenta* (Leipzig, 1903), 2: 314, nos. 1071–75. The citation quoted in the text is from Origen (fr. 1074): ὅτι τοὺς σπερματικοὺς λόγους τοῦ θεοῦ ἡ ὕλη παραδεξαμένη ἔχει ἐν ἑαυτῇ εἰς κατακόσμησιν τῶν ὅλων.

104. Skytobrachion = "Leather-Arm": perhaps an allusion to the quantity of his published work. In my discussion of him I am heavily indebted throughout to Rusten's exemplary monograph, esp. 1–21, 93–101. Most important, I accept his careful arguments leading to the conclusion that Skytobrachion's work can "be dated roughly to the period between 270 (the approximate date the θεοὶ ἀδελφοί were introduced) and 220 B.C. (P. Hibeh 2.186)," with a midcentury median, and by his comparison of Diodoros's summary with the citations of Dionysios in the scholia to Apollonios to demonstrate the generally close and faithful nature of that summary: see 13, 28, 93.

To begin with, and most noticeably, his text is, as we might expect, heavily rationalistic throughout. Here he had ample precedent to guide him, going back a long way. Hekataios of Miletos (540?–480), trying to sort out Hellenic origins, is best known for his caustic comment that "the Greeks have a lot of stories that I find risible":[105] but risible or not, he does not reject them outright, merely trims away implausible fat from what he sees as the solid bone of tradition. What about Herakles bringing up three-headed Kerberos from that cave at Tainaron (*FGrH* 1 F27 = Paus. 3.25.5–6)? Hekataios can dispose of such an improbability: the "dog" was really a dangerous snake known as "the hound of Hades" because its bite was instantly fatal.[106] Herodotos and Thoukydides both similarly historicized myth. Thoukydides, indeed, not only takes the historicity of the Trojan War for granted, but solemnly builds it into his thesis of developing sea power.[107] The systematization of this popular industry was particularly associated with the name of Palaiphatos, possibly a student of Aristotle's.[108]

Most of the "Palaiphatan" rationalizing glosses that have come down to us follow a regular pattern. The Chimaira (Pal. xxviii) was really a volcanic mountain in Anatolia, the flanks of which were haunted by a lion and a serpent. Monsters are sometimes changed into ships (Pegasos) or rapacious courtesans (Skylla, the Sirens, Kirké). This last category is interesting in that it demonstrates the close affinity that such rationalizations could have with allegory, which made these temptresses into abstract symbols of seduction (Buffière 1956, 237). Even petrifaction was assimilated to the "real" world:

105. *FGrH* 1 F1 (= Demetr. *De eloc.* 12): οἱ γὰρ ʽΕλλήνων λόγοι πολλοί τε καὶ γελοῖοι, ὡς ἐμοὶ φαίνονται, εἰσίν.

106. The hands-on traveler and topographer Pausanias pointed out about five centuries later that "there is no road leading underground through the cave, nor is it easily credible that the gods have any underground dwelling into which souls gather." Later mythographers offered other solutions. For Palaiphatos (xxxix), Kerberos was thought to be three-headed because the dog came from Trikarenia, and Herakles rescued it when it was shut up (for stud purposes) in the Tainaron cave. Ps.-Herakleitos (xxxiii) explained the three heads by Kerberos having two puppies that always ran close beside him. In the *Excerpta Vaticana* (v), the dog belonged to Aïdoneus, king of Thesprotia [!], and was stolen, then rescued by Herakles and given to Eurystheus. Kerberos clearly presented an intractable problem.

107. Hdt. 1.1–5 passim; Thouk. 1.1–4, 8–11 passim. Cf. Murray, 93–115; Finley, 14–19; Nestle, 514–28; Dowden, 46–47. Rusten (93–94) stresses the significance, in this context, of Thoukydides' treatment of Agamemnon and Minos (1.9, 1.4), and reminds us that though "Palaiphatan" stories "are often viewed with contempt by modern scholars as the products of a decadent and misguided ingenuity," in point of fact "rationalistic reinterpretations of myth were actually a feature of the earliest Greek historiography" (cf. Hekataios above).

108. Palaiphatos's original five-book work *On Incredible Matters* (Περὶ ʼΑπίστων) is lost, but we possess a later digest based on it, as well as two other similar late collections (one attributed to Ps-Herakleitos, the other the so-called *Excerpta Vaticana* or *Anonymus de Incredibilibus*), all edited by Festa as vol. 3.2 of *Mythographi Graeci* (Teubner). On Palaiphatos in general, see Festa, xxxiii–xlvi (esp. on the four *Souda* entries s.v. Παλαίφατος), and Buffière 1956, ch. 10, 228–48.

the belief (itself apparently engendered by a rock formation) that Niobe had been turned to stone grew from the fact that a statue of the mourning mother was erected over the grave of her dead children (Pal. viii; cf. Buffière 1956, 239 and n. 48). Most characteristic of all is Palaiphatos's explanation of centaurs (Pal. i; Festa, 2–5). When Ixion was king of Thessalia, the crops of Mt. Pelion were being devastated by herds of wild bulls. Some youths from a mountainside village called Nephélé ("Cloud"), hearing that a reward was offered for dealing effectively with this nuisance, got the idea of mounting horses (hitherto only harnessed to carts) and going after the bulls with hunting javelins. As a result they were nicknamed Kentauroi—that is (by one of those false etymologies so dear to Greeks through the ages), "bull-prickers". It was these proto-cowboys who, when invited to the Lapith feast, got drunk and disgraced themselves. The myth that they had been sired by Ixion on a Hera-like cloud (νεφέλη, Diod. Sic. 4.69.5) was explained as a misunderstanding of the valley dwellers, who cried: "The Kentauroi [bull-prickers] are descending on us from Nephélé [the village]," just as the distant sight of them suggested the notion of a creature half horse, half human.

Skytobrachion's *Argonautai* falls precisely into this pattern, attempting, in Rusten's words (93–94), "to explain the fabulous stories connected with the heroes as misunderstandings of perfectly ordinary events, by putting forward a version which preserved τὸ εἰκός, i.e. something which could actually have happened but was late 'mythologized' into an improbable fantasy." He even anticipates one instance of a favorite "Palaiphatan" gloss, the notion that mythical animals are often no more than human names. Thus, the "bull" that made off with Europa was really a conquering general named Tauros (Pal. xv). This useful device, the onomastic homonym, allows Skytobrachion to explain away both Aiëtés' fire-breathing brazen bulls (ταῦροι, *tauroi*) and the unsleeping serpent (δράκων, *drakon*) that guarded the Fleece: the *tauroi* were in fact fierce Taurian guards (presumably to be thought of as wearing brazen armor and breathing metaphorical fire and slaughter), while the sacred grove was watched over (simple error!) by a sentinel named Drakon. Similarly with the magical flying ram (κριός, *krios*): one of the two rationalizations here reported identifies this "Krios" as Phrixos's *paidagogos*, who was sacrificed (no reason given) on arrival in Kolchis, and, equally mysteriously, flayed. Since an oracle stated that Aiëtés would die should the flayed skin be removed, the king had it gilded to convince the sentinels that it was worth guarding [!] (47.2–3, 5).[109] The alternative explanation makes this *krios* a ship with a ram as figurehead, from which Hellé fell overboard in the throes

109. All references to Skytobrachion's *Argonautai* are to the relevant chapter and section in Diodoros, bk. 4. Since Rusten's monograph is not widely available, I have not used the numbers he assigns to this and other texts in his collection of the fragments. It is worth noting (Rusten, 94) that the names Drakon and Krios did actually exist, while the Tauroi (as the myth

of *mal de mer* (47.4).[110] It is surprising that Skytobrachion does not, like Strabo (1.2.39, C. 45) and others, rationalize the expedition as a colonizers' quest for gold.

There are, as we might expect, some notable divergences from the traditional narrative. The entire episode on Lemnos is omitted, perhaps as improper: one of Skytobrachion's most remarkable achievements is to systematically eliminate throughout what had been the Ur-myth's strongest motivating factor—that is, sex. Medeia—uncanny virgin, enchantress, full of old divinity—is rationalized into a liberal humanist's dream. Skytobrachion, like Diogenes before him, finds her clever, but no magician. Rather than a witch, she is presented as a skilled medical herbalist, who rapidly heals any Argonaut's battle wounds (48.5). At high risk to herself, she helps her father's victims escape from prison. Arrested for these activities, she breaks loose at the time of the Argonauts' arrival and seeks refuge with them. Her relationship with Jason is based on mutual self-interest (46.4) rather than passion: no arrows of Eros here. Nor do we hear a word about the murder of Apsyrtos: only the monstrous behavior of Pelias (50.1–2, 6) can bring this Medeia to kill, after years of selfless work for mankind's benefit.[111] Even after persuading Pelias's daughters to cut their father up and boil him, she delicately avoids staying on to witness the butchery (52.1–4). It is not even a case (hinted at by Apollonios) of all passion spent: in this Shavian world, reason is promoted as a desirable substitute for all the passions, sex included.

Skytobrachion also reveals an interesting streak of something familiar to us from the political myth of Panhellenism, and recently the subject of several interesting studies: [112] the systematic effort at Hellenic self-definition by

---

of Iphigeneia reminds us) were a real tribe. On the other hand, why Pelias should have gone to the trouble of sending an expedition to fetch back a servant's flayed skin, gilded or not, is a question left unaddressed.

110. Skytobrachion displays a certain amount of inconsistency. Though his rational mind cannot accept a flying ram, he seemingly has no trouble with a sea monster that picks off coastal victims (42.3), presumably an early version of the Giant Squid legend. Similarly, he has no hesitation about accepting oracles, the Samothrakian mysteries, the miraculous calming of storms, or equally miraculous twin stars descending above the Dioskouroi (Rusten, 95, with nn. 9–120). Social pressures may well have applied here: even the most determined ancient rationalist is unlikely to have exposed himself to a possible public charge of atheism.

111. In the same way, years later in Corinth, it takes Jason's betrayal (54.7) to evoke the innate barbarian savagery that her character has hitherto kept under control.

112. See E. Hall, *Inventing the Barbarian: Greek Self-Definition through Tragedy* (Oxford, 1989); P. Georges, *Barbarian Asia and the Greek Experience: From the Archaic Period to the Age of Xenophon* (Baltimore, 1994); P. Cartledge, *The Greeks: A Portrait of Self and Others* (Oxford, 1993), ch. 3, "Alien Wisdom: Greek and Barbarian," 36–62. Cf. also my paper on "The Metamorphosis of the Barbarian: Athenian Panhellenism in a Changing World," in the *Festschrift* for Professor Ernst Badian, *Transitions to Empire in the Greco-Roman World, 360–146 B.C.*, ed. R. W. Wallace and E. M. Harris (Norman, 1996), 5–36.

contrast with the Barbarian Other. From the very beginning, it is emphasized that the inhabitants of the Black Sea region are fierce, savage, murderous, and liable to kill foreign travelers (40.4). Against them stands Herakles, Hellene par excellence, and famous civilizer in distant lands, who deals appropriately with savagery wherever it may be found. To do this he, not Jason, leads the expedition, and stays with it throughout (41.3, 49.6). An unexpected landfall in the Tauric Chersonese (44.7, 47.2) is probably inserted to justify the existence of those "Taurian" guards, and to emphasize the local practice of sacrificing strangers (ξενοκτονία). Skytobrachion, like Herodoros, Kallimachos, and the dramatists,[113] sends the Argonauts (as we have seen) home by their outward route, with stops at Byzantion and Samothraké now rather than earlier. The voyage over, Herakles founds the Olympic Games, proceeding thence to further glory with a band of devoted young followers—not alone: rationalism forbids (53.4–7). It is hard not to see this treatment as in some sense propaganda for Ptolemy II's vigorous program of colonial expansion.[114]

Rusten claims that Skytobrachion has seemingly "offered a radically new version of an old story,"[115] but the radicalism (if that is what it was) consists in revising the Argonautic myth to conform with every intellectual trend then in fashion. The contrast with Apollonios's *Argonautika* is striking and throws into prominence—something that Apollonios's Kallimachean use of aitia and other literary devices tends to obscure—what we may term, to coin a paradox, the *Argonautika*'s quite astonishingly independent traditionalism. No wonder it irritated the intellectual pundits of the day: it must have come like a direct assault on many of their most cherished beliefs. The one basic characteristic both versions share is an ethnocentric and ultimately political assumption of the fundamental superiority of Hellenism to any other culture. Thus for Apollonios, as for Skytobrachion, the quest for the Fleece is seen as a Hellenic venture to the world's end, a confrontation between Greek civilization and barbarian savagery, deepened in Apollonios's case by the increasingly outré and alien tribes encountered along the southern shore of the Black Sea during *Argo*'s outward voyage, and described in such vivid, not to say anthropological, detail.

113. Soph. *Scyth.* fr. 547 Pearson; Eur. *Med.* 432, 1263; Herodoros *FGrH* 31 F10; Kall. fr. 9 Pf.

114. On lavish celebration of this policy, see Theokr. 17.85–94, and for the background, Green 1993, 146. In Skytobrachion, the familiar ploy of a Hellenic mission (whether of conquest, enlightenment, or one followed by the other) among the savage *barbaroi*, a theme exploited by orators and politicians ever since the Persian Wars, comes across very clearly.

115. Rusten, 101. He goes on to say that it "certainly lacks the grandeur of epic or tragedy, but is not on that account without value. The owner of P. Hibeh 2.186, if he was ever caught reading it by others *with more learned tastes* [emphasis mine], had no reason to apologize." Skytobrachion in fact is so in line with every learned fad of the era that I wonder whether Rusten may not have written those words tongue in cheek.

There may, as I say, be a political element at work here: Ptolemy II not only nursed expansionist dreams, but liked to think of himself, *qua* Alexander's successor, as a protector of Greeks and Greek interests. The underlying belief, however, rested on the basic Hellenocentrism, or Panhellenism, that had been a constant factor in Greek affairs at least since the Persian Wars.[116] The geographical boundaries might have expanded—Alexander had, of course, opened up the "inhabited world" (οἰκουμένη) in a wholly unprecedented fashion—but this merely sharpened the Hellenic appetite for conquest and empire. The new world that emerged had also produced a deep sense of deracination among emigrant Greeks, above all in the intellectuals of Alexandria. Though domiciled in Egypt, they held consciously aloof from the indigenous culture, creating their own, in a sense, at second hand. Mutatis mutandis, they faced the same agonizing dilemma as their ancestors in fifth-century Athens. Some years ago I formulated this dilemma in the following terms: "How, asked the Psalmist, shall we sing the Lord's song in a strange land? And how, in their luxurious enclave or ghetto, were these Egyptian (or Cyrenaic) Greeks to maintain the matrix of sustaining myth that grew up amid warring Mycenaean baronies in central Greece and the Peloponnese? The retreat from reality into a complex aetiological obscurantism must, for such déraciné intellectuals, have offered an almost irresistible temptation."[117]

Reason dictated a rejection of the heroic past; but emotion cried out for a return to one's ancient roots. The cry of "Big book, big evil" (μέγα βιβλίον, μέγα κακόν) was matched by an ever-increasing addiction to aetiologizing; mythos fought a stubborn rearguard action against logos: "Credo quia impossibile est." What Apollonios attempted in the *Argonautika* was a reconciliation of opposites, an epic geste as experienced by heroic yet vulnerable human beings. His decision to frame his narrative as an epic poem in itself represents a decision of great significance. The Kallimachean rejection of this genre owed at least as much to social and historical realities as to literary theory. Hunter (1993, 154) sees the central issue very clearly:

> The decision to write *epic* in such a society, even (or particularly) an epic which constantly sets out to explore the cracks in what are set up as Homeric certainties, carried special weight. . . . [T]he status of epic as embodiment and transmitter of traditional values is in constant tension with the novelty and literariness of Apollonius' project. . . . Apollonius must emphasize fracture and discontinuity both within the "heroic" age itself and between the past and the present, *as well as* the unbroken chain which bound his readers to the pre-Homeric heroes of his story.

116. In addition to the sources cited in n. 112, see Fusillo, 162–67, and Hunter 1993, 159–60, who also cites Rice, *Grand Procession of Ptolemy Philadelphus*, 106–7.
117. Green 1993, 214 (originally published in 1990, the text was in fact complete by 1984).

Skytobrachion, by rejecting both epic form (in favor of prose narrative: I've always thought of him as the E. V. Rieu of antiquity) and most aspects of the mythical that clashed with his circumscribed rationalism, refashioned the Argonaut legend as an unremarkable adventure story, which not only lacked "the grandeur of epic or tragedy" (Rusten, 101) but virtually wrote the heroic age out of existence. This was to ignore the problem rather than grapple with it.

Apollonios, far bolder, sought no such easy and dishonest palliatives. Among the most remarkable features of his narrative are that it never falls back on rationalism and that it is also virtually free of allegory.[118] He writes as though that particular intellectual tradition, of cosmetic patching for unwilling skeptics, had never existed. Marvels of every sort—the Clashing Rocks, Aiëtës' fire-breathing bulls, the Sown Men, Talos, the Nereïds, Medeia's magic—are accepted without demur, as integral features of the heroic unknown. There is no attempt, for instance, to *explain away* the Clashing Rocks, in the style of some modern scholars–for example, as memories of encounters with icebergs in the Arctic;[119] nor to eliminate their awkward physicality by allegorizing them as some sort of moral hazard. Apollonios was, however, forced to accept one addition to the legend made necessary by exploration: the fusing of the rocks once they had been successfully navigated (2.604–6). Pindar (*Pyth.* 4.210–11) was right to describe this necessary end of an archaic belief as a τελευτάν, a kind of death (Braswell, 293).

In sharp and deliberate contrast, the exploring Hellenes who penetrate this barbarous Bronze Age world of wonders and magic are drawn very much as the poet's contemporaries: enterprising yet vulnerable, wholly Hellenistic in their reactions, and human to a fault.[120] This confrontation of old and new—logos, as it were, exploring mythos—is what, operating simultaneously on social, mythical, and literary planes, gives Apollonios's narrative its penetration and originality. The one great anomaly among the Argonauts is, of course, Herakles, who himself embodies the outsize virtues and vices of the heroic age. Despite the Argonauts' protestations, several times

---

118. Hunter 1993, 80–83, 154, makes an attempt to find "near-allegories" in, e.g., the Harpies or Iris; but neither these examples, nor his suggestion that the Argonauts' adventures in Libya (bk. 4) are "a kind of allegory of the Alexandrian Greeks lost in the cultural desert of North Africa," do I find really convincing.

119. See J. G. Frazer's edition of Apollodoros (London, 1921), vol. 2, app. 5, 355–58. He is probably right in his assumption that the Clashing Rocks are an archetypal fairy tale: parallel versions are recounted by (among others) Rumanians, Russians, and Eskimos.

120. We may note that the one supernatural item that actually accompanies them is *Argo*'s "speaking beam," part of the tradition at least as early as Aischylos's day (fr. 36 Mette), "carpentered into the forekeel" by Athena herself (1.524–27), and silent throughout the voyage until, with dramatic force all the greater for its rarity of utterance, it conveys Zeus's wrath at the murder of Apsyrtos (4.585–88).

reiterated,[121] it is clear that they are much happier regretting his absence than dealing with his monstrous and unmanageable presence. There is a nice ambiguity here. The new age must come to terms with its past; but there are some features of that past, symbolized all too graphically by Herakles, the reinstatement of which would produce social chaos. On the other hand—politics again—he had to be handled with care: he was claimed as an "ancestor" by the Ptolemies, and thus much written about by Alexandrian court poets.[122] Dealing with his violent, emotional, and intermittently comic character thus presented a problem in the ethics of patronage on top of everything else.[123]

The wistful longing for Herakles' superhuman aid, as Burkert sees (210), bears all the marks of a wish-fulfillment fantasy: perhaps not wholly surprising in those who habitually hired mercenaries to do their fighting for them. To interpret the traditional myth in terms of human psychology, even while embracing its magical elements, meant, first and foremost, dropping Herakles, "bestial and godlike" (Feeney, 98), from the narrative, leaving him to slouch off through Mysia towards ultimate deification. What would have become of the *Argonautika*'s moral issues and dramatic tension, let alone of Jason's complex relationship to Medeia, had this lumbering demi-deus ex machina been there at every turn to eliminate the opposition?[124] This is the obvious reason why most versions of the myth, Apollonios's included, remove him from the narrative at an early stage of the expedition.[125] The paradoxes of Herakles' nature have also led scholars, both ancient and modern, to extrapolate a moral, civilizing aspect of him to offset the guzzler, rapist, and murderer. Cynics and Stoics, indeed, turned him into a kind of muscular saint (Feeney, 105–8). But this is surely no more than an attempt (of the sort with which we are now all too familar) to clear up some of his more embar-

---

121. E.g., at 2.145–53, 774–95; 3.1232–34; 4.1436–82, esp. 1458–60.

122. See J. Rostropowicz, "Das Heraklesbild in den Argonautika des Apollonios Rhodios," *Act. Class. Univ. Sci. Debre.* 26 (1990): 31–34.

123. This, however, seems not to have proved overmuch of a deterrent: see, e.g., Kall. *H.* 3.145–61, and Theokr. 17.26–33. More difficult to deal with was Hera's notorious distaste for Herakles, since of course she figures throughout Apollonios's poem as the Argonauts' patron.

124. In point of fact, we get a pretty clear answer to this not entirely rhetorical question from Skytobrachion's version of events: see Diod. Sic. 4.48–49 passim.

125. The testimonia are conveniently tabulated by Clauss 1993, 176 and n. 1: Herodoros even claims (*FGrH* 31 F41) that Herakles never sailed with the expedition at all, being at the time enslaved to Omphalé, thus reminding us of his internal antitheses: as Burkert says (210), "the glorious hero is also a slave, a woman, and a madman." We see, however, that Ap. keeps him around long enough to get some fun out of making this polyphiloprogenitive stud upbraid his comrades (1.865–74) for dallying too long in the beds of the Lemnian women. Hunter 1993, 33–34, is sensible about this: whatever the speech put in Herakles' mouth may be, it is certainly not, as has been suggested (Fränkel and Vian ad loc.) an old-fashioned declaration of misogyny by a high-minded heroic pederast.

rassing archaic features by means of allegory,[126] a pitfall Apollonios carefully
—and characteristically—avoids.

For some time now the *communis opinio* about the *Argonautika* has stressed
its acute literary self-consciousness, and in particular the way in which it
echoes, varies, or subverts Homer (see the commentary for innumerable instances). We hardly need telling that as a scholar Apollonios wrote on Homeric epic (Pfeiffer, 140–45). Though I am not primarily concerned here with
literary problems (see Preface, pp. xiii–xiv), this erudite awareness is important for evaluating the *perspective* that Apollonios gives to his quest into
past time, his evocation of the heroic age, even his aetiologizing search for
roots. In *creative* time, Apollonios wrote some four centuries after Homer and
inherited him: as Eliot once remarked of past writers, "We know more than
they did; and they are that which we know." But in *mythic* time, of course,
historically considered, the Argonauts' expedition to Kolchis belonged to
the generation *before* the Trojan War: Cheiron's wife cradles the baby Achilles
as she waves them on their way (1.556–58). Thus by a kind of mythic inter-
textuality, knowledge can jump forwards as well as backwards, offering Apollonios an irresistible opening for deadpan narratological jokes (for a neat
example, see 4.784–90, with n. ad loc.) and the modern scholar enlightenment regarding ancient chronological awareness.

Yet the most crucial element in the Argonauts' Unknown, as for the entire mythical era—above all by way of validation, belief, and instrument of
cultural definition—had to be the divine (τὸ θεῖον): primarily as godhead,
i.e., major and minor divinities, but also embracing marvels (θαύματα),
magic, and the numinous in all its various manifestations. It would be remarkable had Apollonios *not* been affected by three centuries of rationalizing criticism in the area of religion: the remarkable thing is how little impact it actually had on his work. Xenophanes' lethal dismissal of divine
anthropomorphism (Kirk-Raven-Schofield frs. 167–69) has produced a certain awkwardness (perhaps calculated; certainly sometimes witty) over the
physical aspects of deity. Athena is weighty (cf. Hom. *Il*. 5.838–39) but can
still travel by cloud (*Arg*. 2.538–40), and at the Clashing Rocks she thrusts
Argo through with one hand while bracing herself against a rock with the
other (2.598–99). Are the Argonauts thought of as seeing her? Probably not
(Feeney, 74), any more than they see the Nereïds performing a similar function in the Straits of Messina (4.930–64). What is their relative size? We aren't
told, but this passage makes us wonder.

It is true that Hera, Athena, and Aphrodite, during their famous meeting at the beginning of book 3, bear more resemblance, *pace* Feeney (78),
to the gossiping Alexandrian ladies of Theokritos (*Id*. xv) than to Homeric

---

126. As in the famous moral lesson, attributed to Prodikos by Xenophon (*Mem*. 2.1.21–33)
of "Herakles at the Crossroads".

deities. Similarly, in the delineation of Triton, as Feeney says (79), "the norms of anthropomorphism are adhered to in order to be destabilized." But such instances of mild literary mischievousness apart, what strikes one most forcibly is the all-pervasive degree of Apollonios's *anti*-rationalism, confronted with which "Xenophanes and Plato would have recoiled in disdain" (Feeney, 67). Indeed, in many ways the *Argonautika* can be read as a subtle indictment of Protagoras's assertion "Man is the measure of all things", the arrogance and inadequacy of which, after the events of the past two centuries, were becoming increasingly hard to deny.

Here, surely, is the common factor linking a whole range of symptoms apparent throughout the poem: above all, that pervasive sense of human uncertainty, shiftlessness, and ignorance in the face of an unknown that— despite all the advances of science, despite Euhemerism's scaling-down of the Olympians as mere deified kings or generals—extends from divine motivation to the unpredictability of the future, from magic and other counternatural powers to the gaping cracks in the fabric of the old heroic ethos. Judged by these criteria, Jason's much-debated "inadequacy" or "resourcelessness" (ἀμηχανία), far from being a flaw (tragic or not) could be interpreted as a realistic acceptance of man's limitations—a view supported by the constant subversion of the poem's initial heroic optimism. "Heroic promise is constantly cast into shadow by what can only be called a negative, melancholy, almost 'autumnal' tone" (Pike, 29).[127]

Zeus, notoriously, is never seen in the poem, and recognition of his divine will (at least prior to the murder of Apsyrtos) remains fragmentary (Feeney, 58–62, 65–67; Hunter 1993, 79–80)—though at the same time his generational struggle for divine power may be quietly illuminating the all-too-similar deadly strife among Alexander's Successors.[128] Euhemerism, it becomes clear, could cut both ways. Hera works out her revenge against Pelias by using Medeia as an unconscious agent: the emphasis in the *Argonautika* on human decision-making is undercut by the lack of knowledge on which such decisions are based, the arbitrary and unpredictable machinations of the gods. "For the most part, Apollonius' characters struggle in a cloud of ignorance and doubt" (Hunter 1993, 79; cf. Knight, 288). Phineus demonstrates the inadequacy of human prophecy, the ineluctable force of divine vengeance (2.250–51, 314–16). This ignorance recalls the atmosphere in

127. This point is well developed by my former student Greta Ham in an as yet unpublished paper, "*Amechania* and Predestination in Apollonius Rhodius," where she points out that not only do ἀμηχανία and its cognates refer more often to other characters than Jason (including such powerful figures as Peleus and Kirké), but that "rather than characterizing any particular individual, Apollonius employs ἀμηχανία as part of a larger discussion of the human condition."

128. Feeney, 68–69, perceives Ap.'s emphasis on struggle and usurpation in references to Zeus, but does not draw what seems to me the inevitable political conclusion from it.

tragedy. Deity no longer, as in Homer, consorts with mortals. These archaic gods are remote, unknowable, and in epiphany, as Apollo over Thynias, terrifying.[129] As Knight says (289), "all these features show how Apollonius draws on Homer while reducing contact between gods and men."

We see, then, that despite its topdressing of up-to-date literary fashions, the *Argonautika* is in fact a remarkably consistent and thorough reversion to that archaic worldview consciously discarded by the intellectual pioneers of the Periklean age—on the dead end of which allegorists and rationalists were still hopefully battening. The quest for roots had come up with some more-than-aetiological answers: no accident that in this epic we are still reminded (not so gratuitously as has sometimes been assumed) of the nasty fate suffered by Prometheus (2.1246–59). Like Euripides at the close of his life, when he wrote the *Bacchai*, Apollonios had seen, with deadly clarity, that reason alone was not enough, that the dimension of the unknown formulated by myth had shrunk surprisingly little. There is no discussion here of whether Homer's gods "were 'real' or were 'metaphors' to be allegorized away" (even then an old chestnut: Hunter 1993, 80): their power, tangible existence, and inscrutable control of mortal affairs permeate the entire narrative. Whether Eros is symbolized passion or conscious entity, or both at once, Apollonios cleverly leaves ambiguous (3.275–84), with the clear implication that the either/or question is meaningless: what remains real is the *impact* of that force on its human target, which resonates through all that follows with a series of appalling aftershocks.

Perhaps most remarkably, the Fleece itself, the raison d'être of this entire epic geste, remains a complete (and highly numinous) mystery. The full reason for its Grail-like desirability, which can send a shipload of the brightest and best to Kolchis and back, is never explained. We are not even told what generates its unearthly magical glow (4.172–73, 177–78, 185). Apollonios, speaking of its "ruddy blush like a flame" (173), clearly has in mind a deep metallic red-gold such as that of the royal *larnax* from Tomb II at Vergina: what substance are we looking at here? We can safely ignore, as does Apollonios, the numerous and bathetic rationalizations (Braund, 23–25). This Fleece was a magical symbol: of supernatural power, of entitlement, above all of kingship. The bravest thing Jason ever does in this poem is to con-

---

129. See 2.669–79. Many scholars have pointed out that Apollo's visitation here would inevitably evoke comparison with his murderous attack on the Greek camp in the *Iliad* (1.43–52): see, e.g., Feeney 50–51, 75. But the demonstration of supernatural power at Thynias, sometimes seen as a welcome contrast to Homer's dark assault, is in fact at least as awe-inspiring. To rationalize this epiphany as no more than "a poetic version of sunrise" (Hunter 1987, 52–53, repeated 1993, 80) is to lapse into the kind of flaccid symbolism favored by Palaiphatos and Skytobrachion—not to mention the egregious Max Müller, who characterized Herakles' pyre on Oita as one more beautiful sunset (F. M. Müller, *Chips from a German Workshop*, 4 vols. [New York, 1869], 2: 88).

summate his marriage on it (4.1141–43), an act as potentially dangerous as laying impious hands on the Ark of the Covenant.

Apollonios was not, as we have seen, wholly immune to the pressures of his age; but these were restricted, in the first instance, to necessary changes imposed by the expansion of geographical knowledge—that is, by a genuine, and physical, diminution of the unknown. He does not, for example, indulge arbitrarily in what came to be called "exoceanism" ($\dot{\epsilon}\xi\omega\kappa\epsilon\alpha\nu\iota\sigma\mu\acute{o}s$), wandering off the known map, which was badly mauled during his lifetime (Romm, 194–96). His journey home for the Argonauts, even though it works its way into Switzerland by way of the Po, returning to the Mediterranean (via a nonexistent confluence: see note on 4.629–44) down the Rhône, never strays off into the Ocean so remorselessly deconstructed by Herodotos—at one point, indeed (4.1141–43), Hera in person turns *Argo* back—and carefully follows the track of Odysseus's western wanderings as identified by earlier writers.[130]

Apollonios's concessions to Kallimachean fashion—the self-conscious literary irony, the constant aetiologizing—do not for one moment affect his basic approach to the past. At heart, he embraces the ancient epic tradition (certainly as regards its nonhuman conventions and ethos) with a courage that, in the skeptical mid third century, can only astonish us, and that is more than enough to explain the tradition, true or false, of his famous alleged quarrel with Kallimachos–scorning to euhemerize the gods; not questioning the *aitia* (origins, causes), but accepting and embodying them; not rationalizing or allegorizing clashing rocks or fiery brazen bulls, but taking them in his stride as an integral part of those "high and far-off times" (as Kipling so precisely defined them in his *Just-So Stories*), which exist no longer, yet must be preserved forever in men's memories, a guard against intellectual hubris, a reminder and validation of everything it meant to be a Greek (Green 1993, 206–15). That is why the intellectually fashionable Skytobrachion survives only in epitome, whereas Pindar and Apollonios have lived through the centuries to delight and inspire us still today.

---

130. It is a nice point—setting mythical chronology (Argonauts before Odysseus) against writers' time (Apollonios after Homer)—as to whether this "western route" is to be thought of as having been laid out by Odysseus or the Argonauts. The tendency in antiquity (when both were treated as historical) was to give preference to the Argonauts; the balance today (when both are regarded as "mythical" in the modern sense) has swung towards Odysseus. See, e.g., Beye 1982, ch. 4; further bibliography in Romm, 194 n. 51.

The Argonautika

Book I

Starting from you, Phoibos, the deeds of those old-time mortals
I shall relate, who by way of the Black Sea's mouth and through the
cobalt-dark rocks, at King Pelias's commandment,
in search of the Golden Fleece drove tight-thwarted Argo.

For Pelias heard it voiced that in time thereafter   5
a grim fate would await him, death at the prompting
of the man he saw come, one-sandaled, from folk in the country:
and not much later—in accordance with your word—Jason,
fording on foot the Anauros's wintry waters,
saved from the mud one sandal, but left the other   10
stuck fast in the flooded estuary, pressed straight on
to have his share in the sacred feast that Pelias
was preparing for Poseidon his father, and the rest of
the gods, though paying no heed to Pelasgian Hera.
The moment Pelias saw him, he *knew,* and devised him a trial   15
of most perilous seamanship, that in deep waters
or away among foreign folk he might lose his homecoming.

Now singers before my time have recounted how the vessel
was fashioned by Argos with the guidance of Athena.
What I plan to do now is tell the name and family   20
of each hero, describe their long voyage, all they accomplished
in their wanderings: may the Muses inspire my singing!

First in our record be Orpheus, whom famous Kallíope,
after bedding Thracian Oiágros, bore, they tell us,

hard by Pimpleia's high rocky lookout: Orpheus,   25
who's said to have charmed unshiftable upland boulders
and the flow of rivers with the sound of his music.
Wild oaks still form a memorial to that singing:
on the Thracian shore they flourish, marching in order,
dense-packed, just as Orpheus long ago bewitched them   30
with the sound of his lyre, brought them down from Pieria. Such was
Orpheus, whom Aison's son Jason persuaded to join him,
at Aison's advice, on his quest, and gave him warm welcome:
Pieria's royal lord, the Bistonians' monarch.
Soon, too came Asteríon, begotten of Kométes   35
by Apídanos' turbulent waters, who had his dwelling
in Peirésiai of Thessalia, under a lofty mountain,
where mighty Apídanos and divine Enípeus
have their juncture, uniting in one from remote beginnings.
After them, leaving Lárissa, there followed that Polyphémos,   40
Eílatos's son, who once, among the sturdy Lapiths,
when the Lapiths were arming themselves against the Centaurs,
fought as a youth; though now his limbs were heavy
with age, his spirit remained a warrior's as always.
Nor did Iphiklos tarry long in Phylaké, he being   45
Jason's uncle, Aison having married Alkimédé
of Phylaké: her kinship, that marriage bond, compelled him
to enroll himself in the company. Nor did Admétos,
king over sheep-rich Phérai, hang back there under
the peaks of Thessalia's Chalkodónian mountains;   50
nor did Hermes' two sons, Erytos and Echíon,
skillful tricksters both, rich in broad wheatfields,
stay behind in Phthiótis, while Aithálides, their third brother,
joined them on their departure. (Eupolemeia, fathered
by Myrmidon in Phthia, had him by the Amphryssos;   55
the other two Antianeira bore, Menétes' daughter.)
There came too, leaving wealthy Gyrton, Korónos,
Kaineus's son, a brave man, yet not his father's equal:
for Kaineus, as singers tell, was among the living
still when destroyed by the Kentaurs: that day he drove them   60
back, alone of the heroes; and when they rallied
they could neither force him to yield, nor yet dispatch him,
but unbowed, unbroken, he went into earth down under,

crushed by a shattering hail of heavy pine trunks.
Mopsos came too, the Thessalian, whom Apollo,   65
Leto's son, had made skilled in bird omens, above all mortals,
and Eurydamas, Ktímenos' son, who had his dwelling
in Dolopian Ktímené, by Lake Xynias. Actor
ordered forth his son Menoitios from Opous
to go with the flower of the heroes. There followed   70
Eurytion, and valiant Erybótes, the sons
one of Téleon, the other of Actor's scion, Iros—
it was far-famed Erybótes whom Téleon engendered,
Eurytion, Iros. With these as third went Oileus,
peerless in prowess, skilled at harrying foemen   75
from the rear, when he'd broken their ranks. Next, out of Euboia
Kanthos set forth: him Kanéthos son of Abas
sent, at his own eager wish, yet he was not ever
to come back home to Kerinthos, but fated to perish,
he, together with Mopsos, that prince among diviners,   80
in the course of their Libyan wanderings: so true it remains that
trouble lies never too distant for men to encounter,
since in Libya it was those two were given burial,
a place as far from Kolchis as is the distance
to be seen between the Sun's rising and its setting.   85
Next after him Klytios and Iphitos were mustered,
lords of Oichalia, sons to hard-bitten Eúrytos,
Eúrytos, offered a bow by far-shooting Apollo, yet getting
no joy of the gift, since he chose to compete with its giver.
Next came the sons of Aiakos, yet not together,   90
nor from one place, for they dwelt far apart and distant,
from Aígina, after slaying their brother Phókos
in a witless moment. Peleus set up his home in Phthia,
while Télamon moved to Salamis, Attika's island.
After them, from Kekropia, came the warrior Boútés,   95
son of brave Téleon, and Pháleros, stout spearman—
Alkon his father released him, though he had no other
sons to support his old age and livelihood,
and sent him forth, his best-beloved, his only
son, to earn fame among those feisty heroes.   100
But Theseus, who surpassed all the sons of Erechtheus,
an invisible bond held back, down under Tainaros, whither

he'd gone on his vain quest with Peirithoös: that couple
would have made their task's fulfillment far easier for them all.
Tiphys too, Hagnias's son, now left his Thespian canton   105
of Siphai; skilled he was to predict a rising
storm out on the broad sea, saw hurricanes coming,
could steer a ship's course by sun or stars! Tritonian
Athena herself it was called him forth to the assembly
of heroes, and glad they were to have him come among them;   110
Athena, too, it was planned their swift ship, and with her
Argos, Arestor's son, laid it down to her instructions,
which was how it came to be the finest of all vessels
that ever under oar power made trial of the seaways.
Phleias too came from his home in Araithyréa   115
where he enjoyed great wealth by favor of his father
Dionysos, holding land and hearth at the springs of Asópos.
From Argos came Tálaos and Areïos, sons of Bias,
and mighty Leódokos: these three the Neleid
Pero bore, for whose sake the Aiolid Melámpous   120
endured a heavy affliction in the stables of Iphiklos.
No, nor do we hear that the power of stout-hearted Herakles
made light of the strong appeal by Aison's son Jason:
at the time he got the news of the heroes' mustering
he'd passed Lyrkeian Argos on his way from Arkadia,   125
bringing a wild boar, live, that had browsed in Lampeia's
thickets, beside the great marsh of Erymánthos,
and at the very entrance to the Mykenaian assembly
had dumped it, wrapped in chains, from off his great shoulders,
and himself, as he willed, in defiance of Eurystheus,   130
set forth, and with him Hylas, his fine squire,
in the bloom of youth, to care for his bow, bear his arrows.
Next came a descendant of godlike Danaos,
Nauplios. He was the son of Naubolos's son Klytonéos,
and Naubolos's father was Lernos, and Lernos, we know, the son of   135
Proitos, whom Nauplios sired: before that, Poseidon
had bedded the Danaïd maiden Amymoné, got her
with Nauplios, who excelled all mortals in seamanship.
Idmon the seer came last of all those dwelling
in Argos: for he learnt his own fate from the bird signs,   140
yet set forth, lest his good repute be impugned by the people.

He was no true son of Abas, but begotten rather,
to add to the number of the famous Aiolids,
by Leto's son, who himself taught him divination,
how to read signs from birds and in burnt offerings.   145
From Sparta Aitolian Leda sent strong Polydeukes,
and Kastor, skilled in the breaking of swift-footed horses:
in the house of Tyndareus she bore them, her twin darlings,
at a single delivery, nor did she now deny their
prayers: her choice for them now was worthy of Zeus's offspring.   150
The sons of Apháreus, Lynkeus and arrogant Idas,
came from Aréné, both overconfident in their mighty
muscles: and Lynkeus besides excelled in sharpness
of eyesight—if the report be true that this hero
could easily discern even what lay underground.   155
With them set forth Periklymenos, son of Neleus,
eldest of all the children that were born in Pylos
to godlike Neleus: Poseidon granted him boundless
strength, and the gift to assume whatever form he prayed for
when he was engaged in the shock and press of battle.   160
Amphídamas and Képheus came from Arkadia,
whose dwelling was Tegea, the estate of Apheidas,
both Aleos's sons; and with them, a third companion,
Ankaios went, dispatched by his father, Lykourgos,
the elder brother to both, who himself, already   165
aging, was left in the city to care for Aleos, sending
his son to accompany his brothers. So there went Ankaios,
dressed in a local bearskin, and swinging an enormous
two-edged axe in one hand, since his arms had been hidden
by Aleos, his grandfather, in the back of a granary,   170
in a last attempt, even now, to stop him from going.
There came too Augeias, whom rumor made the offspring
of Helios. He was king over Elis and its warriors,
proud in his wealth; he longed to see the land of Kolchis,
and King Aiëtés himself, the Kolchians' leader.   175
Astérios and Amphion, Hyperásios' sons, came
from Achaian Pelléne, which Pellen their grandfather
once founded upon the craggy brow of Aigialós.
After these, quitting Tainaros, there came Euphémos,
whom Európé, strong Tityos's daughter, bore to Poseidon   180

to be a swifter runner than all other mortals:
he'd speed along on the ocean's gray and swelling
surface, never dipping his nimble feet, but would follow
his liquid trail, wetting nothing beyond the soles. Two other
sons of Poseidon followed: the one, Ergínos,   185
had left far behind the citadel of lordly
Miletos; the other, Ankaios, proud of bearing,
the seat of Samian Hera; both vaunted their expertise
in seamanship and war. After these there joined them,
journeying from Kalydon, the son of Oineus,   190
valiant Meleágros, and Laoköon with him,
Laokoön, brother to Oineus, yet not by a single
mother, for him a servant girl bore, and Oineus
sent now, an old man, to serve as his son's guardian,
so that while still a boy, Meleágros entered the daring   195
assembly of heroes: no better man, I think, ever
would have joined them save Herakles himself, had he only
waited among the Aitolians one year longer to grow up.
With him on the same journey came his mother's brother,
Iphiklos son of Thestios, to be his companion,   200
well skilled both as spearman and in close combat.
With him too was Palaimónios from Olénos:
son of Lernos by title, but by bloodline of Hephaistos,
which was how he came to be lame of both feet. Yet no one
dared to sneer at his person or courage: so he too was
    numbered   205
in the roll of the heroes, to boost Jason's reputation.
From the Phokians came Iphitos, son to Naubolos, grandson
of Ornytos: now Jason had once been this man's guest-friend
when he traveled to Delphic Pytho in quest of an oracle
for his voyage: it was there that Iphitos entertained him.   210
Zétes and Kalaïs came, the sons of Boreas, whom once
Oreithyia, Erechtheus's daughter, bore to Boreas in remotest
rough-wintered Thrace: it was hither that Boreas the Thracian
snatched up and carried her off from Kekropia, while she
circled in dance along the banks of Ilissos, took her   215
far away, to the place men know as Sarpedon's
rock, hard by the waters of the river Ergínos,
and there he swathed her in dark clouds and possessed her.

Their sons now, soaring, beat dark wings, a wonder
to see, bright with gold scales, vibrating from their temples   220
and either foot; and about their shoulders, curling
down from crown and nape, blown hither and thither,
their blue-black locks streamed in the wind. Nor was Akástos,
stout Pelias's own son, of a mind to linger   225
in his father's house, or Argos, who worked at Athena's orders,
but both were soon to be numbered in the muster.

Such was the tally of all who gathered to Jason's aid.
Men dwelling round about knew these heroes, every one,
as Minyans, since most of them—and those the better   230
part—claimed to be in line from the daughters of Minyas:
and Jason himself, indeed, had Alkimédé
for mother, who was a child of the Minyan Klymené.

Now after their servants had stowed all the gear in readiness
that oared ships carry aboard, when men are driven   235
to make voyages over the salt deep, then they marched
through the city down to their vessel, by that headland
called Págasai of Magnesia. A crowd of onlookers
hurried along beside them, but they themselves shone out
like stars amid clouds. And thus would people comment,   240
watching the heroes flash past in their armor:
"God above, what's Pelias planning? Where can he mean to
send such a crowd of heroes from all Achaia? The very
day of their coming they could waste Aiëtés' palace
with deadly fire, should he not surrender the Fleece—"   245
"But they can't avoid the voyage—" "Much toil and trouble
for those who go—" So they talked, up and down the city.
But the women kept begging the gods, hands raised to heaven,
to grant them a homecoming such as they would hope for,
and thus would one, weeping, lament to her neighbor: 250
"Poor Alkimédé, sorrow, for you too, late yet certain,
has come, nor have you finished your life in happiness.
Aison too is greatly unfortunate: better, surely,
for him had he long since, wrapped in his funeral shroud,
lain underground, in ignorance of this wretched contest!   255
Better, too, for Phrixos, when virgin Hellé perished,
to have sunk in the black swell, ram too: but no, that frightful

monster framed human speech, to cause thereafter
troubles for Alkimédé, hard pains without number."
Such was their talk as the heroes reached the harbor.   260
Already a crowd of servants and maidservants had gathered:
Jason's mother's arms were around him, and sharp distress
pierced every woman there; while his father, bedridden
by age the destroyer, wept with them, blanket-swaddled.
Jason was doing his best to allay their terrors   265
with words of encouragement: he bade slaves bring his war gear,
and they brought it, walking in silence, eyes downcast.
But his mother stayed as she'd been from the first, arms clasped
close about him, and wept still more sorely, like a girl who
is glad, when alone, to hug her gray-haired nanny   270
and cry, a girl with no other protectors living,
but leading a harsh life, ruled by a stepmother
who abuses the girl with countless harsh reproaches,
so that while she weeps, the heart within her is strangled
by grief, and she cannot discharge all her surging sobs: 275
just so, embracing her son, did Alkimédé
weep without stint, and spoke thus in her anguish:
"Would that upon the day when I heard, to my sorrow,
King Pelias utter his baneful proclamation
the breath had left me at once, I'd forgotten my troubles,   280
so that you with your own hands might have interred me,
my child: that alone was what I had left to hope for
from you; with all other returns for nurture I'm surfeited.
But now I, once revered among Achaian women,
shall be left like a slave in the empty palace, wasting   285
unhappily away with longing for you, in whom once
I took such delight and pride before, for whom alone
I undid my girdle the first and last time: the goddess
Eilethyia entirely begrudged me numerous progeny.
Alas for my fate: not even in my worst dreams   290
could I have guessed that the flight of Phrixos would destroy me."
Thus she would wail and lament, and the serving women
stood sobbing all around her. But he, Jason,
addressed her with words of cajoling consolation:
"Do not inflict such grief and misery on me, mother: 295
it's overdone, you can't stop trouble coming

with tears, all you can do is add sorrow to sorrow.
The woes gods hand out to mortals are unforeseeable,
so accept the lot they give you, despite your heartfelt
sorrow: bear it, be firm, have faith in Athena's   300
covenants, in the god's oracles (since Apollo
has spoken most favorably), in these heroes' aid.
What you must do now, you and your serving women,
is to sit quiet at home. Don't be a bird of ill omen
for the ship. My servants and kinsmen will escort me thither."   305
With that he strode out of the house on his way: like Apollo
issuing forth from his incense-fragrant temple
on most holy Delos, or in Klaros or Pythian Delphoi,
or in wide Lykia by the streams of Xanthos,
thus did Jason move through the throng, the clamor   310
of voices cheering him on. There met him agéd
Iphias, priestess of Artemis, the city's protector,
and kissed his right hand; yet she could not have converse with him
for all her desire—since the crowd now swept him onward—
but was left there on one side, being an old woman,   315
by the younger folk, while he was carried far away.
Now when he got beyond the city's well-built streets,
and reached the headland of Págasai, where his companions
were awaiting him, assembled beside *Argo,* their vessel,
he stood at the harbor's edge, and they gathered before him.   320
Then they glimpsed Akastós and Argos in the distance
on their way down from the city, and all were astonished
to see them coming, in defiance of Pelias. One, Argos,
Arestor's son, had a bull's hide, black-ruffed, slung
from shoulders to ankles, while the other wore a splendid   325
double mantle, the gift of Pelopeia, his sister.
Still, Jason held off from asking them detailed questions,
and made the whole muster sit down together in assembly.
So there, on the furled sails and on the unstepped
mast, they took their places in order. Then the son of   330
Aison addressed them with words kindly and prudent:
"All the gear that's needed for fitting out a vessel
is ranged here in good order, ready for departure;
no need then, on that score, still to hold back from
our voyage, so long as following winds blow for us.   335

Come, friends, since we'll have a joint return to Hellas
and a joint outbound voyage to Aiëtés' kingdom—
because of this, without prejudice, choose the best
man among you as leader, to look after all details,
to settle quarrels, make agreements when we're in foreign parts."   340
So he spoke. The young men's eyes turned to bold Herakles
sitting there in their midst, and with one voice they all
urged him to take command. But he, from where he sat,
raised his right hand and said: "Let no man offer
this honor to me: consent I will not, and, further,   345
I shall stop any other man from rising. Let the person
who mustered this host have its leadership as well."
Such were his high words, and all expressed approval
of Herakles' fiat. Then warlike Jason himself
rose, joyful, and spoke thus to his eager listeners: 350
"If, then, you entrust me with the protection of your honor,
nothing remains, as before, to hold us from our journey.
So now let us first propitiate Phoibos Apollo
with sacrifice, then at once prepare our meal. Meanwhile,
until my servants arrive—my byre keepers, whose business   355
is to search the herd for good oxen and drive them hither—
we could drag our ship down to the sea, load all the tackle
aboard her, cast lots to match up oars with benches.
At the same time let us erect a seashore altar
to Apollo of Embarkations, who through oracles promised   360
to signal and show me the sea routes, should I preface
with sacrifice in his honor my enterprise for the king."
So he spoke, and was first to set hand to the work. Persuaded,
up they all got, piled their garments together in heaps
on a smooth flat reef, beyond reach of the sea's waves,   365
though it bore the briny marks of storms in winter.
Then the ship, in accordance with Argos's admonitions,
they first whipped about with well-inwoven cable,
pulling it taut at both ends, to keep her timbers
tight-doweled, and proof against all salt-surge violence.   370
Next they dug out a space the width of the vessel's beam,
and lengthways from prow to sea's edge, the whole distance
she was going to move, dragged onward by their hands;
and as they advanced, they dug continually deeper

below keel-level, and in this track laid polished   375
rollers, tilting the hull to sit on the first of these
and slide forward down the shipway. Along each side,
port and starboard, they lashed the oars, reversed, to the benches,
with a cubit of handle outjutting on either side,
and themselves stood ranked in order, hands and chests   380
pressing the handles together; and Tiphys meanwhile
went aboard, to spur on their efforts at the proper moment.
A great shout of command he gave, and on the instant,
throwing their whole weight, with one thrust they maneuvered
the ship from its resting place, then advanced, feet braced—   385
forward, heave upon heave, till Pelian *Argo*
responded with ease, and they ran beside her, cheering,
and under the massive keel the rollers groaned
with the friction, and all around dark smoke coiled up
at the weight of her. As she entered the water, they hauled hard   390
on hawsers to check her forward course, then fitted
the oars for rowing, put aboard mast and well-made
sails, rigging, and stores. When all this was accomplished,
and every detail most skillfully taken care of,
then they next cast lots to apportion the rowing benches,   395
two men to each bench. But the central place, amidships,
they selected for Herakles and, over the other heroes,
Ankaios, who dwelt in Tegea's citadel.
To them alone they assigned that midmost seating
at once, without casting lots, and with one accord   400
to Tiphys they entrusted their well-keeled vessel's helm.
Next, close to the sea's edge, they prised up pebbles
and heaped them into an altar, on the shore, for Apollo
Lord of Shores and of Embarkations; then they quickly
overspread it with seasoned olive logs.   405

Meanwhile Jason's cattlemen came back, driving before them
two steers from the herd, and his youngest comrades dragged them
up to the altar, while others readied the aspergent
waters, the crushed barley for sprinkling beasts and altar,
and Jason, invoking Apollo as ancestral god, now prayed: 410
"Hear me, Lord, you who dwell in Pagasai and Aisónis,
that has its name from my father; you who promised me, when

I consulted your Pythian oracle, to show me this venture's
end and accomplishment, having been yourself to blame
for my whole ordeal—now in person bring ship and comrades   415
safe to their goal, and back to Hellas. For you hereafter
as many of us as get home will make splendid recompense,
an ox for each man, on your altars, with countless offerings
that I'll bring you, besides, to Delphoi, and to Ortygia.
But come, now, Far-Shooter, accept this our sacrifice,   420
our very first gift, the voyage-price we offer
for our vessel: may I, Lord, through thy counsel and wisdom,
cast off for a sorrowless future, and may a favoring
wind blow upon us, let us sail through calmest seas."
As he prayed, he sprinkled the barley, while two heroes,   425
proud Ankaios and Herakles, girded themselves
to tackle the oxen. Herakles with his club smote
one in mid-forehead. It sank earthward, a dead weight.
Ankaios sliced through the massive neck of the second
with his bronze axe, severed those powerful tendons,   430
and it fell too, pitching forward on both horns.
Then quickly other heroes cut throats and flayed off hides,
butchered the beasts into joints, severed the sacrificial
thighs, wrapped them all together in thick fat, burnt them
over split kindling, while Jason poured libations   435
of unmixed wine, and Idmon saw with pleasure
the flames of sacrifice glowing on every side, the fateful
thick smoke curling skyward in dark eddies. On the spot
he bluntly declared the purpose of Apollo, Leto's son:
"For you, the gods' fate and destiny is to return here   440
bringing the Fleece, though ordeals beyond number
await you before that, in your going and coming.
But *my* destiny is to die through a god's hateful fiat,
far away in some part of Asia's continent. This
fate I already knew, through bad-luck bird signs,   445
yet still I left my fatherland, to embark on
this ship, and by so doing keep my good fame at home."
So he spoke; and the young men, hearing his prophecies,
felt sorrow for Idmon, but joy in their own return.
At the hour when the sun is past his scorching zenith,   450
and mountain shadows are moving across ploughland

as the sun declines into evening dusk, now all
upon the sand spread foliage in deep layers
along the gray seashore, and laid themselves down upon it
ranged each in order; beside them were set endless   455
dishes and tasty wine that cupbearers poured out
from pitchers. And soon they began to tell one another
such fancy tales as young men often delight in
over food and wine, before ugly excess's onset.
But Jason sat at a loss there, endlessly brooding   460
on every last detail, with a downcast air;
and Idas, observing this, loudly rallied him:
"Son of Aison, what's this great plan you're turning over
in your mind? Speak your thoughts to us all. Or is it terror
that's got to you and unstrung you, such as undoes cowardly men?   465
Be this furious spear my witness, with which I garner
more glory in battle than any—and not even
Zeus aids me as much as my spear—no deadly harm
will befall you, no task remain unfulfilled, with Idas
behind you, even supposing a god should block our path;   470
such a protector you're bringing in me from Aréné!"
With that, he clutched his brimming cup in both hands,
and tossed down the sweet draught neat, wine slopping over
his lips and blue-black beard. A general hubbub
of protest arose, and Idmon now spoke out openly: 475
"Mad fool, have you long nursed such pernicious thoughts,
or is it the unmixed wine that swells that presumptuous
heart in your breast to undo you, makes you slight the gods?
There are other words of comfort with which a man might
put heart in his comrade: what you said was sheer arrogance.   480
Such stuff, we're told, Aloeus's giant sons sputtered
against the blessed gods—and you're far from their equal
in courage—yet *they* both fell to the swift arrows
of Leto's son Apollo, mighty though they were."
So he spoke, but loud laughed Idas, Aphareus's son,   485
and squinnying at him, answered with taunting words:
"Come now, tell me this by your divinations,
if the gods are planning for me just such a doom
as your father handed out to the sons of Aloeus!
And figure how you'll escape from my hands in safety   490

if you're caught out uttering silly false predictions."
So angrily he reproved him. Their quarrel would have worsened
had their comrades, and Jason himself, not called on them to stop,
and Orpheus, lyre raised in his left hand, not begun singing.   495
He sang how, in the beginning, earth, sky, and sea, confounded
in a common mass together, were, as the result
of deadly disruption, separated one from the other;
how in the heavens forever fixed courses were assigned
to the stars and the movements of sun and moon; how mountains   500
rose up, how rivers loud-rushing over gravel,
with their nymphs, came into being, and all creeping creatures.
And he sang how at first Ophíon and Ocean's daughter
Eurynomé were masters over snowy Olympos,
and how he yielded up his honor to strong-armed Kronos,   505
she to Rhea, and both sank under Ocean's waves;
for a while they lorded it over the Titans, blessed gods,
while Zeus was still youthful, still childish in understanding,
hidden deep in the cave of Dikte; nor had those earthborn
Kyklópés yet shored up his power with the fulminous   510
bolt, with thunder and lightning, tools of Zeus's glory.
So he sang, then stopped his lyre and his immortal voice;
but when he'd ceased, all heads still eagerly craned
forward, ears straining, held still and spellbound; such
enchantment did he shed on them with his singing;   515
and not long thereafter they mixed libations for Zeus,
as ritual prescribed, and standing there poured them over
the blazing tongues, then settled to that night's sleep.

But when radiant dawn looked out with eyes of brightness
on the high peaks of Pelion, and the morning   520
breeze stirred the sea, left the headlands calm and clear,
then Tiphys arose, and roused up his companions
to board the ship, and set their oars for rowing.
Then a terrible cry rang out from the harbour of Págasai
and from Pelian *Argo* herself, in her passion for departure,   525
since one divine beam was run through her, of Dodóna oak,
that Athena had carpentered into the heart of the forekeel.
Then they took their seats on the benches, one after the other,
each in the place where the lot had set him to row,
and settled down orderly, with their arms beside them.   530

On the midmost thwart, Ankaios and Herakles' great might
sat; nearby he dumped his great club, and beneath his
feet the ship's keel plunged deep. Now the hawsers
were being hauled in, wine poured on the sea; but Jason
wept as he turned his eyes away from his native land.   535
Just as youths who dance for Apollo, either in Delphoi
or else in Ortygia, or by Ismenos's waters,
stand round the altar and, keeping time together
to the thrum of the lyre, stamp swift feet on the ground, so
these to Orpheus's lyre struck with their oar blades   540
the deep sea's chopwater, sent whitecaps surging back.
On this side and that the dark brine bubbled with foam,
boiled terribly under the thrust of these mighty heroes.
As the ship moved, their arms gleamed flamelike in the sunlight,
and the long wake shone ever white behind them, like some   545
track seen dwindling away across the green savannah.
On that day all the gods in heaven were spectators
of the ship and this race of demigods, valiantly steering
over the deep. On the topmost peaks of Pelion,
the nymphs gazed in amazement as they witnessed   550
Athena of Iton's handiwork, and the heroes themselves,
fists gripping and plying the oars. From his mountain summit
Cheiron, Phílyra's son, came down to the seashore,
and where the waves break brine-gray, in the shallows
splashed fetlock-deep, great forehoof waving them on their way,   555
wishing them safe return from their journeying; and beside him
his wife bore Achilles, Peleus's son, firm-cradled
in the crook of her arm, held him up to his dear father.

Now when they had passed beyond the harbor's protective headland—
helmed by the cunning skills of Hagnias's prudent son   560
Tiphys, whose hands directed the polished steering oars
with mastery, keeping the vessel steady on her course—
then they stepped the great mast in its midships box, secured it
with stays both fore and aft, drawn taut on either side,
and bent the sail on, hauled it high up to the masthead;   565
and a keen wind filled it, and they clewed the sheets to polished
cleats set at intervals along the bulwarks,
and ran on, quiet and steady, under the long headland
of Tisai, while Orpheus played and sang a pleasing

lay to them of Artemis, great father's daughter,   570
savior of ships, who had under her protection
those sea-heights and the land of Iolkos; and the fishes
followed them, great mixed with small, leaping up out of the briny
depths, to skitter along the liquid sea-ways. Just as
in the tracks of a rustic herdsman sheep by the thousand   575
hurry back to their steading, glutted with good grass,
and he goes ahead of them, skilfully playing a country
air on his shrill pipe, so the fishes followed,
and an ever-freshening breeze blew the vessel onward,   579
till Skiathos showed in mid-sea, and further distant,   583
bright through clear air, the whole Magnesian coastline,
with its towns, and the tomb of Dolops. There, towards evening,   585
they were driven by contrary winds to beach their vessel,
and at dusk, as a swell got up, in Dolops's honor
they burnt joints of sheep for the dead. Two days they lingered
idle upon the shore there, but on the third refloated
their vessel, hauling aloft its ample canvas: men still   590
refer to that beach as Aphétai, the "departure point" of *Argo*.
Soon the rich Pelasgian wheatfields sank in the misty   580
distance. Still pressing on, they sailed past the cliffs of
Pelion, left Cape Sepias below the horizon.   582
From there they continued their voyage, passing Meliboia,   592
seeing its craggy heights, its gale-swept shoreline.
As dawn came up, they sighted Homólé, lying
flush with the sea, and sailed past it: not long after   595
they skirted the outflow of the Amyros estuary.
From there they glimpsed Eurymenai, and the sea-swept
ravines of Olympos and Ossa; on they voyaged,
running before the wind, reaching by nightfall
the hills of Palléné, beyond Kanastron's headland.   600
Next day early, as they were sailing, the mass of Thrakian
Athos rose up before them. Though its distance from Lemnos
is as much as a well-found merchantman sails in a morning,
yet its highest peak casts a shadow as far as Myrína.
All that day until dusk the breeze blew strong and steady,   605
and the ship's sail bellied out; but with the last fading
rays of the sun, the wind dropped, and it was under oars
that they came to Sintian Lemnos's rocky shoreline.

There, in the previous year, the whole city had been undone
pitilessly, at one stroke, through transgression by its women: 610
for the men had grown disgusted with the wives they'd married
and put them away, conceiving instead a savage
passion for the girl captives they rounded up while raiding
the Thracian mainland opposite, since Aphrodite's
terrible anger pursued the wives for too long neglecting   615
her worship. Ah, wretched women, jealous past satiation,
to their mischance! Not content with the slaughter of husbands
     and captives
for bedding together, they slew every male, to escape
retribution in after time for this terrible mass murder.
Alone of them all, Hypsípylé, daughter of Thóas   620
the ruler over this people, spared her aged father,
and set him afloat on the sea, in a hollow chest,
to give him a chance of survival; and fishermen brought him
to the island once called Oinoíe, but Síkinos thereafter,
from that Síkinos whom the Naiad Oinoíe   625
bore after bedding with Thóas. But now these women
of Lemnos found it easier to herd cattle,
put on bronze armor, plough the fields for wheat,
than to devote themselves to Athena's domestic
labors as in the past. Yet, notwithstanding,   630
time and again, they would turn their gaze across the
broad sea in fearful dread; were the Thrakians coming?
So when they saw *Argo,* quite close, being rowed to their island,
at once they donned war gear, passed out of Myrína's gates
in a crowd together, hurried down to the seashore   635
like raw-flesh-eating Mainads, saying it was the Thrakians
who had to be coming. With them went Thóas's daughter
Hypsípylé, wearing her father's arms. Sheer lack of
plans struck them dumb, such terror loomed above them all.
But meanwhile from their ship the heroes sent forward   640
Aithálides, swift herald, to whom they entrusted
their embassies, and the staff of Hermes, his father,
who'd given him an indelible memory for all matters:
not even now he's crossed the unspeakable whirlpools
of Acheron has forgetfulness overrun his spirit,   645
doomed by fate to immutable alternations, numbered

now among underworld dwellers, and now with living
men in the sunlight. But what need is there for me
to rehearse at length Aithálides' whole story?
He it was now who sweet-talked Hypsípylé into receiving   650
these travelers, day being far gone, for the hours of darkness;
nor at dawn, with a norther blowing, did they loose their hawsers.

Now the women of Lemnos came into town and seated
themselves in the place of assembly as Hypsípylé had ordered.
Then, when at last the whole crowd was gathered together,   655
she made this speech among them, with intent to persuade:
"Come, my friends, let us offer agreeable presents
to these men, things that men should have to carry on a ship,
food and sweet wine, to keep them outside our towers
for good and all, lest pursuing their needs among us,   660
they find out the truth, and spread unpleasant reports,
far and wide, of the great deed we did, since even such strangers
will not find it at all to their liking, should they learn it.
This, then, is the plan we've thought of; but if any
one else among you can offer a better, let her   665
stand up now: that's the reason I called this meeting."
So she spoke, and sat down again, on her father's
stone seat of office. Then there rose Polyxo, her own nurse,
halting on feet all shriveled with age, and propping
herself with a stick, yet urgent to speak before the assembly;   670
and by her sat four virgins, all unmarried
despite the white manes of hair that covered them. She stood
in the midst of the assembly, barely raising her neck,
with an effort, between stooped shoulders, and spoke as follows:
"Gifts indeed, as our Queen Hypsípylé is minded,   675
let us send to these strangers, since to give is better.
But you—what plan do you have to preserve your lives
if there fall upon you an army of Thrakians, or some other
ill-wishers? Such troubles are common among mankind,
as witness this crowd that's arrived so unexpectedly.   680
And even if some god deflects your present danger,
countless other woes remain, much worse than warfare.
When the women now ancient have perished, and you, the younger,
arrive at hateful old age without any children,

how then will you live, poor creatures? Will the oxen   685
yoke themselves of their own accord for you, through the deep
ploughland drag on the ploughshare, cleave the furrows,
and, prompt at the year's turning, bring in the harvest?
For myself, though the Fates have shrunk from me so far
in repulsion, I predict that sooner than this next year's out   690
the earth will have covered me, that I'll have had my proper
funeral honors before calamity strikes home.
But you younger ones must, I tell you, pay close attention
to this problem—for now a way of escape lies open
before your feet: entrust your houses, all property,   695
our fine city's government, here and now, to these strangers."
So she spoke, and cheers filled the assembly, for her counsel
pleased them. At once after her Hypsípylé rose once more
and spoke in answer as follows: "If this proposal
is pleasing to every one of you, I shall send,   700
here and now, a messenger down to the vessel."
With that she addressed Iphínoë, standing beside her;
"Off with you, Iphínoë, to the man who's the commander
of this expedition, tell him to come among us
and hear, from me, a decision of my people   705
that'll be to his liking: bid the rest, too, freely enter
our land and city in friendship, if they so wish it."
With that she dismissed the assembly, then started homeward,
while Iphínoë went to the Minyans, who asked her
with what purpose she'd come among them. Straight away,   710
in response to all their questions, she spoke as follows:
"Hypsípylé, daughter of Thóas, has sent me to you,
with an invitation for whoever may be in command here
to hear from her a decision taken by her people
that'll be to his liking; and she bids you others freely,   715
if you like, to enter our land and city in friendship."
So she spoke, and all were pleased by her fateful message,
believing that Thóas was dead, and his well-loved daughter
Hypsípylé now ruled. So quickly they sent Jason
on his way, and all made ready to come themselves.   720
He pinned about his shoulders a double purple mantle,
Pallas Athena's handiwork, that the goddess gave him
herself, when she first set up the timber cradle

for *Argo* and taught them to measure the cross-thwarts with the rule.
You could more easily turn your eyes on the rising   725
sun than look straight at that mantle in its fiery redness;
for its middle part was flame-red, but all its borders
deep purple, while top and bottom were embroidered
with many a cunning image, skillfully wrought.
There, first, were the Kyklópés, crouched at their endless task,   730
sweating out for Lord Zeus a bright thunderbolt: already
it was near to complete, still lacking but a single
radiant shaft, which they with their iron hammers
were beating out, a hot blast of raging fire.
There, next, were Amphion and Zéthos, the two sons   735
of Asópos's daughter Antíope. Nearby lay
Thebes, towerless still. In eager haste they'd just
laid the foundations. Now Zéthos, seemingly with effort,
was hefting on one shoulder a lofty mountain peak,
while Amphion came behind him, playing his golden lyre,   740
and a rock twice as large followed after in his footsteps.
Next there was worked the deep-tressed Kytheraian goddess,
clutching Ares' swift shield, while from her shoulder
the tunic, fastened there, hung loose to the forearm,
falling below the breast; and there, in the polished brazen   745
shield, facing her, could be seen her exact reflection.
Next on it there came a rough cattle pasture: rustlers
were fighting over the cattle with the sons of Eléktryon—
the latter in their defense, the former, Taphian pirates,
attempting to lift them: the dew-wet field was sodden   750
with their blood; the few herdsmen were overwhelmed by numbers.
And on it was worked a race between two chariots:
the one ahead was driven by Pelops, shaking the reins,
while the passenger at his side was Hippodameía;
in pursuit of them came Myrtilos, whipping his horses   755
onward, while Oinomáos, clutching a poised spear
beside him, as the wheel's axle snapped in the nave, lurched sideways
and fell, still eager to send his spear through Pelops's back.
And on it Apollo was figured, Phoibos, as a boy
not yet fully grown, but shooting—because of that shameless   760
attempt to strip the veil from his mother—huge Tityos,
child of divine Elára, nursling reborn from Earth;

And on it was Phrixos the Minyan, seemingly attentive
to what the ram said, and the ram shown as though speaking;
seeing them you'd keep silent, embrace the deception,   765
in the hope of hearing from them some word of wisdom—
and long indeed might you gaze with this hope in mind.
Such was the gift of the goddess, Itonian Athena.
In his right hand Jason took one spear, a fine long flyer,
that Atalanta once gave him as a guest-gift on Mainalos,   770
eagerly coming to meet him, for great was her desire
to follow that quest. But by free choice he refused her,
fearing the harsh rivalries engendered by passion.

So Jason strode on to the city, like the bright star
that brides-to-be, sequestered behind new curtains,   775
watch rising above their houses, eyes adazzle
at its fine red glow as it shines on them through the blue-black
night air, and the maiden is gladdened in her yearning
for the young buck now far distant among foreign
fighters, to whom her parents are holding her betrothed.   780
Like that star, in the messenger's tracks now strode the hero,
and when they passed the gates and entered the city,
the commoner women thronged after them in their delight
with this stranger; but he kept straight forward on his way,
eyes fixed on the ground, till he reached the splendid abode   785
of Hypsípylé. At his appearance the maids threw open
the double doors, with their snugly fitted leaves;
and then Iphínoé hurriedly led him across
a fine entrance hall, and seated him on a burnished
chair in front of her mistress, who, with sidelong glances   790
and virginal blushing cheeks, for all her modesty
still contrived to make him a wily, coaxing speech:
"Stranger, why have you all sat waiting so long like this
outside our towers? There are no men now dwelling
in this city, they've migrated to the Thrakian mainland   795
and are ploughing the wheatfields there. Let me tell you truly
the whole sum of our woes, make you familiar with them.
When Thóas, my father, was king over this city,
then raiders from here would sail over, attack the Thrakians
living across there, sack the steadings from their ships,   800

and bring back loot in abundance, along with captive
women. Thus was accomplished the wrath of a dread goddess,
Kypris, who struck these men with a lethal madness:
for they came to abhor their wives, and in the grip of
this folly drove them off, out of house and home,   805
sleeping instead with their spear-won captive women,
the wretches! Long we bore it, hoping they yet might return,
in the end, to their senses: but no, things just got worse,
our troubles doubled, for they dishonored their home-bred
legitimate offspring, instead raised a crop of bastards.   810
So unmarried girls and with them their widowed mothers
would wander neglected up and down the city,
and no father paid the least heed to his daughter,
even if with his own eyes he saw her maltreated
by some arrogant stepmother; nor were mothers kept safe,   815
as before, by their sons from insult and dishonor,
nor did brothers feel responsible for a sister.
It was only the captive women who claimed attention,
at home, when dancing, in the market, at festivals,
until some god gave us the self-respect and courage   820
no longer to let them enter our halls upon returning
from the Thrakians, so that either they'd revert to decent ways,
or take themselves off somewhere else, captive women and all.
Then they, reclaiming every male child that was left
here in the city, went straight back to the snowbound   825
ploughlands of Thrakia, and there they are living still.
So do *you* abide among us! If it be your pleasure
to choose to settle here, then the perquisites and honors
of my father, Thóas, would all be yours; and I cannot think
you'd find fault with our terrain, since of all Aigaian   830
islands this is the richest, the most fruitful.
So come now, away to your ship, and tell your comrades
what I have said; don't hang back outside the city!"
Thus she spoke, glossing over the fact, the act of murder
done on their menfolk. He answered her as follows: 835
"Hypsípylé, most gladly would we accept your welcome
offer, which matches so well with our own desires.
Let me, then, return to the city, after I've related
each detail in order. But the monarchy and the island—

these must be your own care. My refusal's not made   840
lightly or scornfully: there are harsh trials I must face."
With that he clasped her right hand and at once departed
the way he had come; and a swarm of young girls, rejoicing,
skittered round him on all sides till he was out of
the city gates. Then later—when Jason had recounted   845
Hypsípylé's whole message on summoning him—they came
down to the shore at a smart trot in their waggons,
bringing all sorts of presents. They found it easy enough
to fetch all the heroes away as guests into their houses,
since—out of regard for Hephaistos, the jack-of-all-trades,   850
that Lemnos might thereafter be restored, repopulated
with males—Aphrodite had stirred each man to sweet desire.
So Jason set out on his way to Hypsípylé's palace,
and the rest to where chance might take them, all except
Herakles: he volunteered to stay aboard the vessel,   855
with a few chosen companions. Soon the city
was a scene of merriment, full of dancing, feasting,
the smoke from roasting meat; above all other
immortals it was Hera's famed son and Aphrodite
herself that with sacrifice and chant they propitiated.   860
So from day to day they made repeated postponement
of their sailing; and long indeed would they have stayed there
had Herakles not assembled his companions, apart
from the women, and addressed them reproachfully in these words:
"You wretched creatures, is it murder of kin that keeps us   865
far from our country? Was it for lack of weddings
that we came thence hither, scorning our native ladies?
Is it our pleasure to dwell here, sharing out rich Lemnian lots?
We'll not win renown cooped up for all this time
with a passel of foreign women, nor will some deity   870
grab the Fleece if we beg him to, make us a present of it.
Let us go back each to his own, and leave this fellow
in Hypsípylé's bed all day, till he's remanned Lemnos
with his sons, and got himself greatly talked about."
So he chided the company, and no one dared   875
to look him straight in the face, or give him an answer,
but without more ado, fast breaking up their assembly,
they made ready to leave; and the women, when they learnt it,

hurried to them. Just as bees buzz around fine lilies,
swarm out from their rocky hive amid a smiling   880
dew-wet meadow, and flying from bloom to bloom
suck their sweet harvest; so now with loving greed
the women in tears flung their arms around their menfolk,
with hands and words bidding each one farewell,
and praying to the blessed gods to grant them safe homecoming.   885
So too did Hypsípylé pray, Jason's hands in hers,
while her tears streamed down for the sharp loss of his leaving:
"Go, and may the gods bring you back with all your comrades
unharmed, and bearing the Golden Fleece to the king,
as is your dearest wish! But this island and my father's   890
scepter will still be yours, if even once you've
returned you should ever choose to come back here later:
you could easily gather a vast following for yourself
from other cities. Yet you will never nurse such a plan,
and my mind sees that things will not happen in this manner.   895
At least when you're far away, and after your homing,
remember Hypsípylé!—and leave me your instructions,
which I'll gladly carry out, should the gods grant me a child."
Admiring and disconcerted, Jason answered her:
"Hypsípylé, may all this turn out as you want it   900
by the will of the blessed gods! But curb your more hopeful
desires where I'm concerned: enough for me, should Pelias
grant it, to dwell in my homeland—only may heaven
bring me through my ordeal! But should I not be fated
after long voyaging to return to Hellas, and you should   905
bear a son, then send him when grown to Pelasgian
Iolkos, to heal the grief of my parents—if he find them
alive still—and so that they may, though the king be absent,
stay settled in their own home and be cared for." Thus he spoke,
and was first man aboard the ship: then the other heroes   910
followed, and sitting in order grasped the oars
with strong fists, and Argos freed off the stern cables
from under their sea-washed rock. Then they all forcefully
struck the sea's surface with their long sweeps of pine.
Towards evening, at Orpheus's behest, they beached their vessel   915
on the island of Atlas's daughter Elektra, that by learning
those secret rites, with their benign initiations,

they might steer in greater safety across the chilling deep.
Of such rites I say no more, but bid farewell to
the island itself and its indwelling deities, whose   920
are the mystery cults, which here we may not mention.
Thence, moving briskly, they crossed the depths of the Black Gulf
with the Thrakian coast to port, and away to seaward
the island of Imbros. Just as the Sun was setting
they rounded the Chersonésos's jutting promontory.   925
Here they caught a stiff southerly wind and to the following
breeze bent their sail, thrust into the racing channel
of Athamas's daughter. They left the open sea behind them
at dawn and by nightfall were steering under the lee of
Rhoiteion's headland, with Ida firm on their starboard bow.
Leaving Dardania, they set course for Abydos,   930
passing Perkóté next, and Abámis's sandy strand,
and sacred Pityeia. Indeed, in one single night,
their ship zigzagging upstream, they now traversed
the whole of the darkly turbulent Hellespont.   935

Within the Propontis there stands a beetling island,
just offshore from the fertile Phrygian domain,
sloping down to the sea, with sea-washed isthmus,
and sheer on the landward side. Its shores possess double
promontories. It lies north of the Aísepos River,   940
and dwellers round about call it Bear Mountain.
Once it was inhabited by savage and violent
aboriginals, an astonishing spectacle for their neighbors,
since each had six great powerful arms to brandish,
two springing from his stout shoulders, while the four   945
below were fitted to his monstrous rib cage.
But the isthmus and plain were peopled by Doliónes,
fine men, over whom there ruled a hero, Aineios's son,
Kyzikós, whom the daughter of divine Eusóros,
Ainété, bore. Yet never, fearful monsters though they were,   950
did the aboriginals harry them, through Poseidon's succor,
since the Doliónes could claim him as their first ancestor.
Hither *Argo* sailed onward, sped by Thracian winds,
and the Fair Haven welcomed her as she ran before them.
It was here, too, in accordance with Tiphys's counsels,   955

that they dumped their small anchor stone, left it below a spring,
the spring of Artákia, chose another that suited them,
a massive one; but the first, by Apollo's oracles,
the Ionian Neleids afterwards consecrated,
very properly, in the shrine of Jasonian Athena.   960

All together, the Doliónes, and Kyzikós in person,
came out to meet them in friendship, after they'd ascertained
what their race was, and why this voyage; hailed them hospitably,
issued an invitation to row on further, cast their
mooring hawsers ashore inside the city harbor.   965
There they set up an altar to Apollo of Landings,
building it by the shore, and made sacrifice on it.
The King himself gave them the sweet wine that they lacked,
and sheep besides; for he'd learnt from an oracle that when
a band of god-born heroes arrived, he must straightway   970
welcome them in friendship and take no thought for war.
On his cheeks, as on Jason's, the first fine stubble sprouted;
nor as yet had he gotten children to be his pride,
for the wife in his household still remained innocent
of childbirth—Perkosian Merops's daughter, rich-tressed   975
Kleité, whom he'd lately won with rich gifts, and brought
across from her father's home on the mainland opposite.
Yet, notwithstanding, he left his bride's bed and bower
to share their feast, casting all fear from his heart.
They questioned each other in turn: from them he discovered   980
the goal of their voyage and Pelias's behests;
they learnt from him about all the surrounding cities,
the whole gulf of Propontis; but there was nothing
he could tell them of what lay beyond, though they longed to know.
So at dawn some went up high Dindymon, to view for themselves   985
the lie of that sea, while at the same time others
moved the ship from its previous moorings to Bar Harbor,
and the route they took is still called Jason's Way.

But the aborigines, charging around the mountain,
with showers of rocks to the bottom began to dam   990
Bar Harbor mouth, as though trapping a sea beast inside.
Now the younger men had been left behind there, and with them
Herakles, who at once strung his back-bent bow

and shot them down one by one, while they in turn
heaved up and hurled huge, jagged rocks. And doubtless   995
these grim freaks too were bred up by the goddess Hera,
Zeus's bedmate, to be a new labor for Herakles.
Soon the rest joined him, hurrying back before they'd
scaled the lookout peak, true warrior heroes,
and slaughtered the aborigines, repelling   1000
their charges with arrows and spear thrusts, till they'd brought down
every last one of these stubborn, frenzied attackers.
As when long timbers, lately felled with the axe,
are laid out in rows by the woodmen at the surf line
to soak, and thus support the solid dowels; so these   1005
were stretched out, side by side, at the narrow entrance
of the brine-gray harbor, some grouped with heads and breasts
awash in the surf, their nether limbs spreadeagled
over the shore, while others by contrast had heads
cushioned on sand and feet thrust into the sea: 1010
but both lots were food for fish and for scavenging vultures.
So the heroes, having purged the terror from this ordeal,
now slipped the ship's moorings as the wind got up
and over the swell of the sea pursued their voyage.
The ship ran all day under canvas; but at nightfall   1015
the steady breeze dropped, and a contrary hurricane
whirled them about and drove them right back once more
to their kind hosts the Doliónes. They disembarked
in the dead of night. That stone is still called sacred
round which in their haste they looped their mooring hawser.   1020
Nor was there one among them who saw that they'd returned
to the same island, while darkness prevented the Doliónes
from knowing it was the heroes come back again—they may well have
thought that Pelasgian raiders, fierce Makrians, had landed,
so put on their armour and sallied forth to combat.   1025
Ash spears and shields clashed one against the other,
like a swift blast of flame that falls upon dry bushes
and crests there. The noisy pandemonium of battle
fell now, fearful, raging, upon the Dolionian people:
nor was their king, overriding his fate, to return   1030
home to his bridal bed and marriage chamber,
but as he turned to face Jason, Jason sprang

and ran him straight through the breast, and the bone shattered
under the spearpoint, and he on the sand, in spasms,
accomplished his destiny. That destiny no mortal   1035
is allowed to escape; a great barrier fences him all around.
So his fate caught him that night, though he thought himself beyond
any bitter blow from the heroes, and shackled him fast
as he fought them. Many others were slain in his defense:
Herakles dispatched Telekles and Megabrontes,   1040
Akastos brought down Sphódris, and Peleus overpowered
Zelys and Géphyros, so swift in the press of battle,
while Télamon, that fine spearman, killed Básileus, and Idas
struck down Prómeus, and Klytios Hyakinthos,
and the two sons of Tyndáreus Megalossákes   1045
and Phlógios, and beside them Oineus's son saw off
Artákes, that front-rank fighter, and dashing Itymoneus—
all of them honored today by the natives with hero cults.
But the rest turned tail and ran, like a cloud of frightened
pigeons taking flight before swift-winging falcons,   1050
and through the gates they all tumbled, a noisy mob,
and at once the city was filled with groans and lamentation
as the battle backed up. But at dawn both sides acknowledged
their deadly, incurable error: harsh grief swept over
the Minyan heroes as they saw Aineios's son,   1055
Kyzikós, lying before them, roiled in dust and blood.
For three whole days they tore their hair and lamented,
they and the Doliónes together. But then after
they'd circled his corpse three times in their brazen armor
they entombed him with honor and contested in funeral games,   1060
as ritual demands, on the plain called the Meadow, where still
to this day his tumulus stands for posterity to witness.
No, nor did his wife Kleité live on, survive her husband's
decease, but compounded bad with worse by knotting
a noose around her neck. Her death the very   1065
nymphs of the woods and groves lamented; all the tears
that from their eyes dropped earthbound on her account were gathered
by the goddesses into a spring, which men still call
Kleité, illustrious name of that unhappy bride.
This, then, was the grimmest day that upon the women   1070
and men of the Doliónes Zeus ever sent; there was not

one of them had the heart for food, and long thereafter
their grief left them indifferent to the work of grinding,
so that they kept alive by eating food just as it was,
uncooked; and so even now, when the Ionians dwelling   1075
in Kyzikós make their annual libations, to this day they
grind the grain for the offering cakes at the public mill.

From this point there arose fierce storms that lasted
twelve days and nights together, holding the heroes
back from their voyage. But on the following night,   1080
when all the rest were sleeping, during the last watch,
overcome by exhaustion, with Akastos and Mopsos,
Ampykos's son, to watch over their heavy slumbers,
then over the golden head of Jason, Aison's son,
a halcyon circled, with its shrill cry predicting   1085
an end to the driving gales; and Mopsos understood,
hearing it, the good omen of this shore-loving bird; and then
the goddess changed its course once more, so that, down-swooping,
it perched there aloft on the figurehead of their vessel;
and Mopsos shook Jason awake at once, as he lay there   1090
bedded down on soft sheepskins, and spoke to him as follows:
"Son of Aison, needs must that you climb up to rugged Dindymon's
shrine, and propitiate the Mother of all the blessed
gods where she sits enthroned; and then the raging
storms will die out: such the word I lately got   1095
from the sea-halcyon as it circled above your sleeping
body, and told me the truth as to every detail.
For on her the winds and sea and earth's foundations
all depend, and the snowy bastion of Olympos;
and to her, when she climbs great heaven from her mountains,   1100
Zeus himself, son of Kronos, gives place, and all the other
blessed immortals honor that terrible goddess."
So he spoke, and welcome were his words to Jason,
who rose from his couch rejoicing, and hastened to rouse
all his companions, and when they were up, informed them   1105
of what Mopsos son of Ampykos had predicted. Straight away
some of the younger men drove oxen from the byres
and led them up to the sheer peak of the mountain,
while others, slipping their hawsers from the Sacred Rock,

rowed on to the Thrakian Harbor, and then, leaving   1110
a few comrades aboard, themselves made the ascent.
Before their eyes there appeared, as though close enough to touch,
the Makrian heights and the whole coast opposite Thraké,
while far in the haze they could see the Bosporos gap
and the ridges of Mysia; on the other side, the Aísepos   1115
River, the Nepeían plain, the city of Adrasteía.
There they found a massive vine stump, reared in the forest,
dead and dried out: this they cut away, to fashion
a sacred image of the mountain goddess, and Argos
carved it with elegance, and they set it up on that rugged   1120
summit, under the shade of the topmost oaks
that had taken root there, far above all the others.
Then they heaped up a gravel altar, hung it with garlands
of oak leaves, and offered up sacrifice, invoking
Dindyméné the mother, Lady of many names,   1125
dweller in Phrygia, and Títias and Kyllénos—
who alone are called fate-dispensers, and coadjutors
of the Idaian mother, out of that whole crowd
of Daktyls on Kretan Ida, long ago brought to birth
in Dikté's cave by the nymph Anchiálé, clutching   1130
fistfuls of earth from Oiaxos in either hand.
With many prayers Jason besought the goddess to avert
this hurricane, poured libations on the blazing
victims; at Orpheus's command, the young men all together,
with measured leap, danced the war dance in full armor,   1135
beating their swords on their shields, that that ill-omened
cry might be scattered and lost in air, of the people
keening still for their king. From that day Phrygians
have propitiated Rhea with bull-roarer and kettledrum.
Such undefiled offerings surely won the goddess's   1140
prayable ear: appropriate signs appeared now—
trees dropped fruit in abundance, around their feet
Earth of herself brought tender herbage to blossom,
and wild beasts, leaving their lairs and woodland thickets,
came forward wagging their tails. Yet another marvel   1145
the goddess produced: though before no water had flowed on
Dindymon, now for them, on the spot, a constant
spring burst from the parched rock, and local people

have called it, ever since then, the Spring of Jason.
And then, on Bear Mountain, they made a feast to honor   1150
the goddess, hymning Rhea, mistress of many names;
and at dawn the winds dropped, and they rowed on from the island.
Then rivalry stirred up each one of the heroes
to be the last to quit rowing; for all around them
the still air had smoothed the eddies, lulled the sea to sleep.   1155
Reliant on this calm, they drove the vessel forward
by their own might: as it sped through the deep, not even
Poseidon's own storm-swift horses could have caught it.
Then, when whitecaps were whipped up by the furious winds
that begin to blow off the rivers before nightfall,   1160
exhausted, they eased their efforts. But Herakles drew them
on by the force of his hands, all laboring together,
and made the vessel's strong-built timbers tremble.
However, when in their haste to make the Mysian coast, they
had sighted and were passing the Rhyndakos estuary   1165
and Aigaíon's great barrow, then, just beyond Phrygia,
while heaving and furrowing back the sea swell's tumult,
Herakles broke his oar, fell sideways with one splintered
half still clutched in both hands, while the sea's backwash
swept the other fragment away. He sat up, speechless,   1170
glaring around: his hands were not used to being idle.
At the hour when a ploughman or gardener, much relieved,
gets home to his cottage, ravenous for supper,
and on the threshold, knees buckling with exhaustion,
sunburnt, dust-caked, contemplates his toil-worn   1175
hands, and calls down many curses on his belly:
then was the time they reached the habitations of Kios
by Mount Arganthónios and the Kios River's outfall.
They came as friends, so the Mysians who occupied that region
gave them warm welcome, furnished them with provisions   1180
to meet their needs: sheep, and wine in abundance.
Then some brought in dry firewood, others balefuls
of leaves and scythed grass from the meadows to spread as couches,
while others again spun firesticks, or mixed wine
in the great bowls, or worked to prepare dinner,   1185
after sacrificing at dusk to Apollo as Lord of
Embarkations. But Herakles, wishing his comrades pleasure

of their feast, went off to the woodland with the purpose
of getting himself an oar well suited to his grip.
So, casting about, he found a fir, not burdened   1190
with too many branches or excess of foliage,
but more resembling a poplar, with its tapered trunk,
both in length and in thickness. Quickly he laid aside
his bow and quiver of arrows on the ground,
and stripped off his lion skin. With his brassbound club   1195
he gave the fir tree a blow that shook it to its roots;
then with both hands, confident in his muscle,
gripped it around the bole, legs spread, thrust with one mighty
shoulder, leaned in, and, rooted deep though it was,
tore it free of the ground, along with the earth masses   1200
that had held it fast. As when a tearing wind squall,
at the winter setting especially of deadly Orion,
can swoop, out of the blue, down on a ship's mast
and tear it loose from its forestays, quoins and all,
so he lifted that tree. Then, picking up bow and arrows   1205
and club, he put on his lion skin and set out back.

Hylas meanwhile, with bronze pitcher, had left his comrades
in search of some spring's hallowed flow, to draw
water enough for supper, make all else ready,
briskly and in good order, against Herakles' coming;   1210
for Herakles himself had inbued him with such habits,
after taking him as a child from the house of his father,
godlike Theiódamas, whom he pitilessly slaughtered
among the Dryopians in a quarrel over a plough-ox.
Theiódamas was ploughing the length of a fallow field,   1215
heavy-burdened with troubles; but unwilling though he was,
Herakles made him hand over one of his oxen,
for he wanted some lame excuse to war on the Dryopians
since they lived without the slightest regard for justice—
but this tale could lead me too far astray from my theme.   1220
Hylas, then, came to a spring that was known as The Fountains
by local inhabitants. Just now, as it chanced, the dances
of the nymphs were being held there; for it was their custom,
that of all nymphs who dwelt around that lovely mountain,
ever to honor Artemis with nocturnal song.   1225

Now all whose haunts were hilltops or mountain torrents,
the guardian wood nymphs, these were ranged apart;
but one water nymph had just swum up to the surface
of the sweet-flowing spring. Before her she saw young Hylas
in a blushing glow of sweet gracefulness and beauty: 1230
for on him the full moon, shining clear from heaven,
now cast its light. Aphrodite fluttered her senses,
leaving her stunned, scarce able to gather her wits.
But the moment he dipped his pitcher in the current,
crouching over sideways, and the brimful stream rang loud,   1235
as it hit the echoing bronze, then she at once
slipped her left arm round his neck from above, in urgent
longing to kiss his tender young mouth, and with her
right hand drew down his elbow, plunged him into mid-eddy.
Of all the band of heroes, one only heard his cry: 1240
Polyphémos, Eilatos's son, as he advanced down
the same path, awaiting mighty Herakles' return;
and he took off and went near The Fountains, like some savage
beast whose ears have caught the distant bleating of sheep,
and on fire with hunger, he follows, yet does not meet with   1245
any flocks, for the shepherds have already penned them
safe in the fold, and he howls on in his frustration
till he tires: so now Polyphémos shouted despairingly
all round the spot, till he lost his voice; then, drawing
his great sword with dispatch, started out in pursuit,   1250
afraid Hylas was caught by wild beasts, or that men had trapped him
alone, and were dragging him off, an easy prey.
There on the trail, still brandishing naked sword in fist,
he ran into Herakles himself, now hurrying shipward
through the darkness, easily knew him, told him at once,   1255
out of breath, heart pounding, the whole sad calamity:
"My friend, I shall be the first to bring you bitter tidings:
Hylas went to the spring, but has not come back in safety—
either brigands have seized him, are dragging him away,
or wild beasts are savaging him: I heard his cries."   1260
So he spoke; and at the words sweat rained down Herakles'
temples, and under his gut the black blood boiled.
In fury he threw down his fir trunk, and went sprinting
along the path, wherever his feet might take him in his haste.

As when a bull, stung up by the gadfly, cringes,   1265
leaving meadows and marshland, caring nothing
for herdsmen or herd, but presses on, now without stopping,
now standing still, lifting his massive neck
and bellowing, goaded by that damnable sting; so he
in his urgency would now keep his lithe knees ceaselessly   1270
moving, and now would give over from his efforts
to shout, till the echoes rang, in that huge voice of his.

As soon as the morning star rose clear above the topmost
peaks, the wind gusted down, and Tiphys quickly
urged them aboard, to make good use of the land breeze;   1275
then straight away they embarked with a will, and raised the
ship's anchor stones, and hauled hard on the sheet-lines.
The sail bellied out in the wind, and they, rejoicing,
were borne away from shore, past Poseidon's headland.
At the hour when dawn's gray half-light first shines in the heavens,   1280
rising from the horizon, and paths become visible,
and dew-pointed meadows glitter brightly, then they
perceived that, all unknowing, they'd left those two ashore.
Then a fierce quarrel broke out among them, with noisy shouting,
because they had sailed away, leaving there behind them   1285
the best of their comrades. But Jason, amazed and at a loss,
said never a word, one way or the other, but sat there
bowed under his heavy load of ruin, in silence,
consuming his spirit. Then Télamon, furious, shouted:
"Yes, sit there easy, small wonder, it suited you nicely   1290
to leave Herakles behind! This scheme was all your doing,
to stop his fame throughout Greece from eclipsing yours,
if it be that the gods grant us a safe homecoming!
But what's the point of talk? I'm going back, despite those
comrades of yours who planned this treachery with you."   1295
So saying he sprang at Tiphys, Hagnias's son, his
eyes aglint with fury like bright twists of raging fire;
and indeed they would have turned back to Mysian territory,
thrusting across the gulf against the relentless
roar of the gale, had not the two sons of Thrakian   1300
Boreas stopped Télamon short with a harsh reproof—
headstrong fools! who suffered a grim requital thereafter

at Herakles' hands, since they'd held back the search for him.
For on their way home from Pelias's funeral games
he killed them in sea-girt Tenos and piled up earthen   1305
barrows above them, each surmounted by a column
and one of these—a great marvel for men to behold—
sways under the breath of blustering Boreas.
These things came to pass thus in time thereafter.
But out of the briny depths there now appeared to them   1310
Glaukos, the sage interpreter of divine Nereus,
and heaving up high his shaggy head and shoulders
clear to the waist below, he grasped the ship's sternpost
with powerful hand, and cried to his eager audience:
"Why so determined, against great Zeus's counsels,   1315
to bring bold Herakles to Aiëtés' citadel?
In Argos his fate is to toil hard, for presumptuous
Eurystheus, fulfilling a total of twelve labors,
then to share hearth and home with the gods—if he accomplish
a few more still: so let him occasion no regrets.   1320
Likewise with Polyphémos, who, the destined founder
of a famous Mysian township on the Kios estuary,
will meet his measure of doom in the Chalybes' vast land.
But a goddess, a nymph, through love for Hylas, has made him
her husband: it was for *his* sake those two went off, were left." 1325
With that he dived down, wrapped himself in the restless
wave, and around him dark water boiled in seething eddies,
washing the hollow ship onward through the salty depths.
And the heroes rejoiced, and Télamon, Aiakos' son,
was at Jason's side in an instant, impulsively clasped his hand 1330
in his own, embraced him, exclaiming, "Son of Aison,
do not be angry with me if through my thoughtlessness
I acted a little foolishly: it was grief that drove me to utter
words arrogant and intolerable. Come, let us offer
my error to the winds, be good friends as before."   1335
Then Aison's son made him this careful answer:
"Friend, indeed you did abuse me with ill words,
making a claim in public that I'd acted unscrupulously
against a kindly man. Yet I shall not long nurse bitter
resentment, hurt though I was, since not over flocks of   1340
sheep or other possessions were you goaded to fury

but for a man, your comrade. And I hope that if ever
the need arose you'd defend *me* against some attacker."
So he spoke, and they sat down, united as before.

But of those two, by Zeus's counsel, one, Polyphémos,   1345
Eilatos's son, was fated to found and build among
the Mysians a city with the river's name, while the other,
Herakles, toiled at Eurystheus's labors. He threatened
to ravage the Mysians' land on the spot, if they failed
to discover the fate of Hylas, be he dead or living.   1350
They chose, and gave him as pledges, the people's noblest
sons, and swore an oath that they would never
cease from their toilsome search: which is the reason
why to this day the people of Kios ask after
Hylas, Theiódamas's son, and maintain an interest   1355
in well-built Trachis: for there was where Herakles settled
the boys they sent him from Kios to be taken as hostages.

All day and throughout the night a strong wind drove their
ship on her way; but as the dawn was breaking
a dead calm fell. Then, noting where a foreland   1360
stood out from a curve in the coast, very widespread to the eye,
they bent to their oars, and landed there by sunrise.

Book II

Here were the ox stalls and cattle pounds that belonged to Amykos,
the Bebrykians' arrogant king (whom on a time Mélïé bore,
that Bithynian nymph, after bedding with Poseidon,
sire of their race)—most presumptuous of mortals,
who laid down, even for strangers, an outrageous ordinance   5
that none should go on their way till they'd made trial of him
at boxing; and many the neighbors he'd dispatched. So now too
down he came to the ship, in his insolence scorning
to ask them who they might be, or the reason for their voyage,
but stood there among them all, and spoke straight out: 10
"Pay attention, sea-tramps: there are things you need to know.
It's the custom that no foreigner who disembarks here
among the Bebrykians sails away again till he's fought
a bout with me, put up fists against fists. So pick
the best man you have in your company, set him down   15
right here before me to fight it out as a boxer.
But should you ignore my ordinances, trample them underfoot,
then you'll find yourselves in bad trouble, with no way out."
So he spoke in his arrogance, and as they listened
wild anger gripped them. His threat struck Polydeukes hardest   20
and at once he stood up as his comrades' champion, saying:
"Hold on now, whoever you claim to be, don't show us
your nasty violence! We shall go by the rules as you state them.
I myself, here and now, gladly accept your challenge."
So he spoke, bluntly. The king glared at him, eyes rolling,   25

79

like some lion struck by a javelin, with the hunters
closing in on it in the mountains; though surrounded
it pays no heed to the throng, and has eyes only
for the man who hit it first, but failed to kill it.
So the son of Tyndáreus took off his closely woven   30
fine-textured mantle, which one of the Lemnian women
had offered him as his guest-gift; and the king threw down
his thick dark cloak, pins and all, and the herdsman's rough-cut
staff of wild mountain olive that he carried.
Then they cast around, and lit on a place that pleased them,   35
and made their respective companions sit on the sand, well apart
from each other. These two shared nothing in form or stature,
for the one seemed some monstrous offspring of grim Typhóeus
or of Earth herself, such as she bore aforetime
in her fury at Zeus; but the other, Tyndáreus's son,   40
was like the star in heaven that twinkles brightest
as it shows through the first evening darkness. Such was the son
of Zeus, still growing the first down on his cheeks,
eyes still bright with gladness; but now his power
and fierceness swelled like a beast's, and he shadowboxed,   45
testing whether his hands were as quick as they'd been before,
or whether the labor of rowing had left them sluggish.
But Amykos made no tests; he stood apart in silence,
eyes fixed on his adversary, spirit leaping
with the urge to crack his torso, spatter the lifeblood.   50
Between them the henchman of Amykos, Lykóreus,
set down at their feet, on either side, a pair of
knuckle straps cut from rawhide, tanned dry, toughened.
Then Amykos vauntingly challenged Polydeukes:
"Take whichever pair you prefer; be my guest; no drawing   55
of lots—that way you can't blame me afterwards.
But put them on quickly now: you'll learn, and tell others,
how far I rank above all men in cutting dry rawhide
and spattering with blood the cheeks of my opponents."
So he spoke, but the other made no answering retort.   60
Without argument, quietly smiling, he picked up the pair
that lay at his feet. Then Kastor and Bias's giant son
Tálaos came, and quickly bound the knuckle straps
round his fists, exhorting him to display his prowess;

while the king's two squires did the same for him, not knowing,   65
poor fools, that this was the last time, that his luck had ended.
But when the two were squared off, all strapped and ready,
at once they lifted up weighty hands in front of
their faces, and set about one another with eager fury.
Then the Bebrykians' king, like some wild sea-comber   70
cresting against a swift ship—yet the ship by a hair's breadth
dodges it through the skill of a clever helmsman,
though the wave is all set to break inside the bulwarks—
so he, breathing terror, pursued Tyndáreus's son,
never giving him respite, while his quarry, unscathed   75
through his skill, kept dodging the onslaught. But as soon as he'd
    sized up
the king's rough boxing style, its weaknesses and strengths,
then he stood his ground and went at him, blow for blow.
Just as when ships' timbers are forced onto pointed dowels,
layer over layer, by carpenters banging them home   80
with mallets, and blow after blow continually resounds,
so the cheeks and jaws of both these combatants sounded
when struck, and an endless noise of grinding teeth was heard
and they went on slamming each other, neither giving ground,
till each was gasping, done in by lack of breath   85
and they drew apart a little and wiped off the ample
sweat from their foreheads, still panting with exhaustion,
then both went at it again, like a couple of bulls
in furious rivalry for a heifer out at pasture.
But as Amykos stretched up there to his full height,   90
rising on tiptoe like an ox butcher, and bringing
his heavy hand slamming down on him, Polydeukes sidestepped
the blow, withdrawing his head, so that he caught the forearm
glancingly on one shoulder; then whipping in, knee past knee,
he drove home over the ear a blow that shattered   95
the inner bones. Agonized, down sank the king; the Minyan
heroes cheered; his spirit poured forth, was gone.
The Bebrykians, far from careless of their king's fate, now charged
Polydeukes in a body, made to attack him, brandishing
their rough clubs and assegais; but his comrades closed ranks   100
in front of him, stood there with keen blades drawn
from their scabbards. First Kastor struck a man on the head

as he bore down on him, and the skull, split lengthways,
dropped in halves on either shoulder. Polydeukes himself
dispatched the hulking Itymóneus and Mimas,   105
laying one in the dust with a jump and a swift kick
under the breastbone, stopping the other at close quarters
with a right-handed cross-cut over the left eyebrow
that tore off the lid, leaving the whole eye exposed.
Oreites, Amykos's squire, a man proud of his muscle,   110
wounded Tálaos, Bias's son, in the flank, but failed to
kill him off, for the bronze point merely grazed the skin,
passing under the belt, not piercing to the belly.
Aretos too came on at Iphitos, Eúrytos's steadfast
son, and dealt him a blow with his hard cudgel;   115
but an ill fate had not yet doomed him; Aretos rather
was destined soon to perish on Klytios's swordpoint.
Then Ankaios, the daring offspring of Lykourgos, waving
a huge axe, and with his left hand wrapped inside the
skin of a black bear, rushed furiously into the thick   120
of the Bebrykians; and there joined him in his charge
Peleus and Télamon, and with them went warlike Jason.
As on a day in winter the gray wolves, coming down,
will panic the countless flocks in the sheepfolds, undetected
by the sheepdogs' keen noses or even by the shepherds,   125
and go looking for what they can first jump and carry off,
eyeing the whole mass at once, and the sheep run huddling
together, tumbling over each other; so these heroes
spread fearful panic among the high-riding Bebrykians.
And as shepherds or beekeepers smoke out an enormous   130
swarm of bees in a rock, and they to begin with
buzz around in great confusion inside their hive,
but very soon, suffocated by the smudge-black
smoke coils, fly out all together, so the Bebrykians
no longer held firm, or resisted, but fled in all directions   135
throughout Bebrykia, bringing news of Amykos's death—
poor fools, all unaware that another unlooked-for trouble
was close upon them; for their orchards and villages
were even then being plundered by their enemy, Lykos,
and his Mariandynian spearmen, in the king's absence,   140
since this iron-rich region made for endless feuding.

And while they were raiding the farmyards and cattle pounds,
the heroes had already rounded up great flocks of sheep
and were driving them off: and thus one would speak to another:
"Just think what these folk would have done in their cowardice   145
if some god had made it possible to bring Herakles hither!
If you want my opinion, had *he* been here, I'm certain
there'd have been no boxing contest: when that fellow
came spouting his ordinances, a blow from that great club
would have made him forget his pride, and the ordinances as well.   150
Yes, we left him ashore, didn't think of him for one moment,
but sailed off into the blue, and each one of us will realize,
now he is far away, how great was our mad folly."
So he spoke: but all this had been done by Zeus's counsels.

There they stayed through the hours of darkness, tended the wounds   155
of the injured, offered sacrifice to the immortals,
and got ready a great dinner: nor did sleep overtake
any man by the wine bowl and the blaze of the sacrifice.
Their fair brows they garlanded above with laurel
from a tree by the shore, round which their hawsers were lashed.   160
Tunefully in measure they sang as Orpheus led them
on his lyre, and the wind stilled, and their singing held the
coast spellbound with their praises of Zeus's Spartan son.
But when the sun shone on the dewy hilltops, rising
from the eastern horizon, and waking shepherds, then   165
they cast off their hawsers from the laurel's trunk, and stowed
all the plunder aboard that they needed for their voyage,
and a good wind blew them into the turbulent Bosporos.
There a wave like a sheer mountain reared up in their path,
looking as though it would charge them, surging ever   170
higher, above the clouds; you'd think it impossible
to escape a grim fate; in its fury it overshadows,
cloudlike, the vessel amidships; yet, not withstanding,
it can be laid low if you've come by a clever helmsman.
So, thanks to the skills of Tiphys, they too came through,   175
terrified, but unscathed. On the following day,
they moored their ship over against the Thynian shore.
There on the coast was the home of Phineus, Agénor's son,
who above all men endured most terrible misery
through the prophetic gift that earlier Apollo   180

had bestowed on him: he had no scruples about revealing
to men, precisely, the divine will of Zeus himself.
So Zeus afflicted him with interminable old age,
and took the sweet light from his eyes, and would not let him
enjoy the countless dishes that his neighbors always   185
brought to his house, when they'd come to learn the will of heaven;
instead, there swooped down on him, through the clouds, suddenly,
Harpies, forever snatching the food from mouth or hands
with their crooked beaks. Sometimes not a crumb was left him,
at others just enough to let him live and suffer;   190
but then they spread over it all a putrid stench, that no one
could bear when filling his gullet, or even when keeping
their distance, so foul the smell of his dinner's remnants.
The moment he heard the company's voices and footsteps,
he sensed that these passers-by were the ones at whose coming,   195
so Zeus's oracle said, he would get joy of his victuals.
He struggled up from his bed, dreamlike, spiritless,
and tapped his way to the door on bony feet,
huddling over a stick, feeling the walls, joints shaking
from weakness and age: his parchment skin was cured   200
with dirt, only the skin cobbled his bones together.
Out of the house he came, knees buckling, and collapsed
on the courtyard threshold. Blood rushed to his head, the ground
seemed to swim under his feet. He lay there speechless,
swooning, unstrung. When they saw him, the heroes gathered   205
and stood round in wonderment. Then he, with labored
shallow breathing, made this prophetic utterance:
"Listen, you foremost of all the Greeks, if truly
you are they whom, by a king's chill ordinance, Jason   210
is leading, aboard the ship *Argo,* after the Fleece—
yes, it's you for certain: my mind by its prophetic
insight still knows all matters—ah, Lord Apollo,
even in harsh affliction I give you thanks for that!—
by Zeus of the suppliants, that icy foe to human   215
transgressors, for Phoibos's sake, for Hera's, in whose care
above that of all other gods you travel, I beseech you,
help me—save an ill-fated man from outrage,
don't sail away and abandon me with indifference
in the state you see! For not only has some Fury   220

kicked out my sight, while I drag on a weary old age
whose end eludes me, but another most bitter trouble,
worse than the rest, hangs above me: Harpies, swooping from somewhere
unknown and deathly, snatch the food from my lips;
I have no wise plan for my rescue; no, more easily   225
could I escape my own thought, when I long for dinner,
than them, so swift their flight through the air. And even
supposing they leave me some morsel of food, it breathes
the stench of decay, its smell is too strong to be borne:
no mortal could stand coming near it, even for a little,   230
though his heart were forged of adamant. But a bitter
necessity, never satisfied, forces me to remain,
and remaining, to put the filth in my accursed belly.
Them it is heaven's decree that the sons of Boreas
shall restrain; and not as strangers will they drive them off me,   235
if I am that Phineus once renowned among men,
for wealth and prophetic skill, and my father was Agénor,
and when I ruled the Thrakians I brought their sister
Kleopatra home as my bride, and paid well for her."
So Agénor's son spoke, and deep grief seized each one of   240
the heroes, and, more than any, the two sons of Boreas.
Wiping away their tears they approached him, and now thus spoke
Zétes, grasping the hand of the distressed old man:
"Poor wretch! I'll swear there's no other soul alive
more god-hated than you! Why are so many griefs laid on you?   245
Sure, you offended the gods, damned by your thoughtlessness
and your knowledge of prophecy: hence their great anger. Yet
our mind is distraught within us, eager though we are
to help you—if indeed some divinity's granted us this honor—
for all too plain to mere earthlings are the stern reproofs   250
of the immortals. Therefore we will not avert the coming
of the Harpies, much though we long to, until you take an oath
that we shall not, because of this act, lose heaven's favor."
So he spoke, and the old man fixed on him his vacant staring
eyeballs, and made response with the following words: 255
"Hush, now, don't get such ideas in your head, my child.
Witness the son of Leto, who with good will taught me
the mantic art; witness, too, the ill-starred fate that's mine,
and this dark cloud over my eyes, and the underworld

gods—should I die thus perjured, may I forfeit their favor—   260
that this aid will bring down on you no wrath from heaven."
So after this oath the two were eager to defend him.
At once the younger heroes prepared the old man a feast,
a final prey for the Harpies; and the two stood by,
ready to swing their swords at them as they swooped down.   265
And indeed, the very moment the old man touched his victuals,
at once, like bitter blasts or lightning flashes,
suddenly out of the clouds they sprang, with a raucous
scream, dove greedily down on the food. The heroes
shouted at them in mid-flight; but they, after gobbling   270
the whole lot down, sped away into the distance
over the sea, still screaming. An unbearable odor
was left there. And behind them the two sons of Boreas,
swords drawn, raced in pursuit, for Zeus had implanted in them
inexhaustible strength. Without Zeus, though, they'd never have come   275
remotely near the Harpies, who regularly outstripped
the west wind's blasts on their way to Phineus, and back again.
As when, on some mountain range, trained hunting dogs,
on the track of horned goats or deer, run at full tilt,
straining hard, but always a little behind them,   280
vainly snapping their jaws, reaching out with their teeth,
so Zétes and Kalaïs, crowding fast on their heels,
reached out for them, in vain, with the tips of their fingers.
And indeed, against the gods' will, they'd have torn them to pieces,
overtaking them far off, above the Floating Islands,   285
had not swift Iris seen them, and, darting down from heaven
out of a clear sky, restrained them with these words:
"It is not ordained, sons of Boreas, that you should harry
the Harpies, great Zeus's hounds, with your swords; but I myself
will swear to you that they'll never come back to touch this man."   290
So saying she took an oath, over a poured libation
of Styx water, to all the gods the chillest and most awful,
that never again would these creatures come near the dwelling
of Phineus, Agénor's son, since thus it was fated.
So they yielded before the oath, and turned to hasten   295
back to the ship; which is why men now call those islands
Turning, instead of, as they once did, Floating.
Then the Harpies and Iris parted: they flew back to

their lair in Minoan Krété, but she went winging
up to Olympos, soaring high on her swift wings.   300
Meanwhile the heroes cleaned off the old man's dirt-encrusted
skin, and sacrificed sheep, all carefully chosen,
that they'd brought away with the plunder taken from Amykos.
Now when they'd set a great dinner in the palace,
they sat down and feasted; and Phineus feasted with them   305
as he'd dreamed of doing, harpy-ravenous, cheering his spirit.
Then after they'd taken their fill of drink and dinner,
they stayed up all night awaiting the sons of Boreas;
and the old man sat in the midst of them, by the hearthstone,
and told them the ends of their voyage, their quest's accomplishment: 310
"Listen now: not everything is it right for you learn
exactly, but I'll not conceal what's allowed by heaven.
I was blinded by folly once, rashly declared the purpose
of Zeus to the end, all in order; but he himself wishes
to show men prophetic pronouncements that are lacking   315
completion, so they may still need to seek the will of heaven.
First of all, on departing from me, you'll see the two cobalt-
dark rocks, at the point of the two seas' meeting-place,
and through those rocks no one, I tell you, has yet made passage.
For they are not firmly based, with fixed foundations,   320
but constantly come clashing, one against the other,
at a single point; and above, a huge influx of the sea
crests boiling; harsh resounds the roar from the wild headland.
So now you'll mark my advice, and obey it, if you truly
are using good sense on this journey, with respect for the blessed   325
gods, not mindlessly taking your own path to destruction
in pursuit of some youthful impulse. First, then, I bid you
make trial with a dove; this will serve you as an omen.
Send it on ahead of the ship. If it flies safely
through the rocks to the Black Sea beyond, delay no longer   330
yourselves, no longer hold off from trying the passage,
but get a good grip on your oars, pull all together
and cleave through that narrow sea-strait, for your lives
will depend less on prayer than on the strength of your arms.
So let all else go, toil boldly at what will profit   335
you best—not that I mind your praying to the gods beforehand.
But if the dove perishes at the midpoint of its flight,

then turn back, since it is preferable by far
to yield to the immortals: you could not escape a frightful
destruction by the rocks, not if *Argo* were ironclad.   340
Wretches, do not dare to transgress my divinely sanctioned
behests—no, not if you think me three times as hateful
to the heavenly host as I am, or even more, still do not
dare to sail on with your ship in defiance of the omen.
As these things chance, so will they be. But if you escape   345
the clash of the rocks unscathed, and enter the Black Sea,
then straight away, keeping the Bithynian coast to starboard,
sail on, watching out for breakers, till you double
the swift-flowing river Rhebas and the Black Headland,
and come to harbor at the island of Thynias.   350
From there, after covering no great stretch of sea,
beach your ship on the Mariandynian shoreline opposite.
Here there's a steep path leading down to Hades,
Acherousia's long, high headland juts out before you,
and eddying Acheron cuts through the headland's base   355
to discharge its waters from a gigantic gorge.
Close after this you'll sail past the hilly coastline
of the Paphlagonians, whose first king was Enéteian
Pelops, from whom they account themselves descended.
There is a cape that faces the ever-circling Bear,   360
sheer on all sides, and people call it Kárambis,
and above it the blasts of the north wind are split asunder,
so high in air it towers, facing out seaward.
When you've rounded this, you see the stretch of the Long Beach
ahead; and beyond the Long Beach's furthest point,   365
past a great promontory, the Halys River discharges
with a fearful roaring; close after it, but smaller,
the Iris winds to the sea in limpid eddies.
Further on, a large and dominant elbow headland
runs out from the coast. Then the Thérmodon estuary weeps   370
its waters into a peaceful bay by Themískyra's headland
after wandering through a broad continent. Next follows
the plain of Doias, and near it the three cities
of the Amazons; after these, of all men most miserable,
the Chálybes, who possess a rough and unyielding land,   375
toilers, whose business is with the working of iron.

Near to these dwell the sheep-rich Tibarenes, past the
Genétaian cape of Zeus the Strangers' Friend. Then, marching
with these, come the Mossynoikians, who inhabit in turn
the tree-grown plain and the lower mountain slopes,   380
building on plank foundations their wooden dwellings
and the well-made towers for which they have a special   381a
term, *mossynes,* and from which their own name is taken.   381b
Sailing past these, you must land on a rugged island—
after using all your skills to drive off a vast mass of
utterly ruthless birds, which in countless numbers
haunt this deserted isle. Here, once, a stone temple   385
was built, or so they tell us, by two queens of the Amazons,
Antíopé and Otréré, when they were campaigning.
For it's here, from the bitter sea, that advantage will come to you,
which I may not divulge. So my intent is friendly
in bidding you stop there. But what need for me once more to   390
transgress by letting my prophecies tell the whole story through?
Beyond this island, across on the facing mainland,
the Philyrians have their grazing; above them, further on,
dwell the Makrónes and, next, the Becheirians' vast tribes,
and after them as neighbors come the Sapeires,   395
and marching with these, the Byzerians, beyond whom, at last,
are the Kolchians themselves, warlike men. But still continue
your journey by ship, till you touch the sea's inmost gulf,
where through the lands round Kyta and from the far-distant
Amarantian mountains and the plain of Kirké   400
turbulent Phasis propels his broad stream seaward.
Drive your ship as far as that river's outfall,
and then you'll see the battlements of Kytaian Aiëtés,
and the shady grove of Ares, where the Fleece is,
spread out on the top of an oak tree, watched by a serpent,   405
a fearful creature to look at, ever gazing round, on guard,
nor by day or night does sweet sleep close his fierce eyes."
So he spoke, and at once fear gripped them as they listened.
For long they remained struck speechless. Then, finally, Jason,
the hero, spoke, at a loss, and weak-willed in this crisis: 410
"Old man, now you've rehearsed the limits of our laborious
voyage, and shown us the token, trusting to which we'll pass
through those fearful rocks to the Black Sea. But whether, having

escaped them, we'll later win our day of returning
to Greece—that's another thing I'd most gladly learn of you.   415
How must I act? How traverse all that sea route over again,
unskilled, and with unskilled companions? And Kolchian Aia
lies at the furthest limits of sea and earth."
So he spoke, and the old man answered him in these words:
"My child, as soon as you've come through those deadly rocks,   420
take heart: a divinity will guide your homeward voyage
from Aia, and going to Aia you'll have guides in plenty.
But, my friends, keep well in mind the devious succor
to be had of the Kyprian goddess, Aphrodite. On her depends
the success of your venture. Now question me no further."   425
So spoke Agénor's son; and on the moment, the two
sons of Thrakian Boreas came darting down from heaven
and grounded their nimble feet on the threshold. All the heroes
sprang up from their seats when they saw them both appear.
In response to their questions, Zétes, still panting and out of breath   430
from his exertions, recounted what a huge distance
they'd chased the Harpies, whom Iris had stopped them killing,
yet favored them, as a goddess, with that oath; how the Harpies in terror
had fled back to their vast cavern on Dikté's cliff face.
Joyful then in the house were all the companions,   435
and Phineus himself most of all. Then, quickly, Jason,
Aison's son, brimming over with good will, thus addressed him:
"Some god it surely was, Phineus, who took compassion
on your miserable sufferings, and sent us here from so
far away, to let the sons of Boreas rescue you;   440
and if he also put light back in your eyes, why then
I think I'd rejoice as much as if I were coming home."
So he spoke, but Phineus answered, with downcast look:
"Son of Aison, that is irrevocable, no cure exists for it
now or hereafter: my eyeballs are seared away to blankness.   445
Instead, may the god grant me a quick death; after dying
I'll have my share, then, of all that delights the heart."
So these two spoke in half hints one to the other;
and no long time after, while they were yet talking,
the first dawn broke. Then neighbors began to assemble   450
round Phineus, men who before this had flocked there daily,
bringing him each time a share of their own food:

and to all comers, even the poorest, the old man would steadfastly
prophesy, bringing release to many from their troubles
by his mantic art; in return they would visit and care for him.   455
With them now came Paraibios, dearest of all men
to Phineus, and glad he was to see the heroes
there in the house; for once, earlier, Phineus had predicted
that an expedition of heroes from Greece to Aiëtés' city
would make fast its hawsers there in Bithynian soil,   460
and by Zeus's will would stop the Harpies' visitations.
The rest, then, the old man made happy with sage counsel
and sent on their way; Paraibios alone he invited
to stay there with the heroes. And quickly he dispatched him
with orders to fetch them his choicest sheep. The moment   465
he'd left the great hall, with gentle graciousness
Phineus spoke out among the assembled rowers:
"My friends, not all men are arrogant, it would appear,
nor forgetful of benefits. Such a one is this man,
who came here to discover what doom was laid on him: 470
for when he did most work, and toiled the hardest,
then it was that lack of substance, ever increasing,
would wear him down, and each successive day
dawned worse, and he saw no respite to his labors.
The truth was, he was paying a grim atonement   475
for an offense of his father's, who, felling trees
alone in the mountains, made light of a nymph's prayers,
a hamádryad, who besought him, weeping, with abundant
entreaties, not to sever the stock of an oak tree
coeval with her, in which her whole long life had been spent;   480
but he, in his youthful brashness, cut it down regardless.
So to him and his children thereafter the nymph assigned
a doom without recourse. I myself, at his arrival,
knew the offense: I told him to build an altar
to the Bithynian nymph, and on it make sacrifice   485
of atonement, and pray to escape his father's fate.
So, since his release from this god-sent doom, he's never
forgotten or slighted me: he's so urgent to aid my troubles
that he hates to go—it's hard to get him through the doorway."
So spoke Agénor's son: and soon after back from the flock   490
came Paraibios, driving two sheep. Then up stood Jason,

up, too, the sons of Boreas at the old man's bidding,
and quickly, invoking the name of Oracular Apollo,
made sacrifice on the hearth, as day was just ending,
while the younger companions prepared an agreeable feast.   495
Then when they'd feasted well, they all retired to sleep,
some in groups in the house there, some by the ship's hawsers.

At dawn the Etesian winds got up. Now these blow over
the whole earth in equal measure, a benison from Zeus.
For a certain Kyréné, they say, once tended sheep   500
among men of former times, beside the Peneios marshland,
enjoying virginity, an inviolate bed. But Apollo
carried her off, as she watched her flock by the river,
far from Thessalian soil, and put her among the nymphs
who dwelt in Libya, by the Mount of Myrtles.   505
To the god she there bore Aristaios, called "The Hunter"
and "The Shepherd" by Thessalians, rich in grain-fields.
Herself, out of love, Apollo made a nymph there,
long-lived and a huntress; but his infant son he removed
to be brought up in Cheiron's cave; and when he reached manhood   510
the goddess-Muses arranged a marriage for him,
and taught him the arts of healing and divination,
and made him the keeper of all their sheep, that pastured
on Athamas's plain in Phthia, and around towering
Othrys, and by Apídanos's sacred stream.   515
But when out of heaven the Dog Star was burning up the islands
of Minos and for long their inhabitants got no relief,
then at Apollo's behest, they called upon Aristaios
to rescue them from this scourge. At his father's bidding
he left Phthia, and settled on Keos, taking with him   520
those Arkadian folk whose lineage is from Lykáon;
and he built there a great altar to Zeus the Rain God,
and on the mountaintop offered due sacrifice to both
the Dog Star and Zeus son of Kronos. That is the reason
why Zeus sends the Etesian winds to cool the earth   525
for forty days, and on Keos the priests still offer
sacrifices before the rising of the Dog Star.
So the story is told; and so the heroes remained there
by constraint; and daily the Thynians would send them
guest-gifts beyond counting, as a favor to Phineus.   530

But at last, after building an altar to the Twelve
Blessed Ones on the seashore opposite, and making
sacrifices upon it, they boarded their vessel, ready
to row, not forgetting to take with them, in the charge of
Euphémos, a timorous dove, huddling close for fear,   535
gripped in his fist. They cast off their twin hawsers,
and their departure did not pass unnoticed by Athena.
At once she hastened to set her feet on a light cloud
that would bear her onward at once, huge though she was,
and set off, Black Seaward, with friendly thoughts for the rowers. 540
Like a man wandering far from his hometown—as often
we mortals perforce must endure to—who finds no country
remote, but every city lies there clear to his view,
and he'll picture his own home, and there flash before him
the sea and land journeys at once, and in the speed of   545
his thought, his eyes strain after now one, now the other—
with such speed did Zeus's daughter, darting earthward, set her
feet on the Thynian shore of the Inhospitable Sea.

When they reached the narrow throat of that twisting passage,
walled in on either side by a rough rockface,   550
and a turbulent current boiled up under the vessel
as she advanced, and they urged her on, terrified,
while already the knock of the rocks in violent collision
kept assaulting their ears, and the sea-washed cliffs resounded—
then it was that Euphémos scrambled up, still clutching   555
his dove, and made for the prow, while at a word from
Tiphys, Hagnias's son, the rest now slowed the strike-rate
of their rowing, the better to charge the rocks afterwards
drawing on all their strength; and as they rounded the last
bend, in that instant they saw the rocks drawing open,   560
and their hearts were confounded. Then Euphémos released
the dove on her flight, and every head was craned
to watch her as she went; straight on and in between
the rocks she fluttered, and they both came roaring back
to crash one against the other. An explosion   565
of salt spray boiled up like a cloud; then fearfully thundered
the sea, and all about echoed the vault of heaven.
The hollow caverns boomed, while under jagged reefs
surged in the brine, and high as the cliff's summit

spat up the white spume of the seething breakers.   570
Then the ship spun with the current. The rocks sheared off
the dove's tipmost tail-feathers, yet she darted clear
unscathed, to loud cheers from the oarsmen, and a shouted
command from Tiphys himself to row hard, for the rocks were
parting once more. They toiled, panic-stricken, till the tidal   575
reflux, boiling back, bore them forward between rock
and rock, and then the most awful terror gripped them
one and all, for over their heads hung destruction inexorable.
And now, as to right and left the wide Black Sea appeared,
there rose up before them a wave, enormous, sudden,   580
arching like a sheer crag; and they, when they saw it,
shrank back, heads averted, for it seemed about to
plunge down on the ship's whole length and overwhelm them.
But Tiphys moved quicker, easing her round as she labored
with their rowing, and the wave's mass rolled away under the keel,   585
yet bore up the vessel's stern, swung her far back beyond the
rocks, and high aloft she was carried. Then Euphémos
strode between comrade and comrade, shouting to them
to bend their full strength to the oars, and they, with a cheer,
sliced through the water. Yet for every yard rowed forward   590
the ship was driven back two, and the heroes' efforts
made their oars bend till they looked like the curve of a bow.
But then a wave from behind, looming over, rushed upon them,
and their vessel sped forward like a long surfing missile
over the hollow sea on that swift rough crest. But midway   595
between the Clashing Rocks a maelstrom held her. On either
side the Rocks shuddered and thundered, while her timbers
ground to a halt. Then Athena, left hand jammed against a massive
rock, with her right thrust *Argo* through and onward,
and the vessel sped, airborne, like a swift-winged arrow;   600
yet still the Rocks, as they violently met, sheared off
the tip of her curving poop, with its ornament. But Athena,
once they were clear, unscathed, sped back to Olympus;
and the rocks fused into each other, forever rooted
in the same spot, as the gods had decreed should happen   605
the first time a man looked on them, and got his vessel through.
Then at last they breathed again, quit of their chilling
terror, and gazed around them at the sky, the widespread

expanse of sea; for indeed they'd been saved, they thought,
from Hades. The first to break the silence was Tiphys: 610
"It's my belief that we owe our survival of this hazard
to the vessel we sail in—thanks, above all, to Athena,
who when Argos was clamping its dowels breathed in divine
strength to the ship's hull: no way can *Argo* be caught.
Son of Aison, since the god has allowed us to escape through   615
the rocks, you need no longer so fear your king's
commandment; for Phineus, Agénor's son, assured us
that our future ordeals would be easily accomplished."
As he spoke, he urged the ship onward, fast, through open waters,
along the coast of Bithynia. To him Jason   620
replied in soothing terms, yet with sidelong purpose:
"Tiphys, why comfort me thus in my sorrow? I committed
through my own folly an appalling, irreparable error.
When Pelias made his commandment I should have refused
this quest flat out, on the spot, even if it meant   625
enduring a pitiless death, torn limb from limb.
But now overwhelming fear and sorrows past bearing
weigh me down: I dread to sail this vessel over
the chilling paths of the sea, dread the moment when we'll
step ashore on dry land. There are enemies everywhere.   630
Always from each day's ending I keep my grievous vigil
night long—ever since you first assembled for my sake—
pondering every detail. It's easy for you to talk
with just your own life to take care of. For myself
I care not a jot; but for this man and that, for you and   635
all my other comrades I fear, lest I fail to bring you
back home unharmed to the soil of Hellas." So he
spoke, making trial of the heroes; but they all shouted
bold words of encouragement, and his heart was warmed within him
by their utterance, and he went on, straightforward now, "My friends,   640
my confidence gains strength from this brave display of yours.
So now, not even were I to traverse the chasms
of Hades, will fear get a grip on me, since you stand
firm amid grievous perils. Still, now we've sailed
clear of the Clashing Rocks, such another peril   645
I doubt we'll meet hereafter, provided we follow
the instructions of Phineus exactly on our voyage."

So he spoke, and with that they gave over their discussion
and bent to the harsh inexorable rowing. Soon
they came to Rhebas's swift-flowing stream, the lookout crag   650
of Kolóné, and not long after rounded the Black Headland,
and passed the Phyllis's estuary, where aforetime
Dipsakos in his dwelling welcomed Athamas's son,
with the ram, when he fled from Orchomenos's citadel.
Him a meadow-nymph bore; nor was overhigh ambition   655
his pleasure, but willingly he dwelt with his mother,
tending his flocks along his father's riverside pastures.
Quickly his shrine, and the spreading river-meadows
and the plain beyond, and Kalpes with its deep current
came into view and receded. A windless night followed   660
the day, and still they labored on at their tireless oars.
Just as work oxen toil mightily, cutting their furrow
through the damp earth, while sweat rolls abundantly down
from their flanks and withers, and as they labor under
the yoke, their eyes roll round wildly, their breath is fetched   665
in short dry gasps incessantly, and all day long
they strain on, planting strong hooves in the sod—like them
the heroes kept heaving their oars through and out of the water.

At that moment when darkness is ebbing, yet light's divine
brightness has not yet come, when an impalpable glimmer   670
suffuses the night, what waking men call wolf-light,
they entered the harbor of Thynias, barren island,
and stumbled ashore, exhausted by their grievous
labors; and here there appeared before them Apollo, Leto's
son, on his way back from Lykia to the swarming   675
Hyperboreans; and golden, framing either cheek,
the clustering curls outfloated as he strode.
His left hand grasped a silver bow, and about his shoulders
was slung a quiver of arrows, to hang at his back. His footsteps
shook the whole island. Shock waves surged up the shore.   680
When they saw him, helpless terror gripped them: not a single
man dared look straight into the god's magnificent eyes,
but they all stood staring groundward as he dwindled
airborne into the distance, out over the sea. At last
Orpheus it was found his tongue, and addressed the heroes: 685

"Come, let us call this place the holy island
of Dawntime Apollo, since here he revealed himself
to us all, passing by at dawn; we will offer what sacrifice
lies to hand, build a shoreside altar. And if hereafter
he grant us a safe return, unscathed, to Thessaly,   690
then we'll kill horned goats, and lay out their thighs for him.
But meanwhile, I bid you entreat him with burnt fat and libations—
Be gracious, O Lord, be gracious, Who wert manifest unto us."
So he spoke. And some straightway began to build an altar
with loose stones, while others ranged over the island, seeing   695
if they could catch a glimpse of fawns or wild mountain
goats, such as pasture by dozens in deep forest.
And Leto's son gave them good hunting, and on the consecrated
altar they piously burned both thigh bones of each
victim, with invocations to Dawntime Apollo, and round   700
the offerings, as they burned, they made a broad dancing floor,
singing, "All hail, fair healer, fair healer Phoibos
all hail", and with them Oiagros's noble offspring
struck his Thrakian lyre, and began a clear-pitched song
of how once, below Parnassos's rocky scarp, Apollo,   705
while still a beardless youth, rejoicing in his tresses,
slew with his bow the monstrous beast Delphynes.
(Pardon me, Lord: may Thy locks remain ever unshorn,
ever inviolate, since heaven decrees it, and none save
Koios's daughter Leto may caress them with loving hands.)   710
And the nymphs of Párnassos, Pleistos's children, kept cheering
him on with the cry "*Ié, Healer!*" against the dragon,
and hence came the lovely refrain of this hymn to Phoibos.
Now when with dance and song they'd honored the god, next
they took an oath over holy libations, touching   715
the sacrifice as they swore ever to help one another
in concord of spirit; and still there stands in that place
the shrine of beneficent Concord at which they labored
as a worshipful gesture to so noble a goddess.
When the third morning dawned, they caught a blustering   720
westerly wind, and sailed on from that rocky island.
Next on their starboard side the Sangários River's
outflow, the fertile ploughland of the Mariandyni,
the Lykos estuary and the Lake of Flowers

came into sight and were gone, while taut in the wind   725
the sheets and all the rigging trembled as they sped on.
But the wind dropped during the night, and they were grateful
when they made haven, at dawn, by the Acherousian
headland, which rears up sheer with beetling cliffs,
facing out to the sea of Bithynia, and below,   730
firm-rooted, lie sea-swept reefs, and all about them
the rolling breakers thunder; but on the summit
widespreading plane trees grow, and sloping inland
from that great promontory runs a hollow
woodland valley, where lies the cave of Hades   735
arched over with rocks and bracken, and from it an icy
breath that ever exhales from its chill recesses
deposits a constant layer, all around, of glittering frost
which is melted again by the midday sun. And never
does silence rule sovereign over that grim headland,   740
but there's a continual murmur of sounding breakers
and the rustle of leaves stirred up by the winds from the cavern.
Here too flows the outfall of Acheron, which forces
its way through and out of the headland into the Eastern
Sea, and a deep ravine channels it down from above.   745
In after time it was renamed the Mariners' Haven
by Megarians of Nisaia, on their way to settle
in the land of the Mariandyni; for indeed the river saved them
and their ships as well, when caught in a fearful storm.
Here, now, the heroes steered under the Acherousian headland   750
and made landfall over against it, as the wind fell.

No long time passed before Lykos, the ruler of that country,
and the Mariandyni learnt of the heroes' arrival:
earlier rumors had named them as Amykos's slayers,
so their reception included a formal pact of friendship,   755
and Polydeukes himself they welcomed like a god,
mobbing him from all sides, since they for overlong
had been warring against the haughty Bebrykians.
So all together they went up into the city
to the palace of Lykos, enjoying this day of friendship   760
with feasting and pleasant talk. Now Aison's son
told Lykos the name and lineage of every
one of his comrades, and Pelias's commandments,

and how they were entertained by the Lemnian women,
and their dealings in Doliónia with King Kyzikós,   765
and how they reached Kios in Mysia, where they left Herakles,
though much against their will; and the prophecy of Glaukos
he related, and how they'd slain the Bebrykians
and Amykos; he told of Phineus's sufferings
and predictions, of their passage through the cobalt-dark Rocks,   770
of their meeting on the island with Leto's son. As he listened
Lykos was enthralled; but the matter of Herakles'
abandonment saddened him, and thus he addressed them all:
"Ah, my friends, what a man that was, from whose assistance
you've wandered away, cleaving your long sea track   775
to Aiëtés! I know him well—I saw him here in my father
Daskylos's house, where he stopped as he came through Asia
on foot, bearing a trophy, the girdle of warlike
Hippólyté; when he met me, the first down was on my cheeks.
And here, at the games in honor of Priolas my brother,   780
slain by the men of Mysia—and to this day our people
still mourn him with grieving dirges—Herakles competed
in boxing, and defeated that strongman Titias—
Titias, who was the toughest and the most handsome among
the young men—and slamdashed his teeth all over the ground.   785
Together with the Mysians he brought under my father's
rule the Mygdonians, whose ploughland marches with ours,
and subdued the tribes of Bithynia, land and all, as far as
the estuary of the Rhebas and Kolóné's high lookout crag;
and those Paphlagonians, Pelops's descendants, who live   790
in a loop of dark-watered Billaios, surrendered without a fight.
But now that Herakles dwells far off, the Bebrykians
and Amykos in his arrogance have long despoiled me,
slicing off chunks of my land, till they've advanced
their boundary stones to deep-flowing Hypios's water meadows.   795
Still, thanks to you, they've been punished; it wasn't, I tell you,
without the will of the gods that I launched my attack against
the Bebrykians on the day that you, son of Tyndáreus,
killed that man. So now whatever requital I'm able
I'll gladly repay you. Such is the duty of weaker   800
men when the others, the stronger, take action to help them.
To follow you all as companion on this your expedition

I will send my son Daskylos: with him aboard, you'll
get a friendly welcome from all as you sail these waters
till you reach the Thermodon estuary. In addition,   805
for the sons of Tyndáreus, high on the Acherousian headland,
I'll raise a tall shrine, a landmark that sailors, far out
on the deep, shall see and honor with their prayers.
And for them hereafter, as for gods, outside the city
I'll set aside some acres of the plain's rich ploughland."   810
So all day long they pleasured themselves with feasting;
but at dawn they trooped briskly down to the ship, and Lykos
went with them himself, brought countless gifts for the journey,
and sent forth his son from home to sail as their companion.

Then it was that fated destiny struck down Abas's son   815
Idmon—an expert diviner, yet his divinations did nothing
to save him; necessity forced him onward to his death.
For in the river marshes there lurked amid the reed beds,
cooling his flanks and vast belly in the mud,
a monstrous and deadly beast, a white-tusked boar, a terror   820
even to the nymphs of the meadows. No man had knowledge
of its lair: it ranged alone through those broad marshlands.
As Idmon was going along the high muddy riverbank,
suddenly, out of nowhere, the great boar barreled
up from the reeds and at him, slashed with impetuous   825
force clean through his thigh, severed bone and tendons.
With a piercing scream he collapsed. His comrades answered
the wounded man's cry in chorus. Quickly Peleus
hurled a javelin after the brute boar as it scuttled
back marshward. It charged once more. But Idas ran it   830
through, and snarling, impaled on the spear, it fell.
The beast they left on the ground there, where it had fallen,
but Idmon, gasping his life out, his grieving comrades bore
back to the ship, and in his comrades' arms he died.
All thought of their voyaging was now forgotten,   835
and for three long days they remained there, making lamentation,
in mourning for the dead man; but on the fourth
they gave him a splendid funeral, and King Lykos
and his people shared in the rites. Over the grave they slit
the throats of countless sheep, proper honor to the departed,   840

and Idmon had his barrow raised in that place, and above it
a marker, still there for men of later days to see,
a ship's spar of wild olive, leaves sprouting from it,
a little below Cape Acheron. But (if this too I must,
at the Muses' insistence, declare straight out), though Phoibos   845
directly commanded the Boiotians and Nisaians
to venerate this hero as guardian of their city,
and build on a site surrounding the spar of old wild olive,
they to this day pay honor, not to that pious
Aiólian Idmon, but rather to Agaméstor.   850
But who else was it died? since now once more the heroes
heaped up a high barrow for a departed comrade,
and the markers of both men can be seen to this day.
It was Tiphys, Hagnias's son, who died, they say: his fate
let him voyage no further, but a rapid illness   855
put him to sleep here, far away from his own country,
on the day his companions buried the body of Abas's son.
Such loss, on top of their grief, they found unbearable;
and indeed, when they'd performed these obsequies besides,
soon after, hopeless and helpless, they lay down on the shore,   860
silent, close-wrapped in their cloaks, indifferent
to food or drink, their spirits downcast with sorrow,
since their venture was turning out so wide of what they'd hoped.
And indeed the grief they felt would have delayed them
yet longer, had not Hera put an overplus of courage   865
into Ankaios, whom by the waters of Imbrasos
Astypálaia bore to Poseidon, and who was an expert
steersman: eagerly now he made his approach to Peleus:
"Son of Aiakos, what's so fine about loitering here forever
on foreign soil, our struggle abandoned? It isn't so much as   870
a first-class fighting man that Jason's taking me after
that Fleece, all the way from Parthenia, but for my shipboard
expertise: so don't worry one jot about our vessel.
Besides, there are other skilled mariners here—we can safely
put any one of them at the helm, there's no danger   875
they'll mess up our voyage. Quick, now—get this message across,
show confident, urge them all to remember our task."
So he spoke, and Peleus's heart reached out to him in joy,
and without hesitation he then made them this speech:

"Good friends, why cling so vainly to pointless sorrow?   880
These men, surely, have met the fate they were allotted;
but there are steersmen yet to be found in our company,
and plenty of them. So let's not delay our venture,
but throw off your misery, rouse yourselves, and to work!"
Then Aison's son in his shiftlessness made him answer: 885
"Son of Aiakos, where are these steersmen of yours? The ones
we reckoned in time gone by to be skilled performers
are crushed even more than myself by the weight of their grief.
For us I foresee a fate as grim as awaits the dead
if we're neither to make our way to dread Aiëtés' city   890
nor ever again to thread those rocks and make landfall
back in Hellas, but rather an evil fate will enshroud us
ingloriously here, and we'll grow old all for nothing."
So he spoke; but Ankaios most eagerly undertook
to steer the swift ship, for Hera so impelled him.   895
Then after him Ergínos, Nauplios, and Euphémos
all got up, hot to be helmsman; but these others
were turned down—most of the crew gave their nod to Ankaios.
At dawn on the twelfth day, then, they embarked, accompanied
by a powerful westerly tailwind blowing for them.   900
Briskly they rowed her out from the Acheron River
and with trust in the breeze raised sail: a great spread of canvas
bellied out ahead, and under fair skies they cut their
sea track and quickly reached the estuary of the Fairdance
River, where Dionysos, they say, Nysaian offspring   905
of Zeus, returning from India to settle in Thebes,
held secret rites and dances before a cavern
in which he lodged for those solemn and holy nights,
since when the local inhabitants have called the river
Fairdance, and referred to the cavern as the Lodge.   910
Next they sighted the barrow of Sthénelos, Aktor's son,
who on his way home from warfare most valorous
against the Amazons, as companion to Herakles,
was struck by an arrow, and died there on the dunes.
For now they advanced no further, since Perséphoné   915
herself released the weeping spirit of Aktor's son,
which had begged her to let him see, if only for a little,
men of his own kind. From the barrow's summit he watched

the ship, looking just as he'd done when he went to war, his helmet
gleaming bright, four-bossed, with its scarlet crest.   920
Then down into gloom and darkness he sank once more, while they
stood amazed at the sight. Then Mopsos, Ampykos's son,
a prophet inspired, bade them land and propitiate
the dead man with libations. Quickly they struck sail,
threw out hawsers, and on the beach paid respects to Sthénelos's tomb,   925
poured out drink offerings, sacrificed sheep to his shade.
In addition they raised an altar to Apollo, Protector
of Ships, and burnt thigh bones on it; here too Orpheus
dedicated his lyre—hence the place's name of Lyra.
Then the wind got up strong, and at once they hurried   930
aboard, and hauling the sail down bent it taut
to both sheet-lines; and *Argo* was driven onward
with speed into the deep, as a hawk is swiftly carried,
wingspan outspread to the breeze, never stirring its pinions,
poised and silently gliding through the clear bright heavens.   935
On they sailed, past the sea-bound outflow of that gentle
river Parthenios, in which the virgin daughter
of Leto, on her way heavenward after hunting,
cools her body with its delightful waters.
Speeding on then after dark still further, without pause,   940
they sailed past Sésamos and the high Erythínian rocks,
Króbialos and Krómna and thick-wooded Kytóros.
From there with the sun's first rays they doubled the headland
of Kárambis, and then, a long day's toil into night,
bent to their oars and rowed the whole stretch of Long Beach.   945
Soon they made landfall on the Assyrian coast, where Zeus
himself settled Sínope, Asópos's daughter, bestowing
on her (tricked by his own promise) the boon of virginity,
since indeed he yearned to possess her, and swore she should have
whatever her heart desired as a gift from him: 950
so she in her cunning asked to retain her maidenhead.
In the same way she fooled Apollo (he too had this passion
to bed her), and after them the Halys River. No man
from now on ever downed her in sweet embracement.
Here the three sons of noble Deïmachos of Trikka—   955
Deïleon and Autólykos and Phlógios—still dwelt
ever since they'd wandered away from Herakles; they now,

when they saw this expedition of heroes make its landfall
rushed out to meet them, revealed their identity,
had no wish to delay there longer, but the moment   960
a good nor'-wester got up, went aboard the heroes' vessel.
Then, all together, borne on by the swift breeze,
they cruised past the Halys River, past the Iris's neighboring
outflow and Assyria's silted delta. That day,
standing well to sea, they doubled the Amazons' headland   965
and harbor, where once the hero Herakles ambushed
Melanippé, Ares' daughter, and by way of ransom
her sister Hippólyté gave him her gaudily woven
girdle, and he sent home his captive unharmed.
In the bay of that headland now, at the Thérmodon's outfall,   970
they ran ashore, for a rough sea rose against their passage.
No river resembles this one, from none other issue
so many scattered tributaries: reckon them up
and the total count would only be lacking four
to tally a hundred—yet there's only one true source   975
for them all: it comes tumbling plainward from a lofty
range that's known, men say, as the Amazonian mountains.
From there it spreads straight over a rising inland
plateau, so that its streams flow always in tortuous
channels, twist this way and that, wherever they best can   980
find a path down to low-lying ground, some distant,
some close at hand. Many tributaries remain nameless,
their outflow untraced. But a few merge with the Thérmodon,
make an open noisy discharge into Unfriendly Pontos
under that curving headland. The heroes might have lingered   985
to mix it up with the Amazons—no bloodless battle there,
for neither civil nor law-abiding by nature
were those Amazons who occupied the Doiantian plain,
but cared for nothing but war and grievous outrage,
being by race the offspring of Ares and the nymph   990
Harmonia, who bore Ares these war-hungry daughters
after lying with him in a glen of Akmon's grove—
had Zeus not given them back their strong nor'-wester,
and running before it they cleared the headland's haven,
where the Amazons of Themískyra were arming for war   995
(for they did not all share the same city, but dwelt scattered

across the countryside in three separate tribes:
here the Themiskyréans, at this time ruled by
Hippólyté, there the Lykastians, and lastly
the Chadésians, javelineers). So all next day   1000
and the following night they ran on, past the coast of the Chálybes.
These people engage in no ploughing with oxen, they never
busy themselves with cultivating honey-sweet fruit, they do not
lead forth flocks to pasture in the dew-wet meadows;
rather they squeeze out a livelihood by hacking into   1005
the stubborn earth for its iron ores. There's no morning
dawns for them without toil, but rather amid sooty
flames and black smoke they work their heavy shifts.
Next, soon, they rounded the headland of Genetaian Zeus
and held their course past the land of the Tibarénoi.   1010
There, when the women bear children to their menfolk
it's the husbands who take to their beds, and lie there moaning,
heads tightly swathed; the women cook them meals
and prepare for them the baths that follow childbirth.
From here they came to the Holy Mount and the land   1015
where up in the hills the Mossynoikoi inhabit
those wooden huts, *mossynes,* after which they're named.
Their customs and laws all differ from those of others:
What it's normal to do quite openly, in public
or in the marketplace, all such things they perform   1020
in the privacy of their homes: but whatever *we'd* keep private
this they enact, without blame, on the public highway,
not even blushing to couple there: like free-ranging
swine in herds, unabashed by the bystanders,
they pick any woman they fancy, and mate with her on the ground.   1025
Their king, enthroned in the loftiest *mossyn,* dispenses
honest justice to all his many subjects—poor wretch;
since should he err but once in making a judgment
they'll keep him shut up all that day without any food.
Coasting past these, they set their course in the lee   1030
of Ares' island, and all day long toiled at the oars,
for round about dawn the gentle breeze had fallen.
Then, suddenly, they sighted, swooping through the air,
one of the birds of Ares that populate that island:
it shook out its wingspread over the speeding ship   1035

and let fly a pinion at it, that plummeted into the left
shoulder of noble Oileus. As it hit him, the oar
slipped from his hands, and his comrades gaped in wonder
at the sight of this feathered missile. Erybótes, sitting next him,
drew it out, and bandaged the wound with his baldric,   1040
laying aside his scabbard. Then, after the first,
another bird appeared, swooping down; but Klytios,
son of Eúrytos, hero, drew his arching bow,
loosed a swift shaft at the bird, and struck it: spinning
it tumbled seaward close to the swift ship.   1045
Then Aleos's son Amphídamas addressed them thus:
"The island hard by us is Ares'—you all must know it
now that you've seen these birds. But to make a landing
arrows, I reckon, will help us little. We must contrive
some more effective device, if you intend—bearing   1050
Phineus's injunctions in mind—to disembark here;
for not even Herakles, when he came to Arkadia,
was able with bow and arrow to clear the Stymphalian mere
of its floating birds—I myself witnessed this—
but stood on a high rock shaking a bronze rattle,   1055
and at its clatter the birds, screeching in helpless
terror, flew far away. So now let us too
think up some such contrivance—and having myself
already thought of one, let me tell it to you: put on
your heads your tall-crested helmets, then by turns   1060
half of you bend to the oars, the other half with polished
wood spears and shields provide protection for
the ship, and all in chorus raise a tremendous shout,
so that the birds may be scared by this unwonted clamor
by the nodding plumes and all your spears uplifted;   1065
and then, as we reach the island, make a mighty
clangor by banging your shields." Such were his words,
and the plan he proposed seemed effective to them all,
and on their heads they set the brazen helmets,
fearsomely gleaming, and over them crimson flared   1070
the crests, and half of them sat to the oars, while half
with spears and shields made a cover for their vessel.
And as when a man roofs his house over with tiles,
to make it a fine home and protect him from the rain,

and each tile, row upon row, fits snugly into the next,   1075
so they, locking shields together, roofed the ship over;
and such a shout as goes up from a battalion
of warriors advancing, when the ranks engage,
now went up from the ship, and filled the heavens.
As yet they'd seen none of the birds, but when they came close to   1080
the island, and beat on their shields, then in their thousands
the creatures took off, fled terrified hither and thither.
As, when the son of Kronos unleashes a dense hailstorm
out of the clouds on town and homestead, those dwelling
beneath it, hearing the rattle of hail on the rooftops   1085
sit relaxed, since the stormy season has not caught them
off guard, but they've strengthened their roofs in anticipation—
so thick a shower of pinions did the birds launch at them,
flying high over the sea to the far peaks of Skythia.

What, then, was Phineus's purpose in bidding that noble   1090
band of warrior-heroes put in there? What kind of succor
was destined to befall them in response to their desires?

The sons of Phrixos were traveling from Aia, country
of Kytaian Aiëtés, bound for Orchómenos's citadel,
aboard a vessel of Kolchis, bent on winning their father's   1095
boundless wealth: when dying he'd laid this journey on them.
That day, indeed, they'd come very close to the island,
but Zeus stirred up a driving northerly gale,
marking with rain the Great Bear's sodden orbit.
Now all day long it blew gently, barely ruffling   1100
the leaves on trees' outermost branches, high in the mountains;
but at night, with monstrous violence, it screamed down seaward,
its blasts high-cresting the waves. The sky was darkened
with flying spume, and through those thick scudding clouds
not one star shone clear: black murk blanketed everything.   1105
Soaked through, scared stiff by the prospect of a grim end,
the sons of Phrixos were whirled at random by the waves:
the force of the gale had shredded their canvas, then broke
the vessel in two as the breakers pounded its hull.
But then, by the gods' prompting, the four of them clambered   1110
astride a huge beam, one of many that floated loose
when the ship broke up, pegged together with pointed dowels;

and wind and wave bore them onward to the island
in sore distress, after running so close to death.
Then came a tremendous cloudburst: rain lashed down   1115
on the sea and the island and all the mainland across
from the island, where dwelt the arrogant Mossynoikoi,
and the force of the waves thrust the sons of Phrixos, massive
beam and all, up across the island's shoreline
in the dark of the night. The deluge sent by Zeus   1120
ceased at sunrise. Soon the two groups approached each other
and met: it was Argos who spoke first. "In the name
of All-Seeing Zeus, we beg you, whoever you may be,
to treat us with charity, help us in our distress!
A fierce hurricane, swooping down seaward, scattered the timbers   1125
of the wretched ship in which of necessity we'd embarked
and were ploughing the deep. So now we're your suppliants, ask you
to find us clothes for our nakedness, take us with you,
show compassion for men like yourselves in their misfortune,   1130
respect strangers and suppliants for the sake of Zeus,
the protector of strangers and suppliants, both of whom
are Zeus's concern—and his eye may well be upon us now."
Then Aison's son, in reply, convinced that the predictions
of Phineus were being fulfilled, questioned him skillfully: 1135
"All these things we'll be glad to provide for you, right away.
But come, tell me now, and truly, in what country
you live, and what necessity forces you to travel
overseas, and what names you're known by, and your race."
So Argos answered him, helpless in his distress: 1140
"That a certain Phrixos, an Aiolid, came to Aia from Hellas
is undoubtedly true—you may well know it already.
This Phrixos arrived in the citadel of Aiëtés
riding a ram, that had been transmuted, made golden
by Hermes—and indeed you can see its fleece to this day,   1145
hung in an oak, spread over the thick-leafed branches.   1145a
This ram he then sacrificed, on its own instructions,
to Zeus (out of all his titles) as Fugitives' Patron. Aiëtés
welcomed him in his palace, and, rejoicing at heart,
let him wed his daughter Chalkíope, asked no bride-price.
These two are our parents. Phrixos himself just lately   1150

died at a great age in Aiëtés' home: straightway,
respecting our father's behests, we have set out
for Orchómenos, to lay hands on Athamas's possessions.
Oh yes—since you also want to know our names,
this man is Kytíssoros, and this other is Phrontis,   1155
this Melas: as for myself, you can call me Argos."
So he spoke, and the heroes rejoiced at such an encounter,
and took care of them, still much amazed. Thereupon Jason
addressed them once more, as was fitting, in these words:
"Since you are kin to us on my father's side   1160
your prayers for help in distress we look on kindly,
for Krétheus and Athamas were brothers, and now I,
the grandson of Krétheus, together with these companions,
am voyaging from Hellas to Aiëtés' city.
But of these things we'll converse together hereafter—   1165
first let's find clothes for you. I reckon it's by heaven's
intention you fell thus destitute into my hands."
With that he gave them clothes from the ship to put on,
and then all together they went to the temple of Ares
to offer up sheep as a sacrifice, and eagerly assembled   1170
round the altar, that stood there outside the roofless temple
and was built of loose stones. (Inside was set a sacred
black stone, to which once all Amazons used to pray;
nor, when they came across from the mainland, were they sanctioned
to burn offerings on this altar of sheep or oxen; rather   1175
they dismembered horses, of which they tended abundant herds.)
Now when they'd made sacrifice and finished feasting,
then Aison's son spoke among them, and thus began:
"Zeus truly observes every action, nor do we mortals
escape his regard, be we never so pious or law-abiding;   1180
for just as he saved your father from a murderous
stepmother and—far from her—gave him abundant wealth,
so too he rescued you, unscathed, from a deadly
tempest. Now all of you, safely aboard this vessel,
can voyage here or there, wherever you please—to Aia,   1185
or else to the wealthy city of holy Orchómenos.
For our ship Athena crafted, and trimmed its timbers—brought down
from Pelion's heights—with the bronze axe, and Argos

worked at her side. But yours the fierce surge shattered
before you even approached those rocks that all day long   1190
crash one against the other in the Black Sea's narrows.
So come, do you in your turn now lend us assistance
and pilot our voyage, who are eager to seize and bring back
to Hellas the Golden Fleece, since I go to make atonement
for Phrixos's near-sacrifice, Zeus's wrath at the Aiolids."   1195
He spoke thus to persuade them, but they heard him in horror,
expecting they'd get from Aiëtés a far from friendly welcome
if they meant to take off with the ram's Fleece. So now Argos
spoke out, much vexed at their pursuit of this matter:
"Friends, such poor strength as we can raise will never weaken,   1200
no, not one whit, in your support, when need arises.
But his murderous ruthlessness forms a fearful weapon
for Aiëtés: that is why I deeply dread this voyage.
He boasts that the Sun is his father; all around him countless
tribes of the Kolchians dwell; he might match himself   1205
for his terrible war cry and hulking strength with Ares.
And indeed, quite apart from Aiëtés, it's no easy matter
to lay hands on the Fleece—so monstrous a serpent, deathless
and sleepless, coils guard about it, born to Earth herself
on Kaúkasos's scaurs, beneath the Typhaónian rock,   1210
where Typháon, the story goes, struck by a thunderbolt
from Zeus son of Kronos, and raising stout hands against him,
rained from his head hot death-drops: then, thus stricken,
he reached Nysa's plain and mountains, where to this day
he lies, deep-sunk, under Lake Serbónis's waters."   1215
So he spoke, and at once pallor drained the cheeks of many
when they learnt the venture's magnitude. But straightway Peleus
answered with bold encouragement, and thus spoke:
"Good friend, don't try to scare us out of our wits with your tales!
We're not so bereft of strength that we are unable   1220
to deal with Aiëtés, make trial of him under arms:
No, I reckon we too can boast skill in warfare, we who
are on our way thither, near kin to the blood of the blessed
gods: so, if he refuse us his friendship and the Golden Fleece,
have no great fear that these Kolchian tribes will help him."   1225
Thus in turn they addressed each other, until the time
when, satiated with feasting, they retired to sleep.

And as they woke at dawn a gentle breeze was blowing,
and the sails, as they hoisted them, bellied out in the wind,
and quickly the isle of Ares faded behind them.   1230

As night was drawing on they passed Phílyra's island:
here Ouranos's son Kronos—in the days when he ruled over
the Titans on Olympos, and Zeus was still a nursling
in that Kretan cave, looked after by the Kourétés
of Ida—lay with Phílyra, cheating on Rheía. The goddess   1235
caught them in mid-act; Kronos sprang out of bed
and fled, assuming the form of a horse with flowing mane,
while Phílyra, Ocean's daughter, shame-struck, abandoned
her home and favorite haunts, went away to the mountainous
Pelasgian ranges, and there brought forth huge Cheiron,   1240
through that biform engendering half horse, half god.
From here they sailed past the Makrónes, the endless coastline
of the Becheirians, the arrogant Sapeires,
and after them the Byzerians: ever they sheared their swift
sea path forward, borne on by the light tailwind.   1245
Then, as they voyaged, the Black Sea's remotest landfall
rose into view, and behind it the towering peaks
of the Kaukasian mountains, where, limbs close-fettered
by galling chains of bronze to the harsh rocks,
Prometheus fed with his liver an ever-returning eagle.   1250
This creature they glimpsed at evening, flying over the ship's topmast,
cloud-high, with sharp-whirring pinions; yet despite its distance
it shook all the sails with its wing-beats, speeding past.
For it did not share the nature of birds of the heavens,
but the long quill-feathers it flapped were like polished oars.   1255
And not long after they heard the agonized outcry
of Prometheus, as his liver was lacerated: the clear air
rang with his screams, till they saw the eagle speeding
back the same way from the mountain and its feast of raw flesh.
At last, after nightfall, the skills of Argos brought them   1260
to the estuary of the Phasis, and the Black Sea's furthest bounds;
then smartly they lowered the sails and unstepped the yardarm
and stowed them away in the hollow mast-crutch; next
they let down the mast itself, laid it back lengthways, got out
the oars, rowed into the river's strong current, that yielded,   1265

boiling, to their advance. On their left hand they had
steep Kaúkasos and Aia's Kytaian citadel, on
the other the plain of Ares and the god's sacred grove,
where the ever-watchful serpent lay guarding the Fleece
that was spread out on an oak tree's leafy branches.   1270
And Aison's son himself poured out into the river
from a golden cup libations of pure wine, sweet as honey,
to Earth and the country's gods, and the spirits of heroes
now dead, beseeching their kindly and propitious
assistance, praying they'd welcome the vessel's mooring-cables.   1275
Upon that Ankaios spoke among them as follows:
"We have reached the country of Kolchis and the river
of Phasis: time now to take counsel among ourselves
whether with sweet talk we should make trial of Aiëtés
or whether some other approach will best secure our ends."   1280
So he spoke; and by Argos's advice, Jason now gave orders
to row the ship into a backwater, thickly wooded,
close to their point of entry, and let her ride there
at anchor. This place was where they settled for the night,
and after a while to their eager eyes the dawn appeared.   1285

Book III

Now come, Erató, stand by me, and tell me how Jason
brought the Fleece back from Kolchis to Iolkos
through the love of Medeia: for you yourself belong
to Kypris's team, you bewitch with your cares of passion
unbroken virgins, your very name's erotic!   5

So the heroes stayed out of sight, waited in ambush
among the clustering reed beds; but they'd been spotted
by Hera and Athena, who retired to a chamber
well apart from Zeus himself and the other immortals
and took counsel together. First Hera sounded out   10
Athena: "Daughter of Zeus, let's begin with your opinion—
what's to be done? Will you work out some trick that lets them
get the Golden Fleece from Aiëtés and take it back to Hellas?
It seems unlikely they could deceive and sweet-talk him
into agreement, he's so appallingly arrogant—yet   15
no possible line of approach should be left untested."
So she spoke, and instantly Athena made answer:
"I too, Hera, was debating such matters in my mind
when you put your blunt question to me; but as yet,
though I've weighed up numerous plans to boost the heroes'   20
spirits, I still don't feel I've hit upon the right one."
With that, eyes fixed on the ground before their feet,
both sat there, each brooding in private, till Hera quickly
came up with a new proposal, and broke the silence:

"Come, let's both go call on Kypris: when we've found her   25
let's urge her to tell her son (supposing he'll obey her)
to aim one of his shafts at Aiëtés' drug-wise daughter,
charm *her* into love for Jason. If he follows
her suggestions, I reckon he'll get the Fleece back to Hellas."
Such her words; the shrewd suggestion pleased Athena,   30
who once more made her an accommodating answer:
"Hera, my father bore me to know nothing of such pangs,
nor do I know any need that can charm a man's desires;
still, if this project pleases you, then I'd be willing
to follow—but *you* must accost her, and do the talking."   35
So she spoke, and up they both got, and made their way
to Kypris's big house, which her lame husband built for her
when first he brought her home from Zeus as his bride.
Entering through the courtyard, they stood in the colonnade
of the chamber where the goddess tended Hephaistos's bed.   40
He himself had gone off early to his forge and anvils
in a roomy recess on the Wandering Island, where with fire blast
he wrought all manner of intricate objects; but she was left sitting
alone in the house, by the door, on a well-turned chair.
She'd let her hair tumble loose on each white shoulder   45
and was teasing it out with a golden comb, about to braid it
into long plaits; but when she saw them there before her
she stopped, and invited them in, and got up from her chair
and made them sit down on recliners; then settled herself too,
gathered up her mane of hair, still uncombed, with a ribbon,   50
and smiling, ironic, addressed them thus: "Dear ladies,
what occasion, what purpose is it that brings you here
after so long an absence? Why both of you? Hitherto
I've had few visits from you, high goddesses that you are."
To her Hera delivered this answer: "Very witty, I'm sure;   55
but what concerns us here is a serious problem.
Already Aison's son and his crew, in hot pursuit of
the Fleece, have their ship at anchor in the Phasis River.
For all of them, since the moment of action's at hand,
but above all for Aison's son, our anxiety's terrible.   60
Him, even should he voyage to the nether regions
of Hades, to free Ixion from his brazen chains,
I will protect, with all my limbs' innate strength,

so that Pelias, who in his arrogance left me unhonored
with sacrifice, may not make mock of me by escaping   6₅
his evil fate. Besides, long before this Jason had won my
great love, ever since at the estuary of the flooded
Anauros he met me (I was testing men's righteousness)
on his way home from hunting: all the mountains and lofty
peaks were being powdered with snow, while down their gulleys   70
water cascaded in thunderous torrents. I'd taken
the likeness of an old woman: he felt sorry for me,
heaved me up on his shoulders, bore me through the rapids.
Hence the unfailing high honor in which I hold him. Nor will
Pelias pay for his outrage unless you grant Jason   75
a safe homecoming." This speech left Kypris dumbfounded,
awestruck at the sight of Hera entreating her,
so now it was with gentle words she made answer:
"Revered goddess, may you encounter nothing more vile than
Kypris, if I make light of your most urgent appeal   80
either in word or deed, whatever can be effected
by these weak hands of mine—and I ask no favor back."
Thus she spoke, and Hera gave a considered response:
"It's no lack of force or hands has brought us to you—
relax, don't fret, just tell that boy of yours to charm   85
Aiëtés' virgin daughter with passion for Aison's son.
For if she wishes him well and gives him good counsel,
I think he'll easily capture the Golden Fleece
and get back to Iolkos, for she's guile incarnate."
Thus she spoke, and Kypris now addressed them both: 90
"Athena and Hera, he'd certainly do *your* bidding
rather than mine: for you, despite his shamelessness,
there'll be some faint glimmer of shame in his eye, but for me
he cares nothing, always provokes me, treats me with contempt.
And indeed, thus plagued with his naughtiness, I was minded   95
to smash up his bow and nasty-sounding arrows
in public! The threats he uttered when he was angry!—
that if I don't keep my hands right off him while he's still
in control of his temper, later I'll have only myself to blame."
Thus she spoke, and the goddesses smiled, exchanged glances   100
one with the other. Much chagrined, she went on:
"Others find my troubles a joke—I certainly can't tell them

to everyone: bad enough that I know them myself.
But now, since this is a plan that you both cherish,
I'll do my best to coax him: he won't refuse me."   105
Thus she spoke; and Hera clasped her slender hand,
and with a fleeting smile responded slyly:
"Just so, Kythereia: in this business, as you yourself say,
act with dispatch—and don't be cross, don't wrangle
with your boy in your anger: he'll change his ways in time."   110
So saying she rose from her chair, and Athena likewise,
and both hurried off back home. But Kypris
went checking the nooks of Olympos in search of Eros.
She found him some way off, in Zeus's tree-rich orchard,
not alone: Ganymédés kept company with him, whom earlier Zeus   115
had set up in heaven, a hearthmate to the immortals,
being entranced by his beauty. The two of them were playing
at knucklebones—golden ones—as boys in the same house will;
and already greedy Eros was clutching a fistful
in his left hand, holding them tight, close under his breast   120
as he stood erect there, a sweet blush mantling
the bloom of his cheeks. But Ganymédés was crouched down
beside him, silent, dejected: just two dice left, and he threw them
one after the other, maddened by Eros's snickering,
and losing both in a trice, like all their predecessors,   125
took himself off, empty-handed and hopeless, failed
to notice Kypris approaching. She stopped before her son,
chucked him under the chin, and sharply addressed him:
"What are you grinning at, you unspeakable little horror?
Did you cheat him again, win unfairly, cash in on his innocence?   130
Listen now: if you're willing to do the job I tell you,
I'll give you one of Zeus's most beautiful playthings,
that his dear nurse Adrasteia fashioned for him
when he was still a babbling infant in that cave on Ida:
a well-rounded ball, than which you'll get no better   135
toy, not even from Hephaistos's hands. Its rings
have been fashioned of gold, and over each are basted
twin segment-edges, all the way round, with seams
camouflaged, since over each one runs a spiral
pattern of cobalt. If you toss this ball up to catch it,   140
like a meteor it unleashes a gleaming airy trail.

This I shall give you—if you will shoot Aiëtés' virgin
daughter full of desire for Jason. And don't you loiter,
otherwise my gratitude will be much diminished." Thus
she spoke, and Eros, hearing them, welcomed her words.   145
He tossed aside all his playthings, and, two-fisted,
seized the goddess's robe on both sides, hugged her close,
begged her to give it him *now*, on the spot. She countered
with gentle words, pinching his cheeks, then drew him
towards her, kissed him, and replied as follows: 150
"Your dearest head, and my own, now be my witness
that, yes, I'll give you this present, I won't cheat you,
so long as you put a shaft into Aiëtés' daughter."
Such her words. He collected his knucklebones, dropped them—
after counting them carefully—in his mother's dazzling lap,   155
then slung from a golden baldric the quiver he'd left leaning
against a tree trunk, took up his curved bow, hurried
on his way out of great Zeus's rich fruit-laden orchard,
and then passed on, out through the airy portals
of Olympos. From there a vertiginous sky-borne path   160
runs downward: the peaks of two high-towering mountains,
roof to the world, support this vault of heaven
where the rising sun's first rays glow blushing-red.
Down below he could see, in the course of his long flight,
now fertile stretches of farmland, teeming cities,   165
the lines of rivers; now mountains and the surrounding sea.

The heroes meanwhile, still lurking off upriver
in their backwater, were holding a shipbench assembly.
Aison's son himself was addressing them: they listened
quietly, rows of them, each in his proper place.   170
"Friends, what I shall tell you remains my personal
viewpoint: the final decision on action is yours.
This is a common venture, and common to all alike
is the right to speak out. The man who keeps silent counsel—
let him know that he alone robs this group of its homecoming.   175
The rest of you stay aboard here quietly, under arms,
while I proceed to Aiëtés' palace, taking
with me the sons of Phrixos and two companions. When
we meet him, I'll start by sounding him out, to learn

whether he's willing to yield us the Golden Fleece in friendship   180
or will rather, relying on force, make light of our approach.
This way, by learning his malice first from himself
we'll decide if we're going to fight him, or if some other
plan, once we've said no to battle, will serve us better.
We should not—at least not without some prior persuasive talk—   185
just strip him by force of his own possession: far better
to approach him first, win him over with clever discourse.
Often what prowess could barely achieve, words will smoothly
and decorously effect, ease a victory by pressure
applied at need. Aiëtés once welcomed blameless Phrixos,   190
as he fled his stepmother's wiles and sacrifice by his father,
since everyone everywhere, even the most shameless,
respects and observes the code of Zeus as Guest-Protector."
So he spoke, and the youths unanimously applauded
this speech by Aison's son, with no dissenting voice.   195
Then he called on the sons of Phrixos, and Télamon and Augeias,
to accompany him, and himself took the herald's staff
of Hermes, and quickly they crossed the swampy reed bed
between their ship and dry land, and emerged on a sea bank,
a neck of the plain known as Kirké's. There in abundance   200
long stands of willow and tamarisk grow, with trussed-up
corpses suspended from their topmost branches,
for still, to this day, the Kolchians hold it taboo
to cremate their males when deceased, nor is it permitted
to bury them underground, raise a barrow over them: 205
only to wrap them up in the untanned hides of oxen
and hang them from trees, well outside the city. Yet earth
has equal rights with air, since they prescribe burial
for their womenfolk: such is the custom they established.
As the heroes advanced now, Hera, to do them a favor,   210
spread a thick mist through the city. That way they could reach
Aiëtés' palace unseen by the crowds of Kolchians. Soon
they left open countryside, reached Aiëtés' city
and palace: then Hera scattered the mist again.
They stood in the entrance, agape at the royal courtyard,   215
the wide gateways, the columns rising in ordered lines
around the walls, and, roof-high, a stone cornice
supported on brazen capitals. Unhindered,

they made their way over the threshold. Close alongside
high-climbing garden vines, crowned with green foliage,   220
were in full bloom, and there beneath them bubbled
four ever-flowing fountains, their channels dug
by Hephaistos, one of them gushing milk, one wine,
while the third gave forth a stream of fragrant oil,
and the fourth discharged pure water, hot (it's said) at the setting   225
of the Pleiades, but from their rising spouted up
out of the hollow rock, chill as ice crystals.
Such were the marvelous works that subtle craftsman
Hephaistos had made for the palace of Kytaian Aiëtés.
Bronze-hooved bulls, too, he'd forged for him, with brazen   230
mouths, from which they breathed out bright fearful bursts of flame,
and a plough besides, in one piece, of unyielding adamant,
made as repayment for Helios, who'd picked him up
in his chariot when he was weary from battling the Giants.
There too was the wrought-iron inner-court gate, and beyond it   235
chambers to left and right with well-carpentered double doors,
and the whole length along each side an elegant colonnade.
Crosswise on either wing stood other loftier buildings:
in one of these, the tallest of all, was the dwelling
that Lord Aiëtés occupied, he and his consort,   240
while another belonged to Aiëtés' son Apsyrtos.
(Him a Kaukasian nymph, Asteródeia, bore, before
Aiëtés took Eidyia, the youngest-born daughter
of Tethys and of Ocean, to be his lawful bedmate,
and the young Kolchians called him Phaëthon, the Bright One,   245
because he outshone all his bachelor coevals.)
In the others dwelt the handmaids and Aiëtés' two daughters,
Chalkíope and Medeia. Medeia they encountered
on her way to visit her sister in her chamber:
for Hera had kept her at home. In the normal way she spent   250
little time in the house, but was busy all day long
at Hekaté's temple, she being the goddess's priestess.
When she saw them at hand, she cried out. Chalkíope heard her
clearly. The maids, throwing down their yarn and spindles,
all hurried outside in a pack. But when Chalkíope   255
emerged with them, and found her own sons standing there,
she flung up her arms in joy; and they likewise

greeted their mother, embraced her when they saw her
out of sheer happiness. Then, sobbing, she addressed them:
"So, after all, even though you heedlessly left me here,   260
you weren't destined to wander far, but fate brought you back again!
Poor me, what a passion you conceived for Hellas,
through some wretched infatuation, at the behest of Phrixos
your father! On his deathbed he bequeathed most hateful sorrows
to this heart of mine. And why should you take off and travel   265
to this city, Orchómenos (whoever Orchómenos may have been),
for the sake of Athamas's wealth, leave your mother thus grieving?"
While she spoke, Aiëtés was the last to appear: his wife
Eidyia was there already, had hurried out when she heard
Chalkíope's voice. Very soon the entire courtyard   270
was buzzing with people. Of the servants, some now busied
themselves with a hefty bull, while others chopped up dry
firewood, or heated bathwater: there was no one
shirked the hard work in obeying the king's orders.

Meantime through a gray mist came Eros, invisible,   275
an itch, a sting, like the gadfly that swarms up against grazing
heifers, and that's known by ox herds as the breese.
Under the hall-door lintel he quickly strung his bow,
and pulled from the quiver a shaft unhandselled, quick
with trouble; then, stepping swiftly, he crossed the threshold   280
unseen, glancing sharply around, and crouched, a tiny figure,
at Jason's very feet; settled his arrow's notch
to mid-bowstring, then with both arms drew the bow
and let fly at Medeia, striking her heart speechless.
Back up then he darted, out of the high-roofed hall,   285
cackling with laughter. Like a flame that shaft burnt under
her maiden heart: endless bright open glances
she darted at Jason, her breath fetched quick and labored
from her heaving breast, all else was forgotten, her spirit
flooded over in that sweet ecstasy. As a woman, a hireling,   290
whose business is the spinning of wool, will heap
dry kindling around a smoldering firebrand, to tease out
a bright flame under her lean-to when it's still dark,
crouching close over it, and the flame, amazingly,
flares up strong from that little brand, consumes   295

every scrap of the kindling—so Love the destroyer
blazed in a coil round her heart, her mind's resistless anguish
now flushed her soft cheeks, now drained them of all color.
When the servants had set out food ready before them,
and they'd scrubbed themselves bright and clean in warm bathwater,   300
then they eagerly took their fill of food and drink;
and afterwards Aiëtés interrogated his daughter's
sons, addressing them in the following manner:
"Sons of my daughter and Phrixos—a man I honored
more than any other guest I've had in my palace—   305
what brings you back here to Aia? Did some disaster
cut you off in mid-journey? You paid me no attention
when I warned you about the boundless length of the voyage,
though I knew it, had traveled it once, whirled in the chariot
of my father the Sun while escorting my sister Kirké   310
to that land in the west, and we reached our journey's end
on the coast of Tyrrhenia's territory, where to this day
she makes her home, a long haul from Kolchian Aia.
But why waste time on stories? Tell me now, plainly,
what tripped up your plans? These men accompanying you,   315
who are they? And just where did you land from your hollow vessel?"
To these questions Argos, alarmed for Jason's expedition,
made haste to reply before his brothers could speak,
reassuringly, being in any case the eldest:
"Aiëtés, our ship was too soon ripped asunder   320
by a raging hurricane—we clung to its beams for dear life
and the waves tossed us up on the strand of Enyalios's island
in the thick of the night. But some god came to our rescue,
for not even the birds of Ares, that till then had made
their home on that barren island, not even them   325
did we find still: no, these men had driven them headlong,
though they'd only disembarked there the previous day. For sure
it was Zeus's will, in his pity for us—or some act of fate—
that made them delay there, since they gave us food and clothing
the moment they heard the illustrious name of Phrixos—   330
and your own, for it's to your city they were journeying.
And if you're minded to learn their purpose, I'll not hide it.
Desirous of driving this man here far from his country
and holdings, because in might he outshone beyond measure

every one of the sons of Aiolos, a certain   335
king sent him journeying hither on a hopeless quest, avowing
that the Aiolid clan would never be free of implacable
Zeus's heartbreaking fury and gall, of pollution past bearing
and punishment due over Phrixos, till the Fleece came
to Hellas. *Their* ship had Pallas Athena for builder—   340
far different from those found here, among the men of Kolchis,
of which *we* chanced on the worst, for wind and rough water
utterly broke her apart. But that other stays bolted
solid, though gales should blast her from every quarter,
and sails as sweetly on with the crew laboring nonstop   345
over the oars as when she runs before a tailwind.
And in her he's assembled the flower of all Achaia's
heroes, and after a long haul—many cities,
sea upon sea—has made it to your realm, hopes for that gift.
But as *you* please, so shall it be, since he's not come here   350
with violent intent, no, he's ready to recompense you
amply for this present, having heard from me of your bitter
foes the Sarmatians, will subdue them to your rule.
Now, if (as I'm sure you do) you want to know the names
and lineage of your guests, then I shall oblige you.   355
This man, for whose sake the others gathered from Hellas,
they call Jason, the son of Aison, Krétheus's grandson—
and if he really is of the stock of Krétheus,
then he'd be our kinsman on the father's side,
for both Krétheus and Athamas were Aiolos's sons,   360
and Phrixos was the offspring of Aiolid Athamas.
And this one you see here—you may have heard tell of him—
is Augeias, Helios's son; and this Télamon, whose father
was Aiakos—Aiakos, whom Zeus himself engendered.
So too with all the rest: each one of his companions   365
on this quest is son or grandson to an immortal."
Thus Argos, persuasively; but the king as he heard him out
caught fire at these words, rage surging high in his breast,
and made furious answer, angered above all else
at Chalkíope's sons, since it was for their sake, he reckoned,   370
that the heroes had come; in his transport his eyes glared fierce
under his brows as he shouted: "Out of my sight, you scourings!
Pack up and begone with your tricks, go back home from this country,

before some of you see a Fleece and a Phrixos to your sorrow!
You were all plotting this from the start, in Hellas—but not for
    the Fleece!   375
Oh no, it's my crown and my kingdom that you're here for!
I tell you, if you had not first eaten at my table
I'd have cut out your tongues and chopped off your hands—yes, both—
and sent you on your way furnished with feet alone
to deter you from making another attempt hereafter   380
and as recompense for your lies about the blessed gods."
So he spoke in his wrath, and the temper boiled up fiercely
in Télamon's breast, and the spirit within him was urgent
to make a defiant—and deadly—response; but Aison's son Jason
held him back, spoke first himself, with words of appeasement: 385
"Aiëtés, don't jump to conclusions about this expedition—
it's not for the purpose you fear that we've come here to your city
and dwelling, nor did we choose to. Who'd willingly traverse
such a spread of sea to rob foreigners? No, it was heaven's prompting
and the cold-blooded fiat of an arrogant king that forced me.   390
Show favor to these your suppliants, and throughout all Hellas
I'll spread word of your godlike renown. More: we are ready
and eager to make you swift recompense through warfare,
whether it be the Sarmatians or some other people
you're minded to subdue and make part of your kingdom."   395
Such his utterance, gentle and soothing; but the other's spirit
was debating in his breast between two courses:
whether to rush them and slaughter them, there and then,
or else to make trial of their strength; and the latter, as he pondered,
he took for the better way, and so made answer: 400
"Stranger, no need to bore us with endless details—
if you're truly of heavenly lineage, or, even otherwise,
men no whit worse than I am, you who've set out
after foreigners' goods, I'll give you the Fleece to take, if you like,
once I've made trial of you. Against good men I bear no grudge   405
such as (you say) is borne by this king in Hellas.
The trial of your strength and courage will be a challenge
which I, despite its dangers, can fulfill bare-handed.
I have here, out at pasture on the plain of Ares,
two brazen-footed bulls, mouths gusting gouts of flame: 410
this team I yoke and drive over Ares' field, stubborn and fallow,

a four-acre stint, and as I cut each furrow to its turning
I scatter along it not the seed-corn of Demeter
but the teeth of a fearful serpent, that grow and are bodied forth
as armored men; and these I slaughter promptly,   415
laying them low with my spear as they crowd me from all sides.
At dawn I yoke the oxen, and evening is come by the time
I've finished my harvesting. And you, if you do the same,
can bear off the Fleece that same day to this king you speak of—
but till then don't expect me to give it you: it's unseemly   420
for a man of proven valor to yield to a coward."
So he spoke. But Jason, eyes fixed on the ground before him,
sat there speechless, unmoving, at a loss in this crisis.
Long he considered the problem, tried every angle, yet dared not
boldly take up the challenge, so huge a task it seemed.   425
At last, playing for advantage, he replied as follows:
"Aiëtés, it's your right to press me hard in this matter.
So, this ordeal of yours, outrageous as it is,
I too shall dare, though death be my destiny, for nothing
will weigh more chill upon man than vile necessity,   430
such as forced me to travel hither at a king's commandment."
So he spoke, shiftless and thunderstruck; but Aiëtés
replied with these terrible words to him in his distress:
"Go now to your company, since you're so hot for hard work!
But if your nerve cracks, if you fail to yoke the oxen,   435
or shrink back in fright from that deadly harvesting,
then *I* shall wind up the business to warn off others,
make them shake at the thought of bearding men better than themselves."
Such were Aiëtés' blunt words, and Jason rose from his chair
and Augeias and Télamon after him; Argos followed   440
alone, having signaled his brothers to stay there
a while longer. But he and the heroes quit the throne room,
and marvelously amid them all the son of Aison stood out
for beauty and grace; and on him the maiden, glancing
round her bright veil, now gazed in stealthy wonder,   445
pain smoldering in her heart, while like a creeping dream
her mind fluttered after his footsteps as he departed.

So the heroes, much distressed, went their way from the palace,
while Chalkíope meanwhile, keeping clear of Aiëtés' rage,

had taken her sons and gone quickly to her chamber,   450
and Medeia likewise followed, pondering much in her heart,
all the obsessions the forces of love will arouse: before
her eyes the whole scene played again, over and over—
his appearance, his carriage, the great cloak he was wearing,
the way he spoke, how he sat on his chair, his manner   455
of leaving: there couldn't be, she thought, mind in turmoil,
another such man; endlessly in her ears there echoed
the sound of his voice, the mellifluous words he'd spoken,
and dread seized her on his behalf, lest the oxen or Aiëtés
with his own hands should destroy him: she mourned as though   460
he were slain outright already, and in her anguish a round
tear ran down her cheek, stirred by most grievous pity.
Softly sobbing, she forced out these unhappy words:
"Stupid creature, why so grief-stricken? This man is doomed to perish,
so whether he's the flower of all heroes or some lesser   465
mortal, let him go hang! Yet would that he'd got clear
unharmed! Ah Goddess, Lady, daughter of Perses,
make it happen! May he cheat death, get back home! But if
he's doomed to be overcome by the oxen, let him learn this
first: that I, at least, take no joy in his ill fortune."   470
Thus was the girl's heart riven by passionate anguish.

But when the heroes were clear of the city and its people,
going back along the road they'd followed from the plain,
then Argos addressed himself to Jason in these words:
"Son of Aison, you'll find fault with the counsel that I'm going   475
to give you; but in a crisis no suggestion should be neglected.
There's a girl—you've heard me mention her already—
skilled in drug-magic, taught by Hékaté, Perses' daughter.
If we could but win her, I think there'd be no panic
about your defeat in the contest; yet I have a terrible   480
fear lest my mother may not help us in this matter.
Nevertheless, I'll go back again, entreat her on our behalf
since a common destruction hangs over us all alike."
So with good will he spoke, and Jason made this answer:
"Friend, if that's how you feel, I'll not oppose you.   485
Off with you to your mother, sway her with your clever
words, stir her to action: sad hopes we have indeed

if we've entrusted our homecoming to women." So he spoke,
and soon they reached the backwater. There their comrades
questioned them, rejoicing, when they saw them arrive.   490
But Aison's son, distraught, addressed them thus:
"My friends, against us the heart of implacable Aiëtés
is dead set in wrath; it'd serve no useful purpose
for me, or you, to drag through all the details.
He told us that here on the plain of Ares there pasture   495
two brazen-footed bulls, mouths gouting gusts of flame;
with these he bade me plough a field of four acres,
and said he'd give me seed, from a serpent's jaws, with the power
to raise up earthborn men, armed with bronze; and that same
day I must slay them. This challenge—there being no other   500
better plan to put up—I undertook outright."
So he spoke. All felt such a test defied achievement,
and long they eyed each other, brooding and speechless,
downcast, at a loss, in bewilderment. Finally Peleus
made this resolute speech before the assembled chieftains: 505
"Time now to take counsel for action. The way I see it,
there's less profit in talk than in the strength of our arms.
So if you are minded to yoke Aiëtés' oxen,
son of Aison, and play the hero, if you're hot for hard work,
then you must honor your promise, make yourself ready;   510
but if your heart places less than absolute reliance
on your valor, then neither commit yourself, nor sit there
looking hopefully round at the rest of us. For myself,
I'll not hold back: the worst we can suffer will be death."
So spoke Aiakos's son, and Télamon's heart was stirred: 515
quickly he rose, all eagerness, and third, after him, Idas
sprang proudly up, and next, the twin Tyndaridai,
and with them Oineus's son, ranked among those heroes
already into their prime—though his cheeks were still innocent
of the first fine down—such vigor uplifted his spirit.   520
The rest held back and kept silent. Thereupon Argos
spoke as follows to those who were eager for the contest:
"Friends, this is our last resort. Still, I think you may well
get some support in good time from my mother. Wherefore,
eager to go though you are, hold back here in the ship   525
a little while yet, as before, since to show patience

is better than recklessly opting for an evil fate.
There is a certain girl, brought up in Aiëtés' household,
to whom the goddess Hékaté granted preeminent skill
in the lore of all drugs that Earth or Ocean breeds: 530
with these she can quench the hot blast of unwearying fire,
halt rivers dead when they're roaring down in spate,
control the stars and the Moon's own sacred orbits.
To her, as we walked the path hither from the palace,
our minds turned: might it be possible that my mother,   535
being her sister, could get her to aid us in this venture?
And if this plan wins your approval too, I'll go back
this very day once more to the palace of Aiëtés
to try my luck—and maybe, some god backing me, luck out."
So he spoke, and the gods of their good will gave them a sign.   540
A nervous dove, in flight from a hawk's violence,
plunged, terrified, out of high heaven into Jason's lap,
and the hawk impaled itself on the sternpost. Quickly Mopsos
declared his prophetic insight, there before them all:
"This sign has been fashioned for you, friends, by the will of heaven: 545
nor is there any better way to read its meaning
than to carry our tale to the maiden, busily ply her
with every kind of persuasion. She's not, I think,
indifferent—if Phineus spoke true when he said that our return
would hang on Kypris the goddess. It was her gentle bird   550
that flew clear of death. As the heart and spirit within me
presage from this omen, so may it be accomplished!
Come, my friends, call on Kythereia to aid us,
and now do as Argos advises, without delay."
Such his words, and the young men applauded, recalling   555
the instructions of Phineus. Idas, Apháreus's son, alone
sprang up, voice raised in implacable fury, shouting:
"What? Is it with women that we've voyaged hither,
the way we're begging Kypris to be our savior?
No longer do you look to the war god's might, it's doves   560
and hawks you have your eye on to save yourselves from contests!
Begone with you, take no thought for deeds of warfare,
but plan to cajole weak girls with supplications!" Thus
he spoke in his passion, and many of his comrades
murmured under their breath, yet none spoke out against him.   565

So after a while he sat down, still enraged; and Jason
at once spoke his own mind, by way of encouragement:
"Let Argos, since this pleases all of you, make his way
back from the ship. We ourselves shall shift from this creek
and openly moor by the shore. Indeed, it's no longer   570
fitting to skulk away hidden, as though shrinking from combat."
So he spoke, and at once dispatched Argos on his way
with all speed back to the city. Then the rest hauled aboard
the anchor stones on the command of Aison's son, and rowing
a short way out of the backwater, ran the ship ashore.   575

Aiëtés meanwhile at once called the Kolchians to assembly
in their customary meeting place, some way off from his palace,
with schemes for deceit past bearing, great griefs for the Minyans.
He vowed that the moment his oxen had torn to pieces
the man who'd agreed to sweat out the harsh ordeal,   580
he'd axe the thicket crowning that wooded cliff top
and burn the ship, crew and all, make them bubble up,
frying, the harsh arrogance of their wanton schemes.
For he'd never have welcomed Aiolos's son Phrixos
to his hearth and home, despite the man's sore need,   585
though he outshone all guests in good manners and piety,
had not Zeus in person sent his messenger from heaven,
Hermes, to see that Phrixos got a friendly reception.
Much less would any pirates invading his territory
sit there unscathed for long, men who made it their business 590
to lay thieving hands upon other men's possessions,
to scheme and deceive in secret, and raid the steadings
of herdsmen in wretched and cowardly attacks.
And he privately told himself that fitting retribution
would be paid by these sons of Phrixos for coming back as henchmen   595
of a miscreant crew whose sole unscrupulous object
was to rob him of throne and honor; for once a baneful
oracle of his father the sun god had informed him
that he must needs avoid the deep deceit, the scheming
of his own offspring, destruction in many guises   600
(that was why he'd sent them, as they wished, to Achaia,
at their father's request—a long trip). But as for his daughters,
he had not the slightest fear that they or their brother

Apsyrtos would devise some hateful plot against him,
being sure this curse was fulfilled in Chalkíope's sons.   605
Then he announced to his countrymen, fiercely angered,
his ungovernable designs, bade them with threats keep watch
over ship and crew, let not one man escape disaster.

Argos meanwhile, returning to the palace of Aiëtés,
begged his mother with all the persuasion at his command   610
to pray Medeia to aid them. Indeed she herself
had thought of this earlier, but fear choked back her spirit
lest perhaps her efforts to win her proved vain and out of season,
with Medeia scared of her father's murderous wrath; or else,
if she yielded to prayer, lest their deeds become public and manifest.   615

The maiden lay stretched on her bed, where profound slumber
had brought her relief from her torments. But at once destructive
deceitful dreams, such as prey on an overwrought girl, assailed her.
She fancied the stranger had undertaken the contest
not on account of his longing to bear off the ram's Fleece,   620
nor was this why he'd voyaged to the city
of Aiëtés, no; but to take *her* away to his home
as his wedded wife. She dreamed, too, that she herself
wrought with the bulls, effortlessly accomplished
the task set—and that her own parents ignored their promise   625
since it was not their daughter they'd challenged to yoke
the oxen, but Jason himself; and hence a fierce altercation
put her father at odds with the strangers, and both sides left
the decision in her hands, to decide as she thought best—
and she on impulse, rejecting her parents, gave her verdict   630
to the stranger. Sharp anguish pierced them, they shouted out
in their fury. The clamor made sleep loose its hold on her.
She started up, shaking with fear, and glanced wildly round
the walls of her chamber; it was all she could do to steady
the heart in her breast as before. She exclaimed out loud: 635
"Wretch that I am, how scared these bad dreams have left me!
I'm afraid some great evil may be brought here by this coming
of the heroes—my heart's aflutter for the stranger—
let him court some Achaian girl, far off among his own
people, leave me to virginity and my parents' house—   640
No. Despite everything, I'll brazen my heart, no longer

hold aloof; I'll make trial of my sister, see if she asks me
for aid in the contest, through grief for her own sons:
that would quench the sharp agony in my heart."
With those words she rose, and opened her chamber door,   645
barefoot, in only a shift, with a sudden determination
to visit her sister, and so she crossed the threshold.
But long she waited there, in the hall outside her room,
held back by shame: changed her mind, went back inside,
came out once more, and again retreated within,   650
her feet taking her this way and that without firm purpose.
Each time she stepped out, shame checked her, sent her back;
yet bold desire spurred her onward, though barred by shame.
Thrice she made the attempt, thrice checked herself: the fourth time
she fell face down on her bed, writhing. Just as when   655
a bride in her chamber mourns the lusty husband
on whom she'd been bestowed by brothers and parents,
yet cannot, for shame and trained modesty, hold converse
with all her attendants, but sits grieving in a corner
when some ill chance has destroyed him, before either had a chance   660
to enjoy each other's resources, and she, all on fire inside,
weeps silently as she looks on her widowed bed,
in fear lest married women mock and revile her—
like her Medeia lamented. In the midst of her mourning
up came one of the maidservants, suddenly noticed her—   665
a girl, her young attendant, who promptly passed along
the word to Chalkíope, as she sat there with her sons,
figuring out just how to win her sister over.
The story was unexpected, and retailed by a servant:
yet not even so did she disregard it, but rushed in surprise   670
straight from her room to the room in which Medeia
lay torn with anguish, cheeks hidden in her hands.
But when she saw her eyes all dabbled with tears she exclaimed:
"Ah me, Medeia, what caused these tears you're shedding?
What's happened to you? What sharp grief has pierced your heart?   675
Is it a plague from heaven that's run full circle
through your frame? Or have you heard some deadly threat
against me and my sons from our father? How I wish
my parents' home and this city were out of my sight, that my dwelling
lay at the world's end, where the very name of Kolchis   680

was unknown!" So she spoke, and her sister flushed: though eager
to answer, long she stayed silent from virginal modesty.
One moment the words rose up, reached the very tip
of her tongue; at the next they fluttered back deep in her breast.
Often they rushed to her longing mouth for utterance,   685
yet failed to articulate speech; then at last, since shameless passions
were urging her fiercely on, she said, with guile:
"Chalkíope, my heart's in a flutter for your sons,
lest Father now destroy them along with the strangers.
While dozing just now in a brief and broken slumber   690
such a horrible dream I had—may some god prevent its
fulfillment, and may you get no grief on your sons' account!"
She spoke, trying out her sister, to see if she'd make first move
in entreating aid for her sons; and pain past bearing
flooded Chalkíope's heart with the most dreadful   695
terror at what she'd heard, and thus she answered:
"I too have come here to further all these matters,
in the hope that you'll help think up, and implement, some aid.
But swear by Earth and Heaven that whatever I tell you
you'll keep close in your heart, and act together with me!   700
By the blessed gods I beseech you, by yourself and your parents,
not to see them destroyed, horribly, by an appalling
fate—if you do, I'll return after death with my dear
sons from Hades and haunt you, an avenging Fury."
So she spoke, and at once burst into a flood of tears,   705
sank down, and with both arms clasped her sister's knees,
dropping her head in her lap: then both made piteous
lamentation over each other, and throughout the house
there arose the shrill wail of women's anguished grieving.
It was Medeia who first addressed her stricken sister: 710
"Ah, my dear, what cure can I bring you, the way you're talking
of terrible curses and Furies? Would it were surely
within my power to bring your sons salvation!
Witness that mighty oath of the Kolchians, by which you
urge me to swear, by great Heaven and, set thereunder,   715
Earth, the gods' mother, that with all the strength that's in me
I'll never, if you ask what's achievable, fail you."
Such her words, and Chalkíope made her this answer:
"Would you not dare, for this stranger, who seeks your help himself,

to contrive some trick or ruse that would surmount the ordeal   720
for the sake of my sons? Argos, too, approached me
on his behalf, with a plea that I seek your aid—
I left him there in my room while I came on over."
So she spoke, and the girl's heart leapt for joy within her,
her lovely face flushed right up, she melted, a mist swirled   725
in front of her eyes, and she made answer as follows:
"Chalkíope, whatever is your and your sons' pleasure,
that I will do. May the dawn never again rise shining
into my eyes, may you see me living no longer,
if I set greater store on anything than your life   730
or the lives of your sons, who have been as brothers to me,
more than just kin or playmates; so too I regard myself
as your sister, yes, but also as your daughter,
since, just as you did for them, you raised me to your breast
as a baby—or so my mother always used to tell me.   735
Go now, but say nothing about my support, let me honor
my promise to you without my parents' knowledge: I'll go
at dawn to Hékaté's temple, bring back for the stranger
over whom this quarrel arose magic potions to charm the bulls."
So Chalkíope left the chamber, and went back, and informed   740
her sons of the help her sister had promised. But Medeia,
once alone, was seized by shame and wretched terror
at what she planned for a man in defiance of her father.
Night soon darkened the earth, and out on Ocean
sailors looked up from their ships to the stars of Orion   745
and the Great Bear, while travelers and gate porters
longed for a chance to sleep, and a profound torpor
enveloped some mother whose children had all perished:
throughout the city even the dogs ceased their barking,
human voices fell silent: stillness possessed the deepening gloom.   750
But on Medeia sweet sleep could get no hold, kept
wakeful as she was by worrying over Jason
in her longing for him, and dreading the great might of the bulls
that would bring him an ill fate there on Ares' ploughland.
Close and quick now beat the heart in her bosom,   755
as a shaft of sunlight will dance along the house wall
when flung up from water new-poured into pail or cauldron:
hither and thither the swiftly circling ripples

send it darting, a *frisson* of brightness; in just such a way
her virgin heart now beat a tattoo on her ribs,   760
her eyes shed tears of pity, constant anguish
ran smoldering through her flesh, hot-wired her finespun
nerve ends, needled into the skull's base, the deep spinal
cord where pain pierces sharpest when the unresting
passions inject their agony into the senses.   765
Her mind veered: now she thought she'd give him the magic stuff
to quell the bulls; now not, but would herself die with him;
then the next moment that she'd neither help him nor perish,
but rather just stay put, and bear her fate in silence.
Finally, indecisive, she sat herself down and said: 770
"Wretch that I am, I'm for trouble, one way or the other—
my mind lacks any resource, there's no sure remedy
for this pain of mine, it burns without cess: how I wish
I'd been killed already by the swift shafts of Artemis
before I'd ever set eyes on him, before Chalkíope's sons   775
had gone to Achaia: it was a god or some Fury
brought them thence hither, for us sore grief and weeping.
Let the contest destroy him, then, if it's his destiny
to die on that ploughland! For how could I set up my magic
drugs and my parents not know it? What tale can I tell them?   780
What deception, what crafty scheme will there be to help me?
How catch him alone, approach him, away from his companions?
And suppose him dead—not even thus can I hope, with my
bad luck, for relief from these sorrows: it's then, when bereft of life,
that he'd do me most grievous harm. . . . Ah, let modesty go hang,   785
and my good name with it! Saved by my intervention
let him take off, unharmed, for anywhere he chooses—
and then, the very day that he triumphs in his contest,
may I find death, either stretching my neck from a roofbeam
or swallowing drugs that destroy the human spirit.   790
Yet even so, when I'm dead, there'll be nods and winks, reproaches
at my expense, the whole city will broadcast my fate
far and wide, my name will be common coin, bandied
to and fro, with vile insults, on the lips of our Kolchian
women—"This girl who cared so much for some foreign   795
man that she died, this girl who shamed home and parents,
overcome by sheer lust—" What reproach shall I not suffer?

With my blind infatuation would it not be better
this very night to slough life off, here in my chamber,
a sudden end, unexplained, and so escape all censure,   800
before committing such deeds, unspeakable, infamous?"
With that she fetched out a casket, in which were stored
drugs of all kinds, some healing, others destructive,
and setting it on her knees she wept, raining endless
tears down over her bosom, a flood, a torrent,   805
as she bitterly mourned her fate. A yearning seized her
to choose some lethal drug, and then to drink it,
and she actually started to lift the hasps of the casket,
poor girl, in her eagerness; but then, on a sudden,
a deathly fear gripped her heart of loathsome Hades,   810
and long she froze, numb and speechless, while around her
all life's delectable cares caressed her vision.
She remembered the many delights that exist among the living,
she remembered her happy companions, as a young girl will,
and the Sun grew sweeter to look on than ever before   815
once she truly reached out to all these things with her mind.
The casket she raised from her lap and put away once more,
transformed by the promptings of Hera, wavering no longer
between decisions, but impatient for dawn to break
quickly, that moment, so she could give him the spellbinding   820
charms as she'd covenanted, and meet him face to face.
Time and again she unbolted and opened her door
watching for first light, and happy she was when daybreak
brightened the sky, and folk began stirring in the city.
Meanwhile, Argos instructed his brothers to stay where they were   825
so they could check on Medeia's intentions and mediations,
while he himself left them, and made his way back shipwards.

The moment the maiden saw dawn's first faint streaks appearing,
with both hands she gathered and tied up her blonde tresses,
which had been loose and floating in careless disarray,   830
and rubbed her cheeks dry, brightened her complexion
with fragrant ointment and then put on a splendid
dress, fitted out with elegant, well-turned brooches,
and over her beautiful head arranged a silvery

veil, and there, pirouetting round her chamber,   835
she trod the ground in forgetfulness of the heaven-sent
sorrows now dogging her, and others to come hereafter.
So she called on her maids—there were twelve of them all told
who slept in the corridor outside her scented chamber,
girls of her age, not yet sharing their beds with men—   840
quickly to yoke the mules, harness them to the wagon,
to convey her to Hékaté's splendid shrine. Then while the servants
were making ready the wagon, Medeia meanwhile
took from the depths of the casket a special potion,
something that men refer to as the Promethean charm.   845
Were a man, after first placating with nocturnal sacrifice
Hékaté, Maiden only-begotten, to smear it on his body,
of a surety he'd be invulnerable to strokes of bronze,
wouldn't cringe back from blazing fire: no, for one day
in both prowess and physical might he'd surpass all others.   850
The first time the plant sprang up was when that flesh-guzzling eagle
sent raining down earthward on the scaurs of the Kaúkasos
the bloody ichor Prometheus shed in his agony.
Its flower grew a cubit tall, and in appearance
and color much resembled the Korykian saffron,   855
sprouting from double stems; but its subterranean
root had the texture of flesh, just freshly severed.
Its blackish sap, like the ooze from a mountain oak,
she'd gathered, to make her drug with, in a Kaspian seashell,
after bathing first in seven perennial freshets,   860
and seven times calling on Brimo—roarer and rearer,
Brimo, night-wanderer, chthonian sovereign over
the dead—on a moonless night, wrapped in a black mantle.
A bellowing cry from underground made the dark earth tremble
as that Titan-sprung root was severed; Iapetos's son   865
himself groaned aloud at the pain that knifed into his being.
She plucked the root out, concealed it in the fragrant
band that was wound about her divinely lovely bosom.
Now she hurried out and mounted her quick wagon,
and two handmaids went along with her, one on either side,   870
but she herself took the reins, holding the well-crafted
whip in her right hand, and drove through the town, while the others,

her maids, at the wicker back-rail, ran along behind
down the broad avenue, their fine skirts kilted up
as high as their untanned thighs. The way that Leto's daughter,   875
by the sunwarmed stream of Parthenios, or fresh from
her bath in the Amnisos river, standing high
in her golden chariot, goes driving through the mountains
drawn by swift-footed roe-deer, to run down
the steaming, savory hecatomb she's smelt from a distance,   880
and behind her follow the nymphs, her attendants, some assembling
at the Amnisos streamhead itself, others coming from the woodlands
and peaks with their endless rills, while round her savage
beasts, whining, fawn in terror as she passes:
so these raced on through the city, and on either   885
side folk shrank back, avoiding the royal maiden's gaze.
But when she'd passed beyond the well-paved city streets,
and driven across the plain, and reached the temple,
then, prompt and eager, she stepped down from the quick-running
wagon, and spoke as follows to her attendants: 890
"My dears, it's a frightful mistake I've made, not realizing
I shouldn't come out among these foreigners—they're scattered
all over the countryside, the whole of the city
is panic-stricken. That's why none of the women
have showed up now who before would gather here daily.   895
Still, since we've made the journey, and no one else is around,
let's enjoy ourselves to the full with pleasurable games
and gather up flowers here in this grassy meadow,
and then take off back at the usual time. What's more,
you could all of you go home today with a pile of presents   900
if you'll only support this scheme that's so close to my heart.
For Argos is trying to talk me astray, and so is
my sister herself, Chalkíope—but you must keep silent
about what I tell you now, lest it come to my father's ears.
That stranger who took on the ordeal with the bulls—they're saying   905
that I ought to rescue him from so deadly a contest
in return for gifts. Well, I've agreed to their proposal,
and told *him* to meet me alone, away from his companions;
so if he brings gifts, we'll share them with each other
and be giving him in return a different, deadlier potion.   910

When he comes, then, withdraw from my presence." Such her words,
and this crafty proposal of hers found favor with them all.

Now the moment Argos heard from his brothers that Medeia
had set out at first light for Hékaté's holy temple,
he went to Jason, drew him aside from his companions,   915
and led him across the plain; there with them followed Mopsos,
Ampykos's son, skilled at reading the significance of bird signs
as they came up, skilled adviser to setters-out on journeys.
Never yet had there been such a man among those of former times,
not of those descended from Zeus himself, nor of all the   920
heroes sprung from the blood of the other immortals,
as the wife of Zeus made Jason upon that day
both in appearance to look on, and for charm of converse.
His very comrades, gazing on him, were astonished
at his radiant grace, and Mopsos took heart for their journey,   925
though already, perhaps, with foreknowledge of how all would come
    to pass.

Now by the track over the plain, and near the temple,
there stands a poplar, crowned with thick leafy foliage,
where chattering crows would cluster and find a roosting place,
and one of these amid many, clapping its wings   930
up in the topmost branches, at Hera's instigation
cawed mockingly: "Here's a dim seer, can't even figure out
what little children know, that a girl will never utter
words of endearment or love addressed to any
young man when others, strangers, are in attendance!   935
Get lost, badmouth, bad prophet: neither Kypris
nor the sweet Loves fill *you* with favor or inspiration!"
So it cawed, carpingly; but Mopsos smiled at hearing
this godsent birdsooth, and spoke thus: "Son of Aison,
be off with you now to the shrine of the goddess, where you'll   940
find the girl waiting, with a most warm welcome for you
through the promptings of Kypris, who'll help you in the contest
just as Agénor's son Phineus foretold. But we two meanwhile,
Argos and I, shall stay here, awaiting your return
safely out of the way. *You* must deal with her, single-handed,   945

be her suppliant, talk her round with close-knit speeches."
Such his knowing advice, and both at once assented.

Medeia could not remove her thoughts to other matters
whatever games she might play: not a one that she embarked on
caught her attention for long. She quickly found them boring,   950
kept helplessly chopping and changing. She couldn't hold
her eyes quietly on her attendants, but was forever
looking round up the road, peering into the distance.
The times her heart snapped in her breast, when she couldn't be sure
if the sound that scampered by her was wind or footfall!   955
But soon enough he appeared to her in her longing
like Seirios, springing high into heaven out of Ocean,
a star most bright and splendid to observe in
its ascent, yet a sign to flocks of unspeakable disaster:
in such splendor did Jason appear to her eager gaze,   960
yet his coming started the ill-starred miseries of passion.
The heart dropped out of her breast, of their own accord
her eyes misted over, a warm blush mantled her cheeks.
Her knees she lacked strength to shift, forward or backward,
while her feet were nailed to the ground. Her attendants meanwhile   965
had all retired to a distance, away from them both.
Silent and speechless the two were left face to face
like oaks or tall pine trees, side by side in the mountains
standing deep-rooted and quiet, while a calm
stillness prevails, but then a breeze comes blowing   970
and stirs them to endless murmuring converse: so these two,
stirred by the winds of love, would talk to one another.
Perceiving that she'd been made the victim of some heaven-sent
twist to the mind, with comforting flattery Jason addressed her:
"Young lady, why so in awe of me? Because I'm alone?   975
I'm not like some of those other loudmouthed braggarts
you'll find around, nor was I before, when still dwelling
in my own country. So, girl, no need for such modesty—
feel free to ask or tell me whatever you've a mind to.
No, since we've come together with friendly motives,   980
on holy ground, where deception's unthinkable,
speak openly, ask what you will—only do not beguile me
with sweet-sounding talk, since at the beginning you promised

your own sister to give me the drugs to enhance my strength.
By your parents I implore you, by Hékaté herself,   985
by Zeus, who extends his hand to guests and to suppliants;
both as suppliant and as guest I come before you here,
kneeling perforce through my need, since alone, without you,
I'll never come out on top in this grievous contest.
And to you I'll make return later for your assistance,   990
as is right and proper for distant dwellers to do,
promoting your fame and good name; so too will the other
heroes spread your renown when they're back in Hellas,
with those heroes' wives and mothers, who maybe already
are sitting there on the sea strand, and making lament for us: 995
their weary load of sorrow you could scatter to the winds.
Indeed, Theseus too once was saved from a nasty ordeal
by the kindness of Ariadné, Minos's maiden daughter,
whom Pasiphaë, child of the Sun, bore to him; but Ariadné,
once Minos had calmed his anger, boarded a vessel   1000
with Theseus and fled her country. Her even the immortals
loved dearly, and as witness to her in mid-heaven
a starry crown, that men now speak of as Ariadné's,
orbits all night long among the sky's constellations.
So to you too gratitude will accrue from the gods, should you rescue   1005
such a great crew, heroes all; for your appearance
suggests that you're of a sweet and friendly disposition."
Thus he spoke, flattering her; and she, with lowered gaze,
smiled sweet as nectar, and the heart within her melted,
she soared on his praise, looked up directly at him,   1010
yet couldn't decide how to begin their discussion
but felt the urge to blurt out everything at once.
First, though, without hesitation she took from her fragrant breast-band
the drug, and he quickly laid hands on it, rejoicing.
And indeed she'd have gladly drawn out all the soul from her breast   1015
and given it to him, exulting in his great need for her:
such the sweet flame that Eros sent flashing forth
from Jason's fair head, and ravished away her eyes'
bright glances: melting, it warmed the heart within her
just as dewdrops, a necklace around rose trees,   1020
melt and dissolve when warmed by morning sunlight.
Both of them now kept their eyes downcast on the ground

out of modesty, now again stole glances at one another,
from beneath bright brows exchanged their smiles of yearning.
Finally, with great effort, the maiden addressed him thus: 1025
"Listen carefully. This is the way I'll work your rescue.
When you go to my father, and he furnishes you
with the deadly teeth from the dragon's jaws for your sowing,
then wait for the midpoint that divides the passing night,
and after washing yourself in the flow of the tireless river,   1030
alone, apart from the others, wrapped in a dark cloak,
dig a round pit, and over it cut the throat of
a ewe and sacrifice it, burning the carcass whole
on a pyre that you've stacked up high at the pit's brink,
and sweeten with offerings Hékaté, Perses' only daughter,   1035
pouring out from a cup the bees' hive-garnered produce.
Then, when you've appeased the goddess, forgetting nothing,
turn away and retreat from the pyre. You must not let the sound
of footsteps impel you to turn, to look behind you,
no, nor dogs barking, lest you abort the spell   1040
and yourself fail to return in good order to your comrades.
Then, at dawn, steep this drug in water, strip off naked,
and rub it all over your body like oil: within it
there'll be great strength and unlimited prowess—it's not men
you'd think of matching yourself with, but the immortal gods.   1045
On top of this, see that your spear and shield are sprinkled,
and your sword too: then you'll be proof against the spear points
of the earthborn men, against the irresistible onrush
of flame from the deadly bulls. Yet you'll not stay immune
for long, but for one day only: still, never back off   1050
from the contest. And I'll tell you something else to help you:
As soon as you've yoked the tough oxen, and speedily
with might and main ploughed over that stubborn fallow,
when along the furrows the giants come sprouting up
from the serpent's teeth that are sown in the black glebe,   1055
the moment you see a mass of them rise from the ploughland,
then covertly toss a big stone among them: like ravening
hounds round their quarry, they'll kill each other over
the stone; and then do you with all haste betake yourself
to the battle. As for the Fleece—win the contest, and you'll carry it   1060
off back from Aia to Hellas, a long, long haul. Still, after

you leave here you'll go where you choose, where your pleasure
   takes you."
So she spoke, and silently, gaze lowered groundwards,
she let the hot tears drop wet on her sweet fair cheeks
in sorrow that he would soon be gone far away from her,   1065
wandering over the deep. Then with sad words she once more
addressed him, but face to face, and catching hold of
his right hand, for now the shame had left her eyes:
"Remember, if you one day accomplish your homeward journey,
Medeia's name, as surely as I'll remember yours   1070
far away though you'll be. So tell me, please, just where
is your home? Along what sea route will you now steer
your vessel? Will you come near wealthy Orchómenos
or skirt the isle of Aiaia? Oh yes, and who's this maiden
you spoke of before, this bright and famous daughter   1075
of my father's sister Pasiphaë?" So she spoke,
and over him too, as the girl's tears moved his heart,
stole Love the destroyer, and with hidden meaning he said:
"Too true it is, I think, that neither at night nor by day
will I ever forget you, if I but cheat fate, if I really   1080
escape unscathed to Achaia, and there's no further
worse challenge that Aiëtés flings down before us.
But if it's your pleasure to learn about my country
I'll tell you, for indeed my own heart's minded
to do just that. There's a land ringed with lofty mountains,   1085
teeming with sheep and cattle, where Prometheus,
Iápetos's scion, engendered noble Deukálion,
who was the first to build cities and raise up temples
to the immortal gods, first to be king among men:
and those dwelling along the marches call it Haimónia,   1090
and in it there lies Iolkos, my city, and many others
besides, where men have not even heard the name
of the isle of Aiaia: yet there's a story that Minyas
set out thence—Minyas, Aiolos's son—and founded
Orchómenos, that city that marches with the Kadmeians.   1095
But why am I telling you all this idle gossip
about our home and about the daughter of Minos,
the far-famed—that's the splendid title they gave
to the lovely maiden whom you're asking about—Ariadné?

I could wish that, just as Minos then came to terms with Theseus   1100
on her account, so your father might be a friend of ours."
So he spoke, caressing her with his sweet proposals.
But her heart was rubbed raw by the bitterest pangs of anguish,
and grieving, she embraced him with her urgent words:
"In Hellas perhaps it's fine to hold by your covenants: 1105
but Aiëtés is not such a man as, so you assure me,
is Minos, Pasiphaë's husband, nor can I compare myself
with Ariadné; so, no talk, please, of guest-friendship.
No: all I ask is, when you get back to Iolkos,
remember me, just as I, in despite of my parents,   1110
will remember you. And from far off may there reach me,
when—if—you forget me, some divine voice, some winged courier,
and then may tearing storm winds snatch me up skyward
and carry me to Iolkos, far out over the deep,
to reproach you face to face, remind you it was by *my*   1115
favor that you escaped. Ah yes, it's *then* I'd desire,
out of the blue, to make claim on your hearth and home!"
So she spoke, while the piteous tears ran streaming
down her cheeks; and he then guilefully answered her:
"Silly girl, let the storm winds blow themselves out wherever,   1120
and your winged courier too: you're talking airy
nonsense! If you come our way, to the land of Hellas,
honored among women and by men respected
shall you be: indeed, they'll tend you as a goddess,
since it was thanks to you that their sons accomplished the journey   1125
home once more, that their brothers and other kinsmen
and a passel of hearty husbands were saved from disaster;
and our bed in the bridal chamber shall be tended
by you, and no other barrier shall keep us from our love
till the death decreed by fate enfolds us about."   1130
So he spoke, and at those words the heart within her melted,
yet shuddered to contemplate such deeds of destruction.
Unhappy creature! Not for long was she destined
to refuse to dwell in Hellas, for thus Hera mediatrix
planned, that Aiaian Medeia, forsaking her native land,   1135
might come to sacred Iolkos as trouble for Pelias.

By now her handmaids, observing her from a distance,
were silently worried: time was running short

for the girl to hurry back home, rejoin her mother.
But she'd no thought yet of leaving, such joy had her heart   1140
found in his physical beauty and persuasive discourse,
till Jason, tardily circumspect, broke the silence:
"Time to be going now, or else the sun will have sunk
before we know it, and some outsider take note of
this whole affair. But we'll come back, we'll meet again here."   1145
So the two made trial of each other, thus far, with gentle
converse, and then they parted. Jason took off in haste
back to the ship and his comrades, full of joy,
and she to her handmaids. These all came hurrying up
and flocked around her, but she was oblivious to their presence,   1150
for her soul had winged up cloud-high, and her feet were left
to bear her back of themselves, and up onto the wagon.
With one hand she grasped the reins, with the other her inlaid
whipstock, to drive the mules. At a gallop they sped
cityward to the palace. When they got there, Chalkíope   1155
distraught for her sons' sake, tried to ask her questions;
but Medeia, completely unstrung by being back home again,
neither heard the words, nor was minded to offer any answer.
She huddled there on a low stool, set at the foot of her bed,
cheek resting crosswise on the palm of her left hand, eyelids   1160
framing damp staring eyes, as she brooded over
the enormity of the deed that her counsel had abetted.

But when Aison's son once more rejoined his comrades
in the spot where he'd left them to make his solitary venture,
they set off back together, he recounting to the other   1165
heroes all that had happened. They arrived in a body
at the ship, where the rest of the crew, as they came in sight,
welcomed and quizzed them. Jason told them all Medeia's
wily plans, and showed them the fearful drug: but Idas
sat aloof, alone of his comrades, biting back fury. The others,   1170
happily for the moment, since night's darkness restrained them,
now went about their own business. But at daybreak
they dispatched two envoys, to go and ask Aiëtés
for the seed: first Télamon himself, beloved of Ares,
and with him Aithálides, Hermes' illustrious son.   1175
Off they went, and on no vain mission: at their coming
lord Aiëtés gave them, for the ordeal, the perilous

teeth of Aonia's dragon, that in Ogygian Thebes,
Kadmos, when he arrived there on his quest for Európa,
slew, as it kept watch over the spring of Ares   1180
(and there too he settled, by the guidance of the heifer
that Apollo's oracle gave him to lead him on his way).
But its teeth the Tritonian goddess dashed from the dragon's jaws
and gave, half as a gift to Aiëtés, half to its slayer.
So after sowing his share in the Aonian plainland   1185
Agénor's son Kadmos founded an earthborn people
of all that were left by the spear after Ares' harvesting:
but Aiëtés now handed out his, to be taken to the ship—
quite readily, being convinced that Jason would never
accomplish the full task, even were he to yoke the oxen.   1190

The sun, far off, was sinking beneath the darkened earth,
away in the west, beyond Ethiopia's furthest peaks,
and Night was yoking her horses, while the heroes
bivouacked on the ground, by the stern cables. But Jason,
as soon as the stars of bright-shining Heliké the Bear   1195
had declined, and the air was still in the high vault of heaven,
went away to a lonely spot, like some furtive footpad,
with all that he needed. He'd fixed every detail beforehand
during the day: a ewe, and milk besides, from some flock
Argos now brought him; the rest he'd found himself on board.   1200
But when he sighted a spot that was well away from traffic
of men's feet, clear to the sky, by the clean river meadows,
then first of all he ritually bathed his body,
so tender and smooth, in the sacred river, and round him
wrapped a dark cloak once given him as a present   1205
by Lemnian Hypsípylé, a memento of much love-making.
A cubit deep then he dug a pit in the ground,
and piled up firewood, and over it cut the sheep's throat,
and laid it out trimly on top and lit the kindling
with a torch thrust in below, and poured on mixed libations,   1210
appealing for aid in his struggle to Hékaté the Roarer.
Then, his invocation made, he stepped back; from the uttermost
depths the dread goddess heard him, and approached the
sacrifice Jason had offered. Her whole person was entwined

with terrible serpents and oak-leaf saplings; countless   1215
torches dazzled and flared, while all around her
a pack of clamorous hellhounds bayed shrilly. All the meadows
shook at her footfall, and awestruck wailing arose
from the nymphs of marshland and river, all those that hold
their dances along the meadows of Amarantian Phasis.   1220
Fear gripped Aison's son, yet his feet took him away
without ever a backward glance, till in his going
he came among his comrades; and already high over snowy
Kaúkasos early dawn, rising, had cast her light.

And now Aiëtés fitted in place, about his breast,   1225
the stiff corselet that Ares gave him after slaying
with his own hands Phlegraian Mimas, and on his head
he put the golden helmet, four-crested, equal in
brilliance to the dazzling haloed luminescence
of the Sun when first he climbs up out of Ocean;   1230
his hide-layered shield he brandished, along with his fearful
unmatchable spear—not one of the heroes remaining
could have withstood it, now that they'd abandoned Herakles
long since and far away: only he could have matched it in battle.
Close by stood Phaëthon, holding ready his strong-built   1235
chariot with its swift horses for him to mount; and he mounted,
and took the reins in his hands, and drove from the city
along the broad highway, eager to be present
at the testing; and behind him a huge crowd followed on.
Just as Poseidon travels, mounted high in his chariot,   1240
to his festival at the Isthmus, or to Taínaron, or the waters
of Lerna, or to the grove of Hyantian Onchéstos,
and afterwards oftentimes he drives to Kalaúreia,
to Pétra in Thessaly, or forested Geraístos:
such a one to behold was Aiëtés, the Kolchians' chieftain.   1245

Meantime, carrying out Medeia's instructions, Jason
steeped the drugs in water, and with this sprinkled his shield
and massive spear, but his sword above all; and round him
his comrades exerted their strength on his arms, yet could not
bend that spear even a little, but just as it was   1250

it remained, unbroken and hard for all their violent handling.
Then, raging against them still with insatiate fury, Idas,
Aphareus's son, slashed the butt with his great sword: but its edge
sprang back in recoil like hammer from anvil. The heroes
cheered together for joy, with high hopes of the contest.   1255
Then Jason sprinkled himself; and force coursed through him,
terrible, fearless, ineffable. His arms swung to and fro,
bursting with vigor, in the full strength of manhood.
Just as a warhorse, in its eagerness for battle,
paws the ground, caracoles, whinnies, proudly arches   1260
its neck, ears sharp and erect, rejoicing in its power,
so did the son of Aison exult in his limbs' force,
time and again leaping high, this way and that,
hands brandishing brass-bound shield and spear of ash.
You'd say it was winter lightning, quick-branched in all directions   1265
down from the lowering heavens, a bright zigzag
out of clouds pitch-black and loaded with the coming rainstorm.
No longer then were the heroes minded to postpone
the moment of trial, but sitting in order on the benches
speedily rowed their vessel towards the plain of Ares.   1270
It lay a short way upstream, across from the city,
about as far as the winning post is for a chariot
from the starting gate, when the kinsmen of some dead monarch
offer footrace and horse-race prizes in his honor.
There they found Aiëtés and the rest of the Kolchians: 1275
these latter standing to watch from the spurs of the mountainside,
while the king paced up and down along the riverbank.
Now Jason, the moment his comrades had made the stern cables fast,
sprang forth from the ship, and bearing shield and spear
advanced to the contest; and with him he took the gleaming   1280
bronze helmet brimful of sharp-pointed teeth
and his sword slung from a baldric: stripped to the waist,
in ways he resembled Ares, in ways Apollo
of the golden saber. Eyeing the field, he spotted
the brazen yokes for the bulls, and the plough beside them,   1285
adamant-strong, in one piece. Up he came, and fixed his massive
spear by its butt end, and against it propped his helmet.
Then, with only his shield, he went forward to examine

the countless tracks of the bulls. They from some hidden
underground cave, where stood their strong-built stalls   1290
all wreathed about with dark smoke, lurid and thick,
both burst forth together, snorting gouts of fire.
At that sight the heroes all shuddered; but Jason, planting
feet firmly apart, faced their charge, as in the sea a rockbound
reef faces the waves whipped up by endless gales.   1295
His shield he thrust out in their path, and both came charging
against it with mighty horns, and bellowing; yet they failed
to shift it so much as an inch, for all their onset.
As through the holes pierced in a furnace the bronze-smith's bellows,
made from tough leather, now strike out showers of sparks   1300
while they heat up a deadly blaze, now pause in their blowing,
and a fearful roar comes from the fire as it surges upward
from the furnace grate—so the bulls, their mouths exhaling
quick blasts of flame, roared, and a murderous fireball
engulfed Jason, hit him like lightning, but the girl's drugs saved him. 1305
Then seizing the bull to his right by the tip of its horn
he dragged it masterfully, with all his might, till he brought it
under the yoke of bronze, and forced it down on its knees
with a sudden kick, foot against brazen foot. The other
he laid low likewise, felled by a single blow,   1310
and tossing his broad shield aside, with feet set firmly
right and left, he held them both down where they'd dropped
to their foreknees, one on each side. He stooped straight through
the flames, and Aiëtés gaped at his heroic prowess.
Meanwhile Tyndáreus's sons, briefed earlier for this service,   1315
picked the yokes up, and brought them to him for the harnessing.
On the bulls' hump necks he firm-set them; then between the pair
he ran out the bronze pole and made fast its tapering
end to the yokes. While his two helpers now backed off
from the flames and went back to the ship, he recovered his shield,   1320
shouldered it behind him, and took the strong helmet, full
of sharp teeth, along with his irresistible spear. Employing
this as a goad, he jabbed at their flanks, as Thessalian
peasants will goad their oxen, while firmly he guided
the well-wrought plough-handle, fashioned of adamant.   1325
All this time the bulls raged on in monstrous fury, breathing

their fierce fire against him; the blast came surging up
like the roar of a blustering gale, worst of all terrors
to seafaring men, who strike their great sail at its coming.
But soon enough after, forced to move by the spear's urging,   1330
they started off, and behind them the rock-hard fallow
was broken up, sheared by strong bulls and sturdy ploughman;
and a terrible crunching noise arose from the plough's furrow
as the mansize clods were split; and Jason followed,
one strong foot pressing the coulter, and far behind him   1335
kept scattering teeth along the line of new-broken clods,
with many a backward glance, lest that deadly harvest
of earthborn men should rush him too soon; and the bulls
slogged on forward, treading heavy with brazen hooves.
But when the day's last third was still remaining   1340
as it dwindles away from dawn, at the time when weary
peasants wish aloud for the sweet hour of unyoking,
then all the fallow was ploughed by that unwearied ploughman,
four acres though it spread; and he loosed the plough from the oxen.
The beasts he scared off, sent them running across the plain;   1345
he himself went back to the ship, while he yet saw
the furrows empty of earthborn men, and his comrades
pressed round him with heartening shouts. He strode to the river,
filled up his helmet with water and slaked his thirst,
flexed his knees to keep them supple, flooded his great heart   1350
with valiance, raging like a boar that sharpens its tusks
against the men who are hunting it, while from its jaws
the abundant slaver of fury drips groundward. By this time
the earthborn men were sprouting all over the ploughed acres,
and from end to end the precinct of man-slaying Ares   1355
was abristle with stout shields, two-handed spears,
and shining helmets: the gleam reached up from the ground
to high Olympus, clove through the air like lightning.
And as when the earth has had a heavy snowfall,
and gales have then scoured away the clouds of winter   1360
on a moonless night, and all the galaxies in heaven
glint bright through the darkness: so did these warriors shine
as they sprang up out of the earth. But Jason remembered
the counseling he'd been given by guileful Medeia.

He seized from the plain a boulder, enormous, rounded,   1365
a terrible shot-weight of Ares the War God: not even
four sturdy men could have got it up an inch;
but Jason hefted it easily, made a run and hurled it
far into the thick of them, then crouched down behind his shield
unseen, full of daring. The Kolchians shouted loud   1370
as the sea roars, surging over sharp-jagged reefs,
while Aiëtês was struck dumb with amazement by the cast
of the huge shot-weight. The warriors, like eager hounds, now sprang at
each other, roaring for slaughter, and tumbled on the earth,
their mother, skewered by spear thrusts. They looked like pines   1375
or oaks that are shaken down by some fierce gale.
And just as a fiery meteor flashes across the heavens
trailing its furrow of light, a marvel to those
who see it shoot gleaming through the airy darkness,
such was the son of Aison as he charged the earthborn   1380
warriors, bare sword drawn from the scabbard, slashing
at random into the thick of them, mowing them down
with cuts to belly or flanks, some waist-clear, some out as far as
the knees, some that had just completely emerged,
some on their feet already and hurrying to the fray.   1385
And as, when a war breaks out between neighboring peoples,
the husbandman—scared lest the enemy reap his harvest
before him—takes in his hand a curved sickle, freshly sharpened,
and hurriedly cuts the crop while it's still unripe, not waiting
for the sun to parch it out in its proper season,   1390
so now Jason reaped his earthborn crop, the furrows
filling with blood as field channels with springwater.
They fell, some biting the harsh clods with their teeth,
stretched prone, some on their backs, some on an elbow
or side, in appearance like beached dead sea monsters;   1395
and many, struck down before taking one step on earth,
slumped groundward with what torso they'd reached up to heaven,
bowed down by the weight of their weak and heavy heads—
a scene, you might say, like that when Zeus has sent heavy
rain, and nurslings new-set in the vineyard are battered   1400
flat, broken off at the roots, sad toil for the husbandmen;
but dejection and deadly sorrow comes upon the estate's

owner, who planted the slips. Such, at that time,
was the heavy grief that entered King Aiëtés' heart,
and he made his way back to the city with all his Kolchians,   1405
brooding on how he might soonest confound the heroes.

So the day went down, and Jason's ordeal was ended.

Book IV

Do you yourself now, goddess, daughter of Zeus, my Muse,
voice the torments and plans of Medeia: for my own part
I cannot: my inner thoughts spin in dumb distress, uncertain
whether to call it the pain of an ill-starred infatuation
or shameful panic that drove her from her Kolchian homeland.   5

Supported by the finest of his warriors, Aiëtés
spent the whole night planning sheer disaster for the heroes
there in his halls, enraged beyond all measure
at the contest's hateful result; besides, he was certain
that none of this had been done without his daughters' knowledge.   10
And into Medeia's heart Hera cast the most appalling
terror: she panicked like some quick fawn, struck witless
by the baying of hounds in a deep-wooded thicket,
for at once she guessed, truly, that the assistance she'd provided
he'd not missed, and too soon she'd have her fill of trouble.   15
She was scared of her handmaids: they knew too much. Her eyeballs
burned, and a terrible humming rang in her eardrums;
time and again she'd clutch at her throat, or, groaning
in an agony of grief, tear her hair out by the roots.
There and then, indeed, she'd have died, overriding her destiny   20
with a dose of her own drugs, and voided Hera's plans,
had the goddess not stirred her to flee, in her confusion,
with the sons of Phrixos: the fluttering heart in her breast
cheered up, and she took all the drugs that she'd collected

in the fold of her dress and replaced them together in the casket.   25
Then she kissed her bed and the uprights of the double folding doors
on either side, touched the walls, and with both hands sheared off
a long tress, and left it there in her room, as a memento
for her mother of her virginity, and, deeply grieving, said:
"This outspread tress I leave in my place at my departure,   30
Mother: farewell, it's a long road that I'm taking.
Farewell, Chalkíope, and all my home. Ah, stranger,
the sea should have destroyed you before you ever reached Kolchis!"
So she spoke, and from her eyelids the tears came flooding.
Then, just as some captured woman, torn away from a wealthy   35
house—one whom fate has lately taken far from her husband,
one as yet unsubjected to grinding labor, still
lacking all practice in anguish and servile duties—
will pass, distraught, under the harsh hands of a mistress:
so hastened away from her home this charming maiden,   40
and to her of their own accord the door bolts yielded,
swiftly springing back, impelled by her incantations.
Barefoot she hurried on through the narrow alleys,
left hand holding her mantle at brow level, to conceal
her face and sweet cheeks, while with her right she lifted   45
the edge of her skirt's hem; and very quickly,
along a blacked-out track, outside the spreading
city's towers, in terror she sped, and not one
sentinel saw her pass: her flight deceived them all.
From here she purposed to make for the ship, being well acquainted   50
with all the ways thither, having often roamed them searching
for corpses and baneful roots, as is the way of women
skilled in drug magic; but now her spirit shivered
in terror. The Moon, Titanian goddess, new-risen
on the horizon, observing her distraught flight, exulted   55
with relish, and thus soliloquized in her heart:
"So, I'm not the only one to rush off to the Latmian cave,
nor do I alone burn up for handsome Endymion!
How many times, you bitch, have your treacherous incantations
left me yearning far from my love, to let you in darkness   60
work at your leisure those magic tricks that you delight in!
But now you too, I fancy, are snared by a like passion,
and some bloody-minded deity's given you Jason

to your grievous hurt. Well, go on, then, learn endurance:
for all your cleverness, it's tears and pain you must bear."   65
So she spoke; but Medeia went hurrying on her way,
and glad she was, when she reached the riverbank,
to see on the further side the campfire that the heroes
had kept blazing all night long to celebrate their triumph.
Then in shrill clear tones she called out through the darkness,   70
loudly, across the river, to Phrixos's youngest son
Phrontis; and he, with his brothers, and Jason himself,
recognized the girl's voice. Their comrades were all struck dumb
with amazement when they figured the truth of the matter.
Three times she called; three times at the crew's urging   75
Phrontis hallooed in reply, and the heroes meantime
had sat to their oars, and were rowing quickly over
to get her. The mooring cables hadn't yet been thrown out
on the opposite bank when Jason sprang light-footed
ashore from the high deck, and after him Phrontis   80
and Argos, Phrixos's two sons, also landed, and Medeia
flung both arms around their knees, and thus addressed them:
"Get me out of here, friends—rescue me in my misfortune,
and yourselves, from Aiëtés: already the whole business
is public knowledge, past mending. Let's make our escape   85
in the ship, before *he* can harness his swift horses!
Oh, I'll give you the Golden Fleece, when I've lulled its guardian
serpent asleep—but do *you*, in the presence of your comrades,
stranger, invoke the gods to witness those solemn vows
you made me; nor when I've voyaged far from here   90
leave me despised and dishonored through lack of guardians."
So she spoke in her grief; but the heart of Aison's son
knew great joy, and at once he gently raised the suppliant,
unclasped her arms from his knees, spoke words of comfort:
"Poor girl, let Olympian Zeus himself, and Hera,   95
Zeus's bedmate, goddess of marriage, bear me witness
that I'll set you up in my home as my wedded wife
when our voyaging's done and we reach the land of Hellas."
So he spoke, and straightway clasped her right hand in his;
and at that she bade them row the swift ship to the sacred   100
grove without further ado, so that while there still was darkness
they could seize the Fleece and remove it against Aiëtés' will.

Then word and deed became one to the eager heroes:
they took her aboard and at once pushed off their vessel
from the bank, and a loud clatter went up as they all settled   105
down to their oars, and thrust hard. She started backwards,
hands stretched out to the shore, in sheer despair; but Jason
spoke words of comfort to her, and kept her grief within bounds.
At the hour when huntsmen scale off sleep from their eyes,
men who, trusting their hounds, never slumber the night through   110
till the dawn breeze is near, but anticipate first light
lest it erase the spoor and scent of their animal quarry,
lancing down with its pale white rays—then it was that Jason,
Aison's son, and Medeia stepped ashore from their vessel
into a grassy meadow known there as the Ram's Rest,   115
where first the beast folded its weary knees, as it carried
on its back the Minyan scion of Athamas. Hard by
stood the fire-blackened base of the altar that long before
Aiolid Phrixos had raised up to Zeus of the Fugitives,
sacrificing that wondrous creature, all gold, just as benevolent   120
Hermes at their encounter had bidden him; and now
it was there, prompted by Argos, that the heroes set them down.
The two of them followed a pathway that brought them to the sacred
grove, in search of that vast oak on which the Fleece
was spread out, just like some cloud that blushes ruddy gold,   125
caught by the fiery rays of the sun at its rising.
But straight ahead of them the vigilant serpent was watching
with sleepless eyes, stretched out its enormous neck,
aware of them as they advanced, and hissed horribly. All around
echoes rang through the vast grove, down the long water meadows.   130
People heard it who dwelt in areas of Kolchis
far from Titanian Aia, near the Lykos estuary—
Lykos, a river that branches from loud-rushing Araxes
and carries its sacred waters to Phasis; then cresting onward
together, they have their outflow in the Kaukasian Sea.   135
Fear struck at newly delivered mothers, and around their
tiny infants, still sleeping in their embrace, they tightened
agonized arms, as the hiss left the babes atremble;
and as when from smoldering brushwood countless soot-black
eddies of smoke go spiraling skyward, each   140
ascending directly after the other, wafted

aloft from below in rings, so then did the monster
undulate its enormous coils, with their protective
armor of hard dry scales. Now as it writhed
Medeia forced it down there, holding it with her eyes,   145
in sweet tones calling on Sleep, supreme among gods,
to charm this fearful creature, then invoked the night-wandering
Queen of the Nether World for success in her venture.
Jason followed behind her in terror; but already
the dragon, charmed by her spells, was relaxing the long spine   150
of its sinuous earthborn frame, spreading out its countless coils,
as some dark wave, stealthy and noiseless, rolls over
a sluggish expanse of ocean; yet still it struggled
to rear up its frightful head, still obstinately urgent
to wrap its killer jaws round the pair of them together.   155
But she with a branch of juniper, newly severed,
dipping it in her potion, chanting strong spells, drizzled
her charged drugs in its eyes, and their most potent odor
enveloped it, laid it unconscious. Its jaw dropped where it lay,
in one last spasm, and far behind it those endless   160
coils lay stretched out, through the dense trunks of the forest.
Then Jason, at the girl's urging, reached into the oak tree
and brought down the Golden Fleece; but still Medeia stood there
smearing the monster's head with her salves, till Jason
forced her to get moving, to make tracks back to their ship,   165
and so they hurried away from Ares' shadowy grove.
As a full moon climbs the sky, and its risen brightness
shimmers down on the garret bedroom of some young creature
who catches it on her fine dress, and the heart within her
lifts at the sight of that pure radiance, so now Jason   170
was filled with joy as he hefted the great Fleece in his hands,
and over his fair cheeks and brow the bright glint of its texture
cast a ruddy blush like a flame. In size it equaled
the hide of an ox, a yearling, or of the stag
that huntsmen know as a brocket—such its dimensions,   175
and golden throughout, and the hanging top nap of it
was heavy with flocks of wool. Brightly the earth
gleamed ever in front of his feet as he strode on forward.
So he went, now wearing the Fleece draped off his left shoulder
from the nape of his neck to his ankles, now holding it rolled up   180

tight in his hands, to feel it, fearing most greatly
lest some being, man or god, should come and spirit it from him.

Dawn was already breaking over the earth when they made it
back to the company. At the sight of the great Fleece gleaming
like Zeus's lightning, the young men were amazed; each one   185
started forward, eager to touch it, to hold it in his hands.
But Jason kept back the rest of them, flinging over
the Fleece a new woven mantle. Then he spread it out in the stern,
and seated Medeia on it, and addressed them all as follows:
"No more delaying now, friends: hoist sail for home!   190
Now at last the endeavor for which we dared this perilous
voyage, laboring sore with harsh suffering, is fulfilled
easily, thanks to all this young lady's counseling.
Her I shall take back home, according to her wishes,
and make her my wedded wife. But *your* duty to this   195
good helper of yourselves and of all Achaia must be
prompt rescue: for, I'm certain, Aiëtés with much uproar
will bar our seaward passage out of the river.
Now, half of you sit to the oars through the length of the vessel,
each second man in order; let the rest hold up your ox-hide   200
shields, a quick barrier against enemy assaults,
a protection for our homecoming. At this hour we hold everything
in our own hands—children, dear country, aged parents;
upon this venture of ours now hangs the fate of Hellas,
whether she'll be cast down or achieve great glory."   205
So he spoke, and put on his armor, and they all cheered him
with impassioned enthusiasm. He from the scabbard plucked
his sword, and with it slashed the stern-hawsers through,
and took his post there, armed, close to Medeia,
beside Ankaios the steersman, while his rowers drove the vessel   210
onward, bursting their muscles to get clear of the river.

By now high-handed Aiëtés and everyone in Kolchis
had learnt the truth of Medeia's passions and actions.
They thronged to assembly in arms, as numberless as whitecaps
cresting out at sea, whipped up by winter gales,   215
or as leaves drifting groundward from dense-packed forest branches
during the leaf-fall month—who could reckon their sum? So these
in countless hordes came streaming along the riverbank,

furious, shouting. There in his well-built chariot
Aiëtés stood, high over them, drawn by the horses   220
that Helios gave him, like gales of wind for swiftness,
his left hand holding aloft a rounded shield,
his right a huge pine torch, while beside him his massive
spear stood, couched at the ready. The horses' reins
were firm in Apsyrtos's hands. But already the vessel   225
was clearing its way out to sea, thrust on by brawny
rowers and by the great river's seaward current;
and the king in his surfeit of anguish raised arms to heaven,
calling on Zeus and the Sun to bear witness to such wicked
deeds, shouting fearful threats against all his people: 230
that unless they forthwith caught the girl—either after
she landed, or having found the ship on the high seas still,
and fetched her back to let him glut his soul, so eager
for revenge against all these wrongs—their heads would pay for it
when they'd borne his full wrath, all the measure of his ruin.   235
So spoke Aiëtés, and on that same day the Kolchians
launched their ships from the slipways and loaded the tackle aboard
and that same day put to sea: nor would you credit
that such a force was a fleet; no, rather it seemed an endless
cloud of birds, flight after flight, came screaming over the deep.   240

Swift now, in accordance with the goddess Hera's wishes,
a following wind blew strongly, speeding Medeia
towards the Pelasgian land, a disaster for Pelias
and his house. So, on the third day, they made fast their hawsers
on the shoreline of Paphlagonia, at the Halys river's mouth: 245
for she bade them disembark and offer propitiatory
sacrifices to Hékaté. Now all that the maiden purposed
in preparing this offering—may none know the essence of it,
and may my spirit never urge me to put it into verse!—
I shrink in awe from uttering; yet the shrine the heroes   250
built there for the goddess by the breakers' edge
stands to this day, a sight for men of a later age.
Then quickly Jason recalled, and with him all the other
heroes, how Phineus had told them their voyage back from Aia
would take another course, but one unknown to them all.   255
So when Argos addressed them, they all gladly listened.

"We were bound for Orchómenos, which is where that unerring prophet,
whom you earlier met, foretold you should make landfall.
For another sea route exists, which priests of the immortal
gods have made known, those sprung from Triton's daughter Thébé.   260
All the star clusters wheeling in heaven were then still nonexistent,
no one then could have answered questions about the sacred
race of the Danaäns: only Arkadians existed,
Arkadians who (so it's rumored) were living even before
the moon, in the hills, eating acorns. Nor was the Pelasgian   265
land then ruled by Deukálion's lordly line,
in the days when Aígyptos, mother of earlier mortals,
was known as the Land of Mists, rich in fertile
harvests, and Nile, the broad-flowing stream by which
all the Land of Mists is watered; there from Zeus never   270
comes enough rain; it's Nile's flooding makes crops grow.
Starting here, they say, one man traveled the whole
journey through Europe and Asia, trusting in his people's
force, strength, and courage: countless the cities
he founded as he advanced, of which some are inhabited   275
yet, and some not: many ages have passed since then.
Aia indeed stands fast still, along with the descendants
of the men whom he settled there to dwell in Aia:
these indeed keep their ancestors' written records,
tablets on which are marked all routes and boundaries   280
of water and dry land, for circumnavigators.
One river there is, the northernmost branch of Ocean,
broad and deep enough for a merchantman to sail through;
Istros they call it, and have mapped its furthest course.
For a long stretch this river cuts through boundless ploughland   285
single and solitary; far off, beyond the North Wind's
gales, its springs burst forth roaring in the Rhipaian mountains;
but when it reaches the marches of Thraké and Skythia, there
it divides: one stream discharges its waters in the eastern
sea on this side, the other winds back, shears through   290
a deep gulf branching out of the Trinakrian sea,
the sea that borders your territory—if it's truly there,
in your territory, that the spring of the Acheloös rises."
So he spoke, and the goddess vouchsafed them an auspicious
portent, at sight of which they all roared their approval,   295

ʊιat this was the route they should take: for a shooting star blazed
its sky trail far beyond them, where they'd find their passage.
Here, then, they left Lykos's son, and, with great rejoicing,
hoisted sail and stood out to sea, setting their course
by the mountains of Paphlagonia; but they did not round   300
Cape Kárambis, for the wind and that trail of heavenly fire
held steady until they reached the Istros's great estuary.

Of the Kolchians, some, pursuing a vain quest,
sailed out of the Black Sea through the cobalt-dark Rocks;
but the rest, with Apsyrtos commanding, made for the river,   305
taking a short cut, coming in by the Fair Mouth,
getting ahead of the heroes after crossing that land neck
into the furthest gulf reaching back out of Ionian
waters. There's an island, Peuké, framed by Istros,
three-cornered, its broad base reaching the delta,   310
its apex facing the current, dividing the outfall
into two separate streams: the one that they call Narex,
while the other—the southern stream—is the Fair Mouth. Up this
    channel
Apsyrtos and his Kolchians hastened, anticipating
the Argonauts as they rounded the island's northernmost shore,   315
making the long haul. From the river meadows rustic
shepherds fled, leaving their teeming flocks, in terror
at the ships, believing them beasts sprung from the monster-haunted
depths, for never before had they set eyes on seagoing vessels,
none of them, not the Skyths who march with the Thrakians, not   320
the Sigynnoi, not the Traukénioi, not the Sindians, who today
people the vast desert plain that lies around Laurion.
but when they'd passed Mount Angouron, and, lying well beyond
Angouron, the high spur of Kauliakós (round which
Istros divides his stream, flows on one side and the other   325
into the sea), and the Laurion plain, then at last
the Kolchians debouched into the Sea of Kronos,
and to stop the fugitives blocked off every route.
Now the heroes came down the river behind them, as far as
the two Brygean islets of Artemis, lying close by.   330
On one of them stood the sacred shrine; it was the other
on which, in their flight from Apsyrtos and his people

that they landed, since their pursuers had left these, out of many,
inviolate, through their respect for Zeus's daughter; the others,
crowded with Kolchians, barred every outlet to the sea,   335
and Apsyrtos had massed his men on the shores of neighboring islands
as far as the river Salángon and the Nestaian marches.

So there and then the Minyans, being few against many,
would have fought a grim battle and lost: but before that moment
they came to terms, thus avoiding this great clash, taking oaths   340
that the Golden Fleece—since this Aiëtés himself had promised,
if they triumphed in all his contests—they should keep
for ever, and with full right, no matter whether
they took it by guile, or openly, in the king's despite;
but Medeia—for here was the real bone of contention—   345
should be set apart, placed in ward with Leto's daughter,
till one of the royal lawgivers issued his verdict,
whether she must turn back to her father's home
[or to the rich city of holy Orchómenos]   348a
or follow the heroes to the land of Hellas. So when
Medeia had figured all this out in her mind,   350
then the sharp pangs of distress came violently shaking
her heart, and at once she drew Jason aside, away from
his companions, took him off some distance, until
they stood well apart; then face to face addressed him
with hurting words: "Jason, what is this plot you've all   355
worked out on my account? Has success left you quite forgetful?
Have you no regard for all the speeches you made me
when necessity pressed you so hard? Where now are your oaths
by Zeus of the Suppliants gone, where your honey-sweet promises?
They let me ditch all restraint, with shameless determination   360
lose my country, my house's good name, my very parents,
all that I held most dear, so that now I'm carried
far from them, adrift on the deep with the mournful halcyons,
all on account of your trials, so that—thanks to me—you've come safe
through your ordeal with the bulls and the earthborn men.   365
Lastly, the Fleece, too, when all was discovered, you got
through my infatuation, and a killing shame I brought
upon women everywhere! So it's as *your* wife, *your*
daughter, too, I tell you, *your* sister, that I now follow

you to Hellas! Defend me then willingly, always, do not   370
abandon me, leave me behind when you go to these royal judges—
only give me protection! Stand firm in that just agreement
we entered upon together, or else without hesitation
take your sword and slash through this throat of mine, bring me
a fitting reward for my acts of insensate folly! Harsh man,   375
what if this lawgiving king to whom you've both entrusted
so unfeeling an arbitration should return me by his judgment
to my brother? How then shall I face my father? A shining
reputation indeed! What chastisement or heavy
sentence shall I not suffer for those grievous crimes   380
I committed, while *you* are enjoying your homecoming?
May *she* bar you from this, Zeus's consort, the Queen of Heaven
on whose support you pride yourself! Remember me one day
when suffering's squeezed you dry: then may the Fleece like a nightmare
fade into nether darkness! The moment you reach your homeland   385
may my Furies drive you out again, in revenge for all
I've suffered from your stubborn cruelty! No way can my words
fall to earth unfulfilled, for you've broken a mighty oath
in your hard-heartedness: it's not long you'll be mocking me,
not long you'll be left in peace, for all your sworn covenants."   390
So she spoke, on a rolling boil of heavy anger, minded
to set the ship ablaze, burn up everything publicly,
then fling herself into the raging fire. But Jason,
in alarm, then addressed her thus, with honey-sweet words:
"Easy now, dear lady: I too dislike this business—   395
but we're searching for some way out, to put off fighting,
so vast a cloud of foemen, a fiery noose,
now rings us on your account. All this country's inhabitants
are eager to aid Apsyrtos, to see you carried home
like some captive woman, taken back to your father, while we   400
would all of us, if we came to grips with them, perish
by the most horrible deaths, with yet ghastlier suffering
in store for you, if, dying, we left you as their prey.
But this treaty will bait the device by which we'll lure *him*
on to his ruin—the folk around him won't be so hostile,   405
helping the Kolchians out because of you, once the prince—
your guardian, your blood brother—has been removed.
Then, with only the Kolchians left, I'll not shrink from head-on

battle against them, if they deny me free passage."
Such his fawning words, and this her deadly answer: 410
"Listen well now: needs must, after such shameless actions,
plot this through too, since from the beginning I erred
through my fault, contrived ill designs at a god's urging.
Do you in the press of fighting avoid the Kolchians' spears,
while I persuade *him* to entrust himself to your hands   415
with sweet talk. So, welcome him, give him rich presents
and somehow maybe I'll coax the heralds, on their departure,
to leave him alone with me, to accept my proposal.
Then, if you relish the job—I couldn't care less—
kill, and set up a battle against the Kolchians."   420
So these two in connivance fashioned a great snare
for Apsyrtos, brought out to him guest-gifts in abundance,
and bestowed on him, among them, Hypsípylé's sacred
purple robe that the Graces, those goddesses, fashioned on sea-girt
Dia for Dionysos, who afterwards gave it   425
to Thóas his son, who left it in turn to Hypsípylé,
and she made it over to Jason, a fine-wrought guest-gift
to carry off with much other rich stuff. You could never
get enough of the pleasure of handling or gazing at it,
and a heavenly scent still clung to it from the occasion   430
when the king of Nysa himself lay down on it to sleep,
half-tipsy with wine and nectar and clutching the lovely
breasts of Minos's virgin daughter, who'd followed
Theseus from Knossos, and was left by him on Dia.
But when Medeia had told the heralds her false tale—   435
to cajole him, as soon as she reached the goddess's temple
as agreed, and night's black darkness was spread around them,
to come there and work out a plot with her, by which
she'd seize the great Golden Fleece and go back home
to the palace of Aiëtés (for it was by brute force   440
that the sons of Phrixos had given her to these strangers
to carry off)—after beguiling them thus, she scattered
her potent drugs down the wind, drugs that could fetch
a distant beast of prey from the steepest mountainside.

Merciless Love, great affliction, great bane to all mankind,   445
from you come wretched quarrels, ordeals and lamentation

and, surging in over these, other griefs beyond counting:
up now, you god, take arms against my enemies' sons
as once you cast hateful frenzy into Medeia's heart!
How then when he came to her, did she wickedly dispatch   450
Apsyrtos? That forms the next theme of my story.

So when they'd left Medeia behind in Artemis's temple
as the pact required, each group ran their vessels ashore
separately from each other; but Jason hid in ambush
waiting for Apsyrtos, and then for his companions.   455
Apsyrtos, ensnared by Medeia's most fearful promises,
quickly in his vessel crossed over the roiling water
and under a dark night sky disembarked on the sacred isle.
Alone he went to that meeting, began sounding out
his sister—like some fragile child approaching   460
a swollen wintry torrent that grown men would not cross—
to see if she'd contrive some snare to entrap the strangers;
and the two of them reached agreement on every detail
at the very moment Jason sprang from close ambush,
drawn sword upraised in one hand. Quickly Medeia   465
turned her eyes away, face hidden behind her veil,
desperate not to see her brother cut down, murdered,
whom Jason now, like some butcher axing a great horned bull,
sighted and struck, beside the shrine once raised
to Artemis by those Brygoi across on the mainland,   470
and there in its portico, down on his knees, the hero,
gasping his life out, cupped the black blood in both hands
as it gushed from the wound, spattered his flinching sister's
white-silvered veil and robe with clots of crimson.
With one sharp sidelong glance the all-powerful pitiless   475
Fury perceived the deadly deed they'd accomplished;
but Jason, the hero, lopped the corpse's hands and feet,
thrice licked up blood from the killing, thrice spat the pollution
out from his teeth, right atonement for treacherous murderers,
then buried the flaccid corpse out of sight where, to this day,   480
its bones still lie in the Apsyrtians' homeland.

The Argonauts, all together, when they saw the light
of the torch that Medeia held up as their signal to approach,

brought their own vessel alongside that of the Kolchians,
and, heroes all, slaughtered the Kolchian crew, like hawks   485
pouncing on doves, or fierce lions charging into
a crowded sheepfold, wreaking havoc among the flocks.
Not one escaped death, they ran through the lot of them
like fire, on a killing spree. At long last Jason
rejoined them, eager to help: but far from needing   490
aid themselves, by this time they were worried on his account.
So now they sat down to thrash out the wisest counsel
for their voyage, and Medeia came across and joined them
in their deliberations. Peleus spoke first: "I tell you—
now, right away, while it's dark still, let's man ship   495
and row out, keeping well clear of the area that's controlled
by our enemies. Come the dawn, when they discover
all that's been done, they'll have (I reckon) no firm
command to unite and drive them on in pursuit of us:
when their leader's lost, men will split into bitter factions—   500
easy then for us, when their forces are divided,
to come back later and drive a passage through."
So he spoke, and the young men applauded the words of Aiakos's
    son,
and boarded their vessel quickly, and bent to the rowing
with vigor, until they reached Elektrís, that holy isle   505
last in the northern chain, near the river Erídanós.

The Kolchians, when they discovered their prince's murder,
went raging in pursuit of the Minyans and *Argo*
the whole length of the Sea of Kronos; but Hera from heaven's
vault held them back with lightning, bright and terrible.   510
Then, at long last—for the thought of their Kolchian homeland
sickened them, the dread of Aiëtés' savage anger—
they scattered, some here, some there, made permanent
    settlements.
Some sought those very islands where the heroes had landed,
and men there are, named for Apsyrtos, who live there to this day; 515
others beside the black depths of the Illyrian river,
close to the tomb of Kadmos and Harmónia, built a fortress,
dwelling among the Enchéleans; others made their home
in the mountains known as "the Thunderers," have lived there ever

since Zeus son of Kronos with his thunderbolts stopped them   520
from making their way across to the island opposite.

But the heroes, once confident that return would bring no dangers,
set forth, and when they reached the land of the Hylleans
made fast their cables ashore, for islands swam up crowding
thick as they sailed, with only a narrow mid-passage   525
to steer through; and now the Hylleans, who'd earlier planned mischief
against them, proved friendly, helping them on their way,
and got for reward an outsize tripod of Apollo.
A pair of these tripods Phoibos had given Jason
to take on that far journey he made perforce, when he came   530
to Delphi with questions for Pytho concerning the voyage
that lay ahead: it was fated that wherever the tripods
were set, that land should remain inviolate always,
unravaged by hostile attacks. So one of them still lies hidden
deep underground, hard by the Hylleans' pleasant city,   535
to keep it for ever removed from mortals' prying eyes.
But no longer alive in that place did they find its ruler
Hyllos, whom lovely Melíté had borne to Herakles
in the Phaiakians' country, when he'd come to Nausithoös's home
and to Mákris who nursed Dionysos, to get himself washed clean   540
of his children's horrible murder: it was here, in hot passion,
that he seduced the daughter of the river Aigaíos,
the Naiad Melíté, who bore him mighty Hyllos.   543
But when Hyllos became a youth, he no longer wished   546
to stay there under the royal eye of lordly Nausithoös,
but made for the Sea of Kronos, after raising a company
of native Phaiakians (for Nausithoös, true hero,
helped him fit out his voyage), and settled there, till slain   550
by Istrian tribesmen, defending his cattle at pasture.

But, goddesses, how came it that beyond this sea, along
the coast of Ausonia, among those Ligurian islands
known as the Echelon, so many sure traces of Argo's
passing survive to this day? What urgent necessity   555
carried her crew so far on? What winds impelled them?

At sight of Apsyrtos slumped heavily into death

Zeus himself, king of gods, felt rage for what they'd done,
and decreed that only after the arts of Aiaian Kirké
had cleansed them of deadly spilt blood, and they'd suffered woes
    untold   560
would they have their homecoming. This none of the heroes knew:
they were running before the wind, the country of the Hylleans
left far astern, sailing past all those sea-girt Liburnian
islands that not long back the Kolchians had held—
Issa and Dyskélados and enchanting Pityeía.   565
Next after these they coasted by Kérkyra, where
Poseidon established a home for Asópos's daughter,
lovely-haired Kérkyra, far from the land of Phleious,
when he'd carried her off out of love. Sailors far out at sea
seeing its coastline all darkened with shadowy forest   570
called it Black Kérkyra. Sailing on they advanced
past Melíté, basking happily in its warm sea breezes,
and sheer-cliffed Kerossós, and on the horizon
Nymphaía, where once the lady Kalypso, daughter
of Atlas dwelt; and they thought they could make out the haze-dim   575
Thunderer mountains. It was now that Zeus's plans
concerning them, his great wrath, became clear to Hera
and—plotting safe homecoming for them—she raised a hurricane
that whirled them about and carried them headlong back
to Elektrís's rocky island. Instantly, suddenly,   580
in the midst of their running human speech harshly creaked
from the hollow ship's speaking beam, of Dodóna oak,
that Athena had carpentered into the heart of the forekeel,
and deathly terror seized hold of them while they listened
to the voice and the heavy anger of Zeus: for it made plain   585
they'd escape neither the vast sea's hardships nor vexatious
tempests till Kirké should wash them clean of the pitiless
murder of Apsyrtos; and it bade Polydeukes and Kastor
pray the immortal gods to grant them a safe passage
through to Ausonian waters, where they would reach   590
Kirké, daughter of Pérsé and the Sun. Such *Argo*'s
words as dusk fell. Up sprang Tyndáreus's sons,
raised arms in supplication to the immortals,
and made a full prayer; but dejection overpowered
the rest of the Minyan heroes, while *Argo* sped far onward   595

under sail, and brought them upstream into Erídanós,
where once, breast struck by a fiery thunderbolt,
Phaëthon, half-burnt, plummeted from the Sun's
chariot into the reaches of that deep estuary: still
from his smoldering wound heavy vapor discharges skyward,   600
and over this stretch of water no bird with its light wingspread
can cross, but faltering somewhere in mid-passage
falls into the fiery cauldron, while all around
the Sun's virgin daughters, made over as tall poplars,
weep out their plaintive lament, from under anguished   605
eyelids rain down bright drops of amber earthward,
that fall in the sand and are dried there by the sun;
but when the dark delta's waters come flooding up over
the shoreline, driven on by a howling gale, such objects
are whirled out into Erídanós hugger-mugger   610
on the crest of the tide. The Keltoi have attached this legend to them,
that the drops spun away through the eddies are the tears of Leto's son
Apollo, those countless tears he shed in time gone by
when he came to the holy clan of the Hyperboreans,
exiled from gleaming heaven at his father's command,   615
in a fury concerning his son, whom in splendid Lakéreia
divine Korónis bore by the Amyros estuary:
such is the tale that's reported among these people.
But all taste for food and drink now left the heroes,
their hearts were indifferent to pleasure.The whole day through   620
they suffered agonies, sluggish and enfeebled,
from the vile unbearable stench of still-burning Phaëthon
that drifted up from the streams of Erídanós, while during
the night their ears were assailed by piercing lamentation
from the Sun's shrill-keening daughters, whose tears of grief   625
like oil-drops were borne along on the water's surface.

From here they entered Rhódanos's deep-flowing channel
that debouches into Erídanós, and at their confluence
the mingling streams seethe and roar. Out in Earth's furthest
recesses, where are the gates and foundations of Night,   630
Rhódanos has its rising: one branch discharges on Ocean's
shores, while another feeds the Ionian sea; the third
coursing through seven mouths flows into the Sardinian

sea and its vast gulf. From that river they rowed onward
into the stormy lakes that stretch away for ever   635
through the territory of the Keltoi. There they all but suffered
an inglorious fate, for the branch they were following led
out to a gulf of Ocean. None of them was aware
that this was where they were headed, that from it they would never
have got back alive. But Hera, darting down out of heaven, shouted   640
from the Herkynian promontory, and at that cry
all of them shuddered in terror, so fearfully the vast
vault of heaven resounded: the goddess turned them back,
to find the track by which their return home was assured.
So after long traveling they reached the seaswept coastline,   645
coming safe, by Hera's counsel, through countless Ligurian
and Keltic tribes, for the goddess spread about them
a strange uncanny mist every day of their journey, until
steering their way seaward out from the midmost channel
they disembarked safe and sound on the Echelon islands, thanks   650
to the sons of Zeus, in whose honor shrines and altars
were built, and survive: not of that voyage only
did those two act as protectors, but Zeus entrusted vessels
in after time to their charge. From the Echelons they set course
for the isle of Aithália: here they scraped off the abundant   655
sweat of their toil with pebbles. These still litter the beach,
variegated in color, with their quoits and heroic detritus,
in the harbor that's known today as the Bay of Argo.
Swiftly from there they sailed on, across the Ausonian
deep-sea swell, in full view of Tyrrhenia's coastline,   660
till they reached Aiaia, and in its splendid harbor
ran hawsers ashore from the ship. There they came upon Kirké
sluicing her head in seawater to cleanse away nightmarish
nocturnal fears that had preyed on her as she slept:
Every room in her house, each wall she dreamed she could see
    dripping   665
with blood, while flames devoured the innumerable drugs
that till now she'd used to bewitch each stranger who came her way;
but then she quenched this red bonfire with sacrificial blood,
scooping it up in her hands, and the deadly terror left her.
Because of this, at dawn's breaking she'd woken, and now   670
in the breakers' spray was bright-rinsing her clothes, her untressed

hair, while beasts—not wholly like wild beasts in appearance,
nor yet with the bodies of men, but a biform medley
of limbs drawn from both—crowded round her, just as sheep
will press flocking out of the fold behind their shepherd.   675
Such creatures in ages past earth had bred unaided
out of primeval slime, a tangle of mixed limbs,
when as yet she'd not been dried solid by the scouring
of thirsty air, before her moisture was most of it lost
to the parching sun's rays. Time recombined these bodies   680
into fixed species. Such her followers' formlessness;
and boundless astonishment gripped the heroes: in an instant
each one of them, closely scrutinizing Kirké's appearance
and eyes, now recognized her for the sister of Aiëtés.
But she, her nightmare terrors sent packing, in an instant   685
turned about and strode back, with a caressing gesture
compelled them to follow, craftily led them on.
Then the company came to a halt, on Jason's orders,
and waited, indifferent, while he dragged Medeia forward,
both following Kirké along the road till they arrived   690
in her great hall, and she, much puzzled at their coming,
invited them to sit down, on waxed and polished chairs,
but they, silent and speechless, flung themselves at the hearthstone
and crouched there—the proper ritual for miserable suppliants—
she hiding her face in both hands, he having planted   695
his great hilted sword in the ground, the sword with which
he'd killed Aiëtés' son; neither dared meet her gaze,
but stared groundward with lowered eyelids. Kirké instantly
knew their fugitive fate, the bloodshed that defiled them.
So—and through fearful regard for the fiats proclaimed by Zeus   700
of the Suppliants, great flail and great savior of man-slayers—
she set about that ritual employed for purification
of ruthless suppliants claiming the hearth as their sanctuary.
First, in expiation of murder irreparable,
she held out above them the young of a new-farrowed   705
sow whose dugs still were swollen, bloodied their hands
in the flow as she cut its throat. Then with further propitiating
libations, she called upon Zeus: Avenger, Purifier,
Zeus the bringer of succor to blood-guilty suppliants,
and all the polluted scourings were gathered and carried out   710

by her attendant Naiads, who served her in everything.
She meanwhile, inside by the hearth, burnt wineless offerings,
cakes of flour, oil, and honey, offered up prayers
that the terrible Furies would cease from their wrath, that Zeus
himself would look kindly on them, show gentleness to them both,   715
whether they sought the hearth with hands polluted
by a stranger's blood—or even by a kinsman's.
Only when all was accomplished did she make them
get up. Then she seated them on polished chairs, and herself
sat close, facing them, and asked them detailed questions,   720
plunging straight in—Now, what was their voyage in aid of,
where had they come from, what brought them here, to her home,
why seat themselves at her hearth? As she wondered, the frightful
memory of those nightmares invaded her mind,
and the moment she saw Medeia raise her eyes from the ground,   725
she was eager to hear her voice—a kinswoman's, surely,
for all the Sun's descendants were impossible to mistake,
since from under their eyelids they darted a radiance
far in front of them, a brightness like that of gold.
So Medeia, the daughter of savage-hearted Aiëtés,   730
answered each question as she asked it, eager
to please, speaking in Kolchian, explaining the expedition
and the heroes' wanderings, all their toil in those barbed contests,
and the wrong she did at her unhappy sister's urging,
and how, with the sons of Phrixos, she'd taken terrified flight   735
from her father's harsh threats. But of the murder of Apsyrtos
she said nothing—yet fooled Kirké not one whit, who, though
moved by her tears to pity, still addressed her thus:
"Wretched creature, this is a bad and shameful voyage
you've undertaken: not long, I think, will you escape   740
Aiëtés' heavy fury. Very soon he'll reach your homeland
of Hellas, seeking revenge for his murdered son: this crime
you've committed defies compassion. But since you're my suppliant,
my kinswoman too, now you're here I'll inflict no further
suffering on you. Get out, and take the stranger with you,   745
whoever he is, this no one you've picked up to spite your father!
And don't clutch my knees at the hearth: *I* can never condone
the deeds you plotted and did, your disgraceful flight."
So she spoke, and sheer anguish seized Medeia: muffling

her face in her robe she sobbed and wailed, till the hero,   750
taking her by the hand, led her out of the great hall
shaking with fear, and so they left Kirké's house.

But they did not elude the notice of Zeus's wife, for Iris
told her as soon as she saw them emerging from the palace,
since Hera's own orders were to keep watch for the moment   755
when they made for the ship. Now she gave her fresh instructions:
"Dear Iris, come, if you've ever done my bidding,
speed away now, on your light swift wings, to Thetis:
bid her come here to me, up from her briny depths,
for I have great need of her. Next, you must make your way   760
to those island shores where the anvils of Hephaistos
ring brazen under the strokes of his mighty hammers:
tell him to damp down his fire blasts until the *Argo*
is safely past them. Then go also to Aiolos,
Aiolos, lord of all winds born in the high clear heavens   765
and tell him, too, my purpose: let him hold up all motion
of air in the firmament, let not the least breeze ruffle
the deep, except for a gentle western tailwind
until they reach the Phaiakian isle of Alkínoös."
So she spoke, and Iris promptly launched herself from Olympos,   770
light wings outspread, knifed through the air, and plunged
into Aigaian waters, where Nereus has his domain.
First she visited Thetis, and passed on the whole message
that Hera had given her, commanding Thetis's presence;
next she sought out Hephaistos, made him silence his iron   775
hammers that instant, choke off the breath from the smoky
fire blasts. Then, thirdly, Iris called upon
Aiolos, far-famed son of Hippótas. While she was giving
her message to him too, and relaxing from her journey,
Thetis, leaving behind both Nereus and her sisters,   780
rose from the sea to Olympos, to the goddess Hera,
who sat her down close to herself, and made her intentions plain:
"Listen well, Thetis, goddess, to what I have to tell you.
You know how high the regard my heart feels for heroic
Jason, and all the other companions of his quest,   785
and just how I saved them as they threaded the Wandering
Rocks, with their fearfully roaring fiery tempests,

and breakers that crash in spindrift over jagged reefs—
but now it's by Skylla's vast rock, and the fearful eructations
of Charybdis that they must steer. Do not forget, Thetis,   790
how it was I that reared you from infancy, and loved you
more than all other sea nymphs that dwell in the salt depths
because you would not bed, for all his urgent longing,
with Zeus—oh, I know him, that's what he's always up to,
sleeping around with women, mortal or immortal—   795
but out of respect for me (*and* because you were scared silly)
you kept him at bay; and he then swore a tremendous
oath, that no deathless god would ever call you wife.
Yet he still, even so, kept at you, very much against your will,
till reverend Themis spelled out the truth of the matter to him,   800
telling how he was destined to sire a son of better
stuff than his father. So then, even though he still wanted you,
fear made him give over, scared lest some rival oust him
as king of the gods: he wanted to keep his rule forever.
But I gave you for husband the best of earthly men,   805
to let you enjoy a marriage that pleasured your heart
and bear children; I asked to your wedding feast the whole
company of the gods, with my own hands I lifted
the bridal torch, all because of that kind respect you showed me.
And now let me tell you a tale that's sure of fulfillment: 810
When he comes to the plain of Elysion, this son of yours—
who now in the abode of Cheiron the Kentaur
has Naiads as nurses, yearns for his mother's milk—then
his fate's to become the husband of Aiëtés' daughter
Medeia: so go help her, your daughter-in-law-to-be,   815
and Peleus as well. Why this unyielding rage against him?
He was foolish: yet the gods, too, are rendered blind by folly.
Surely at my behest Hephaistos will, I'm certain,
cease from blowing his fire white-hot, while Hippótas's son
Aiolos will hold back the swift blasts of all his winds,   820
save a steady western tailwind until they reach haven
among the Phaiakians. *You* fix them a risk-free voyage:
the rocks and those vaulting waves are your only concern,
and such dangers you and your sisters can well avert.
Don't let them, through sheer fecklessness, go plunging into   825
Charybdis, lest she swallow them down forever,

or sail too close to Skylla's disgusting hiding place—
deadly Ausonian Skylla, whom Hékaté, that night wanderer
known as Krataïs, once bore to Phorkys—lest with
horrible jaws agape she spring on them and destroy   830
the pick of the heroes. I want you to steer their vessel
on that narrow line through the strait that will let them skirt disaster."
So she spoke, and with these words Thetis answered her:
"If, *if* the force of the raging fire, and those violent
tempests in truth shall cease, why then, for my own part   835
I can promise with confidence, even should the waves
run counter, to save the ship: all I need is a light west breeze.
But the journey's unspeakably long—high time I was off
in search of my sisters, who'll help me, and then
on to where the vessel lies moored by its hawsers,   840
so that at first dawn the crew may think of sailing."
With that she sprang up, and swooped down out of heaven
into the swirl of the cobalt sea, crying out to her sister
Nereids to come aid her; and they, when they heard her call,
ran crowding round. Then Thetis announced the commands   845
of Hera, and promptly dispatched them, every one,
to the Ausonian Sea, while she herself, more swift
than a flash of light, or the sun's rays darting up
from the horizon, sped over the water till she reached
Tyrrhenian territory, the shoreline of Aiaia.   850
The heroes she found by their ship, relaxing at archery
and with quoits; so she approached them, reached out, and barely
    brushed
the hand of Peleus, Aiakos's son—her husband.
Yet no one else could discern her, to him alone
was she visibly manifest, and thus she now addressed him: 855
"Waste time here no longer on this Tyrrhenian beach,
but at first dawn cast off the hawsers of your speedy vessel
in obedience to Hera, your helper; for by her orders
all the Nereid maidens are assembling together
to convoy your ship in safety through those rocks that sailors   860
know as the Wanderers: there lies your destined sea route.
But reveal my presence to no one, when you see us approaching
together: keep silent, or you'll make me still angrier
than you did with your recklessness on that other occasion."

So saying she plunged out of sight into the sea's depths.   865
But he was pierced by sharp sorrow, for till this moment
he'd not seen her since she'd fled from his bed and chamber
in a rage, on account of her baby, splendid Achilles;
for nightly in the dark hours she'd flame his mortal
flesh all about with fire blaze, and day by day   870
rub ambrosia into his tender body, to make him
immortal, free his skin from the ravages of age.
But Peleus, roused out of sleep, started up when he beheld
his dear child writhing in flames: he let out a terrible
shout at the sight, the great fool, and hearing that, Thetis   875
snatched back the baby, threw it screaming to the ground,
while she, like some wind embodied, a fleeting dream,
passed swiftly out of the house and flung herself, furious,
into the sea: after that she never once came back.
Sheer amazement now froze his reactions: yet, notwithstanding,   880
all Thetis's behests he reported to his comrades.
They broke off their games at once, ceased from their playing
with a ready will, prepared supper, made up their beds
on the ground, ate their fill, and slept all night as usual.

As Dawn brought up her light to strike the rim of heaven,   885
then, with the onset of a brisk breeze out of the west,
they quit dry land for their benches, cheerfully hauled
their anchor stones up from the depths, clewed in the rest
of the tackle all shipshape, hoisted the great sail,
spreading it taut with the halyards from the yardarm,   890
and a steady wind bore the ship on. Very soon they sighted
lovely Anthemoéssa, the island where those clear-voiced
Sirens, daughters of Acheloös, with their seductive
songs of enchantment destroyed all travelers who put in there.
Terpsíchoré, one of the Muses, a beautiful creature, bore them   895
after bedding with Acheloös; a time came when they served
Demeter's powerful daughter, then still unmarried,
sharing her play: but now to look at they were
formed partly like birds, and partly like young maidens.
Always keeping watch from their lookout above the harbor,   900
many the men they robbed of a honey-sweet homecoming,
wasting away their will. Ruthlessly, now, to these

newcomers too they called out in lily-pure voices, and they
already were on the point of casting hawsers ashore
had not the son of Oiagros, Thrakian Orpheus,   905
quickly seizing and stringing his native lyre,
thrummed out a sprightly theme, all galloping rhythm,
to confuse their listening ears with the buzz and twang
of plucked chords, so that his lyre drowned out the Sirens' singing.
Rolling in from astern the west wind and the echoing   910
waves drove their vessel on, and the singing faded.
Yet, despite all, one of the company, Téleon's noble son
Boútés, his spirit melted by the Sirens' high clear call,
before they could stop him, vaulted from his polished bench overboard,
into the surging breakers, and struck out for the shore,   915
poor wretch—they'd surely have robbed him, there and then, of his
      homecoming
had not the goddess Kypris, the guardian of Eryx,
pitying him as he thrashed in the eddies, rushed to his aid,
snatched him and saved him, to dwell on Cape Lilybéon.

So it was racked with grief that they left the Sirens; yet more,   920
and worse, ship-cracking perils still loomed at the seas' crossroads,
for on one side now they saw the sheer smooth rock of Skylla,
while from the other came the endless roar and upsurge
of Charybdis, and beyond them, under enormous breakers,
loud thundered the Wandering Rocks. Here, earlier, blazing   925
fire jets pulsed from the peaks, high above red-hot rock,
and the clear air was clouded with smoke, so thick that you could not
see the sun's rays. Even now, although Hephaistos
had ceased from his work, the sea still bubbled with hot steam.
It was now that the daughters of Nereus, crowding in from every side   930
came to their aid, while behind them, one hand on the steering oar
stood godlike Thetis, to guide them amid the Wanderers' reefs;
and just as schools of dolphins emerge from the depths in windless
weather, to frolic in circles all round a speeding vessel,
and are glimpsed now ahead of it, now plunging in its wake,   935
now alongside—a source of pleasure to sailors—so the Nereids,
darting forward up out of the deep, close as warp is to woof,
thronged all around the ship *Argo,* while Thetis steered her course.
And when they were close to running upon the Wanderers, then,

quickly hoisting their skirts by the hem to their white knees,   940
high on the very reefs among the pounding breakers
they ran ahead, left and right, in separate groups. Now *Argo*
was slammed from side to side by the riptides, while rough-rearing
waves all around beat wetly into the rockface.
Now like towering crags the Wanderers touched the sky,   945
now deep down below the sea's bottommost foundations
were rooted fast, and the wild swell rose high above them;
while the Nereids—just as girls on some sandy secluded beach,
kilting their skirts up, tucking them into their waistbands,
will play with a nice round ball, each one of them in turn   950
catching it from another, and passing it on again
with a high toss in midair, so it never hits the ground—so
the Nereids passed the swift ship in turn one to another,
skimming it over the wavetops, always taking care to
keep it clear of the rocks, as the roaring tide seethed round them.   955
They had watchers: high on a sheer cliff's summit, standing
erect, one brawny shoulder propped with his hammerhelve,
Lord Hephaistos looked on; and high above the radiant
heaven stood Zeus's consort, so scared by what she saw
that she flung her arms in terror about Athena.   960
For the whole allotted span of a day in springtime,
so long the Nereids labored, heaving the vessel
clear through the thunderous rocks, till the heroes recaptured
a following wind, and sped onward, rapidly coasting
past Thrinákia's meadows, where the sun god's cattle pastured.   965
Here it was that the Nereids, their work for Hera done,
plunged back, like so many shearwaters, into the depths,
while, wafted on the breeze, the mingled bleating
of sheep and lowing of cattle reached the rowers' ears.
The sheep were herded from thicket to dewy thicket   970
by Phaëthousa, youngest of the daughters of Helios,
a silver crook clutched in one hand; following the cattle,
her sister Lampétië brandished a brightly polished
ox goad of mountain copper. These cattle the heroes themselves
saw grazing along the line of the river meadows   975
in pasture and grassy marshland: not a single beast
from that herd was dark-coated, every last one gleamed white
as milk, and trod proudly, glorying in its golden horns.

These they coasted by in the daytime, but when it was dark
they struck out over open sea, in high spirits, till once more   980
Dawn, morning's daughter, shed her light on their voyaging.

An island there is, large, fertile, that fronts the Ionian
strait, in Keraunian waters; and under it—so goes
the story—there lies that sickle (forgive me, Muses
for retelling, with reluctance, the ancient tale!) with which   985
Kronos ruthlessly lopped his father's privates—though others
call it the reaping hook of chthonian Demeter;
for indeed she once had her dwelling in that country
and taught the Titans to harvest the teeming ears of grain,
all out of love for Mákris. So Drépané, "The Sickle,"   990
became the name of this island, the Phaiakians' nurse, and they
themselves today claim descent from the blood of Ouranos.
To them now, long delayed by many troubles, came *Argo,*
with a fair breeze, from the Thrinakian Sea. Alkínoös
and his folk gladly welcomed their arrival with happy   995
sacrifices: in their honor the whole of the city
made holiday—you'd think they were fêting their own sons—
while the heroes themselves went rejoicing through the crowd
as though it was rather in the Thessalian heartland
that they'd landed. But soon a great shout made them strap on their
   armor—   1000
so close, well in sight, had come an enormous host
of Kolchians, who by way of the Black Sea's mouth, and through the
cobalt-dark Rocks, were on the track of the heroes—
insistent on taking Medeia back to her father's home,
no argument: if not, they threatened, they'd unleash   1005
the bloodiest battle, with horrible cruelty and slaughter,
both at once and thereafter, on the coming of Aiëtés.
But Lord Alkínoös reined in their urgent longing
to make a war of it, being firm set to resolve
both sides of this violent quarrel without armed conflict.   1010
In the grip of deadly terror, Medeia made repeated
appeals to Jason's companions, repeatedly flung
her arms round the knees of Arété, Alkínoös's wife:
"Majesty, I beseech you, have mercy, don't give me up
to these Kolchians to be shipped back to my father, not if you're   1015

of the race of mortals yourself—creatures whose purpose
through careless transgressions runs helter-skelter on ruin.
Just so my good sense deserted me—but it wasn't
out of lust! By the sun god's holy light I swear it,
by the rites of Perses' daughter, the virgin night wanderer,   1020
not willingly, not by choice, did I sail away from Kolchis
with men of an alien race: it was hateful fear that forced me
to resort to this flight when I'd erred, and there was no other
way out. My virginity still, as in my father's house,
remains undefiled, unsullied. So pity me, lady,   1025
intercede with your husband for me—and may the immortals
grant you a life of fulfillment, in beauty abounding,
and children, and pride in a never-conquered city."
Thus she entreated Arété, shedding tears; and thus
each warrior in turn of that band of heroes: "*You*—   1030
oh yes, *you*, the best, the bravest—and your ventures
are why I'm now so distraught—I, by whose connivance
you yoked the bulls and reaped that killing harvest
of earthborn men; I, through whom you're now homeward
bound with the Golden Fleece, to Thessaly; I, I who   1035
have abandoned my country, am severed from my parents
and home, from all things that make a life worth living;
yet *you* are going back, you'll live in your own homes again—
thanks to *me!*—you'll have the joy of once more seeing your parents
with your own eyes—but from me some lowering spirit's wrested   1040
such delights, so that I wander, an embarrassment, with strangers.
Go in fear of your pacts and your oaths, go in fear of the Fury
of suppliants, of the gods' vengeance, should I fall into
Aiëtés' hands, to die in agony and dishonor!
No temples, no ramparts are mine: no other protection   1045
can I hold out as my shield save your own persons. Cruel,
ruthless, hard-hearted—do you not feel secret shame
at the sight of me so helpless, arms outstretched to clasp
the knees of a foreign queen? Ah, when you were eager
to get your hands on the Fleece, why, *then* you'd have crossed swords   1050
with the whole Kolchian host, *and* proud Aiëtés: but now,
when they're cut off and isolated, you've forgotten your courage!"
So she spoke, appealing to them; each man that she approached
addressed her with words of comfort, sought to restrain her grief:

they seized their sharp spears and brandished them in their fists,   1055
waved unsheathed swords, swore that they'd not hold back
from protecting her if they got an iniquitous judgment.
While she agonized through the host, Night stole upon them,
Night that beds down men's actions, and spread her drowsy
peace over the whole earth. Yet not one instant's repose   1060
did Medeia get: her tormented heart kept turning
the way a poor working woman will turn her spindle
all night through, while her orphan children whimper round her
in her husbandless widowhood: tears trickle down her cheeks
as she weeps for the miserable fate that's caught her—such   1065
tears wet Medeia's cheeks, and her inner spirit
cringed, impaled on the knifepoints of keenest suffering.

In the city, retired to their palace, as before, the royal couple—
lordly Alkínoös, and that great lady, Arété,
Alkínoös's wife—were debating, in bed, over Medeia,   1070
in the dark; and she, as wife to wedded husband,
clasped him in her embrace and entreated him lovingly:
"Please, dearest, act now, protect this much-put-upon girl
from the Kolchians, do the Minyans a friendly turn, for Argos
and the warriors of Thessalia may be close to our island,   1075
but Aiëtés dwells nowhere near us—indeed, we know nothing
of Aiëtés except by hearsay. But this most unfortunate
young woman has broken my heart with her supplications: oh, sir,
don't give her up to the Kolchians, to be dragged back to her father's!
It was infatuation misled her when she first provided charms   1080
to that man for subduing the oxen—then tried to mend ill with ill
(as we often do when in trouble) by running away
from the weight of her overbearing father's wrath. But Jason—
or so I hear—is bound by strong oaths of her asking
to make her his wedded wife, the queen in his palace.   1085
So, dearest, don't choose a course that will render Jason
forsworn in his oath, nor by your connivance let
this father's harsh resentment outrage his helpless child!
For fathers tend, to a fault, to be jealous of their daughters—
just look how Nykteus treated his lovely Antíopé,   1090
all the trouble that Danaë had, adrift in the deep,
through the criminal acts of her father—and recently, not far

from here, violent Echetos drove bronze needles through
his daughter's eyeballs: now her wretched fate withers her
as she grinds away at bronze corn husks in a shadowy barn."   1095
So she besought him, and his heart was warmed pleasurably
by the words of his wife, and such the reply he made her:
"Árété, I *could* raise an armed force to drive out
these Kolchians, for the girl's sake do the heroes a favor;
but to slight Zeus's upright justice—that I dare not.   1100
Nor is it wise to ignore Aiëtés, as you bid me,
for there lives no mightier monarch than Aiëtés,
and remote though he is, should he wish, he could bring his feud
    to Hellas.
So it is right for me now to render a judgment
that will win all men's approval: I'll not hide it from you.   1105
If she is virgin still, I decree that she be carried
back to her father; but if she's sharing a man's bed
I'll not separate her from her husband, nor if she's bearing
a child in her belly will its enemies get it from me."
So he spoke, and immediately slumber overcame him.   1110
But she took his shrewd words to heart, got up from bed quickly,
and hurried out through the lobby. The women who served her
came running, bustled about at their mistress's heels.
Quietly she beckoned her herald, gave him a message
to Aison's son, recommending, in her thoughtful wisdom,   1115
that he bed the girl, and forgo the appeal he was planning
to Alkínoös—"for the king is going to give his judgment
to the Kolchians, that if she is virgin still, he'll return her
to her father's house, but if she is sharing a man's bed
he'll not cut her off from the joys of wedded passion."   1120
So she spoke, and at once his feet took him out of the hall
to convey to Jason Árété's encouraging words
together with the decree of god-fearing Alkínoös.
The heroes he found by their ship, under arms and keeping watch,
in the harbor of Hyllos, close to the city. He told them   1125
the whole of Árété's message, and each hero's heart
rejoiced, for the news he brought was much to their liking.
Straightway for the blessed gods they mixed a bowl of wine
in due form, and reverently dragged sheep to the altar,

and that very night they prepared Medeia a bridal   1130
bed in the sacred cave that had once been home to Mákris,
daughter of Aristaios, whose skills first pioneered
bee-keeping, and the yield to be sweated from the olive.
She it was who first of all, in Abantian Euboia,
took to her breast Zeus's Nysaian child, and smeared   1135
its dry cracked lips with honey, as soon as Hermes
had rescued it from the fire; but Hera saw her,
and in her fury drove her clean out of the island.
So Mákris settled far off, among the Phaiakians,
in their sacred cave, and brought the inhabitants untold wealth.   1140
There, then, they made up a great marriage bed, and on it
spread the bright Golden Fleece, to honor this wedding
and make it famous in story. For them the nymphs
gathered wild flowers of all colors, brought them bouquets
in their white bosoms. A glow like firelight shone round them,   1145
so bright the light that glittered from the Fleece's golden tufts.
In their eyes it kindled sweet longing; yet though each was eager
to reach out a hand and touch it, awe held them back.
Among them were some known as daughters of the river Aigaios,
others who dwelt round the peaks of the mountain called Mélité,   1150
others again who were wood nymphs, out of the plains: for Hera
herself, Zeus's consort, had sent them, to render Jason honor.
To this day that sacred grotto is still known as the Cave
of Medeia, curtained off with their scented veils by the nymphs
when they made that couple one flesh, while the heroes, brandishing   1155
their war spears in clenched fists (lest some hidden body
of enemies fall upon them, savage them unawares),
heads crowned with garlands of leafy tendrils, sang
the marriage song at the threshold of the bridal chamber
to a clear and tuneful accompaniment from Orpheus's lyre—   1160
though not here, in the realm of Alkínoös, had the hero Jason
looked forward to having his wedding, but in his father's home
when he'd got back safe to Iolkos; and Medeia herself
felt as he did; but necessity forced their union now.
For it's true that we generations of wretched mortals never   1165
get a firm footing on pleasure: some bitter sorrow
insinuates itself always amid the merriment. So

it was with these two: though melting in the heat of their sweet passion,
they still were gripped by fear—would Alkínoös give that judgment?

Now Dawn resurgent with her immortal radiance   1170
dispersed black night through the morning haze, and the island
beaches, the dew-wet paths far off across the plain
laughed in the sun, the streets were loud with voices:
folk were up and about in the city, and the Kolchians likewise,
away at the furthest tip of the Mákris peninsula,   1175
and Alkínoös, promptly, as he had agreed to do,
set forth to pronounce his decree on Medeia. In one hand
he held his gold staff of justice: under its dominion
his subjects throughout the township got upright judgments.
Behind him, armed as for battle, came marching in serried ranks,   1180
file upon file, the best warriors of the Phaiakians.
The women went hurrying out in crowds beyond the ramparts
to get a glimpse of the heroes, and when the field laborers
got word, they came in to join them, for Hera had spread abroad
a report of what was afoot. One brought a chosen   1185
ram, the pick of his flock, one an unworked heifer;
others had jars of wine that they set up, conveniently at hand
for mixing; far off the smoke of burnt sacrifice eddied.
The women brought fine-worked fabrics (as is their custom),
and offerings of gold, and besides these every sort   1190
of adornment with which the newly wed are provided.
They stared in rapt amazement at the peerless heroes'
fine figures and handsome faces, while among them Orpheus
with quick and skillful fingers picked sweet music from his lyre,
tapping one foot to the beat in its fine-worked sandal;   1195
and when he played wedding music all the nymphs together
sang the sweet hymeneal. Then again they'd dance
round in a circle, their singing now unaccompanied,
to honor you, Hera: for you it was put Aréte
in mind to pass on Alkínoös's wisely framed response.   1200

But the king, from the moment he'd pronounced the verdict
of his upright judgment, and the marriage's consummation
was made public, stood firm by his word. Neither deathly fear
nor yet the heavy burden of Aiëtés' fury could shift him—
and he'd bound all parties involved with unbreakable oaths.   1205

So when the Kolchians learnt that their requests were hopeless,
and he gave them his ultimatum: either honor the judgment,
or take their ships and keep far from his harbors and country—
then, dreading the angry reproof of their own king, they begged him
to accept them as allies. And so, there on the island   1210
they dwelt for many years among the Phaiakians, till
the Bacchiad clan, whose ancestral home was Ephyra,
in the fullness of time came as settlers; and then they migrated
across to the mainland. From there they reached the Amantes,
Keraunian mountain dwellers, the Nestaians, and Orikon: 1215
but all this came to pass long centuries afterwards.
And still the Fates and the nymphs receive annual offerings there,
sacrificed in the shrine of Apollo the Good Shepherd
on the altars set up by Medeia. The departing Minyans
got guest-gifts galore from Alkínoös, and many too   1220
from Arété, who also bestowed on Medeia as attendants
twelve Phaiakian handmaids, slaves from the palace.

On the seventh day they left Drépané: at dawn in a clear sky
the breeze blew fresh, and they, with a good tailwind behind them,
sped on their way; but it was not yet fated   1225
that the heroes should make landfall on the shores of Achaia
till at Libya's furthest confines they'd endured more suffering.
Already they'd passed the gulf that bore the Ambrakians' name,
already, sails outspread, they'd voyaged beyond the land
of the Kourétés, beyond the strung-out Echínadés   1230
and their islets, and Pelops's land was just coming into view—
when suddenly, in mid-passage, a raging norther
seized and drove them towards the Libyan sea for nine
whole nights and days, till finally they were carried
far, far within the Syrtes, from which there's no returning   1235
when a vessel is once forced in past this gulf's entrance:
for everywhere there are shoals, everywhere massed seaweed grows
from the bottom; over it all laps a silent layer of spume,
and the sand stretches far into haze. Nothing live stirs there,
no creature winged or creeping. Then they were caught up   1240
by the flood tide—for these waters regularly ebb out
from the gulf, and then come surging back in on the shoreline
with a fierce thunderous roar—and were suddenly driven

so hard up the beach that their keel was scarce left touching water.
They sprang from the ship. Sorrow seized them as they took in   1245
the hazy sky and the ridges of that vast landscape, stretching
unbroken into the distance, like haze itself; no oases,
no tracks, no herdsmen's steadings could they discern
near or far: a brooding silence lay over everything,
and in his deep distress one hero enquired of another: 1250
"What land does this call itself? Where, pray, have the storm winds
    tossed us
ashore? We should have risen above our deadly terror,
followed the same course homeward, steering right through
those rocks: even had we outstripped the destiny Zeus decreed us,
better to set our hearts on greatness, and so perish.   1255
But now what can we do, should the winds enforce even
a short stay here upon us? How barren and desolate
the coast of this endless terrain spread out before us!"
So he spoke, and after him, in helplessness at their evil
case, Ankaios the steersman addressed his grieving comrades: 1260
"We're done for indeed, and by a most dreadful fate—no loophole
from ruin for us, no prospect but to endure the worst,
crouching here on this barren strand, even should a strong wind
start blowing offshore; for looking all round, near and far
at this gulf, what I see are shoals, and a thin top layer of water   1265
that's raked over the gray sandbars into the shallows.
What's more, this our sacred ship would have broken up miserably
long since, and far from the land, without that flood tide
to carry her out of the deep and leave her high and dry.
But now it's rushed back seaward, and all that washes round her   1270
is brine, just clear of the seabed, too shallow for sailing.
That's why, I'm telling you, any hope of getting seaborne
and returning back home is cut off. Let some other man, then,
show off *his* expertise, fill that seat at the steering oars,
if he's so set on rescuing us! But it's clear that after all   1275
our toil, Zeus still will not fulfill our day of returning."
Thus he spoke, weeping, and all who were skilled shipmen
shared his distress, and agreed: the heart of each one of them
froze, and a greenish pallor spread over their cheeks.
Just as men will sometimes wander, like lifeless phantoms,   1280
through the streets of their city, awaiting the dread onset

of war, or pestilence, or some cataclysmic deluge
that floods out the labors of a myriad plough oxen;
when images break out in a spontaneous sweat
of dribbling blood, and men think they hear bellowings   1285
in shrines, or the sun at high noon draws darkness on
out of the firmament, and the sky is bright with stars:
so then the heroes wandered, slouching despairingly,
along that endless strand. Soon evening's shadows
descended. Then most piteously they embraced each other,   1290
made their farewells with tears, before each went his separate way
to lie down in the sand and render up his spirit.
So they scattered hither and thither to their lonely
resting places, and then, heads muffled in their mantles,
foodless and fasting, lay there that whole night through   1295
and on past sunup, awaiting a wretched death. But the women,
separately huddling together, lamented around Medeia.
As when unfledged chicks, left all alone after tumbling
from their hollow cleft in the rocks, keep up a shrill cheeping,
or when, on the overhang, above that mighty river   1300
Paktólos, swans raise their cry, and all around
echoes ring from the dew-bright meadows and the river's fair waters,
so these women, befouling their tawny manes in the dust,
night long lamented, piteously wailing.
And indeed they'd have all been sundered from their lives there,   1305
nameless and blotted out from mankind's knowledge,
those bravest of heroes, their enterprise unfinished;
but their helplessness, their diminution of stature
stirred pity in Libya's guardian-heroines, who
long ago, when Athena sprang gleaming from her father's head,   1310
met her, and bathed her in the waters of Lake Triton.
It was high noon, and Libya was being roasted
by the sun's keenest rays. They gathered beside Jason,
and with their hands gently drew the mantle from his head.
But he turned his eyes away in the other direction   1315
out of awe for these deities; for he alone could see them,
and in his confusion they spoke soothing words to him:
"Poor wretch, why so stricken by absolute helplessness?
We know how you went in quest of the Golden Fleece; we know
the whole tally of your ordeals, all the superhuman   1320

deeds you've performed, both on land and in your sea wanderings.
We are sheep-herding desert goddesses, voiced like mortals,
Libya's guardian-heroines, and her daughters.
Now get yourself up—enough of this sniveling self-pity—
and rouse your companions. As soon as Amphitríté   1325
unyokes the swift-running chariot of Poseidon,
then must you offer full recompense to your mother
for all the long pains she suffered while carrying you
in her belly; and so you'll get home to your hallowed Achaia."
Thus they spoke, and faded from sight where they stood, their voices   1330
dwindling away into silence. Then Jason, casting
his eyes about as he sat on the ground there, spoke as follows:
"Be gracious, great desert goddesses! Yet I cannot entirely
grasp your utterance on our homecoming: I shall assemble
my comrades, and tell it to them. Perhaps we'll discover   1335
some sign touching our route: many heads, better judgments."
With that he sprang up, grimy, sunburnt, and shouted loud
to his comrades, like a lion that goes roaring through the forest
after its mate; and away in the distant mountains
the glens resound to that deep and terrible voice,   1340
while the cattle out at pasture, yes, and their cattle herders
shiver in panic. To them, though, there was nothing alarming—
the voice was their companion's, summoning his friends—
and they gathered round him, dejected, and he made them
sit down, men and women together, by their vessel,   1345
a miserable group, and laid the whole matter before them.
"Listen, my friends: when I was despairing, a trio
of goddesses, clad in goatskins that reached from their necks
down over their backs and haunches, like human women,
came close, stood above my head, and tugged at my mantle   1350
with gentle hand, and uncovered me, and commanded
me to get up myself, and to go and rouse you,
and then to offer full recompense to our mother
for all the long pains she suffered while carrying us
in her belly, as soon as Amphitríté unyokes   1355
Poseidon's swift-running chariot. I have no notion
what this prophecy may portend. They said that they were
Libya's guardian-heroines, and her daughters;
and all we'd endured in the past, whether on dry land

or at sea, they declared they knew, in every detail.   1360
But I saw them no more where they stood, for a kind of mist
or cloud came between us, and made them invisible."
So he spoke; and all his listeners were filled with amazement.
And then the Minyans witnessed the strangest of portents:
out of the sea a monstrous horse sprang landward,   1365
gigantic, with golden mane flying high about his neck;
and lightly shaking the streams of brine from his quarters
set off at a gallop, wind-swift. Then straightway Peleus
announced, rejoicing, to his assembled companions:
"I believe that Poseidon's chariot has just, this moment,   1370
been unyoked by the hands of the god's own wife; and our mother,
I'd guess, is none else than this very vessel
we sail in: it's true she has us forever in her belly,
and groans at the troublesome labors to which we set her.
Now, with unflinching might and stubborn shoulders   1375
let's hoist her aloft and carry her to the interior
of this desert land, where the swift horse sped before us;
for he won't dive under the sand, and his tracks, I'm hoping,
will guide us cross-country to some inland sea lagoon."
So he spoke, and all favored his counsel, judged it apt.   1380

This story belongs to the Muses: I sing in obedience
to those Pierian ladies; and the tale I heard as true
was that you, O bravest by far of all scions of royalty,
through your strength, your endurance, did over the desert dunes
of Libya bear your vessel, and all the gear she carried,   1385
hoisted high on your shoulders, for a full dozen
days and nights on end.

         Of the agony and hardship
that they got in full suffering measure, who could reckon the tally?
Of immortal blood they most surely were, such an exploit
sheer need drove them on to perform: slogging on for ever   1390
till they got her, oh joy, to the waters of the Tritonian
lake, waded in, and lowered her from their massive shoulders.
Then, scattering like a pack of frenzied hounds, they went
in search of a spring, for besides all their suffering and anguish,
a parching thirst lay upon them: they did not dally   1395

along the way. So they reached that sacred plain, where Ládon,
old chthonian serpent, till yesterday had watched over
the apples of purest gold in Atlas's domain, while round him
nymphs, the Hespéridés, went to and fro, sweetly singing;
but when they arrived, he'd already been laid low by Herakles,   1400
and was stretched out against the trunk of the apple tree: only the tip
of his tail was still twitching, from his head down the whole length
of his dark spine he lay lifeless. Herakles' arrows
had left in his blood the rank poison of the Lernaian Hydra,
and on his putrefying wounds flies shriveled and died.   1405
The Hespéridés stood near him, heads cradled in their hands,
white against blonde, shrilly mourning. The Minyans approached them
suddenly, all together. The nymphs, at this quick movement,
instantly, on the spot, became dust and earth. But Orpheus
observed their divine magic, and stood and made them this prayer: 1410
"O fair and beneficent spirits, be gracious, ladies,
whether you're numbered among the goddesses of heaven
or those of the nether realm, or are known as the sheep-herding
desert nymphs: come, O nymphs, holy offspring of Ocean,
make yourselves manifest to us, reveal to our longing eyes   1415
some spring gushing out of the rock, some sacred river
bubbling up from the earth, O goddesses, with which we can slake
our burning insatiable thirst. If we ever make our way
back home in our voyaging to the land of Achaia,
then foremost among all goddesses you'll have our grateful   1420
offerings—gifts past counting, libations, banquets."
Such his prayer, spoken urgently; and at once the nymphs took pity
on their sufferings. From the earth they first of all made grow
seedlings; then from these seedlings there developed
long upward-reaching shoots, then verdurous saplings   1425
that shot up straight and tall, high above the earth:
Hespéré became a poplar, Erythéis an elm,
Aiglé the sacred stock of a willow. Then from these
tree forms they visibly changed back, became the same
nymphs as they'd been before, a rare marvel. Aiglé gave   1430
the heroes, in soft-spoken words, the response they'd hoped for:
"Sure it's a great help entirely to *your* troubles
that this shameless dog showed up here, reft away
our guardian serpent from life, stole the goddess's golden apples

and then took off, but *we've* been left with our hateful grief.   1435
So: it was yesterday that the stranger came, a killer
in physique and temper both, eyes aglint under shaggy brows,
ruthless, wearing the skin of an enormous lion,
all untanned rawhide; he had a stout olivewood club,
and arrows, with which he shot this creature to death.   1440
He too, like all foot travelers in this country,
was parched with thirst when he got here, stormed around everywhere
in search of water. It seemed that he'd never find it.
But there's a standing rock here, beside the Tritonian
lake, and he (did he think of it? did some deity prompt him?)   1445
kicked its base with his foot—and water gushed forth in abundance.
Then down he dropped, chest and both hands pressed in the dirt,
swilling great gulps from the rock-cleft, till he'd sated
his capacious belly, like some beast of burden."
So she spoke, and at once they rushed off, all excitement,   1450
till they found the welcome spring to which Aiglé had pointed the way;
and just as when round a narrow cleft there clusters
a mass of burrowing ants, or just as flies,
descending upon a small smear of sweet-tasting honey
swarm greedily over it—so now, all packed together,   1455
the Minyans jostled around the spring from the rock;
and one, lips all wet-slobbered, exclaimed in his delight:
"Odd chance: remote though he is now, Herakles has rescued
his comrades when they were done in with thirst! If only
we could find him, somehow, somewhere, on our overland journey!"   1460
With that, while they were talking, those best fitted for such a task
sped off on their quest, fanning out in all directions,
for tracks had been swept away by the night winds blowing
over the shifting sand. The two sons of Boreas
had confidence in their wings, while Euphémos relied on   1465
swiftness of foot, and Lynkeus on his farsightedness
and sharpness of vision. The fifth in the group was Kanthos,
driven to make this quest by the destined will of heaven
and his own valiant spirit, to find out from Herakles
just where he'd left Polyphémos, being determined   1470
to quiz him on every last detail about his comrade—
who in fact, after founding a far-famed Mysian city,
in hope of rejoining the quest had gone in search of *Argo,*

a lengthy overland trek, until he reached the country
of the maritime Chálybes; it was there that fate undid him,   1475
and under a tall white poplar his gravestone stands
looking out over the sea. But now only Lynkeus fancied
that he could see Herakles, off in the farthest distance,
the way a man, when the month's new, sees—or imagines
he sees—a sliver of moon through the obscuring clouds;   1480
and hurrying back to his comrades he said no further searchers
should set out: they'd not find him. So presently the others—
Euphémos, that swift runner, and the two sons of Thrakian
Boreas—returned, worn out and empty-handed.
But Kanthos, you the fell death spirits seized in Libya   1485
when you found those sheep out at pasture; they'd a sturdy
shepherd behind them, and when you tried to drive them
off for your hungry comrades, he, in defense of his flock,
laid you low with a sling stone, for he was no feeble creature,
this grandson of Phoibos of Delphoi, this Kaphaúros,   1490
whose mother, chaste Akakállis, Minos long ago
exiled to Libya, gravid with the god's burden,
his own daughter though she was; and she bore to Phoibos
a splendid son, whom they call Amphithémis and Gáramas.
Amphithémis in course of time took to bed a Tritonian   1495
nymph, who then bore him Násamon and Kaphaúros,
who now it was slew Kanthos while protecting his flocks.
Yet he did not escape the heroes' vengeful violence
when they learnt what he'd done. Then the Minyans recovered
Kanthos's rotting corpse, and gave it due burial   1500
with tears and great lamentation. The sheep they commandeered.
There, too, on that very same day, implacable destiny
took Mopsos, son of Ampykos: despite his prophetic skills
he did not escape a grim fate. Death remains ineluctable.
There lay in the sand dunes, avoiding the midday sun,   1505
a dangerous snake—too sluggish to strike unless provoked,
or to dart straight out at someone who backed away in terror:
but the moment its black poison entered any sentient creature
of all that life-giving earth provides with nourishment,
that creature's road to Hades would measure a cubit or less,   1510
even though Apollo the Healer—if I can speak openly—
should doctor it: the least bite would turn out fatal.

For when Perseus, the gods' equal, flew over Libya—
his mother also called him by the name of Eurymedon—
bringing back to the king the Gorgon's head, newly severed,   1515
every last drop of dark blood that hit the ground
generated a brood of those serpents. It was on the endmost
spine of its tail that Mopsos, striding forward,
stepped hard with the sole of his left foot, and the serpent,
writhing in agony round his leg bone and calf muscles,   1520
sank its fangs deep in his flesh. Medeia and her handmaids
fled in terror. But Mopsos palpated the bleeding wound
without discomposure, conscious of no great pain from it—
poor wretch—for already a paralyzing numbness
was spreading through his body, a thick mist veiling his eyes,   1525
and he slumped to the ground in an instant, limbs heavy and helpless,
while a deadly cold seized him. His companions gathered round,
Jason among them, amazed at such terrible destruction;
and once he was dead, he couldn't be left there lying
out in the sun, no, not one moment, for the poison   1530
rotted his flesh from within, his hair sloughed off as mush.
So at once they hurriedly dug out a deep grave
with their bronze mattocks, cut locks of hair in mourning,
both they and the women, in grief at the pitiable
fate of the dead man. Thrice, fully-armed, they marched   1535
around him with all due rites, heaped a high barrow over him.
Then a south wind blew over the sea, and quickly brought them
aboard their vessel. They set off, searching among the channels
for one that would take them out of the lake; but their efforts
were mere guesswork; all day long they sailed on aimlessly.   1540
As a snake writhes its coils along on a crooked track
when the rays of the broiling sun scorch it most fiercely,
and turns its head this way and that, and hisses, and its eyes
glint in its rage like fiery sparks, till at last
it slithers back into its lair though a cleft in the rockface—   1545
so *Argo*, in her vain quest for a navigable outlet
from the lake, advanced hither and thither, hour after hour. Then
     Orpheus
abruptly declared they should off-load Apollo's great tripod
to sweeten the local divinities, win a safe voyage home.
So they went, and set up ashore this offering to Apollo;   1550

and there met them—in the likeness of a young man in his prime—
wide-ruling Triton, who picked up a clod of earth
and offered it to the heroes as a guest-gift with these words:
"Take this, friends, since at present I have no better guest-gift
to put in the hands of those who may entreat me.   1555
But if it's the sea-lanes here that you're after, such as often
men need to know when traveling through foreign terrain,
I'll show you them, for my father Poseidon gave me
expert knowledge of these waters. My rule is over
the coastal region: perhaps even far away you've heard tell   1560
of Eurypylos, born here in Libya, home of wild beasts."
So he spoke, and Euphémos readily stretched out cupped hands
for the clod, and made him the following crafty reply:
"If you chance to know Apis, hero, and the Sea of Minos,
then truthfully answer the question that we ask you.   1565
For not willingly have we arrived here: it was the northern
storms that drove us within the borders of your country,
and then we carried our vessel to the waters of this lagoon
shoulder-high, overland, a sore burden; we've no knowledge
of how to reach open sea, win home to Pélops's land."   1570
So he spoke, and Triton pointed his hand to show them
the distant sea, and the lake's deep estuary, saying:
"Yonder lies the sea channel, where the water is deepest,
unstirring, almost black, and on either side white breakers
shimmer, translucent: midway between the breakers   1575
follow that narrow passage. It will bring you clear through.
The sea out there stretches far beyond Krété, haze-distant
to the sacred land of Pélops. When you've passed from the lake
to the chop of the open sea, then follow the coastline,
sailing close inshore for as long as it runs northward   1580
beside you; but when the landmass curves off, sloping
away to the east, then you'll have an uneventful voyage
if you sail straight out to sea from that long projecting headland.
Go now in joy: no complaints about heavy labor—
limbs fueled by youth shouldn't jib at working hard."   1585
At the end of this friendly speech they hastened aboard,
intent on rowing themselves clear of the lagoon,
and already, in their eagerness, had got under weigh when Triton,

humping the massive tripod, was seen (they thought) to enter
the lake; yet afterwards no one perceived how he vanished,   1590
tripod and all, and so close to them. But their spirits
were cheered by the good omen of having encountered
one of the blessed gods; and Jason, they said, should choose
the finest sheep as a sacrifice to him, chant his praises.
So at once Jason made a quick choice, lifted the victim over   1595
the stern, and then cut its throat, while uttering this prayer:
"Spirit, whoever you are, that appeared by this lakeside,
whether you're Triton the sea monster, or known as Phórkys
or Néreus by the daughters of the salty deep: be gracious,
grant what our heart most craves, to return home safely."   1600
With that prayer he cut the sheep's throat, dropped it over the stern
into the water. At that the god surged up from the depths
in his own person, assuming his true appearance.
As when a man leads out on the broad racetrack
a brisk yet docile colt, one hand in its shaggy mane,   1605
and quickly gets it trotting, neck proudly arched,
obedient to his lead, bit flecked with foam and jingling
responsively as the colt champs down on its steel ends—
so Triton, laying his hands to the stern post of hollow *Argo*,
thrust her on seaward. His body, from the crown of   1610
his head, down his back and flanks, as far as the belly
in shape was wondrously like those of the blessed gods;
but from under his loins there stretched a great sea-beast's tail,
forking this way and that. He thrashed the water's surface
with this spiny flail: its nether tip was divided   1615
into fins that curved like the horns of the crescent moon.
He drove the ship forward till they reached the sea, then set her
on course, and at once plunged into the depths. The heroes
cried out as they witnessed this uncanny portent. Here still
there's a Bay of Argo and memorials of their vessel   1620
and altars dedicated to Triton and Poseidon,
since for that day they rested up. But when dawn broke,
they ran on with bellying sails before a good west wind,
keeping that barren coastline to starboard. Next morning early
they sighted the promontory and the deep sea gulf   1625
that lay beyond the curve of the jutting headland.

At once, as the west wind dropped, the sirocco began to blow
from the southwest, and their hearts rejoiced to hear it.
But when the sun went down, and that shepherd's star
returned that brings respite to all weary ploughmen,   1630
then, after darkness fell, the sirocco died down,
so they struck the sails and lowered the lofty mast,
bent to their smooth-worn oars, and rowed doggedly on
all night long, and next day besides, and after that day another
full night. Remote Kárpathos, craggy and beetling,   1635
welcomed them. From here they planned to make the crossing
over to Krété, the outermost of all Aigaian islands.
But Talos, the man of bronze, by breaking off gigantic
rocks from the massy headland, stopped them from making fast their
mooring ropes ashore, there in Dikté's sheltered haven.   1640
This Talos was a survivor, of Bronze Age stock, folk descended
from ash trees, living now in the age of the demigods;
Zeus gave him to Európé to be the island's watchman,
and on brazen feet, thrice daily, to pace round Krété.
Now the rest of his body and limbs indeed were fashioned   1645
of bronze, and infrangible; but below his ankle tendon
there ran a vein, full of blood, and the delicate membrane
covering it determined the bounds between life and death.
So they, though worn out with fatigue, at once in terror
bent to their oars, backed the ship off from shore,   1650
and in sore distress would have voyaged far from Krété,
afflicted by thirst and exhaustion both, had not Medeia
cried out to them as they began their withdrawal: "Listen:
I believe that I alone can win the mastery for you
over this man, whoever he is, even if his whole body   1655
be fashioned of bronze—unless he should prove immortal.
So hold the vessel at large, out of range of his stone-throwing,
until he submits to me, concedes my mastery."
So she spoke, and they, having got out of missile range,
rested there on their oars, waiting to see what device   1660
she'd contrive against expectation. Covering both cheeks
with a fold of her purple mantle, she ascended
the after deck, and Jason, clasping her hand in his,
led her along the catwalk between the thwarts.

There with her spells she invoked, and placated, the death spirits,   1665
those eaters of life, swift hellhounds, that all around us
circle the air, to pounce upon living creatures.
Thrice now in supplication she besought them with spells,
thrice with prayers, then hardened her will with malice,
and with alien hostile gaze hexed bronze Talos's vision,   1670
teeth grinding in hate-filled wrath against him, while her vehement
fury assailed him with deadly hallucinations.

Zeus, Father, indeed great wonder stirs my spirit
that not only through wounds or disease should annihilation
meet us: some enemies, too, can crush us from a distance!   1675

So Talos, bronze though he was, conceded the mastery
to Medeia's far-reaching magic. While he was hefting
massive rocks to stop them reaching safe anchorage,
he scraped his ankle against a stony spur. The ichor
gushed out like melted lead. Not for long after   1680
did he still stand planted there on that jutting headland,
but like some gigantic pine, high up in the mountains,
that the woodmen with their keen axes have left half-severed
when they trudge back home from the forest, and first it's shaken
by gales of wind at nightfall, then finally, later,   1685
comes crashing down, snapped at the stump: so Talos awhile,
though swaying, held himself upright on unwearying feet,
but weakening at last, fell prone, with an enormous crash.
So that night indeed they bivouacked on Krété,
these heroes; but afterwards, at the first flush of dawn,   1690
when they'd erected a shrine to Minoan Athena
and taken on water, they quickly went aboard
to row out as soon as might be past Cape Salmónis.
But as they were running steady across the great Sea of Krété
night suddenly fell, a terror they call the Shroud of Darkness.   1695
This deadly night was too thick for starlight or moonbeams
to pierce, it came as a black void out of heaven,
or some other blackness, up from the nether depths.
For themselves, they had no notion whether it was in Hades
or on the sea that they were drifting: but still they entrusted   1700
their safe return to the sea, not knowing where it bore them.

Then Jason, hands outstretched, called loudly upon Phoibos
appealing for rescue, while down his agonized cheeks
tears ran. Gifts he promised past counting, he'd bring them
in bulk to the god's shrines—Ortygia, Pytho, Amyklai.   1705

Son of Leto, quickly you heard him, lightly you descended
from heaven to the Melantian rocks, that lie there
out in the deep, and springing on one of their twin peaks
in your right hand you brandished high your golden
bow, and all around it gave off a dazzling light.   1710

So now there was revealed to them one of the Spóradés,
a small island over against the tiny islet Hippoúris,
and here they cast anchor and landed. Very quickly the dawn
came up, bringing light, and they built Apollo a splendid
shrine in a shady grove, and a pebbled altar,   1715
and because of the far-beamed radiance they invoked him as Phoibos
the Radiant, and that rocky island they named Anáphé,
"Revelation," since in their distress Apollo revealed it to them.
They sacrificed such things as men on a desolate beach
could provide for sacrifice; but when they poured libations   1720
of water on blazing faggots, then Medeia's
Phaiakian handmaids, seeing them, could no longer
hold back the laughter that rose within them, so frequent
the sacrifices of oxen they'd seen in Alkínoös's halls.
The heroes scoffed back at them with indecent language,   1725
reveling in the joke, flared up, flung scurrilous insults,
exchanged mockery, all in fun. Because of the heroes' sport,
on that island women still contend against the menfolk
in such raillery, when with their offerings they propitiate
Apollo the Radiant, the guardian of Anáphé.   1730
But when from here too they'd cast off, in calm clear weather,
Euphémos then remembered a dream he'd had that night,
with reverence for Maia's glorious son. It seemed to him
that the god-given clod he held tightly against his breast
was being drenched with streams of white milk, and changing its
    substance,   1735
small though it was, into a living woman,
most like a young virgin, and he lay with her in passion,

aroused uncontrollably; finished, he wept, as though it were
his daughter he'd bedded, whom he was nursing with his milk.
But she addressed him with words of kindly comfort: 1740
"Triton's offspring I am, friend, nurse of your children,
no daughter of yours, for Triton and Libya are my parents.
Set me down in the keeping of Nereus's maiden daughters,
to dwell in the sea off Anáphé. In time hereafter
I'll return to the sun's rays, ready aid for your descendants."   1745
So Euphémos held these words in his heart, and told Jason
the whole business; whereat Jason, going over in his mind
those oracles of Apollo, sighed gently and answered him:
"My good friend, fate has willed you a great and splendid honor!
When you throw this clod into the sea, the gods will make it   1750
an island, and it shall be peopled by your children's
descendants, for Triton handed it to you as a guest-gift,
this piece of the Libyan mainland: it was he, and no other
immortal, who made you this present at your meeting."
So he spoke, and Euphémos did not reject Jason's answer,   1755
but took heart from the prophecy, hefted the clod and flung it
into the deep. From it there rose an island,
Kallísté, sacred nurse to the children of Euphémos—
who'd dwelt in former times in Sintian Lemnos,
then, driven out of Lemnos by Tyrrhenian warriors,   1760
reached Sparta as suppliant colonists; later they quit
Sparta, led by Théras, Autésion's noble son,
to this island, Kallísté. He changed its name to Thera
after himself. But by then Euphémos was long since gone.

From there, swift and steady, over long leagues of deep-sea swell,   1765
they made landfall on Aígina. Here instantly they quarreled,
harmlessly, over the drawing and fetching of water—
who could soonest get it and bring it back to the ship,
since that steady tailwind was blowing, and they longed for home.
There to this day, humping jars abrim with water,   1770
and sprinting against each other, light-footed, in competition,
the youths of the Myrmidons still strive after victory.

Be gracious, my heroes, race of the Blessed, and may these
songs of mine year by year be sweeter for men

to sing! For now I have reached the illustrious conclusion   1775
of your labors, since there befell you no further adventures
as you set sail from Aígina and continued your voyage;
no storms, no tempests opposed you; calmly you coasted
past the Kekropian shore, and Aulis, in the channel
beyond Euboia, and past the Opuntian cities of Lokris,   1780
and joyfully stepped ashore on the beach at Pagasai.

ABBREVIATIONS

Ael.	Aelian: Claudius Aelianus (Ailianos) of Praeneste, anecdotalist (c. A.D. 170–235)
	NA *De natura animalium* (On the Nature of Animals)
	VH *Vera historia* (True Stories)
Aisch.	Aischylos (Aeschylus), tragic poet (525/4–456 B.C.)
	Ag. *Agamemnon*
	Choeph. *Choephoroi* (Libation-Bearers)
	Eum. *Eumenides*
	Pers. *Persai*
	Prom. *Prometheus Bound*
	Sept. *Septem contra Thebas* (Seven against Thebes)
	Suppl. *Supplices* (Suppliant Women)
Alex. Com.	Alexis Comicus, playwright of the New Comedy (c. 375–c. 275 B.C.)
Antim.	Antimachos of Kolophon, epic poet (c. 444–c. 390 B.C.)
Ant. Lib.	Antoninus Liberalis, mythographer (? 2d cent. A.D.)
AP	*Anthologia Palatina*
Ap.	Apollonios Rhodios, epic poet (c. 300–c. 230 B.C.)
	Arg. *Argonautika*
Apollod.	Apollodoros, mythographer (c. 180–c. 110 B.C.)
	Epit. *Epitome*
Apul.	Apuleius of Madaura (C.A.D. 123–? c. 170)
	Met. *Metamorphoses*
Arat.	Aratos of Soloi (c. 315–240/39 B.C.)
	Phain. *Phainomena*

Arist.   Aristotle (384–322 B.C.)
            HA   *Historia animalium*
            Met.   *Meteorica*
            Mir.
            auscult.   *De mirabilibus auscultationibus* (On Marvelous
                          Things Heard)
            Poet.   *Poetics*
            Pol.   *Politics*
            Rhet.   *Rhetorica*

Aristoph.   Aristophanes, comic playwright (c. 450–c. 385 B.C.)

Arnob.   Arnobius of Sicca Veneria, Christian apologist (c. A.D. 270–?
            c. 330)

Artemid.   Artemidoros Daldianos, dream interpreter (late 2d cent.
            A.D.)
            Oneirocr.   *Oneirokrita*

Athen.   Athenaios of Naukratis, belle-lettrist (fl. c. A.D. 200)

Catull.   C. Valerius Catullus, lyric and elegiac poet (c. 84–c. 54 B.C.)

Cic.   M. Tullius Cicero, statesman and orator (106–43 B.C.)
            De div.   *De divinatione*
            ND   *De natura deorum*

Demetr.   Demetrios (identity and date uncertain)
            De eloc.   *De elocutione* (On Style in Oratory)

Diod. Sic. Diodoros Siculus, historian (c. 80–c. 20 B.C.)

Diog. Laert. Diogenes Laertius, philosophical biographer (? early 3d
            cent. A.D.)

Dracont.   Blossius Aemilius Dracontius, Christian poet (late 5th cent.
            A.D.)

Epigr.   *Epigram(s)*

Eratosth.   Eratosthenes, scientist and philosopher (c. 275–194 B.C.)
            Kat.   *Katasterismoi* (Catasterisms)

Etym. Gen. *Etymologicum Genuinum,* ed. G. Berger. Meisenheim am Glan,
            1972.

Etym. Magn. *Etymologicum Magnum,* ed. Thomas Gaisford. 1848. Amster-
            dam, 1967.

Eur.   Euripides (c. 485–406 B.C.)
            Bacch.   *Bacchai*
            El.   *Elektra*
            Hel.   *Helena*
            Hipp.   *Hippolytos*
            HF   *Hercules Furens*

IA	*Iphigenia in Aulide*
IT	*Iphigenia in Tauris*
Med.	*Medeia*
Orest.	*Orestes*
Phoin.	*Phoinissai*

Euseb.   Eusebius of Caesarea, Christian chronographer (c. A.D. 260–340)
       Hist. eccles.   *Historia ecclesiastica*

Eustath.   Eustathius, archbishop of Thessaloníké (12th cent. A.D.)

FGrH   *Fragmente der griechischen Historiker,* ed. F. Jacoby. Berlin, 1923–.

Hdt.   Herodotos of Halikarnassos, historian (c. 485–c. 425 B.C.)

Hes.   Hesiodos of Askra (Hesiod), epic poet (fl. c. 700 B.C.)
       Cat.   *Catalogues of Women (Ehoiai)*
       Scut.   *Scutum Herculis* (Shield of Herakles)
       Theog.   *Theogony*
       WD   *Works and Days*

HH   *Homeric Hymns*

Hippokr.   Hippokrates, physician
       AWP   *Airs Waters Places*
       Morb. Sacr.   *On the Sacred Disease*

Hippol.   Hippolytos, Christian apologist (c. A.D. 170–236)
       Ref.   *Refutatio omnium haeresium* (Refutation of All Heresies)

Hom.   Homer, epic poet (fl. ? late 8th cent. B.C.)
       Il.   *Iliad*
       Od.   *Odyssey*

Hygin.   C. Julius Hyginus (c. 50 B.C.–c. A.D. 20)
       Fab.   *Fabulae*

Kall.   *Kallimachos* (Callimachus) of Kyréné, scholar and poet
       Ait.   *Aitia*
       Dieg.   *Diegesis*
       H.   *Hymns*
       Iamb.   *Iambi*

Lobel-Page   *Poetarum Lesbiorum Fragmenta,* ed. E. Lobel and D. Page. Oxford, 1955

Louk.   Loukianos of Samosata (Lucian), sophistic writer (c. A.D.120–c. 185)
       Philopseud. *Philopseudes* (The Congenital Liar)

LSJ   H. G. Liddell and R. Scott, eds., *A Greek-English Lexicon.*

	9th ed., rev. H. S. Jones and R. Mackenzie, with supplement. Oxford, 1968.
Luc.	M. Annaeus Lucanus, epic poet (Lucan) (A.D. 39–65)
	Bell. civ. *Bellum civile (Pharsalia)*
Lucret.	T. Lucretius Carus, epic-philosophical poet (c. 94–c. 55 B.C.)
Lykophr.	Lykophron, tragic poet and scholar (c. 320–c. 280 B.C.)
Merkelbach-West	*Fragmenta Hesiodea,* ed. R. Merkelbach and M. L. West
Orph. Arg.	*Orphika Argonautika*
Ovid	P. Ovidius Naso, elegiac and epic poet (c. 43 B.C.–A.D. 17/8)
	Her. *Heroides*
	Met. *Metamorphoses*
	Fast. *Fasti*
	Tr. *Tristia*
P.	papyrus
Pf.	*Callimachus,* ed. R. Pfeiffer (Oxford, 1949–53)
P. Oxy.	Oxyrhynchus Papyrus
Pal.	Palaiphatos, paradoxographer (late 4th cent. A.D.)
Paus.	Pausanias, travel writer (fl. A.D. 150)
PGM	*Papyri Graecae Magicae,* ed. K. Preisendanz. 2 vols. Stuttgart, 1928–31. Rev. A. Henrichs, 1973–74
Pind.	Pindar of Thebes, lyric poet (518–438 B.C.)
	Isth. *Isthmian Odes*
	Nem. *Nemean Odes*
	Ol. *Olympian Odes*
	Pyth. *Pythian Odes*
Plat.	Plato, Athenian philosopher (c. 429–347 B.C.)
	Kratyl. *Kratylos*
	Phaidr. *Phaidros*
	Phileb. *Philebos*
	Rep. *Republic*
	Theait. *Theaitetos*
	Tim. *Timaios*
Pliny	C. Plinius Secundus, polymath and antiquarian (A.D. 23/4–79)
	NH *Naturalis historia*
Plout.	Ploutarchos of Chaironeia (Plutarch), biographer and essayist (c. A.D. 45–c. 125)
	Dem. *Life of Demosthenes*
	Lucull. *Life of Lucullus*

Mor.	*Moralia*
Quest. conviv.	*Quaestionum convivialium libri iii* (Dinner-table Problems: 3 books)
Thes.	*Life of Theseus*
PMG	*Poetae Melici Graeci*. Oxford, 1962.
Ps.-Skylax	(?) Skylax of Karyanda, geographer (fl. c. 500 B.C.)
	Peripl. *Periplous* (Circumnavigation)
schol.	scholion or scholiast
Solin.	C. Julius Solinus, geographer (fl c. A.D. 200)
Soph.	Sophokles (Sophocles), tragic playwright (c. 496–406/5 B.C.)

Aj.	*Ajax*
Ant.	*Antigoné*
OC	*Oedipus Coloneus* (Oidipous at Kolonos)
OT	*Oedipus Tyrannos*
Trach.	*Trachiniai*

Stat.	P. Papinius Statius, epic poet (c.A.D. 45–96)
	Theb. *Thebaïs*
Steph. Byz.	Stephanos of Byzantion, grammarian (5th cent. A.D.)
Suet.	G. Suetonius Tranquillus, writer and imperial civil servant (c. A.D. 69–130)
suppl.	supplement(um)
Theokr.	Theokritos (Theocritus), bucolic poet (c. 300–c. 260 B.C.)
	Id. *Idylls*
Theophr.	Theophrastos of Eresos (c. 370–288/5 B.C.)
	HP *Historia plantarum* (Botanical Studies)
Thouk.	Thoukydides (Thucydides), Athenian historian (c. 455–c. 395 B.C.)
Tib.	Albius Tibullus, elegiac poet (c. 50–19 B.C.)
Val. Flacc.	C. Valerius Flaccus, epic poet (? c. A.D. 60–92/3)
	Arg. *Argonautica*
Virg.	P. Vergilius Maro (Virgil) (70–19 B.C.)
	Aen. *Aeneid*
	Georg. *Georgics*
Xen.	Xenophon, Athenian historian (c. 428/7–c. 354 B.C.)
	Anab. *Anabasis*
	Kyn. *Kynegetika*
	Mem. *Memorabilia*

SELECT BIBLIOGRAPHY

Note: Works that I have found of use and interest but do not specifically cite are listed without a short title.

Beye 1982 ——. *Epic and Romance in the "Argonautica" of Apollonius.* Carbondale, Ill., 1982.

Blum Blum, R. *Kallimachos: The Alexandrian Library and the Origins of Bibliography.* Trans. H. H. Wellisch. Madison, Wis., 1991.

Blumberg, K. W. *Untersuchungen zur epischen Technik des Apollonios von Rhodos.* Diss., Leipzig, 1931.

Braswell Braswell, B. K. *A Commentary on the Fourth Pythian Ode of Pindar.* New York, 1988.

Buffière 1956 Buffière, F. *Les Mythes d'Homère et la pensée grecque.* Paris, 1956.

Burkert Burkert, W. *Greek Religion.* Trans. John Raffan. Cambridge, Mass., 1985.

Cameron Cameron, A. *Callimachus and His Critics.* Princeton, 1995.

Carspecken Carspecken, J. F. "Apollonius Rhodius and the Homeric Epic." *Yale Classical Studies* 13 (1952): 33–143.

Clauss 1993 ——. *The Best of the Argonauts: The Redefinition of the Epic Hero in Book One of Apollonius' "Argonautica."* Berkeley, 1993.

Delage 1930b ——. *Biographie d'Apollonios de Rhodes.* Bordeaux, 1930.

Dowden Dowden, K. *The Uses of Greek Mythology.* New York, 1992.

Eichgrün, E. *Kallimachos und Apollonios Rhodios.* Diss., Berlin, 1961.

Feeney Feeney, D. C. *The Gods in Epic: Poets and Critics of the Classical Tradition.* Oxford, 1991.

Finley   Finley, M. "Myth, Memory and History" = ch. 1 (pp. 11–33) of *The Use and Abuse of History.* London, 1975.

Fränkel 1968   ———. *Noten zu den Argonautika des Apollonios Rhodios.* Munich, 1968.

Fraser   Fraser, P. M. *Ptolemaic Alexandria.* 3 vols. Oxford, 1972.

Frazer   Frazer, J. G. *Apollodorus: The Library.* 2 vols. Cambridge, Mass., 1921.

                  Friedländer, P. "Kritische Untersuchungen zur Geschichte der Heldensage: I, Argonautensage." *Rheinisches Museum* 69 (1914): 299–317.

Fusillo   Fusillo, M. *Il tempo delle Argonautiche: Un'analisi del racconto in Apollonio Rodio.* Rome, 1985.

Green 1993   ———. *Alexander to Actium: The Historical Evolution of the Hellenistic Age.* 1990. 2d rev. printing. Berkeley, 1993.

                  Hadas, M. "The Tradition of a Feeble Jason." *CPh* 31 (1936): 166–68.

Händel   Händel, P. "Die zwei Versionen der Viten des Apollonios Rhodios." *Hermes* 90 (1962): 429–43.

Herter
1942a   Herter, H. "Beiträge zu Apollonios von Rhodos." *Rheinisches Museum* 92 (1942): 226–49.

Herter
1942b   ———. "Zur Lebensgeschichte des Apollonios von Rhodos." *Rheinisches Museum* 91 (1942): 310–26.

Herter
1944–55   ———. "Bericht über die Literatur zur hellenistischen Dichtung seit dem Jahre 1921. II: Apollonios Rhodios." *Bursians Jahresbuch* 285 (1944–55): 213–410.

Herter
1973   ———. "Apollonios, der Epiker." In A. Pauly, G. Wissowa, W. Kroll, and K. Ziegler, *Real-Encyclopädie d. klassischen Altertumswissenschaft* (Stuttgart, 1894–Munich 1978), supp. 13 (Munich, 1973), cols. 15–56.

Hunter
1987   ———. "Medea's Flight: The Fourth Book of the *Argonautica*." *Classical Quarterly* 37 (1987): 129–39.

Hunter
1989a   ———. *Apollonius of Rhodes: "Argonautica" Book III.* Cambridge, 1989.

Hunter
1993   ———. *The "Argonautica" of Apollonius: Literary Studies.* New York, 1993.

Huxley   Huxley, G. L. *Greek Epic Poetry from Eumelos to Panyassis.* London, 1969.

Mooney   Mooney, G. W., ed. *The "Argonautica" of Apollonius Rhodius* With introd. and commentary. London, 1912. Repr., Amsterdam, 1964.

Murray   Murray, O. "Herodotus and Oral History." In *Achaemenid History,* vol. 2: *The Greek Sources,* ed. H. Sancisi-Weerdenburg and Amélie Kuhrt, 93–115. Leiden, 1987.

Nestle   Nestle, W. *Vom Mythos zum Logos: Die Selbsentfaltung des Griechischen Denkens von Homer bis auf die Sophistik und Sokrates.* 2d ed. Stuttgart, 1942. Repr., Aalen, 1966.

Palombi, M. G. "Eracle e Ila nelle *Argonautiche* di Apollonio Rodio." *Studi classici e orientali* 35 (1985): 71–92.

Paskiewicz, T. M. "Aitia in the Second Book of Apollonius' *Argonautica.*" *Illinois Classical Studies* 13.1 (1988): 57–61.

Pfeiffer   Pfeiffer, R. *History of Classical Scholarship from the Beginnings to the Hellenistic Age.* Oxford, 1968.

———. *Callimachus.* 2 vols. Oxford, 1949–53.

Romm   Romm, J. S. *The Edges of the Earth in Ancient Thought: Geography, Exploration, and Fiction.* Princeton, 1992.

Rusten   Rusten, J. S. *Dionysius Scytobrachion* [*Papyrologica Coloniensia,* 10]. Opladen, 1982.

Sainte-Beuve, C. A. "De la Médée d'Apollonius." 1845. Repr. in *Portraits contemporains,* 5: 359–406. 4th ed. Paris, 1882.

Segal   Segal, C. *Pindar's Mythmaking: The Fourth Pythian Ode.* Princeton, 1986.

Severin, T. *The Jason Voyage: The Quest for the Golden Fleece.* New York, 1985.

Smiley   Smiley, M. T. "The Quarrel between Callimachus and Apollonius." *Hermathena* 17 (1912–13): 280–94.

Vian 1974   Vian, F., and E. Delage. *Apollonios de Rhodes: "Argonautiques."* Vol. 1. Paris, 1974.

Vian 1980   ———. *Apollonios de Rhodes: "Argonautiques."* Vol. 2. Paris, 1980.

Vian 1981   ——— *Apollonios de Rhodes: "Argonautiques."* Vol. 3. Paris, 1981.

Wendel   Wendel, C. *Scholia in Apollonium Rhodium vetera.* 2d ed. Berlin, 1958.

Ziegler   Ziegler, K. *Das hellenistisch Epos: Ein vergessenes Kapital griechischer Dichtung.* Leipzig, 1934. 2d ed., Leipzig, 1966.

GLOSSARY

NOTE: Names in boldface refer to other entries in the Glossary. The names of Argonauts are preceded by an asterisk (*).

Abantian:	Epithet of the island of **Euboia,** from the name (**Abantes**) of one of its early tribes (see also **Abas**).
Abarnis:	A city in the **Hellespont,** near Lampsakos.
Abas (1):	An **Euboian,** father of *****Kanéthos.**
Abas (2):	An **Argive,** reputed father of *****Idmon.**
Abydos:	City by the **Hellespont,** opposite Sestos, on the **Mysian** coast. Notable as the point from which Xerxes launched his invasion of Greece, and Alexander of Macedon began his conquest of the Persian empire; also in myth as the starting-point of Leandros's ill-fated swim to visit his lover Hero on the further shore. The two cities stand at the narrowest point of the **Hellespontos.**
Achaia, -an:	Mostly used as a synonym for "Greece" or "Greek" in general; but at 1.177 refers to the historical Achaia in the northern Peloponnesos.
Acheloös, R.:	A long river (still the largest in all Greece), the Acheloös has its source in Epeiros and runs south through mountain gorges for 150 miles, forming the frontier between Akarnania and **Aitolia,** and debouching into the Gulf of Corinth.
Acheron, R. (1):	One of the subterranean rivers in **Hades** (q.v.), located in S. Epiros (1.644).
Acheron, R. (2):	A river (also connected with the Underworld) near Herakleia in **Bithynia** (2.355, 743, 901).
Acherousia, -an:	The name of a prominent headland (mod. Eregli), and its surrounding territory, in what was later known as **Bithynia:**

located by Ap. between the territories of the **Mariandynians** and the **Paphlagonians.**

Achilles: Son of *****Peleus** and **Thetis.** "Flamed" by **Thetis** as a baby (4.868–76); subsequently reared by **Cheiron.** The main character in Homer's *Iliad,* and the slayer of Hektor. Destined after his death to become the husband of **Medeia** in **Elysion** (4.811 ff.).

*****Admétos:**   Argonaut, founder and king of **Pherai** in Thessaly. Famous on two counts: (a) as the monarch whom **Apollo** was forced to serve for a year after slaying the **Kyklopes,** and (b) for persuading his wife Alkestis to die in his place (cf. Euripides' play *Alkestis*).

Adrasteia (1):   A city and plain of **Hellespontine Phrygia,** to the west of **Kyzikós** (see map).

Adrasteia (2):   The **Kretan** nymph who nursed **Zeus** in a cave on **Mt. Ida** and gave him a beautiful ball (3.133 ff.) as a toy.

Agaméstor: A local hero of Herakleia Pontika, in the (**Phrygian**) territory of the **Mariandynians** (2.850).

Agénor: Father of **Phineus** and **Kadmos,** son of **Poseidon** and **Libya.** He was also the father of **Európé;** when she was abducted by **Zeus,** he sent his sons in search of her, and ordered them not to return empty-handed. Since **Európé** was nowhere to be found, the sons all settled in foreign countries.

Aia: Originally an early name for the whole area afterwards known as **Kolchis** (q.v.), but for Ap. and later writers the chief city of **Kolchis,** and **Aiëtés'** capital.

Aiaia: Originally regarded as an island, but afterwards a cape of Latium, Monte Circeo, in the **Tyrrhenian** sea, the traditional home of **Kirké.**

Aiakos: Son of **Zeus** (by **Európé** or **Aigina**) and after his death one of the three judges in **Hades.**

Aiëtés: King of **Kolchis,** a son of **Helios** the Sun God; father (by **Asteródeia**) of **Apsyrtos,** and (by **Eidyia**) of **Chalkíope** and **Medeia.** Subsequent to the events of the *Arg.,* he was, according to tradition, deposed by his brother **Perses,** but later restored either by **Medeia** or, more probably, by her son Medos (whose father was Aigeus, whom she married in Athens): Apollod. 1.9.28.

Aigaian: The Aegean; that section of the Mediterranean Sea within the circle of mainland Greece, **Kréte** (Crete), and the western coast of Turkey.

Aigaíon: An **Euboian** giant whom **Poseidon** pursued to **Phrygia** and buried under the island of Besbikos: schol. 1.1165c–d, cf. Vian 1974, 105, n. 2. Besbikos is in fact not all that near the estuary of the **Kios R.,** which formed the Argonauts' immediate landfall (1.1179).

Aigaios: A river, and river god, of **Phaiakia,** father of various nymphs and, in particular, of the Naiad **Melíté** (q.v.).

Aigialos (1): Ancient name ("The Coast") of Peloponnesian **Achaia** (q.v.).

Aigialos (2): See **Long Beach.**

Aígina: An island in the Saronic Gulf, near Athens: originally known as Oinóné, but renamed after Aigina (daughter of the **Asopos R.**), who gave birth there to **Aiakos** (q.v.).

Aiglé: One of the three (sometimes four) **Hespéridés** (q.v.): metamorphoses herself into a willow, 4.1428. Cf. Apollod. 2.5.11.

Aígyptos: Egypt, synonymous for the Greeks with hoary antiquity. The Land of the **Nile** was at once a source of wonder and nervous ridicule (the Greek words for ostrich, crocodile, obelisk, and pyramid originally signified, respectively, sparrow, wall lizard, cooking spit, and a small, pyramidally shaped, bun). Ap.'s reference (4.267–71) to this 'Land of Mists' emphasises the antiquity.

Aineios: Son of **Apollo** and Stilbé: a **Thessalian** who migrated to the **Hellespontine** area and married **Ainété,** daughter of **Eusóros,** king of **Thraké,** by whom he had **Kyzikós** (2) (q.v.).

Ainété: See s.v. **Aineios.**

Aiolos (1): Son of Hellen, king of the **Aiolian** regions "about **Thessalia**" (Apollod. 1.7.3), and father of **Athamas** and **Krétheus,** whose descendants were known as the **Aiolids,** and included *Idmon, Melampous, Minyas,** and **Phrixos.**

Aiolos (2): Son of **Hippótas** and king of the **Aiolian** islands: in Homer, as for Ap., the Lord of the Winds, and (according to some accounts) the great-great-grandson of (1).

Aísepos R.: The largest river of **Aigaian Mysia,** perhaps forming its eastern boundary: it rises in the Kotylos range of **Mt. Ida** and flows northward into the **Propontis** between **Adrasteia** and **Kyzikós.**

Aison: Son of **Krétheus** and father of *Jason. When news came of the return of the **Argonauts,** he was forced to commit suicide by **Pelias** (q.v.).This act was the reason why, by way of revenge, **Medeia** afterwards tricked **Pelias'** daughters into chopping their father up and boiling him, in the belief (which she fostered with some trickery) that this process would make him immortal.

Aisónis: According to schol. 411, the ancient name of "a city in **Magnesia,**" Greece, named after **Aison** (q.v.): the natural inference is that **Iolkos** is meant, since **Aison** was ruler over that city when deposed by **Pelias.** Vian (1974, 251) claims that the schol. identifies it *as distinct from* **Iolkos,** but this is not true: the text simply places **Aisónis** in **Magnesia,** without further comment.

Aithália: The ancient name for the island of Elba, in the **Tyrrhenian Sea.**

	The **Argonauts,** like Napoleon, left evidence (4.654–58) of their presence there.
*Aithálides:	Son of **Hermes** and **Eupolemeia,** half-brother of *Echion and *Erytos, and herald of the **Argonauts.** His father gave him the gift of perfect memory; he also enjoyed the privilege of residing alternately in the upper and nether worlds, and thus became associated with Pythagorean metempsychosis.
Aitolia, -an:	Though its precise boundaries fluctuated during the course of history, **Aitolia** was, basically, that territory on the north side of the Gulf of Corinth lying immediately east of Akarnania and west of Ozolian **Lokris** (see map 1), and bounded on the north by the land of the **Dolopians.**
Akakállis:	A daughter of **Minos,** whose name was apparently **Krétan** for "narcissus" (Athen. 15.681e; Hesych., s.v. ἀκακαλλίς), and who bore various sons by both **Hermes** and **Apollo.** See F. Frost, "Akakallis, a Divinity from Western Crete," *AncW* 27 (1996), 54–57, for a full conspectus of sources. As he nicely remarks, "the fate of Akakallis . . . is always to flee an angry father, and bear children in hiding, children who will found cities."
*Akastos:	A son of **Pelias,** but nevertheless an **Argonaut,** he also was one of the select band who participated in the great Calydonian boar hunt. It was his sisters whom **Medeia,** after the return of the expedition, persuaded to cut up and boil their father in the hope of rejuvenating him, and *Akastos himself who exiled both **Medeia** and *Jason from **Iolkos** as a result. At the funeral games of **Pelias,** the wife of *Akastos (Astydámeia or Hippólyté) fell in love with *Peleus, and when he rejected her advances accused him to her husband of attempted rape. *Akastos went out hunting with *Peleus, waited till he was asleep, then re-moved his weapons and left him. *Peleus survived an attack by the **Kentauroi,** but was rescued by either **Cheiron** or **Hermes,** returned, and killed both *Akastos and his wife. The *Nachleben* of individual **Argonauts** can be instructive.
Akmon:	Brother of **Doias** (q.v.): gave his name to the "**Akmonian** plain" in Asia Minor, where **Ares** had intercourse with **Harmonia.** **Akmon** was probably (Vian 1974, 224) a son of the Lydian deity Manes.
Aktor (1):	A **Lokrian,** brother of Phylakos, and, by **Aígina,** father of *Menoitios and grandfather of Patroklos.
Aktor (2):	A **Lokrian,** or **Phthiotian,** son of **Myrmidon** and Peisidiké, father of **Iros** and grandfather of **Eurytion** (q.v.).
Aktor (3):	The father of **Sthénelos** (2.911 ff.): his provenance and geneal-ogy are quite uncertain.
Aleos:	King of **Tegea** in Arkadia: by Neaira, the father of *Amphí-

damas, *Kepheus, and Lykourgos, whose son *Ankaios went on the expedition in his father's place, despite his grandfather's attempt to prevent this by hiding his armor.

Alkimédé: Daughter of Phylakos and Minyas's daughter Klymené; married to Aison (q.v.), and by him the mother of Jason.

Alkínoös: King of Drépané (i.e., Phaiakia, or Scheria), and grandson of Poseidon; married to Arété, by whom (subsequent to the action in *Arg.*; cf. Hom. *Od.*) he had five sons, and one daughter, Nausikaä.

Aloeus: A son of Poseidon and Kanaké, who by Iphimedeia had two sons, the giants Otos and Ephialtes.

Amantes: Inhabitants of an area of Illyria south of Apollonia in the Keraunian mountains (the "Thunderers"), near the Kolchian foundation of Orikon (q.v.).

Amarantes, -ian: A Kolchian tribe; the Amarantian mountains, probably to be located in Armenia, contained the source of the Phasis R.

Amazons, -onian: A mythical tribe of female warriors, ruled by sister queens, Hippolyté and Antíopé (2), daughter of Ares (qq.v.), and supposedly occupying an area around Themískyra and the Thermodon R. in the Kaúkasos, near Trapezous (modern Trebizond). The Thermodon had its source in the (probably mythical) "Amazonian mountains" (Strabo 11.5.4, C. 504).

Ambrakia, -an: A city on the north shore of the Ambrakian Gulf, on the west coast of mainland Greece between Epeiros and Akarnania. The inhabitants of the city and region were Ambrakians or Ambrakiots.

Amnisos: A town and river in Krété, near Knossós. Eilithyia, the goddess of childbirth, later identified with Artemis, had a cult there in a cave from Mykenaian times onward.

*Amphídamas: Argonaut, the son of Aleos (q.v.).

*Amphion (1): Argonaut, the son (with *Asterios) of Hyperásios, of Pelléné in Achaia, the town founded by their grandfather, the eponymous Pellen, on the heights of Aigialos (q.v.). A similarly eponymous town of Hyperásié (later Aigeiros) is also known.

Amphion (2):   Son of Zeus and Antíopé (1), and twin brother of Zéthos. The two brothers were responsible for building the walls of Thebes: when Amphion played his lyre, the stones magically moved into place and fitted themselves together. Amphion married Niobe: their numerous children were shot to death by Artemis and Apollo, the children of Leto, because both Niobe and her husband (who later suffered for it in Hades) had compared Leto and her two offspring unfavorably with their own brood.

Amphithémis: The Libyan son of Akakállis (q.v.): also known as Gáramas. By the nymph Tritonis, he became the father of Kaphaúros and of **Násamon,** the eponymous ancestor of the Nasamones, a **Libyan** tribe, and was himself the eponymous founder of the Garamantes, who occupied the interior of **Libya,** modern Fezzan (Vian 1981, 198), with their capital at Garama (Djerma).

Amphitríté: A Nereid or Oceanid who became the wife and charioteer of **Poseidon** and the ruling goddess of the sea. When her husband turned his amorous attentions to **Skylla** (q.v.), the ingenious **Amphitríté** poisoned the lady's well, thus metamorphosing her into the six-headed, twelve-footed monster, which subsequently haunted the Straits of Messina, to the considerable annoyance of Odysseus and his crew, among others.

Amphryssos R.: A minor river of **Thessalia,** flowing from **Mt. Othrys** into the Gulf of **Págasai,** and possessing a certain mythological *réclame* as the place where **Apollo** pastured the flocks of **Admetos** (q.v.) during his enforced servitude to that ruler.

Ampykos or **Ampyx:** A son of **Pelias** (interesting enough in itself), and, by Chloris (one of the only two children of **Amphion** and Niobe to escape the arrows of **Artemis** and **Apollo**), father of *Mopsos the seer. Such fascinating interrelationships do much to explain the obsession of Hellenistic scholars with aetiological and genealogical arcana in the field of myth. (Chloris, incidentally, got her name, which means, roughly, "the pale-green one," through having turned that color out of fright at her narrow escape from summary execution.)

Amyklai: A town of Lakonia, near Sparta, and in myth the home of **Tyndáreus** and of **Kastor** and **Polydeukes** (q.v., also n. to 2.40–43). It was famous for its shrine and statue of **Apollo.**

Amykos: Son of **Zeus** by the **Bithynian** nymph **Mélië,** and king of the Bebrykians. Ap. gives the fullest account of him. In some traditions, he is supposed to have invented, or improved, the leather thongs that served as boxing gloves in antiquity, but this may be no more than an inference from 2.58. The scholiast on 2.98 tells us (a view supported by the iconographic evidence) that **Polydeukes** did not kill the king but bound him to a tree—a laurel, as the Ficorini cist suggests, and an anecdote in Pliny *NH* 16.239 confirms. On **Amykos**'s tomb grew a laurel, the so-called *laurus insanus:* if a slip from this was taken aboard ship, it made the crew quarrel incessantly until it was thrown overboard.

Amymoné: A Danaïd, mother of **Nauplios** (1) by **Poseidon,** who rescued her from a satyr (met when she was out in search of water) only to ravish and acquire her himself. But at least he directed her to the wells of Lerna (Apollod. 2.1.4).

Amyros R.: A river in **Thessalia,** emptying into Lake Boibéïs, famous as the place where **Korónis** gave birth to Asklepios. Ap. (1.596, 4.616–17) wrongly identifies it as discharging into the **Aigaian.**

Anáphé:	A small **Aigaian** island in the southern **Spóradés,** due east of **Thera,** and celebrated for its temple (commemorating the event described at 4.1706–18) as the shrine of **Apollo** Aigletes ("the Gleamer"), at the eastern end of the island (ruins of this temple have been overlaid by the monastery of the Kalamiótissa).
Anauros R.:	A river of **Magnesia,** flowing down from **Mt. Pelion** past **Iolkos** into the Gulf of **Págasai.**
Anchíalé:	A nymph in **Krété** who gave birth to the **Idaian Daktyls.**
Angouron, Mt.	On the **Istros R.** (Danube), though the precise location is uncertain: perhaps to be identified with the mountains of the Iron Gates.
***Ankaios** (1):	**Argonaut,** son of the Arkadian **Lykourgos** (q.v.). He subsequently took part in the **Kalydonian** boar hunt and was killed by the boar.
***Ankaios** (2):	**Argonaut,** son of **Poseidon** by **Astypálaia** and king of the Leleges on **Samos.** Ap. clearly distinguishes between ***Ankaios** (1) and (2): see 1.163–71, 185–89. However, they seem to have been confused by some mythographers: though Ap. quite clearly has (2) succeed ***Tiphys** as steersman of Argo, Apollodoros (1.9.23) names (1) to this post, and the confusion is rendered worse by the fact that not only (1) but also (2) was killed by a wild boar. Indeed, the death of (2) gave rise to a famous proverb. It had been predicted that he would not live to taste the wine from his own vineyard; and when he was on the point of doing just that, with a sarcastic gibe at the prophet, news came of a wild boar ravaging the neighborhood, and he postponed his drink to deal with it. "Many a slip 'twixt the cup and the lip," the prophet called after him as he left; and of course he was killed. Lykophron, it hardly needs saying, relates this story when discussing (449) not (2) but (1).
Anthemoéssa:	The "isle of Flowers" where the **Sirens** dwelt. See n. on 4.892.
Antianeira:	The mother (by **Hermes**) of ***Erytos** and ***Echion** (qq.v.).
Antíopé (1):	Daughter either of **Nykteus** (q.v.) or of the river god **Asopos** in **Boiotia;** she became by **Zeus** the mother of **Amphion** and **Zéthos** (qq.v.).
Antíopé (2):	Queen of the **Amazons** (q.v.), who left them to marry **Theseus,** and bore him Hippolytos. When the **Amazons** invaded **Attica, Antíopé** fought and died at **Theseus**'s side. Notable in Ap. for the shrine she built on the isle of **Ares** (2.385–87).
Aonia:	The pre-Kadmean name of Boiotia.
Apháreus:	Brother of **Tyndáreus** and father of ***Idas** and ***Lynkeus** by **Aréné** (q.v.). **Apháreus** is said to have founded a town

in Messenia and named it after his wife. For the cattle-raiding quarrel between his sons and the **Dioskouroi,** see s.v. ***Idas.**

Apheidas: Lord of **Tegea** and father of **Aleos** (q.v.).

Aphétai: A port on the coast of **Magnesia,** so called, it was believed, because it marked the "departure point" of *Argo* (whatever that meant: see n. on 1.591).

Aphrodíté: See **Kypris.**

Apídanos R.: A river of **Thessalia,** the main tributary of the **Enipeus R.** Rising in the mountains of **Phthia,** the Apidanos, after joining the **Enípeus,** empties its waters into the main river of **Thessalia,** the **Peneios.**

Apis: Ancient name for the Peloponnesos: see n. to 4.1564.

Apollo: Major deity of the Olympian pantheon: son of **Zeus** and **Leto,** brother to **Artemis,** associated with flocks and herds (cf. s.v. **Admétos**), medicine, archery, the creative arts, especially music and poetry, and thus, by way of inspiration and the **Muses,** with divination, prophecy, and oracles. His oracular shrine at **Delphoi** was the most prestigious in the Greek world: he, and it, were truly international in the sense of being Panhellenic (he was also closely connected with colonization schemes). By Ap.'s day he had become the patron of intellectual thought generally: guarantor of law codes, favorite deity of philosophers. Originally his ties were to the north (see also s.v. **Hyperboreans**) and Asia (**Lykia**); his supposed association, or even identification, with the Sun seems to have no basis in fact, though it was widely believed in Hellenistic times—as his epiphany over **Thynia** (2.674–715) strongly suggests. Throughout *Arg.,* his favors to **Jason** and his comrades, though remote, remain constant, from encouraging **Delphic** oracles (e.g., 1.301–2, 411–14) to the revelation of **Anáphé** (4.1701–14).

Apsyrtos: Son of **Aiëtés** by **Asteródeia** (according to Ap.), though other sources give a variety of alternatives. Only one of these, however, Apollodoros (1.9.23), suggests that **Apsyrtos** had the same mother, **Eidyia,** as **Medeia.** He is thus to be regarded—certainly in Ap.'s version, and indeed widely elsewhere—only as **Medeia's** half-brother, and by a nymph at that (a point stressed by Sophokles in a lost play, probably the *Kolchian Women,* fr. 546 Pearson). It should be noted, further, that Ap.'s version of events, with **Apsyrtos** as a grown man, older than his sister, and **Aiëtés'** lieutenant and charioteer, is not, insofar as we can judge, the traditional one. It is, indeed, despite the murder, considerably less grisly than that found elsewhere, which (schol. 4.223–30a, d; cf. Apollod. 1.9.24) seems to go back to Pherekydes. There **Apsyrtos** is a mere child, whom **Medeia** cuts to pieces and strews in the wake of their ship to slow down **Aiëtés'** pursuit. This act of course gives added edge to **Aiëtés'** determination to recover his errant daughter, now not only a fugitive but also a murderer; no puzzle, either, as to why Ap. changed the story so radically, to make **Medeia** at worst an accomplice in the killing. To retain the audience's sympathy for her, even vestigially, would have been impossible had he followed Pherekydes' version. (Sophokles in *Kolchian Women*, fr. 343 Pearson, has **Apsyrtos** killed at home in the palace, but does not say by whom.) Note that those **Kolchians** who stayed on the islands and coast of the Adriatic rather than return home and face **Aiëtés'** wrath were known as Apsyrtians.

Araithyréa: The original city (afterwards Phlious) of Phliasia in the NE Peloponnesos, a pocket plateau to the west of Kleonai and Nemea, famous in Homer (*Il.* 2.571) for its vineyards, and watered by the **Asopos R.** (2) (q.v.).

Araxes R.: A river (now the Aras) rising in Armenia and flowing into the Kaspian Sea, until the late nineteenth century by way of the Kyros (Kur). Its relation to the Kyros, the **Lykos,** and the **Phasis** rivers was uncertain in antiquity, and this is certainly true of Ap.: for specific problems, see Commentary where relevant.

*Areïos: Argonaut, son of **Bias** and **Pero,** daughter of **Néleus.** Both **Bias** and ***Jason** were directly descended from **Krétheus,** through his sons Amythaon and **Aison** respectively, and thus were first cousins.

Aréné: Town on the west coast of the Peloponnesos, possibly the site of Samikón (mod. Kleidhí), and named after the wife of **Apháreus.** Two of their sons, ***Lynkeus** and ***Idas,** were Argonauts.

Ares: Son of **Zeus** and **Hera,** the chief war god of the Greeks, traditionally fierce and (in every sense) bloody-minded by nature, but not a central figure in *Arg.*, where his presence and existence are for the most part felt indirectly: e.g., when **Kypris** (Aphrodite) holds his shield (1.743) or **Aiëtés** receives from him the breastplate of **Mimas** (3.1225–27). Several times identified with place, e.g., the bird-haunted islet in the **Black Sea** (2.1031 ff.), the ploughland that forms the scene of ***Jason's** ordeal (3.1270), and the sacred grove where the Fleece is hung (2.1268–69). Cf. also s.v. **Harmonia** (1).

Arestor: There is a small puzzle here. Ap. clearly identifies **Arestor** (1.112, 325) as the father of ***Argos** (1) (q.v.), who was chiefly famous for having helped **Athena** to build *Argo*. He makes a very clear distinction between ***Argos** (1) and **Argos** (2), the son of **Phrixos** (q.v.). But Apollodoros (2.1.3) cites Pherekydes for **Arestor** having been the father of that **Argos** known as Πανόπτης, or "The All-Seeing," the guardian of Io; he also firmly identifies

Argos (2), the son of **Phrixos,** as the builder of *Argo* (1.9.16; cf. schol. Ap. 1–4e). It is possible, considering the dramatic use he made of **Argos** (2), as a character quite separate from the Argonauts, that this switch of responsibilities was deliberate: it seems hard to credit that, with so famous a figure of myth as *Argo's* builder, he would be guilty of simple confusion because the name was the same.

Arété: Sister of **Tyndáreus** (q.v.), queen of **Alkínoös** (q.v.), and better known from her appearance (quite a few years and six children later) in Homer's *Odyssey.*

Aretos: A **Bebrykian,** a boxing second to **Amykos,** killed by *Klytios in the battle following the latter's death at the hands of **Polydeukes.**

Arganthonios, Mt.:   A (variously named) mountain range on the east side of the **Propontis,** forming a peninsula (with a headland known in antiquity as Cape Poseideion) running out between two gulfs, those of Astakos in the north, and **Kios,** on the **Kios R.,** in the south (see map 2).

Argo: The fifty-oared vessel (pentekonter) built by ***Argos** (1) (q.v.; also s.v. **Arestor**) with the aid of **Athena,** who implanted a "speaking beam" into its forekeel, for the expedition undertaken by the **Argonauts** (Apollod. 1.9.16). According to one tradition (schol. Ap. 224–26b), **Aiëtés** commanded ***Argos** to peg the hull with weak dowels so that **Jason** and his crew would perish, but ***Argos** ignored the request. After the expedition, *Argo* was dedicated at the isthmus of Corinth (Apollod. 1.9.27). An earlier tradition (which Ap. has to avoid, but seems aware of: see 1.547 ff. and 4.316 ff., also s.v. **Arestor** above, and n. on 3.340–46) made *Argo* out to have been the first ship.

*Argos (1):   Argonaut, son of **Arestor** (q.v.), and co-builder with **Athena** of the expedition's vessel, *Argo.*

Argos (2):   Eldest son of **Phrixos.** The other three were **Kytíssoros, Melas,** and **Phrontis.** They were en route to **Orchómenos** to claim their inheritance when shipwrecked and rescued by the Argonauts. On both (1) and (2), see s.v. **Arestor,** above.

Argos (city):   Traditionally, the oldest city in Greece, situated about three miles from the sea on the Argive plain, and built—by "Pelasgians," as was believed— below the 900 ft. high acropolis called "Lárissa" (supposedly the Pelasgian term for a citadel). In the *Iliad,* **Argos** is the fief of Diomedes, who holds it from Agamemnon of **Mykenai.**

Ariadné: Daughter of **Minos** and **Pasiphaë,** and granddaughter of **Helios,** the sun god (as was **Medeia**). When **Theseus** came to **Krété** bringing the annual tribute for the Minotaur (**Ariadné's** half-brother), she fell in love with him, and he promised to marry her: she gave him the vital ball of thread that brought him safely out of the Labyrinth after he slew the Minotaur, and fled with him in his ship. But he abandoned her on **Dia** (Naxos). According to one tradition, **Ariadné** was herself killed there by **Artemis;** but the more popular version, used by Ap., has her rescued, and married, by **Dionysos,** who set her wedding crown among the stars as the Corona Borealis.

Aristaios: In the best-known tradition, followed by Ap., son of **Kyréné** (q.v.), a **Thessalian** nymph, granddaughter of the river god **Peneios,** and **Apollo.** Rival claims for his parentage include **Ouranos,** Kárystos, and **Cheiron;** the last-named is generally agreed to have reared him at **Apollo**'s bidding. **Aristaios** seems to have been an extremely ancient Greek—perhaps pre-Greek —pastoral deity, protector of herds and flocks as well as of vineyards and olive groves, averter of drought and burning heat waves. He was also supposed to have first instructed farmers in the art of bee-keeping. His cult was primarily associated with **Thessalia,** but he was also connected with **Boiotia, Arkadia,** and the islands of the **Aigaian,** in particular **Keos** (mod. Kea).

Arkadia, -an: The central state in the Peloponnesos and the largest after Lakonia. Ringed and traversed by mountains (it has been described as "the Switzerland of Greece"), Arkadia has always combined wild remoteness and backwardness (except for one narrow outlet on the W. coast, it is completely landlocked) with areas of great fertility and unspoilt beauty, which helped promote the literary notion of the area as a primitive Shangri-la. This view found confirmation in the tradition of Arkadians as autochthonous **Pelasgians** who referred to themselves as "antemooners" or "pre-selenic" ($\pi\rho o\sigma\acute{\epsilon}\lambda\eta\nu o\iota$), and who compensated for their lack of ordinary exports by regularly sending out their own able-bodied men as mercenaries.

Artákes: **Dolionian** warrior, killed by *****Meleágros.**

Artakia: A spring on **Kyzikós,** near modern Erdek.

Artemis: Daughter of **Zeus** and **Leto,** and twin sister to **Apollo** (q.v.): goddess of the forest, the chase, and wild beasts (probably, as Mistress of Beasts, $\pi\acute{o}\tau\nu\iota\alpha\ \theta\eta\rho\tilde{\omega}\nu$, originally Minoan in origin). Identified with various foreign deities, most notably with a bloodthirsty goddess in the Tauric **Chersonésos** (Crimea) who demanded human sacrifice of her devotees. Ap. introduces her only in indirect ways: as patron goddess of **Iolkos** and **Magnesia,** or as a hunting figure, by the banks of the **Parthenios** or **Amnisos** rivers (2.936–9, 3.877–84), to whom human protagonists are compared.

Asopos R. (1):   A river in the NE Peloponnesos, with its source in the mountains south of Phlious, which flows northward into the Gulf of Corinth through the territory of Sikyonia (1.117).

Asopos R. (2):   A river of southern **Boiotia,** formed by drainage from Kithairon and springs in the Plataian plain. It marked the ancient boundary between Plataiai and **Thebes.** Its course ran eastward by way of Tanagra, and it discharged into the sea near Oropos (1.735).

Asopos: The river god variously associated with both (1) and (2), and thus probably a conflation of two separate deities. Ap. mentions him as the father of **Antíopé** (1), of **Sínopé,** and of **Kérkyra:** the first two are associated with (1), the third with (2).

Assyria: For Ap., a coastal region on the southern shore of the **Black Sea,** extending from **Sinopé** in the west to **Themískyra** in the east: divided by the **Halys R.** and overlapping the loosely defined territory of the **Amazons.** It is the region occupied by the "Syrians" of Herodotos and later known as Kappadokia.

*Asterion: An **Argonaut** from **Thessalia,** son of **Kométes** and Antigone, daughter of Pheres. He took part in the funeral games for **Pelias.**

*Asterios: An **Argonaut** from **Pelléné,** son of **Hyperásios.**

Asteródeia: A nymph of the **Kaúkasos,** and first wife of **Aiëtés** (q.v.), to whom she bore **Apsyrtos.**

Astypálaia: Daughter of Phoinix and Perimédé, and sister to **Európé;** from **Samos.** By **Poseidon,** she became the mother of ***Ankaios** (2) (q.v.).

Atalanta: Daughter of Iasios and **Klymené.** Her father (who wanted a son) exposed her; she was suckled by a she-bear (associated with **Artemis**), and grew up a natural hunter, the swiftest of runners, and a great beauty. Though Ap. does not include her among the Argonauts, other sources (e.g., Apollod. 1.9.16, Diod. Sic. 4.48.5) do; she also took part in the **Kalydonian** boar hunt and the funeral games for **Pelias.** She married Melanion (who tricked her in the race she made him run against her—her hand if he won, his head if she did—by dropping three golden apples in her way: cupidity got the better of her); they were turned into lions for impiously coupling in the sacred grove of **Zeus.**

Athamas: Son of **Aiolos** (1) (q.v.) by Enarété, daughter of **Deïmachos:** his brothers included **Krétheus** and Sisyphos. By the nymph Nephélé ("Cloud"), he had **Phrixos** (q.v.) and **Hellé.** His passion for a mortal, Ino, led Nephélé to return to the gods and ask that he be sacrificed by way of atonement. Ino meanwhile, playing the wicked stepmother with gusto, tried to destroy **Athamas's** children by Nephélé, bribing messengers to the **Delphic** oracle to report, falsely, that **Phrixos** must be sacrificed. It was to preserve her children that Nephélé arranged for their miraculous removal to **Kolchis** on the Golden Ram. For the subsequent history of **Athamas,** see Apollod. 1.9.2.

Athena: Originally a pre-Hellenic protective goddess, **Athena** retained her close association with that function in Athens, as **Athena** Polias, guardian of the city on the Acropolis, her shrine occupying the site of the old Mykenaian palace. Virgin ("Parthenos") in tradition (a characteristic nicely exploited by Ap., 3.32–33), and born from **Zeus's** head (in **Libya,** 4.1309–11: hence the epithet **Tritonian,** q.v.), she was also a warrior goddess, a patroness of arts, crafts, and domestic skills, and, by association, a divine repository of wisdom. With **Hera** she acts as the **Argonauts'** strongest divine supporter in the *Arg.* She is the prime builder (cf. her epithet **Itonian**) of *Argo;* she helps to persuade **Kypris** to make **Eros** fire the fatal arrow of love into **Medeia;** she saves the Argonauts from being crushed by the **Clashing Rocks,** and is with **Hera** at the passage of the **Wandering Rocks.** But it was also she who collected the **Theban** dragon's teeth and gave half of them to **Aiëtés,** thus partly facilitating **Jason's** ordeal.

Athos, Mt.:   The extremity of the Akté peninsula, running out from Chalkídiké between the **Aigaian** and the Singitic Gulf: the headland rises in a sheer mountain some 6,350 ft. high. For the possibility that this peak at sunset could cast a shadow as far as **Lemnos,** see 1.602–4. The peninsula was famous in antiquity for the canal cut through it by Xerxes during his invasion of Greece in 480, and today for the monasteries— accessible only to males— that crowd the headland.

Atlas: A **Titan,** son of **Iapetos,** best known for his supposed role of supporting the sky, or its "pillars," and commonly associated with the Atlas Mountains in NW Africa. He was the father of the **Pleiades,** including **Elektra** (1.916), and of **Kalypso,** the nymph who entertained Odysseus on Ogygia (4.574–75). He was also connected with the **Hespéridés** (q.v.).

Attika: The roughly triangular area bounded on the east by **Euboia** and the **Aigaian,** on the west by the Saronic Gulf, on the north by the mountain ranges of Kithairon and Parnes, and with Cape Sounion as its southernmost point. Originally twelve independent regions, **Attika** became unified under the central control of Athens; according to myth, **Theseus** was responsible for this centralization (συνοικισμός), though in fact it was carried out by the Peisistratids.

*Augeias: Argonaut, of disputed parentage (by birth son of **Helios,** says the scholiast [1.172–73], but by common repute son of Phorbas and Hyrmine [*sic:* = Hermione]; several other possible putative mothers are known), king of the Epeians in **Elis.** Much better known as the proprietor of the stables and cattle pound that **Herakles** cleaned out as his fifth Labor. **Augeias** refused **Herakles** his promised reward, for which **Herakles** later killed him and his sons, and captured **Elis.**

Aulis: Ancient port on the east coast of **Boiotia,** about three miles south of Chalkís, facing **Euboia** across the Euripos channel, and chiefly famous as the site of Agamemnon's sacrifice of Iphigeneia in order to obtain a fair sailing wind to Troy for the Greek fleet.

Ausonia: Ancient Greek name for central Italy and the Campanian coast, which came to serve as a literary synonym for Italy as a whole.

Autesion: One-time king of **Thebes,** son of Tisamenos, great-grandson of Polyneikes, and father of **Théras** (q.v.). At the bidding of an oracle, he left **Thebes** and migrated to the Peloponnesos. His son was **Thevas** (q.v.).

Autolykos: Son of **Deïmachos,** brother of **Deïleon** and **Phlógios,** and founder of **Sinopé** (q.v.): the three accompanied **Herakles** against the **Amazons.** Some sources (but not Ap.) claim him as an Argonaut.

Bacchiads: A powerful, wealthy, aristocratic clan in Corinth during the archaic period. Originally one Bacchis, a supposed descendant of **Herakles** by way of the clan's Dorian "founder," Aletes, had made himself king and established a hereditary monarchy. In 747, the kingship was ended when strong royal relatives took over from a weak ruler, and ran Corinth as an aristocratic oligarchy, until ousted in 657 by the non-Dorian (but equally aristocratic) tyrant Kypselos.

Basileus: One of the **Doliónes** killed during the night action on **Kyzikós;** probably an eponymous hero (cf. 1.1047–48), and perhaps the ancestor of certain "Basileis" who later served there as priests of Perséphoné.

Bear Mountain: This title (in Greek Ἄρκτων Ὄρος, as Ap. calls it, or Ἄρκτων Νῆσος) represents the mountainous part of the island/isthmus of **Kyzikós** (q.v.), culminating in the peak of **Dindymon.**

Bebrykia, -ans: Some ancient sources locate **Bebrykia** on the NE coast of the **Propontis,** others on the south shore of the **Black Sea,** to the east of the **Bosporos** and the **Rhebas R.** A glance at the map shows that, as Delage 1930a saw (117–18), both are likely to have been right, with the **Bebrykians** occupying most of the **Bithynian** peninsula. Theokritos (22.27–29), in making the encounter with **Amykos** take place *after* the passage of the **Clashing Rocks,** is thus not as much in conflict with Ap.'s version as might appear at first sight. Their territory marched with that of the **Mariandynians,** and indeed, at the time of the Argonauts' visit, **Amykos** had extended his rule eastward at the latter's expense as far as the **Hypios R.** (2.791–95).

Becheirians: A barbarous coastal tribe of E. **Pontos,** situated by Ap. between the **Makrónes** and the **Sapeires.** Other sources seem to locate them further W, in the Trapezous area.

Bias: Son of Amythaon, brother to **Melámpous** (q.v.), and father of *Tálaos, *Areïos, and *Leódokos by **Pero,** daughter of **Neleus.** Since Amythaon was brother to **Aison,** both being the offspring of **Kretheus** and **Tyro,** while **Pero** was also, through her father, **Tyro**'s granddaughter, it follows that **Bias, Melámpous,** and **Pero** were all **Jason**'s first cousins. The Quest was more of a family affair than is sometimes recognized.

Billaios R.: A river of **Paphlagonia,** the modern Filiyos Çay, to the east of the tomb of **Sthénelos,** discharging into the **Black Sea** by the town of Tieion.

Bithynia, -an: For Ap., **Bithynia** was loosely equated with the Chalkedon peninsula, its coastline extending from the NE part of the **Propontis** to that part of the **Black Sea** immediately to the east of the **Bosporos.** Later it extended further E, to the western frontier of **Paphlagonia.**

Black Gulf: The arm of the **Aigaian** sea between **Thráké** and the **Thrakian Chersonesos** (Gallipoli Peninsula).

Black Headland: A promontary situated a little to the east of the **Rhebas R.** (q.v.) and the northern outlet of the **Bosporos.**

Black Kérkyra: Not modern Corfu, but rather the island of Korčula, to the north of Dubrovnik.

Black Sea: Identical with the ancient Pontos or Euxine: the great inland sea bounded in the west by **Thráké,** in the east by **Kolchis,** to the north by the Tauric Chersonesos (Crimea), and along its south coast by the various tribes, from **Bebrykians** to **Byzerians,** passed by *Argo* on her outward voyage.

Boreas: The embodied North Wind, generally associated with **Mt. Haimos** in **Thráké,** but also the husband (after rape) of the Athenian **Oreithyia,** daughter of **Erechtheus,** on whom he sired not only *Zétés and *Kalaïs, but also the **Kleopatra** who became the first wife of **Phineus** (q.v.).

Bosporos: The narrow channel linking the **Propontis** and the **Black Sea;** sometimes known as the **Thrakian Bosporos** to distinguish it from the **Kimmerian Bosporos,** in the Crimea, the latter being the strait between the **Black Sea** and the Maiotic Lake (Sea of Azov).

*Boútés: Argonaut, an Athenian, son of **Téleon** (2): there were at least four mythological characters of this name, and it seems probable that the one mentioned by Ap.—who was rescued from the **Sirens**' clutches by **Kypris** (Aphrodite), and taken to **Lilybéon** in Sikelia, where he sired **Eryx** on her—should be distinguished from the more famous son of Pandion and brother of **Erechtheus,** priest of **Athena** and **Poseidon Erechtheus** in Athens, and the reputed ancestor of the Eteoboutadai clan, though they are often confused.

Brygean Isles: A group of islands occupying the (supposed) Adriatic delta of the **Istros R.** (Danube), and sacred to **Artemis.**

Brygoi: Originally a **Thrakian** tribe dwelling in Makedonia, north of Beroia; some of them emigrated to the northern Balkans, and it is these whom Ap. has in mind.

Byzerians: A coastal tribe located somewhere east of Trapezous: for Ap., they are the last people passed by the **Argonauts** before reaching **Kolchis,** but their precise habitat remains quite uncertain.

Chadésians: One of the three tribes of **Amazons** (q.v.): they dwelt near the river Chadesios or Chadisia, from which they took their name, west of the **Thermodon** and **Iris** rivers. A town named Chadesia is also mentioned by our sources.

Chalkíope: Daughter of **Aiétés** and **Eidyia,** and elder (by a wide margin: see n. on 3.260–67) sister of **Medeia.** When **Phrixos** arrived in **Kolchis** after his escape on the magical Golden Ram, **Aiétés** gave him **Chalkíope** as a bride, and she bore him four sons: **Argos** (2) (q.v.), **Melas, Phrontis,** and **Kytíssoros.**

Chalkodonian Mts.: A range in **Thessalia,** otherwise unknown; possibly a single mountain called **Chalkodonion** or **Chalkodonios.** Delage 1930a (41) and Vian 1974 (241) tentatively identify it as the Kara-Dagh ("Black Mountain") massif dominating **Admetos*'s capital of **Pherai.**

Chálybes: A coastal tribe perhaps located near the **Thermodon R.** (their exact whereabouts was much debated in antiquity: see n. on 2.1000 ff.): famous for their mining and working of iron.

Charybdis: A famous whirlpool or maelstrom, on the Sikelian side of the strait between Messana (Messina) and Rhegion (Reggio), and best known from the description in bk. 12 of Homer's *Odyssey.*

Cheiron: A **Kentaur,** son of **Kronos** and **Phílyra** (Hes. *Theog.* 1001–2), preeminent for his sagacity: he was responsible for rearing various heroes, including **Achilles** and **Jason* himself. Through his daughter Endeïs, he was the grandfather of **Peleus,* and was partly responsible for facilitating the latter's ill-fated connexion with **Thetis** (q.v.).

Chersonésos: The modern Gallipoli Peninsula (see map 2): known in antiquity as the **Thrakian Chersonésos** to distinguish it from the Tauric Chersonésos, today the Crimea.

Clashing Rocks: A group of rocks at the **Black Sea** entrance to the **Bosporos,** which supposedly opened and shut of their own volition, making it impossible for ships to pass through safely: hence their name of Συμπληγάδες ("The Clashers"). They were, and still are, often confused with the **Wandering Rocks** (q.v.), which Ap. firmly locates in the Straits of Messina.

Corinth: See s. v. **Ephyra.**

Daktyls: Ap. conflates several accounts of these curious mythical figures:

Phrygian, Milesian, and **Krétan.** The two whom he mentions, **Títias** and **Kyllénos,** were associated with **Miletos.** The former also had connections with Herakleia on the **Black Sea.** The **Daktyls** ("Fingers") best known as acolytes of the Great Mother (**Kybélé**) in **Phrygia** were Kelmis, Damnameneus, and Akmon. The last-named ("Thunderbolt," "Anvil") emphasizes the **Daktyls'** role as metalworkers. They were particularly associated with **Mt. Ida** (1) in **Phrygia,** whence by natural progression later myth also brought them to **Mt. Ida** (2) in **Kréte.** They seem to have combined the functions of metalworkers, sorcerers, and physicians.

Danaë:	Daughter of Akrisios, king of **Argos,** who (having heard from an oracle that she would bear a son who would kill him) shut her up in a brazen tower. She nevertheless became pregnant, seduced either by Akrisios's twin brother and rival **Proitos,** or— the commoner version—by **Zeus,** in the form of a shower of gold that poured down through the roof into her lap. Akrisios, refusing to credit the shower-of-gold story, set her and the son she bore, **Perseus,** adrift in a chest. The chest washed up on the island of Sériphos. For the further adventures of **Danaë** and **Perseus,** see Apollod. 2.4.1–5.
Danaïds:	The fifty daughters of **Danaös** (q.v.); see also **Amymoné.**
Danaös:	A grandson of **Poseidon** and **Libya,** and brother of **Aígyptos.** Traditionally a native of Upper Egypt, he migrated to the the Peloponnesos with his fifty daughters, and became king of **Argos.** Of interest to Ap. solely as the father of one particular **Danaïd, Amymoné** (q.v.).
Dardania:	Territory on the Asiatic coast of the **Hellespontos,** south of **Abydos.**
Daskylos (1):	King of the **Mariandynians** and father of **Priolas** and **Lykos** (q.v.); got the help of **Herakles** against his neighbors the **Mygdonians.**
Daskylos (2):	Son of **Lykos,** who offers him as a guide to the **Argonauts.**
Deïleon:	One of the three sons of **Deïmachos** of **Trikka** (q.v.).
Deïmachos:	From **Trikka,** father of three sons, **Autolykos, Deileon,** and **Phlógios,** all of whom went with **Herakles** against the **Amazons** and met the **Argonauts** at **Sinopé.**
Delos:	Small island at the center of the Kykládes (**Aigaian**), and sacred to **Apollo,** whose birthplace it had been. In the fifth century B.C., it housed the treasury of the Athenian-led Delian League; during the Hellenistic period it achieved great wealth as a commercial entrepôt and slave mart.
Delphoi, Delphic:	Situated on the lower slopes of **Parnassos,** with a marvelous view out over the Gulf of Corinth, Delphoi—for the Greeks, the symbolic center of the world—formed the second great cult center of **Apollo,** the other being **Delos** (see above). It was also

the site of the most famous oracular shrine in the ancient world. See also s.v. **Python.**

Delphynes: The monstrous serpent or dragon slain by **Apollo** at the site of the future oracular shrine of **Delphoi.** See further n. to 2.706–13, and s.v. **Python.**

Demeter: The great Greek grain goddess, daughter of **Kronos** and **Rhea,** and thus sister to **Zeus,** by whom she had **Perséphoné** (or Kóré, "The Maiden").

Deukálion: Son of **Prometheus** and first king of **Phthia** in **Thessalia;** with his wife Pyrrha (daughter of Epimetheus and Pandora), he survived the Flood by divine help, and the two of them then repeopled Greece by throwing stones over their shoulders, which became men and women.

Dia: Early name for the **Aigaian** island of Naxos, where **Ariadné,** abandoned by **Theseus,** became the bride of **Dionysos.**

Dikté, Mt.: Mountain of eastern **Krété** (sometimes confused with **Ida** (2), q.v.), in a cave of which, according to one tradition, the child **Zeus** was reared; also sometimes associated with the **Daktyls** (q.v.), and the refuge of the **Harpies** after their encounter with the **Dioskouroi.** Dikté is also the name of a harbor in eastern **Krété** (4.1640).

Dindyméné: A title of the Great Mother Goddess, Kybélé, derived from the mountain in western Galatia (**Dindymon,** later Agdistis) near Pessinous that was closely associated with her cult, and that lent its name to the peak of **Kyzikós,** which Ap. describes as part of **Bear Mountain.**

Dindymon, Mt.: The peak of **Bear Mountain** on **Kyzikós,** named after the other **Mt. Dindymon** sacred to the Great Mother, **Kybélé,** in central **Phrygia** (Galatia).

Dionysos: Son of **Zeus** and Sémelé; an ancient **Thrakian** deity linked with the vine and ecstatic cults, in particular among women (see also s.v. **Mainads**). Various traditions describe the spread, or reintroduction, of his worship in Greece (e.g., at **Thebes**), and the resistance to it. Ap. knows the legend of **Hermes** entrusting the infant **Dionysos** to **Makris** in **Euboia** (4.540, 1134–38), and of his rescue of **Ariadné** from **Dia** (4.424–34). See also s.v. ***Phleias.***

Dioskouroi: These "sons of **Zeus**" (Διὸς κοῦροι) were **Kastor** and **Poly-deukes** (q.v.); see also s.v. **Tyndáreus,** and Diod. Sic. 4.56.4 for Meio cult as patrons of sailors.

Dipsakos: Son of the **Phyllis R.** and a local **Bithynian** nymph: entertained **Phrixos** (and presumably his magical flying ram too) when the latter was en route for **Kolchis** (2.651–54).

Dodóna: Site of an ancient oracle of **Zeus** in Epeiros, nr. modern Ioannina: the oracle supposedly spoke through the rustling of leaves in the sacred oaks, and it was from one of these that the "speaking beam" came that **Athena** 'carpentered into the heart of the forekeel' of *Argo* (4.582–83).

Doiantian Plain: This πεδίον Δοίαντος seems to have been thought of as lying in **Amazon** territory, perhaps to the east of the **Thermodon R.** and south of **Themískyra.**

Doias: Eponymous hero of the πεδίον Δοίαντος (see above) and brother of **Akmon** (q.v.).

Doliónes, -onian: Inhabitants of the isthmus, plain, and mainland *peraia* of **Kyzikós** (q.v.).

Dolopia, -an: A mountainous canton of **Phthia** in SW **Thessalia,** between the ranges of Tymphrestos and **Othrys.** The **Dolopians** were an ancient tribe, mentioned in Homer (*Il.* 9.484).

Dolops: According to the scholiast (1.587), **Dolops** was the son of **Hermes** and had a prominent barrow, visible from a great distance, on the coast of **Magnesia,** near Peiresiai, though the exact site remains in doubt. He was given heroic honors by the **Argives,** and it seems very probable that he was the **Dolopians'** eponymous ancestor.

Drépané: Ancient title ("The Sickle") for the large Adriatic island on the Balkan side of the Straits of Otranto identified with Homer's Scheria, and known afterwards as **Kérkyra,** Corcyra, or Corfu. See also s.vv. **Makrís** (1) and (2).

Dryopians: One of the oldest (supposedly autochthonous) peoples of Greece, originally occupying the area around Mt. Oita, and extending as far as **Parnassos** and the Spercheios R.; but (as Ap. indicates, 1.1213 ff.) **Herakles** and the Malians drove them out, and they migrated southward to **Euboia,** the **Argolid** peninsula, and the island of Kythnos.

Dyskélados: One of the numerous islands in the NE Adriatic, perhaps (according to Vian 1981, map of the Adriatic) offshore from modern Zadar.

Echelon Islands: Approximate translation of the name of islands in the Bay of Marseilles (Sea of Sardinia) known to the Greeks as αἱ Στοιχάδες: the Romans called them the Ligurian Islands, and today they are the Îles d'Hyères.

Echetos: A king of Epeiros in NW Greece, notorious (as early as Homer's day) for his cruelty. See 4.1092–95 for his blinding and other maltreatment of his daughter.

Echínadés: A group of small islands off the SW coast of Akarnania: already in antiquity the silting caused by the **Acheloös R.** had reduced their number, linking many of them to the mainland (Hdt. 2.10); and today only a few survive.

*Echíon: Argonaut son of **Hermes** and **Antianeira,** brother of ***Erytos,**

	and half-brother of **Aithálides** (q.v.): from **Phthiotis** in **Thessalia.** Both brothers also took part in the **Kalydonian** boar hunt.
Eidyia:	A daughter of **Ocean** and second wife of **Aiëtés** (q.v.), by whom she had both **Chalkíope** and **Medeia.**
Eílatos:	A prince of the **Lapiths** at **Lárissa** in **Thessalia:** by Hippeia fathered *****Kaineus** and *****Polyphemos,** both of whom joined the **Argonauts.** His name is sometimes given as **Elatos.**
Eilethyia:	Ancient Greek goddess of childbirth: her cult probably originated in **Krété,** where for centuries she had a shrine in a cave at Amnisos near Knossos.
Elára:	Daughter of **Orchomenos** and by **Zeus** mother of **Tityos** (q.v.).
Elektra:	One of the seven **Pleiadés,** daughter of Atlas and Pleioné: the island over which she had dominion was **Samothráké.**
Elektrís:	One of a group of islands (**Elektrides**) supposedly at the mouth of the **Eridanos R.** (Po), named for the amber (Greek ἤλεκτρον) found there. In fact, no such islands ever existed. When this became widely known, the fictitious **Elektrides** were relocated on the upper Balkan coast of the Adriatic, where there were islands and to spare.
Eléktryon:	Son of Perseus and Andromeda, and king of **Mykenai.** On his dealings with **Taphian** pirates see 1.747–51. **Eléktryon** was later accidentally killed by Amphitryon.
Elis:	State in the NW Peloponnesos, facing west onto the island of Zakynthos and the Ionian Sea, and bounded on the east by the mountains of **Arkadia,** with Messenia to the south and **Achaia** to the NE. Ruled in the mythical period by **Oinomáos** (q.v.).
Elysion:	Abode of the dead, more commonly known as the "Plain of Elysion" or the "Elysian Fields": sometimes located in the Islands of the Blest, and in sharp and pleasurable contrast to Tartaros, or Hades. Ap.'s interest in **Elysion** is limited to the fact that, traditionally, **Achilles** married **Medeia** there in the afterlife: not, one might have thought, a consummation devoutly to be desired, even at an eschatological level, by either party.
Enchéleans:	An **Illyrian** tribe (their name in Greek, Ἐγχέλεες, means "Eel People") occupying the area of the Keraunian (**Thunderer**) Mountains, north of the Taulantioi and Epidamnos, and connected in myth with **Kadmos** (q.v.) and **Harmónia** (2).
Endymion:	Numerous variants disagree as to his parentage and provenance: the most constant tradition is that he was a beautiful young Kavian shepherd lulled into sleep (whether eternal or not is debated) by Selene, the **Moon,** so that she could steal kisses from him. One account (Paus. 5.1.2) claims that he had no less than fifty daughters by her, which suggests a certain amount of wakefulness.

Enétoi, -eian: The name of a prominent **Paphlagonian** tribe, of which **Pelops** was the reputed ancestor: their exact location was already a matter of debate in antiquity. Ap. follows the version that places them in the area of **Sesamos** (Amastris) and **Kytóros** (Strabo 12.3.8, C. 543); others associated them with Amisos, E. of the **Halys R.**

Enípeus R.:   Major, fast-flowing **Thessalian** river: rises in **Mt. Othrys,** and flows through the Pharsalian plain, where it joins the **Apidanos** (sources differ as to which of the two was the tributary): both discharge into the **Peneios.** As a river god, **Enipeus** was loved by Salmoneus's daughter Tyro: see s.v. **Pelias.**

Enyalios: See s.v. **Ares.**

Ephyra: Ancient name for Corinth, the city controlling both sea and land traffic (between northern Greece and the Peloponnesos and the Saronic and Corinthian gulfs) through its commanding position at the Isthmus.

Erató: One of the nine **Muses,** in Graeco-Roman times associated especially with lyric poetry and hymns.

Erechtheus: Mythical early king of Athens: son of Pandion, and father of—among others—**Kekrops,** Prokris, and **Oreithyia** (q.v.). The Erechtheion on the Akropolis seems to have stood on the site of the original **Mykenaian** palace: there may be a historical strand in the mythical tradition.

*Ergínos: In the tradition followed by Ap., an Argonaut and son of **Poseidon,** a native of **Miletos;** earlier accounts (e.g., Pind. *Ol.* 4.19–28) make him son of Klymenos and lord of **Orchómenos.** Pindar also associates him with an event not mentioned by Ap., the funeral games held by **Hypsípylé** in honor of her father **Thóas,** where **Ergínos,** mocked by the **Lemnian** women for his prematurely gray hair, nevertheless contrived to defeat that wind-swift pair **Zétés** and **Kalaïs** in the footrace. He succeeded **Tiphys** (2.896 ff.) as *Argo*'s steersman.

Ergínos R.:   A river in **Thráké,** possibly a tributary of the Hebros.

Erídanós R.:   At least from the time of Pherekydes, the **Erídanós** was firmly identified with northern Italy's largest river, the Po, though an earlier tradition—as well as the curious myth of **Phaëthon**'s fiery death there, and the **Heliades** with their tears of amber—hints at a more northern, indeed, **Hyperborean,** association. Ap.'s notions concerning the geography of the **Erídanós,** in particular its supposed connection with the Rhine and Rhône were decidedly sketchy.

Eros: The Greek god of love, whose curious and unique distinction was to grow steadily younger from archaic to Hellenistic times, beginning (in the oldest representations we have) as a young adult, but gradually regressing through adolescence to the spoilt and mischievous winged *putto,* complete with bow and arrows, we find in Ap.'s presentation. Originally the child of Ge (Earth) and **Kronos,** or of **Eilethyia,** or even of the cosmic world egg, he is now firmly, and appropriately, the offspring of **Kypris** (Aphrodite), even though—also appropriately—his father remains in doubt: **Hermes** (perhaps because their statues appeared together in most gymnasia)? **Ares** (the most obvious candidate)? even **Kypris**'s own father, **Zeus?** Ap. leaves the matter in doubt, but hints (3.135 ff.) at **Hephaistos,** who was, after all, Aphrodite's husband.

*Erybótes: Argonaut, sometimes known as Eurybates, son of **Téleon** (1): a **Lokrian,** and a skilled physician. He was represented on the Chest of Kypselos (Paus. 5.17.10) as taking part in the funeral games of **Pelias.**

Erymánthos: The name of a mountainous massif on the frontiers of **Arkadia, Achaia,** and **Elis:** from it four rivers descend, including a tributary of the **Acheloös** also named **Erymanthos.** The swamp that formed the haunt of the boar killed by **Herakles** should probably be thought of as lying near the confluence of the two rivers.

Erythéis: One of the **Hespéridés** (q.v.).

Erythinian rocks: A pair of high reddish rocks some ten or eleven miles along the **Paphlagonian** coast, east of **Sésamos** (Amastris).

*Erytos: Argonaut, son of **Hermes** and **Antianeira,** brother of ***Echion** (q.v.) and half-brother of ***Aithalides** (q.v.).

Eryx: A mountain (the modern Monte San Giuliano, 2,184 ft.) and Elymian settlement in western Sikelia, about two miles inland and six from Drepana: best known in antiquity for the great temple of Astarte (Aphrodite, Venus) on its summit, supposedly founded by Aeneas.

Etesian Winds: These "annual" northerly winds—still a regular feature of the **Aigaian** during July–August, and now known as the *meltemi*—were traditionally thought to blow from the time the Sun left Cancer for Leo, and until it entered Virgo, i.e., from the rising of the Dog Star till that of Arktouros. The duration varied according to source; but the most commonly accepted time was that recorded by Ap., i.e., forty days. Cf. note on 2.498, and Vian 1974, 271.

Euboia: The long offshore island lying to the immediate east of **Lokris, Attika** (q.v.), and Boiotia, separated by no more than a narrow channel from the Gulf of **Pagasai** in the north and the island of Andros in the south.

*Euphémos: Argonaut, originally from **Phokis** or **Boiotia,** but latterly dwelling at **Tainaron** in the south Peloponnesos: son of **Poseidon** and **Európé**, and the ancestor (4.1731–64) of Battos of **Kyréné.**

Eupolemeia: Daughter of Myrmidon (the eponymous ancestor of the Myrmidons in **Thessalian Phthia**) and Peisidiké: by **Hermes** the mother of **Aithalides* (q.v.).

Európé (1): Daughter of **Tityos** (q.v.), and by **Poseidon** the mother of **Euphémos** (q.v.).

Európé (2): Daughter of **Agénor** (q.v.), carried off by **Zeus,** in the form of a bull, to **Kréte,** where in due course she bore him **Minos,** Sarpedon, and Rhadamanthys. Her brother **Kadmos**'s search for her took him to **Delphoi** and thence—following a cow—to **Thebes.**

*Eurydamas: Argonaut, son of **Ktímenos,** from **Dolopia** (q.v.).

Eurymedon: A title ("Wide-ruling") of several deities, including **Poseidon, Hermes,** and (4.1514) **Perseus.**

Eurymenai: A **Magnesian** coastal town somewhere near the foothills of **Mt. Ossa;** the exact location remains uncertain (cf. n. on 1.592–8). Pliny *NH* 31.29 records an odd tradition that if thrown into a certain spring there, garlands (*coronae*) underwent petrifaction.

Eurynomé: An **Oceanid.** For Ap. (who probably conflated the traditions of Hesiodos and Pherekydes) the wife of **Ophión,** or **Ophioneus** (q.v.); together they were thought of as preceding **Kronos** and **Rhea** on **Olympos,** and defeated by them for rule over the **Titans.**

Eurypylos: An alternative name or title of **Triton** (3) (q.v.).

Eurystheus: Grandson of Perseus and Andromeda, and the king of **Mykenai** who imposed the Twelve Labors on **Herakles.**

*Eurytion: Argonaut, son of **Iros** and Demonassa, a **Lokrian;** he subsequently took part in the great **Kalydonian** boar hunt, during which he was accidentally killed by his son-in-law **Peleus** (q.v.), who had fled to him for refuge and married his daughter Antígoné when expelled from his own dominions.

Eúrytos: King of **Oichalia** on **Euboia,** near Eretria; by Antioché, the father of **Iphitos* and **Klytios*. A skilled archer, he was even supposed to have instructed **Herakles** in the art. According to Hom. *Od.* 8.226, he was killed by **Apollo** for presuming to rival him as a bowman, and it is this tradition that Ap. follows (1.86–89). According to a more common version, he offered his daughter Iolé to anyone who could outshoot him, confident in his own unbeatable skill. **Herakles** disabused him of this belief, but **Eúrytos** reneged on his promise, fearing lest **Herakles** might kill the children of the union, as he had done previously. This was unwise. **Herakles,** in a fury, captured **Oichalia,** killing both **Eúrytos** and his sons (Apollod. 2.6.1, 7.7), and taking Iolé captive—thus provoking his own death through the jealousy of Deianeira.

Eusoros: Father of **Ainété** (q.v.) and Akamas; the latter commanded the Hellespontine **Thrakian** contingent allied to Priamos during the Trojan War.

Fairdance (Kallichóros) R.:	A river situated a little to the east of Herakleia on the south shore of the **Black Sea**, and possibly to be identified with the Oxines (mod. Tcharuk).
Fair Mouth:	Translation of Καλὸν Στόμα, the southernmost mouth of the **Istros** (Danube), skirting the south side of **Peuké** ("Pine Island").
Fates:	The **Fates,** or Moirai, were traditionally three in number, daughters of **Zeus** and **Themis:** Klotho ("The Spinner": the Fates were thought to spin the "thread" of a person's destiny), Láchesis ("The Getter-by-lot"), and Atropos ("The Irresistible"). They presided at all births and weddings, bringing the varied gifts of fortune to child or bride. In particular, Ap. thinks of them at the wedding of **Peleus** and **Thetis** (so shown on the François Vase).
Furies:	Known in Greece as Erinyes: chthonian pursuing-spirits of vengeance, especially where the blood-guiltiness associated with murder, of kin in particular, was concerned, but with power also over perjurers and criminals generally.
Ganymédés:	Of uncertain parentage; while Kallirhoë is fairly constantly cited as his mother, his father is variously given as Tros (the most popular choice), Laomedon, Ilos, Erichthonios, or Assarakos. There are also two traditions about his elevation to **Olympos.** One, known to Homer (*Il.* 20.231), is that the gods carried him off to be their cupbearer. As early as the *Little Iliad,* however, we find the alternative version, which very soon became standard, that **Zeus,** enamored of the boy's beauty, abducted him (either sending an eagle to do the job or transforming himself into an eagle for the occasion). Once again the ostensible purpose was to employ **Ganymédés** as a cupbearer; but **Zeus**'s ulterior motive is made clear by the Roman corruption of the boy's name into "Catamitus," and indeed we hear that Tros received either a pair of mares or a golden vine (conveyed by **Hermes**) as compensation for his son's rape. See also n. on 3.115–17.
Gáramas:	See s.v. **Amphithémis.**
Géphyros:	A **Dolionian** warrior, slain by **Peleus;** Vian (1974, 99) suggests that his name (its meaning is "Bridge Man") may derive from the bridges thrown across the channel connecting **Kyzikós** with the mainland.
Geraístos:	The SW promontory of **Euboia,** east of **Karystos,** a once-wooded cape (today, Cape Mandili), on which there stood a famous temple of **Poseidon,** with a busy port below.
Giants:	The battle between Gods and **Giants** (Gigantes) was unknown to Homer, who gives a different account of them; but from Hesiod onward they seem to have been regarded as a second generation of the **Titans,** with whom they are often confused, being born of Ge (Earth) from the spilt blood of **Ouranos,** Ge

being incensed at the fate of her earlier children, the **Titans.**
The **Giants** were monstrous creatures, some snake-tailed: their
conflict with the **Olympians** became a regular theme for art,
most notably in the frieze of the Great Altar at Pergamon (c. 230).

Glaukos: A marine deity, of rather odd antecedents: originally a fisher-
man from Anthedon in **Boiotia,** who happened to eat part of
the divine herb sown by **Kronos,** and thus by sheer luck became
immortal. His association with the Fleece legend was closer than
Ap. chooses to indicate: some traditions make him not only the
Argonauts' steersman, but also the builder of *Argo.* Famed for
his trustworthy oracles and erotic adventures, he was commonly
represented in art as a man to the waist but a great fork-tailed
fish below, with hair and beard dripping wet, and chest wreathed
in seaweed. See s.v. **Triton** (3). This iconographic tradition was
clearly drawn on by Ap. See 1.1310–28.

Graces: The **Graces** (or Charites) were, as their name suggests, personi-
fications of grace, charm, and beauty. There are various traditions as to their number, names, and parentage, though **Zeus**
(or sometimes **Apollo** or **Dionysos**) is most often mentioned as
their father. Hesiod identified three of them, called Euphro-
syné, Aglaia, and Thalia, and his version became the most
commonly accepted one.

Gyrton: Town in the plain near **Thessalian Lárissa,** on the r. bank of
the **Peneios R.** Modern identification remains uncertain: both
Tatári and Bakréna have been suggested.

Hades: The Greek underworld and abode of the dead, generally represented as situated physically below the earth's surface, with
various entries (e.g., **Styx, Acheron** [q.v.], Tainaron) leading to
it, a view encouraged by Greece's widespread system of subterranean limestone caves and waterways. These entries were not
restricted to the mainland, or even to Greece: for the "cave of
Hades" near the **Acherousian** headland in **Bithynia,** see 2.735 ff.
and Vian 1974, 276–7, Severin 154.

Hagnias: Father of *Tiphys (q.v.).

Haimonia: The ancient name of **Thessalia.** It was supposedly derived
from the eponymous **Haimon,** son of Pelasgos and father
of Thessalos.

Halys R.:   The main river of Asia Minor: it rises in the Tauros Mountains,
and after an initial SW sweep turns N, forming the eastern
frontier of **Paphlagonia,** and discharges into the Euxine roughly
midway between **Sinopé** and **Themiskyra.** It was most famous
in antiquity as marking the (sixth-century) frontier between
the Lydian empire of Kroisos and that of Persia, crossing which
(the result of misinterpreting a **Delphic** oracle) cost Kroisos his
throne.

Harmonia (1): According to Pherekydes (schol. 2.992), a Naiad who, with **Ares,** produced the **Amazons** (q.v.).

Harmónia (2): Daughter of **Ares** and Aphrodite (**Kypris**), bestowed as wife upon **Kadmos** (q.v.) when the latter was confirmed by the **Olympians** as ruler of **Thebes,** having previously been led to the site by a cow, as foretold through an oracle. At the wedding—to which all the gods came—either **Kadmos** himself, or, in another tradition, Aphrodite or **Athena,** gave her a necklace as a present. This necklace, later inherited by Polyneikes, became notorious for the ill-fortune associated with it. When **Kadmos** and **Harmónia** left **Thebes,** they were promised by another oracle rule over the **Encheleans** (q.v.) if they helped them in their war against the **Illyrians.** This they did, and the oracle was fulfilled. In the end the two of them were metamorphosed into serpents, and translated by **Zeus** to **Elysion** (q.v.).

Harpies (Harpyiai): Originally these "swift snatchers" seem to have been wind spirits (so they appear in Homer), but from a very early time that concept was allied with characteristics taken from scavenging birds—kites and vultures in particular. Hesiod names them as Aello, Okypeté, and Kelaino.

Hékaté: An ancient and mysterious chthonian deity of uncertain origin, possibly pre-Greek. Homer does not mention her. She is closely associated, and often confused, with **Artemis.** According to one tradition, she accompanied **Demeter** in her search for **Perséphoné,** carrying a torch. By Hellenistic times her uncanny and magical aspects were strongly stressed: she haunted graveyards and crossroads, announced by the barking of dogs, and escorted by her own **Stygian** hellhounds.

Heliádes: The sisters of **Phaëthon** (q.v.), whom they helped to harness the chariot of the Sun (**Helios**) when he made his ill-fated attempt to drive his father's chariot across the sky. When **Phaëthon** fell into the **Erídanós** (q.v.), his sisters were metamorphosed into poplars by the riverbank and shed tears of amber in mourning for him.

Helios: The sun god, who, legend had it, drove his fiery chariot across the sky from east to west daily, returning during the night by way of the stream of Ocean in a golden skiff made by **Hephaistos.** To this tradition belongs the episode of the god's son **Phaëthon** (q.v.). **Helios** is otherwise connected with the Argonauts through various descendants, in particular—by **Persé** (or Perseïs)—his son **Aiëtés** and his daughter **Kirké** (whom he escorted in his chariot to **Aiaia** [3.309–13]). **Medeia** was thus his granddaughter, and **Kirké** her aunt.

Hellas: Originally a small area of **Phthiotis** in **Thessalia,** but gradually extended to signify, first, most of central Greece, and latterly, by Ap.'s day, Greece as a whole.

Hellé: Daughter of **Athamas** and **Nephélé,** and sister of **Phrixos** (q.v.). Killed by falling into the **Hellespontos** (named after her) while fleeing with her brother on the golden-fleeced ram provided by their mother to get them away from the machinations of their stepmother, Ino.

Hellespontos: The modern Dardanelles: the channel separating Europe from Asia, and linking the Propontis (Sea of Marmara) with the **Aigaian.**

Hephaistos: **Hera** was supposed to have given birth to **Hephaistos** partheno-genetically (possibly, as one tradition has it, through jealousy of **Zeus**'s having brought **Dionysos** to term without *her* assistance), though **Zeus** is sometimes named as his father. When **Zeus** hung **Hera** from **Olympos** with two anvils tied to her ankles, **Hephaistos** came to her rescue. He was thrown out of heaven for his pains, falling for nine days and nights and landing on **Lemnos** (q.v.), which resulted in his lameness and perhaps dictated his subsequent role as divine smith, artificer, and fire god. (Another variant attributes his fall to **Hera** herself, disgusted by his physical deformities.) He was also associated with volcanic phenomena (see his forge on the **Wandering Island** [3.41–43]), and, a trifle improbably (an allegory of Craftsmanship and Beauty allied?), married to Aphrodite (**Kypris**). In addition to the brazen bulls of **Aiëtés,** he was also variously credited with making the armor of **Achilles,** the necklace of **Harmonia** (2), Agamemnon's scepter, and Pandora, the first woman.

Hera: A pre-Greek goddess of marriage, in myth the daughter of **Kronos** and **Rhea,** and sister (possibly twin sister) as well as wife to **Zeus.** At their "sacred marriage" ($\iota\epsilon\rho\grave{o}s$ $\gamma\acute{a}\mu os$), all the **Olympians** were present: Ge (Earth) made them a present of a tree bearing golden apples, which was subsequently watched over in North Africa by the **Hespéridés** (q.v.). Her quarrels with **Zeus** were proverbial, and may hint at an early conflict between her indigenous cult and that of the Aryan sky god imported by the invaders. In the *Arg.,* she functions throughout as *Jason's divine supporter, having never forgotten his gallant gesture to her when she was disguised as an old woman and he carried her across a river in spate (3.67–73).

Herakles: Behind the enormous accumulation of legend that surrounds this enigmatic figure, there seems to be an original core associating him with Tiryns, **Argos,** and the Perseïd dynasty, which may be based on some actual or quasi-mythical prince from the era, who owed allegiance to **Eurystheus,** king of **Argos** (and joined the Argonauts against the latter's wishes [1.122–32]): he is hero rather than god (though later, exceptionally, admitted to immortality and the company of the **Olympians**). Half of his Labors are located in the Peloponnesos; three others (including the winning of the Apples of the **Hespérides**) seem to be variants on the myth of conquering Death or pursuing a quest to the world's end. His vast physical strength, unruly appetites, and frequent bouts of uncontrollable violence were proverbial. For Ap.'s treatment of him, see various notes ad loc.

Hermes:
A minor **Olympian** deity: associated with trade and commerce, and (by a natural Greek train of thought) also with trickery, thievishness, and deception. Perhaps originating in a primitive roadside cairn or stoneheap ($\H{\epsilon}\rho\mu\alpha$), **Hermes** was best known for his street-corner images (pillar with head and phallus), and for his role as Guide of Souls ($\psi\upsilon\chi\sigma\pi\sigma\mu\pi\acute{\sigma}s$). The son of **Zeus** and **Maia,** he acted for the most part as a messenger for his father, e.g., in the *Arg.*, to **Phrixos** (4.119–21) and **Aiëtés** (3.587–88).

Hespéré:
One of the **Hespérides** (q.v.).

Hespérides:
Guardians of the golden-apple-bearing tree bestowed by Ge upon **Zeus** and **Hera** at their wedding: their names and ancestry are variously given. Ap. names them as **Aiglé, Hespéré,** and **Erytheïs.** Their "garden" was located somewhere in the West: most often beyond the **Atlas** mountains by **Ocean,** but for Ap. in **Libya.**

Hippodameía (1): Daughter of **Oinomáos** (q.v.), king of **Elis.**

Hippodameía (2): Daughter of Atrax and bride of **Peiríthoös** (q.v.).

Hippólyté:
An **Amazon,** daughter of **Ares** and **Otréré,** sister to **Antíopé** (2) and **Melanippé,** and queen of the **Amazons** dwelling around **Themískyra.** The version of her dealings with **Herakles** (involving the famous girdle) given by Ap. at 2.966–69 is one among several: more often, **Herakles** is represented as killing her. In some variants it is she, rather than **Antíopé** (2), who marries **Theseus.**

Hippótas:
Father of **Aiolos** (2) (q.v.).

Hippouris:
One of the southern **Sporádes** (q.v.).

Holy Mount:
A sacred peak ($\iota\epsilon\rho\grave{o}\nu$ $\H{o}\rho\sigma s$) situated in the territory of the **Tibarénoi** (q.v.); a temple of **Zeus**-of-the-fair-winds ($\sigma\H{\upsilon}\rho\iota\sigma s$) stood there.

Homólé:
Thessalian coastal town located near **Mt. Ossa;** probably on the right bank of the **Peneios R.,** near the outflow of the Vale of Tempe.

Hyakinthos:
Dolionian warrior, killed by ***Klytios.**

Hyantes, -ian:
Name of an aboriginal tribe in **Boiotia.** They originally inhabited **Onchestos,** but later were driven out by the **Kadmeians** and founded Hyampolis in **Phokis.**

Hydra:
Mythical nine-headed monster located at **Lerna** in the **Argolid,**

	target of **Herakles**' second Labor: as soon as one head was cut off, two more sprang up in its place. However, **Herakles** finally subdued the creature, and used its gall to poison his arrows with which he killed the serpent **Ladon**, q.v.). The Hydra was probably a mythical personification of the numerous springs and streams that, despite repeated draining schemes since antiquity, still render parts of the area marshy.
*Hylas:	Argonaut, son of the **Dryopian** chieftain **Theiódamas,** and taken on by **Herakles** as his page-cum-minion after he killed the boy's father. For the circumstances of his seduction by a water nymph, see 1.1207 ff.
Hylleans:	An **Illyrian** tribe of uncertain location: Vian (1981, 25) places them a little to the north of the **Liburnian** islands, on the modern Ravni Kotari peninsula, and this seems very plausible. Other theories ad loc. (nn. 4–6).
Hyllos:	A **Phaiakian** by origin, son of **Herakles** and **Melité,** daughter of the river god **Aigaíos** (an alternative tradition makes his mother Deianeira: Apollod. 2.7.7). **Herakles** is said to have pursued and seduced **Melité** while seeking purification on **Drépané** for the murder of his children. Since **Hyllos** chafed under the authority of the island's ruler, **Nausithoös** (the father of **Alkínoös**), he took a colonizing expedition to the **Illyrian** Adriatic, and became the eponymous ancestor of the **Hylleans** (see above).
Hyperásios:	From **Pelléné,** son of Pellen, and by Hypso father of *Asterios and *Amphion.
Hyperboreans:	A mysterious mythical people supposedly dwelling in the far north, in a peaceful sunny enclave "at the back of the North Wind." Ap. knows (4.614–17) of **Apollo**'s sojourn among them during his exile; they have also been connected with the European amber route.
Hypios R.:	A small river with a broad estuary, lying to the east of the larger and more powerful **Sangarios,** in the west part of the territory of the **Mariandynians.** At one time, according to Ps.-Skylax, it formed the boundary between them and the **Bithynians.**
Hypsípylé:	Daughter of **Thóas,** and thus granddaughter of **Dionysos,** a point often forgotten when assessing her character and motives. During the massacre of the **Lemnian** men that preceded the appearance of the **Argonauts** on the island, **Hypsípylé** alone arranged the escape of her father (a fact she concealed from the **Argonauts,** who believed him dead, not least since she offered **Jason** his throne). Her career after the period covered by the *Arg.* is not without interest. At some point after bearing **Jason** twin sons, she was captured by pirates and sold into slavery, ending up in the house of Lykourgos, king of Nemea, as nurse to one of his children, Archemoros. When the expedition

of the Seven against **Thebes** passed through Nemea, Hypsípylé
guided the force to a spring. While she was thus occupied, the
baby was bitten by a snake and died. Amphiaraös obtained a
pardon for **Hypsípylé,** and the Nemean Games were founded
in the dead child's honor.

Iapetos: A **Titan,** son of **Ouranos** and Ge (Earth), and, by a daughter of
his brother Okeanos (**Ocean**)—either Asia or **Klymené**—father
of **Prometheus** (q.v.).

Ida, Mt. (1): Mountain range extending through western **Mysia** and the
Troad, rising to some 4,650 ft. above sea level: heavily wooded,
with many streams and springs (including the sources of the
Skamandros, the Simoïs, and the Granikos), described by
Homer as rich in wild beasts. This last characteristic may partly
explain Ida's consecration to the Great Mother (**Kybélé** or
Rhea) in her capacity as Mistress of Beasts ($\pi \acute{o} \tau \nu \iota \alpha\ \theta \eta \rho \tilde{\omega} \nu$).

Ida, Mt. (2): The central, and highest, point of the mountain range that
forms the backbone of **Kréte;** sometimes confused in antiquity
with **Mt. Dikté** (q.v.) further to the E, and associated from early
times with legends concerning the childhood of **Zeus,** who was
said to have been reared in a cave on the mountain's slopes and
protected by the **Kourétés** (1) (q.v.). The metalworking (**Idaian**)
Daktyls (q.v.) were also located in this area.

*Idas: Argonaut, son of **Aphareus** and **Aréné,** and brother of ***Lynkeus**
(q.v.), with whom he not only took part in the quest for the
Fleece, but also in the great **Kalydonian** boar hunt (where
he traditionally killed the boar that had killed ***Idmon;** see
2.815–34). He was also notorious for having competed with
Apollo for the hand of Marpessa, who (left by **Zeus** with the
decision between them) chose **Idas,** on the reasonable grounds
that **Apollo,** an immortal, would get bored with her when she
grew old, if not before. **Idas** thus enters the pages of mythology
as one of the very few mortals who got the better of a god.
In the long run, of course, this did him little good. He and
Lynkeus got into a cattle-raiding quarrel with the **Dioskouroi**
in **Arkadia;** during the resultant fight, **Idas** killed **Kastor** and
knocked out **Polydeukes** (who had meanwhile killed **Lynkeus**)
before being fulminated himself by **Zeus.**

*Idmon: Argonaut from **Argos,** putative son of **Abas** (q.v.); a prophet
and seer who was taught his mantic skills by **Apollo** (according
to some sources, his father). Like Megistias during the Persian
Wars, he volunteered for the expedition even though he
foresaw his own death during it (1.436–49).

Ilissos, R.: A small river of **Attika,** rising at the north end of the Hymettos
range and flowing south of Athens towards Phaleron Bay:
immortalized by Plato in the *Phaidros* for its beauty, today its

	course lies mostly under concrete, and among rocks and burnt maquis where visible, besides being mostly dry during the summer months.
Illyria:	A loose term for the area roughly congruent with the east coast of the Adriatic, covering what used to be Yugoslavia, plus Albania and northern Epeiros.
Imbrasos R.:	A small river of **Samos,** with its source on Mt. Ampelos ("Vine"). **Hera** was venerated in a nearby shrine. **Imbrasos** was also the name given by some Karian tribes to **Hermes.**
Imbros:	Mountainous island in the northern **Aigaian,** lying west of the **Thrakian Chersonésos,** between **Samothráké** and **Lemnos.** Celebrated in antiquity, like **Samothráké,** for its cults of the Kabeiroi and **Hermes.**
Iolkos:	City of **Magnesia,** at the head of the Gulf of **Pagasai** and on the lower slopes of **Mt. Pelion;** almost certainly identical with **Aisónis** (q.v.). Homeland of *****Jason** and *****Pelias** and assembly point for the **Argonauts.** Traditionally held to have been founded by **Krétheus** and colonized by **Minyans** from **Orchómenos.**
Ionians:	So called from their supposed eponymous ancestor, Ion, son of Kreousa and Xouthos (or possibly **Apollo**), the founder of the original four Athenian tribes. During the eleventh and tenth centuries B.C., after the collapse of the **Mykenaian** kingdoms, they emigrated from mainland Greece (traditionally under **Neleus,** son of Athens's last king, Kodros) to colonize the central part of the eastern **Aigaian** coast, which then took the name of **Ionia.**
Ionian Sea:	Ancient name for what was later known as the Adriatic: the waters between the coast of **Illyria** and Epeiros, and the Italian peninsula.
Ionian Strait:	The channel between **Drépané** (**Kérkyra,** modern Corfu) and the mainland of Epeiros (modern Albania).
Iphias:	Priestess of **Artemis** in **Iolkos:** see 1.311–16.
***Iphiklos** (1):	Argonaut from **Phylaké** in **Phthiotis;** son of **Phylakos** and **Minyas**'s daughter **Klymené,** and brother of **Alkimédé** (q.v.) the wife (according to Ap., basing himself on Pherekydes) of **Aison.** **Iphiklos** was thus also **Jason**'s maternal uncle. By either Diomedeia or Astyoche, he was the father of Protesilaos (the first warrior ashore at Troy) and Podarkes (the leader there of the **Thessalian** contingent). A wealthy cattle baron, he gave his herds to the seer **Melampous,** the brother of **Bias** (q.v.), in return for a magic recipe enabling him to become a father. Since **Neleus** had promised his daughter **Pero** to the suitor (**Bias** being one of them) who brought her the oxen of **Iphiklos,** this deal pleased everybody. **Iphiklos** was also a champion runner, who carried off the prize at the funeral games of **Pelias.**

*Iphiklos (2):	Argonaut from **Aitolia,** son of **Thestios,** and maternal uncle of **Meleagros;** he took part in the great **Kalydonian** boar hunt (along with several other **Argonauts**) as well as the quest for the Fleece.
Iphínoé:	A **Lemnian** woman, represented by Ap. as Queen **Hypsípylé's** envoy to the **Argonauts.**
*Iphitos (1):	Argonaut from **Oichalia** in **Euboia;** son of **Eurytos** (q.v.) and brother of *Klytios. Wounded in the fight with the **Bebrykians,** he was finally slain by **Herakles** during the latter's attack on **Oichalia.**
*Iphitos (2):	Argonaut from Phokis, son of **Naubolos** (2), and **Jason's** host during his consultation of the oracle at **Delphoi.**
Iris:	Daughter of Thaumas and **Elektra** and sister to the **Harpies** (q.v.): the regular messenger of the Olympian deities, and associated with the rainbow, which according to some sources formed her traveling bridge between heaven and earth.
Iris R.:	A sizable river of Anatolia, east of the **Halys,** that rises in the Antitauros range and, after describing a great westward loop, debouches into the **Black Sea** at Ankon, between the **Chadesios R.** and **Themískyra.**
Iros:	A **Lokrian,** son of **Aktor** (2) and Demonassa, and father of *Eurytion (q.v.). When *Peleus accidentally killed *Eurytion during the **Kalydonian** boar hunt, he offered **Iros** his flocks in compensation, but **Iros** refused to accept them. In obedience to an oracle, **Peleus** instead let them loose, and they were devoured by a wolf. The wolf, turned to stone, became a boundary marker between **Lokris** and **Phokis.**
Ismenos R.:	A seasonal torrent, today the Chrysorrhoas, flowing south to north past the eastern gates of **Thebes.** The parallel stream to the west of the city was the Dirké (mod. Plakioussa).
Issa:	One of the **Liburnian Isl.** (mod. Lissa) off the coast of **Illyria** in the Adriatic, lying slightly NW of **Black Kérkyra** and **Melíté.**
Isthmus:	The isthmus of Corinth, famous for the Isthmian Games (alluded to at 3.1241), a festival in honor of **Poseidon,** for which the crown was a wreath of wild celery. Traditionally founded either by Sisyphos or (the version preferred at Athens), by **Theseus,** to celebrate his killing of the brigand Sinis, these Games were officially celebrated every two years from 581 B.C.
Istria, -an:	The large peninsula of **Istria** is situated on the NE side of the head of the Adriatic, between Venetia and **Illyria.** Modern Pola lies at its tip, while Tergeste (mod. Trieste) and Rijeka mark its upper limits.
Istros R.:	The modern Danube: Ap.'s misconceptions concerning its course are, as alert readers will note, considerable.

Iton, Itonian: A **Thessalian** town of **Phthiótis,** located on the south slopes of **Mt. Othrys** and (appropriately) described by Homer (*Il.* 2.696) as "mother of flocks" (μητέρα μήλων). Ap. uses **Itonian** as an epithet of **Athena:** in the context of the building and launching of *Argo,* this seems decidedly more apt here than the MS alternative of **Tritonian** (q.v.).

Itymoneus (1): A **Dolionian** warrior, killed by **Meleagros** (1.1046–47).

Itymoneus (2): A **Bebrykian** warrior, killed by **Polydeukes** (2.105–7).

Ixion: King of the **Lapiths** and father of **Peiríthoös** (q.v.), best known for his attempt to rape **Hera** after receiving kind treatment from **Zeus:** by way of punishment, he was chained for ever in **Hades** to a revolving fiery wheel.

*Jason, -onian: The leading Argonaut; son of **Aison** and **Alkiméde** (other sources vary as to his mother) of the **Aiolid** family in **Iolkos.** On the death of **Krétheus, Aison's** father, and the usurpation of the throne by **Pelias,** the young **Jason** was smuggled away to be brought up by **Cheiron** (q.v.). Ap. picks up the story on his return to claim his heritage—minus one sandal, thus fulfilling an ominous oracle for **Pelias,** who sent him off in quest of the Fleece, the getting of which forms the theme of the *Arg.* On his return to **Iolkos** with **Medeia** as his wife, he found that **Pelias** (not expecting **Jason** ever to return) had forced **Aison** to commit suicide, and that **Alkiméde,** after cursing the killer, had likewise killed herself.

   Jason delivered the Fleece, dedicated *Argo* at the **Isthmus,** and then called on **Medeia** (as he had already done so often in a crisis) to get vengeance for him on **Pelias.** This she did by using her magic tricks to convince **Pelias's** daughters that they could rejuvenate their father by killing him, cutting him up, and boiling him in a cauldron. Guilelessly, they did so, but **Pelias** remained very dead. His son **Akastos** then expelled **Jason** and **Medeia** from **Iolkos;** they went to Corinth, where they lived peaceably enough for ten years. At the end of this time, **Jason,** with an eye to the throne, engaged himself to King **Kreon's** daughter **Glauké** (or **Kreousa**). **Medeia,** thus provoked, sent the prospective bride a poisoned bridal dress (which destroyed the wearer by spontaneous combustion), burned **Kreon** alive in his own palace, killed at least two of her children by **Jason,** and made her escape in a chariot drawn by winged dragons. **Jason** is said either to have killed himself out of grief, or else to have been crushed by the poop of the *Argo* falling on him (he had—apparently on **Medeia's** advice, they meanwhile having become reconciled—lain down to sleep under it). Later sources claim, presumably in the interests of a happy ending, that they finally returned to **Kolchis** and restored **Aiëtés** (q.v. for this episode) to the kingdom he had lost. **Medeia** herself was said to have become immortal and to have married **Achilles** (q.v.) in **Elysion.** The details of **Jason**'s unedifying liaison with **Medeia** after the close of the *Arg.* would have been familiar to all Ap.'s readers, and he continually plays off their knowledge of events subsequent to his own narrative.

Kadmos, -meians: Son of **Agénor** (q.v.) and Telephassa, and brother of (among others) Phoinix and **Európé.** For his journey in search of the latter, and the founding of **Thebes** (the original inhabitants of which were known as **Kadmeians**), see Apollod. 3.1.1–3.4.2 (with Frazer's notes). For his marriage, old age, metamorphosis into a serpent, and ultimate translation to **Elysion,** see s.v. **Harmonia** (2).

Kaineus: A **Lapith,** son of Elatos and father of **Korónos** (q.v.). He was famed (as 1.58–64 shows) for his invulnerability, a gift bestowed in curious circumstances by **Poseidon. Kaineus** had originally been a girl, **Kainis,** of whom **Poseidon** was enamoured. At her request, the god gave her a sex change, and made the resultant male invulnerable into the bargain. Thus the **Kentauroi** could only deal with him by battering him into the ground and burying him.

*Kalaïs: One of the sons of **Boreas,** the other being ***Zétes.** Both were Argonauts. They were also winged, though Ap.'s description of wings at their heads and feet (1.219–221, cf. Hygin. *Fab.* 14) does not agree with that given by Pindar (*Pyth.* 4.183; cf. Braswell, 265–66), who locates their wings on their back, presumably at the shoulders, in what was to become traditional angelic iconography. This is also the favorite pictorial representation (*LIMC*, 3.1, pp. 126–33, s.v. "Boreadai";3.2, pls. 11, 15, 20, 26, 30, 47, 49), though one early Lakonian vase (pl. 6) does show them with ankle wings. Ap.'s account of their death at the hands of **Herakles** (1.1300–8) is taken from Akousilaōs (cf. Apollod. 3.15.2); another version has them perishing during their pursuit of the **Harpies.**

Kalaúreia: Island in the Saronic Gulf, mod. Póros, opposite Pogon (mod. Galatás), from which it is separated by a narrow strait. In the interior of the island, on a saddle between two hills, are the remains of an ancient sanctuary of **Poseidon,** where the orator Demosthenes, in retreat from Antipatros's agents, committed suicide by sucking poison through a reed pen.

Kallichóros R.: See s.v. **Fairdance R.**

Kallíope: One of the Nine Muses, daughter of **Zeus** and Mnemosyne (Memory), whose province was epic poetry. By **Oiágros** the mother of ***Orpheus, Kallíope** was represented iconographically with a stylus and tablet (or papyrus roll).

Kallisté: See s.v. **Thera.**

Kalpes R.: A river of **Bithynia,** about midway (according to Xenophon,

Anab. 6.4.1–3), between Byzantion and Herakleia, i.e., east of the **Phyllis R.;** but passed by the Argonauts before they reached the outflow of the **Sangários.**

Kalydon, -onian: A famous city of south **Aitolia,** between the Euenos and **Acheloös** rivers, near modern Mesolonghi. Nearby Mt. Zygos was the site in the Heroic Age of the great **Kalydonian** boar hunt alluded to more than once in these pages: see, e.g., s.vv. **Atalanta, Meleagros.**

Kalypso: A nymph, daughter (according to Homer, whom Ap. follows) of **Atlas** q.v.), and best known for her seven-year entertainment of Odysseus. In Hesiod (*Theog.* 359) her parents are **Ocean (Okeanos)** and **Tethys,** while Apollodoros (1.2.7) names her father as **Nereus.** There was also debate as to her dwelling place: Homer's Ogygia some located off **Krété,** and see also s.v. **Nymphaia.**

Kanastron: The cape at the tip of the long promontory of **Palléné,** the westernmost of the three parallel promontories extending S. into the **Aigaian** from Chalkídiké (see map 1).

Kanéthos: A **Euboian,** son of **Abas** (1) and father of *****Kanthos.**

*****Kanthos:** Argonaut, son of **Kanéthos,** the only member of the expedition to die in combat: killed in **Libya** by **Kaphaúros** (q.v.).

Kaphaúros: A **Libyan,** son of **Amphithemis (Gáramas)** (q.v.) and a **Nymph** from Lake **Triton** (2): slayer of *****Kanthos,** and then himself slain by the **Argonauts.**

Kárambis, C.: A major headland on the coast of **Paphlagonia,** this cape marked the commencement of the **Long Beach** (q.v.), stretching about 100 miles eastward to **Sinopé.**

Kárpathos: A long, sheer, rocky island (Ap.'s "craggy and beetling," παιπαλόεσσα, is accurate) situated about midway on the sunken land bridge between eastern **Krété** and Rhódos (Rhodes).

Kaspian: A title applied generically (a) to the mountains north of modern Teheran, (b) to the pass ("Gates") leading from NW Asia into the NE provinces of Persia, but most generally (c) to the Kaspian Sea (as at 3.859) and the tribes dwelling round its SE shores.

*****Kastor:** Argonaut; one of the two **Dioskouroi,** brother to **Polydeukes.** For variant details concerning their birth, see Apollod. 3.10.5–7, 4.2.4.8. **Polydeukes** was the skilled boxer, and **Kastor** won renown as a famous horseman. Apart from the quest for the Fleece, they also took part in the **Kaledonian** boar hunt, and attacked Athens in order to rescue their sister Heléné, who had been carried off by **Theseus.** For **Kastor**'s death during the cattle-raiding dispute between the **Dioskouroi** and the sons of **Apháreus,** see s.v. *****Idas.**

Kaúkasos: General name for the great mountain range extending from the

Black Sea to the **Kaspian,** and treated by Ap., loosely, as a mountain somewhere in the region of **Kolchis. Aiëtés'** first wife, **Asteródeia,** was a nymph from the **Kaúkasos;** the serpent that guarded the Fleece was also born here (2.1209–13); and it was, of course, the site of **Prometheus's** famous punishment (2.1248–50). The **Kaúkasian Sea** was the easternmost extremity of the **Black Sea** or Euxeinos (Euxine).

Kauliakós: A rocky eminence supposedly located at the division of the **Istros** (Danube), and by some tentatively placed at the junction of the Danube and Sava.

Kekropia, -an: Originally the name of the early settlement on the Athenian Akropolis, so called after Athens's mythical first king, **Kekrops,** whose tomb was shown in the complex of the Erechtheion (see also s.v. **Erechtheus**); afterwards extended as a synonym for **Attika** generally, especially when the supposed autochthonous origin of its inhabitants was being stressed.

Keltoi: A fairly loose appellation for tribes north of the Mediterranean, ranging from Spain in the west to Galatia in the E. For Ap., they are the peoples inhabiting the territory along the **Erídanos** (Po) and the **Rhódanos** (Rhône).

Kéntauroi: The **Kéntauroi,** or Kentaurs, were mythical creatures combining the upper torso of a man with the four legs and body of a horse. Much addicted to wine and rape, they were notorious for their great fight with the **Lapithai** (1.42 ff.). Cf. also s.v. **Cheiron.**

Keos: A small island some thirteen miles off the coast of SE **Attika,** the nearest of the Kykládes to the mainland.

*Képheus: Argonaut, king of **Tegea** in **Arkadia** (q.v.): son of **Aleos** and Neaira. He had no fewer than twenty sons (and two daughters), but he and they all perished in an expedition against the Lakedaimonians led by **Herakles.**

Keraunian Mts.:   These mountains, the name of which (Κεραύνια) means "The Thunderers," and which I have so translated (see 4.518–20), sometimes also known as "Akrokeraunian," i.e. "The Thunderers of the Cape," stretched along the coast of the Adriatic in Epeiros, to the north of the island of **Kérkyra,** terminating in the lengthy Akrokeraunian promontory. Both mountains and promontory acquired their name from the frequent thunderstorms that supposedly took place in the vicinity: they had a reputation for being hazardous to shipping. Some of the **Kolchians** established themselves there (4.518–21, 575–76, 1214–15).

Kérinthos: A small town of NE **Euboia,** home of ***Kanthos.**

Kérkyra: More commonly known as Corcyra, the modern Corfu: a long (38 m.) narrow island offshore from Chaonia in Epeiros (modern Albania), separated from the mainland by a channel less than 2 m. wide at its northern end. **Kérkyra** is Homer's Scheria; Ap. gives it its ancient name of **Drépané** ("The Sickle"). Not to be confused with **Black Kérkyra** (q.v.).

Kerossós: A small island off the Adriatic coast: not securely identified, but from context (4.561–76) to be located just south of **Melíté,** with a long view across open sea towards **Kérkyra.**

Kios: A coastal town of **Mysia,** on the **Kios R.,** at the head of the gulf of the same name that forms the SE extremity of the **Propontis,** and at the foot of **Mt. Arganthonios** (q.v.).

Kirké: Daughter of **Helios** (q.v.) and **Persé,** sister to **Aiëtés,** and thus **Medeia**'s aunt. (Other versions of her provenance exist, but Ap. follows Homer here.) Some doubt existed as to her location— east or west? **Kolchis** or central Italy? Ap. solves the problem by having **Helios** drive her in his fiery chariot from **Kolchis** to **Aiaia** in Latium (q.v.), which is where **Jason** and **Medeia** encounter her. According to Hesiod (*Theog.* 1011–16, possibly a late inter- polation), she bore Odysseus two sons during his stay with her, Agrios and Latinos. Roman poets were not slow to adopt this alien visitor: Ovid makes her responsible for the transformation of Picus into a woodpecker (*Met.* 14.320 ff.).

Klaros: Site of a famous, and extremely ancient, sanctuary and oracle of **Apollo,** about a mile from the coast near Kolophon in Ionia.

Kleité: Daughter of King **Merops** of **Perkóté,** and newly married bride of **Kyzikós** (q.v.). When her husband was killed in error during a night battle by the **Argonauts,** she hanged herself from grief (1.1063–65), and her name passed to a spring formed from the tears that the **Nymphs** shed over her (1.1067–69).

Kleopatra: Daughter of **Boreas** and **Oreithyia,** and sister to **Chióne, Zétes,** and **Kalaïs.** She was the first wife of **Phineus** (q.v.), and bore him two sons, Pandion and Plexippos. However, he then married Idaia, daughter of Dardanos, who (in classic stepmotherly style) accused **Kleopatra**'s sons of raping her. **Phineus** believed her, and either blinded them himself, or allowed Idaia to do so with her sharp loom shuttle. See Apollod. 3.15.2–3, with Frazer's note.

Klymené (1): Daughter of **Minyas** and by Phylakos (or possibly Kephalos) mother of **Alkimédé** (q.v.).

Klymené (2): Daughter of **Ocean** and **Tethys;** wife of **Iapetos,** to whom she bore, among other offspring, **Atlas** and **Prometheus.**

*Klytios: Argonaut from **Oichalia** in **Euboia;** son of **Eurytos** and brother to ***Iphitos.** He inherited the skill at archery of his father, who according to Homer (*Od.* 8.226–28) was killed by **Apollo** for challenging the god to a shooting match: ***Klytios** himself is shown knocking one of the birds of **Ares** out of the sky with a well-aimed arrow (2.1042–45). Both he and his brother were killed by **Herakles** at the taking of **Oichalia** (late sources put the death of **Eúrytos** on this occasion too).

Klytonéos: **Argive** in origin; son of **Naubolos** (1), king of Tanagra in **Boiotia,** and father of *****Nauplios** (2).

Knossós: Royal city of **Minos** on **Krété;** site of the famous Labyrinth.

Koios: One of the **Titans,** son of **Ouranos** and Ge (Earth); the father, by Phoibe, of Asteria, who became a quail and plunged into the sea to escape the sexual advances of **Zeus,** and of **Leto** (q.v.), who was not so reticent and suffered in consequence.

Kolchis, -ians: Originally known as **Aia** (q.v.), the later name for the region's capital, **Kolchis** was a somewhat ill-defined region on the east coast of the **Black Sea,** lying to the south of the **Kaúkasos** mountains, and separated from the E. tribes of Anatolia by the **Phasis** River, which also served as a trading route into central Asia. (Ap., however, seems to envisage **Aiëtés'** kingdom as extending beyond this boundary.) **Kolchis** was rich in timber and other raw materials for shipbuilding; it also contained numerous different ethnic and linguistic groups. Thus the eastern background for the **Argonaut** myth had a solid grounding in fact—though it is at least dubious whether Herodotos's theory (that the dark-skinned, curly-haired **Kolchians** were descended from the remnants of an Egyptian army) was any more historically plausible than the flight of **Phrixos** on the Golden Ram.

Kolóné: An otherwise unknown rocky landmark situated somewhere between the **Rhebas R.** and the **Black Headland.**

Kométes: Father (by Antigone, daughter of Pheres) of *****Asterion.**

Korónis: A **Thessalian,** daughter of Phlegyas, and by **Apollo** the mother of Asklepios, whom she bore by the **Amyros R.** We should note that Ap. here diverges from the common tradition, according to which **Korónis** during her pregnancy became the lover of Ischys, the brother of **Kaineus. Apollo,** learning of this from a messenger crow (or, according to Pindar, through his own omniscience), sent **Artemis** to kill his faithless lover, and turned the crow black for having brought such bad news. He later rescued the unborn Asklepios from **Korónis's** womb when she lay on the funeral pyre, and sent the child to be reared by **Cheiron** (cf. Apollod. 3.10.3, with Frazer's n., vol. 2, pp. 13–15). Asklepios grew up to be a great physician, and was blasted by **Zeus** for bringing mortals back to life. **Apollo** in return killed the **Kyklopes** who had forged the offending thunderbolt, and was forced as a result to spend time in servitude and exile—in the common version of the myth with **Admétos** (q.v.), but as Ap. has it (4.612–17, citing local **Keltic** tradition), among the **Hyperboreans.** It is not clear why Ap. chose to be so discreet in this particular case. Cf. Vian 1981, 37 with n. 3.

*Korónos: Argonaut, son of **Kaineus** from **Thessalian Gyrton.** His son Leonteus was among the suitors seeking Heléné's hand in marriage, and fought in the Trojan War. **Korónos** himself is sometimes also identified as the man of that name who was killed commanding the **Lapithai** against **Herakles;** but this is uncertain.

Korykos, -ian (1): Name of a cave on **Mt. Parnassos,** by which the **Nymphs** of the region were also known.

Korykos, -ian (2): Name of a promontory and cave on the coast of Kilikia, the cave (according to Strabo, 14.5.5, C. 670–71) being famous for the saffron that grew there.

Kourétés (1): Semidivine beings who protected the infant **Zeus** in his cave on **Mt. Ida** (2) in **Krété** by dancing and clashing their weapons to drown his cries.

Kourétés (2): An ancient, perhaps **Pelasgian,** people; originally settled in **Aitolia,** but later driven out into Akarnania: traditional enemies of the **Kalydonians** (Hom. *Il.* 9.529).

Krataïs: According to Ap., a title of **Hékaté,** whom he identifies as the mother of **Skylla** (q.v.); but other sources give **Krataïs** a separate identity: cf. Apollod. *Epit.* 7.20–21, with Frazer's n. 4, vol. 2, p. 293.

Krété, -an: The great island in the southern **Aigaian,** best known in antiquity for its fabled Bronze Age civilization under King **Minos** (hence "Minoan") based on **Knossós.** For Ap., it was primarily notable as the birthplace of **Zeus** and the home of the **Daktyls,** the **Harpies,** the **Kourétés,** and the bronze giant **Talos.**

Krétheus: Son of **Aiolos** (1), brother of **Athamas** (q.v.), by Tyro, father of **Aison,** and thus **Jason**'s grandfather.

Krobialos: A site on the **Paphlagonian** coast, according to Ap. (correcting Homer, apparently from a geographer or author of a *Periplous*) somewhere between the **Erythinian Rocks** and **Kromna** (see map 3).

Krómna: A village between **Krobialos** and **Kytóros;** later one of several settlements that were combined to form the town of Amastris.

Kronos: Father, by **Rhea,** of **Zeus,** whom his mother hid in a cave on **Mt. Ida** (2) to save from **Kronos**'s murderous attentions, since the latter knew himself fated to be overcome by one of his male offspring. He was, however, most notorious for castrating his father **Ouranos** with a sickle (cf. 4.984–86). For his begetting of **Cheiron** on **Phílyra** (q.v.), see 2.1235–41, and Hes. *Theog.* 1001–2.

Ktiméné: A town of **Dolopia,** the mountainous region lying west of **Phthia** in **Thessalia,** near Lake **Xynias,** and traditionally bestowed by **Peleus** on Phoinix.

Ktímenos: Father of ***Eurydamas,** from **Ktiméné** (see above).

Kyklópés: A group of mythical one-eyed beings, around whom various disparate legends accumulated (e.g., in Homer's *Odyssey*, they are savage giant pastoralists living in Sikelia): Ap. refers only to the Hesiodic legend, according to which the **Kyklopes** were three in number, named Brontes, Steropes and Arges ("Thunderer," "Lightener," "Brightshiner"), famed smiths who made the thunderbolts for **Zeus** (1.509–11, 730–34), and were slain by **Apollo** for having supplied the weapon that destroyed Asklepios (see s.v. **Korónis**).

Kyllénos: One of the **Krétan Daktyls,** attendant of the Mother Goddess of **Dindymon** on **Mt. Ida** (2): cf. 1.1126–31 s.v. **Daktyls**.

Kypris: For Ap., as for Homer, the goddess more commonly known as Aphrodíté ("Foam-Born"?) was always **Kypris,** i.e., "the Kyprian," so called, originally, because of her cult at Paphos on the eastern Mediterranean island of Kypros (Cyprus). Like Isis, she had a number of other important local cult centers, e.g., on **Kythera** (hence her alternative title of **Kythereia** [3.108]) and at Corinth. The goddess of sexual passion (and the patron of prostitutes), rather than of marriage or fertility (though there is some evidence for her occasional association with these more domestic attributes), she was also widely worshipped—like Isis later— as a goddess of the sea and seafaring. This last attribute is mildly puzzling, since her only connection with the sea seems to have been her birth from it (in Hesiod's version, *Theog.* 188–93), or more precisely from the foam-encircled genitals of **Ouranos,** that fell into the waves after his castration by his son **Kronos** (q.v.). In Homer, however, she is the daughter of **Zeus** and Dione, and (as for Ap.) married to **Hephaistos,** with **Ares** as her paramour: she is steadily pro-Trojan, and, by Anchises, the mother of Aineias (Virgil's Aeneas).

Kyréné: A **Thessalian** nymph beloved by **Apollo,** who sired **Aristaios** (q.v.) on her, and conveyed her to **Libya,** where she gave her name to the city of Kyréné. Ap.'s account (2.500–509) draws on Hesiod (frs. 215–17 Merkelbach-West) and Pindar (*Pyth.* 9.1–70), though diverging from the latter in many details, e.g., locating her by the **Peneios R.** rather than near **Cheiron**'s cave on **Mt. Pelion.** Nor does Pindar mention her delivery to the **Libyan** nymphs of the **Mount of Myrtles.** Cf. Vian 1974, 271–72.

Kyta, -aian: In **Kolchis,** traditionally the birthplace of **Medeia,** but commonly used as a simple synonym for **Kolchis** and the **Kolchians** generally.

Kythera, -eian: An island off Cape Malea in the southern Peloponnesos, and according to one tradition the birthplace of **Aphrodíté** (**Kypris,** q.v.), who was thus sometimes known as **Kythereia** or "the **Kythereian**."

Kytíssoros: One of the four sons of **Phrixos** (q.v.) by **Chalkíope,** and (according to Ephoros, Strabo 12.3.10, C. 544), the founder of the town of **Kytóros,** between Amastris and **C. Kárambis.**

Kyzikós (1): A large all-but-island situated on the south shore of the **Propontis,** between the **Aísepos** and **Rhyndakos** rivers. The name was also given its the main city, close to the neck of the isthmus. **Kyzikós** was also sometimes known as Bear Island or **Bear Mountain** (q.v.).

Kyzikós (2): Son of **Aineios** and **Ainété,** married to **Kleité** (q.v.), and king of the **Dolionians.** For the oracle compelling him to entertain the **Argonauts,** his accidental death in night battle against them, and the tradition springing from his funeral rites, see 1.961–84, 1030–39, 1054–62, 1075-77, 1136–38; also Apollod. 1.9.18.

Ládon: The dragon that guarded the golden apples of the **Hespéridés.** Ap. is the only source to name this mythical beast, to which he attributes (4.1398) a chthonian origin. According to Hes. *Theog.* 333, its parents were **Phorkys** and Kéto; Pherekydes (*FGrH* 3 F 16) opts for **Typháon** and Echidna. Cf. Vian 1981, 195–96.

Lake of Flowers: In Greek known as Anthemoeisis (not to be confused with the **Sirens'** island of **Anthemoéssa**), this lake was in the vicinity of the **Lykos** (1) estuary, Herakleia, and the **Acherousian** headland in **Bithynia.**

Lakéreia: A **Thessalian** town, on the **Amyros R.** (q.v.), home of the nymph **Korónis.**

Lampeia: The southern part of the **Erymanthos** massif (q.v.) in **Arkadia.**

Lampétië: A daughter of **Helios** (q.v.) by the nymph Neaira, transported when young with her sister **Phaéthousa** to Sikelia to guard her father's flocks. Cf. n. on 4.964–65, 970–78.

*Laokoön: Argonaut from **Aitolia;** half-brother to **Oineus** and tutor of his nephew **Meleagros.** Unknown to the Argonaut canon before Ap., and only mentioned after him by Hyginus. Cf. Vian 1981, 248–49.

Lapithai: A mountain-dwelling **Thessalian** clan, putatively descended from Lapithes, a son of **Apollo** and Stilbé and brother of Kentauros, the ancestor of the **Kéntauroi.** When **Peiríthoös** was leader of the **Lapithai,** being son of **Ixion** (q.v.) and thus half-brother to the **Kéntauroi,** the latter fought the **Lapithai** for a share in the inheritance. Though they were beaten, the quarrel burst out again at the feast celebrating **Peiríthoös's** marriage to **Hippodameía** (2), when the **Kéntauroi** once again suffered a defeat.

Lárissa: A central **Thessalian** town, strategically situated on the south bank of the **Peneios R.,** in a wide plain, with a strongly fortified citadel, and capital of the district known as Pelasgiotis. It still flourishes under the same name today.

Latmos, Mt.:	A mountain chain of NW Karia, in the hinterland behind **Milétos,** chiefly famous for **Endymion** (q.v.) having been sleeping in a cave there when kissed by the **Moon** (**Seléné**).
Laurion:	A plain, otherwise unknown, somewhere in the Upper Danube basin.
Leda:	An **Aitolian,** wife of **Tyndáreus,** who was impregnated in one night both by her husband, and by **Zeus:** just how she bore the resultant children (normally or from an egg?) and just who fathered which child, are questions that remain uncertain (see s.v. *Kastor and further notes referred to there); but between them **Zeus** and **Tyndáreus** were responsible for the **Dioskouroi** (i.e., *Kastor and **Polydeukés**), Heléné, and Klytemnestra.
Lemnos, -ian:	A northern **Aigaian** island, south of **Samothráké** and NW of Lesbos: volcanic in origin (hence its close association with **Hephaistos** (q.v.), and, apart from its notoriety over the "Lemnian deeds" described by Ap. and others, chiefly notable in antiquity as the place where **Philoktétés** was abandoned with his suppurating and malodorous foot wound.
*Leódokos:	Argonaut from **Argos,** son of **Bias** (q.v.) and **Pero,** daughter of Neleus. Not apparently mentioned before Ap.
Lerna, -aian:	A marshy coastal district at the SW end of the **Argive** plain, with many springs and a grove with shrines sacred to **Demeter** and **Dionysos.** It is mainly remembered as the site of one of **Herakles'** labors, the subjugation of the **Hydra** (q.v.), a myth probably enshrining attempts to drain the marshland and control the numerous springs.
Lernos (1):	An **Argive,** son of **Proitos** and father of **Naubolos** (1).
Lernos (2):	An **Aitolian** from **Olénos;** supposed father of *Palaimónios (who in fact was the son of **Hephaistos**).
Leto:	A **Titan,** daughter of **Koios** (q.v.) and Phoibé: one of the few **Titans** who had a cult in classical Greece, in her case mainly because she was the mother, by **Zeus,** of **Apollo** and **Artemis,** to whom she gave birth on the island of **Delos** when no other island would accept her, and despite every effort by a jealous **Hera** to thwart her.
Liburnian Islands:	A group of limestone islands off the coast of **Illyria,** on the latitude of modern Zadar. Probably formed by volcanic upheaval, they tend to be long and narrow, parallel with the coast, and thus aligned NW–SE (see map 4).
Libya, -an:	Originally the name for coastal North Africa between Egypt and the Pillars of **Herakles:** as geographical knowledge developed, the concept of what lay south of this coastal strip changed, but (despited the reported circumnavigation by Phoinikians [Hdt. 4.42]) remained vague. The north coast, however, had been thoroughly explored by Ap.'s day. The eponymous nymph

Libya, daughter of Epaphos and Memphis, became by **Poseidon** the mother of **Agénor** (q.v.). For other North African eponymous legends see, e.g., s.vv. **Akakállis** and **Kyréné.**

Liguria, -an: The coastal region extending, roughly, from Genoa to Marseilles: for the offshore **Ligurian** islands, see s.v. **Echelon Isl.**

Lilybéon, C.: A promontory on the W. coast of **Sikelia** (Sicily), on which was situated the ancient town of the same name (mod. Marsala).

Lokris, -ians: In Ap., the East, or **Opountian, Lokris,** located on a narrow coastal strip of eastern Greece SE of Thermópylai and opposite **Euboia,** and so named from their chief town, **Opous.**

Long Beach: Translation of the Greek Πολὺς Αἰγιαλός, a stretch of over one hundred miles of the **Paphlagonian** coast between **C. Kárambis** and **Sínopé.** See also n. on 2.943–45.

Lykáon: A king of **Arkadia,** son of **Pelasgos** and **Meliboia.** The father of some fifty sons, he was remembered as both a great civilizer and a great blasphemer (not incompatible qualities: look at **Prometheus**). For attempting to trick **Zeus** with cannibal fare, he and all but one of his sons were either fulminated or (appropriately for the name: λύκος, lykos = "wolf") lycanthropized.

Lykastia, -ans: A canton and town of the **Amazons,** traditionally located somewhere between **Themískyra** and the **Chálybes.**

Lykia: A mountainous country facing on the south coast of Asia Minor, bounded on the west by Karia, to the north by **Phrygia** and Pisidia, where the Tauros Mts form the country's frontier, and to the east by Pamphylia, extending as far as Mt. Klimax. **Lykia** was traditionally associated with the worship of **Apollo.**

Lykóreus: A **Bebrykian,** henchman of king **Amykos.**

Lykos: Son of **Daskylos** (1), and king of the **Mariandynians;** entertained **Herakles** in **Mysia** and was aided by him in a battle against the **Bebrykians,** much of whose territory he acquired. Later received the **Argonauts.**

Lykos R.(1): River near Herakleia and a little W. of the **Acherousian** headland (2.724).

Lykos R. (2): Tributary of the **Phasis R.** in Kolchian territory (4.131–35). It should be noted that there are many rivers of this name in the ancient world, especially in Asia: arguably they were so called from the supposed resemblance of a mountain torrent rushing down to a wolf (λύκος, lykos) attacking a sheepfold.

Lykourgos: Son of **Aleos** (q.v.) and Neaira; a mythical king in **Arkadia,** and father (by whom is variously reported) of, among others, *****Ankaios.**

*****Lynkeus:** Argonaut, son of **Apháreus** (q.v.) and **Aréné,** brother to *****Idas,** and famed for the sharpness and penetration of his sight (he could even see things underground). He was one of those who took part in the **Kalydonian** boar-hunt. For his death at **Polydeukes**' hands during a quarrel over cattle-lifting that he and his brother had with the **Dioskouroi**, see s.v. ***Idas.***

Lyra: The spot near the tomb of **Sthénelos,** to the east of the **Acherousian** headland, where ***Orpheus*** dedicated his lyre (hence the name).

Lyrkeian: Epithet of **Argos** (city) and the Argolid, derived from Mt. Lyrkeion, a range forming the natural boundary between the Argolid and **Arkadia.** See s.v. **Argos** (city).

Magnesia, -an: The eastern coastal part of **Thessalia,** extending from the eastern arm of the Gulf of **Págasai** (and including **Págasai** itself) northward almost to the frontier with Makedonia.

Maia: The eldest of the **Pleiadés,** daughter of **Atlas** (q.v.) and Pleione, and by **Zeus** the mother of **Hermes,** whom she bore in a cave on Mt. Kylléné in **Arkadia.**

Mainads: Female devotees of **Dionysos,** inspired by the god to ecstatic frenzy, during which they tore wild beasts limb from limb and ate them raw.

Mainalos, Mt.: A high (5,015 ft.) mountain range of SE **Arkadia,** forming the frontier between Mantinéa and **Tegea** (see map 1).

Makrians: A **Pelasgian** tribe, at war with the **Doliones,** and located on the mainland near **Kyzikós.**

Mákris (1): An ancient name for the peninsula on the east coast of Corfu (anc. Kérkyra; Homer's Schéria, Ap.'s **Drépané**), between the bay of Garitsa and the Khalikiopoulo lagoon, which formed the site of the ancient city (today known as Palaiópolis), just south of its modern successor. The name derived from **Mákris** (2), q.v.

Mákris (2): A daughter of **Aristaios** (q.v.); she cared for the infant **Dionysos** in **Euboia** when the child was brought to her by **Hermes;** but **Hera** drove her out of the island, and she sought refuge with the **Phaiakians** on **Drépané.**

Makrónes: A wild and primitive tribal group located in the hinterland of eastern **Pontos** near Trápezous: both Herodotos (2.104, 7.78) and Xenophon (e.g., *Anab.* 4.8.3, 5.5.18) give descriptions of them.

Mariandynians: A tribe inhabiting the coastal area of the south shore of the **Black Sea** between the **Sangários** and the **Billaios** rivers (see map 3). Their king was **Lykos** (q.v.), who in Ap.'s account entertains the Argonauts.

Medeia: In Ap.'s account, daughter of **Aiëtés** and his second wife **Eidyia,** by whom he also had had **Chalkíope** (q.v.). Other sources make her mother **Hékaté,** daughter of **Perses.** For her precise relationship to her (half-?) brother, see s.v. **Apsyrtos.** For an outline of some of her activities after returning to **Iolkos**, see s.v. **Jason**. It should perhaps also be noted that after fleeing from Corinth to Athens, she married Aigeus and attempted, unsuccessfully, to poison his son **Theseus**, after which she was expelled from Athens too: clearly you couldn't teach this not-so-old witch new tricks. The number (and paternity) of her children is disputed; but most sources agree that she killed her two children by **Jason**, and that Medus, who helped her (with or without **Jason**) to restore her father to his throne in **Kolchis**, was the son of Aigeus.

Megabrontes: A **Dolionian** warrior killed by **Herakles**; his name means "The Loud Thunderer."

Megalossákes: "Big Shield": a **Dolionian** warrior killed by the sons of **Tyndáreus** (**Kastor** and **Polydeukes**).

Megara, -ians: Natives of **Nisaia**, the port of **Megara** on the Saronic Gulf, colonized the southern **Black Sea** port of Herakleia, on the **Acherousian** headland (2.746–49).

Melámpous: Descendant of **Aiolos** (1), q.v.; son of Amythaön by Eidómené (or Aglaia, or Rhódopé), and brother of **Bias**. Best known for his prophetic powers, and for understanding the language of birds (after having his ears licked out by serpents while he was asleep). See also s.v. **Iphiklos** (1).

Melanippé: An **Amazon**, daughter of **Ares** and sister to **Hippólyté** (q.v.). Once carried off by **Theseus** (Apollod. *Epit.* 1.16), she later commanded the Amazons (Diod. Sic. 4.16. 3–4). She was killed by *Télamon.

Melantian Rocks: A landmark near Thera (Santorini), possibly the islet of Makrá, near **Anáphé**.

Melas: One of the sons of **Phrixos** (q.v.) and **Chalkíope**.

*Meleágros: Argonaut from **Aitolia**, son of **Oineus** and Althaia; he married Kleopatra, daughter of *Idas (q.v.) and Marpessa (once again we have an example of intertwined Argonaut relationships). Though represented by Ap. as one of the youngest, yet bravest, members of **Jason**'s crew (he kills two **Dolionian** warriors, and volunteers to undertake **Aiëtés**' test with the brazen bulls), he is not a leading figure in the *Arg.* (In an alternative version, Diod. Sic. 4.48.4, he is represented as killing **Aiëtés** in battle.) But **Meleágros**'s chief claim to fame was always his participation in the great **Kalydonian** boar hunt, during which he killed the boar (sent by a peevish **Artemis** because of **Oineus**'s failure to sacrifice to her). During a quarrel over the spoils of the hunt, involving **Atalanta** (whom he loved) **Meleágros** killed his mother Althaia's brothers. In revenge she burned the half-consumed log on which the Moirai (Fates) had decreed at **Meleágros**'s birth that his life depended, and he died.

Meliboia: A city on the coast of **Magnesia**, by the southern foothills of **Mt. Ossa**.

Mélié: A **Bithynian** nymph, daughter of **Ocean** (**Okeanos**), who became by **Poseidon** the mother of **Amykos** (q.v.). She seems to have been peculiarly susceptible to seduction by gods or demigods: besides **Poseidon,** Inachos, Seilenos, and **Apollo** all sired offspring on her. Her name ($\mu\epsilon\lambda\acute{\iota}\eta$ = "ash tree") suggests that she was originally a Dryad.

Melíté (1):   A **Naiad,** daughter of the river god **Aigaios,** and by **Herakles** the mother of **Hyllos** (q.v.) on the **Phaiakian** island of **Drépané.** A mountain on the island (4.1150) was named after her.

Melíté (2):   A long narrow island off the east coast of the Adriatic, just S. of **Black Kérkyra.**

Menétés: Father of **Antianeira** (q.v.).

*Menoitios: Argonaut from **Lokris,** son of **Aktor** (1) and **Aígina,** daughter of the **Asopos R.** A friend of **Herakles,** he became by Polymélé the father of **Achilles'** companion Patroklos.

Merops: King of **Perkóté** on the **Hellespontos,** between Lampsakos and **Abydos,** and the father of (among others) Adrastos and **Kleité,** the bride of **Kyzikós** (2). He was a well-known soothsayer, and sometimes known as Makar or Makareus ("The Blessed One").

Miletos: The eponymous founder of the coastal city of that name, in southern **Ionia.** Legend had it that both **Minos** and **Sarpedon** competed for his favors in **Krété** when he was a boy: he preferred **Sarpedon,** and **Minos** went to war because of the affront. The lovers fled to Anatolia, where **Sarpedon** became king of **Lykia,** while **Miletos** settled the city that afterwards bore his name.

Mimas (1):   A **Bebrykian,** killed by **Polydeukes** (2.105–9).

Mimas (2):   A Giant, killed by **Ares** (for variants see note on 3.1226–30), who is supposed to have presented his breastplate to **Aiëtés.**

Minos: King of **Krété;** it is possible that the word represents a title (like "Pharaoh") rather than a personal name, and in any case the myths surrounding him clearly contain recollections of **Minoan** civilization as the archaeologists have recovered it. Traditionally, he is presented as son of **Zeus** and **Európé** (2) (q.v.), and married to **Pasiphaë,** daughter of the sun god **Helios.** When he prayed to **Poseidon** for a sign confirming his entitlement as king, the god endorsed him by sending a bull from the sea to sacrifice. It was so beautiful that **Minos** kept it rather than sacrifice it, whereat **Poseidon** caused **Pasiphaë** to fall in love with it. By the connivance of the craftsman Daidalos, the queen coupled with the bull, and the result of this miscegenation was the Minotaur. Daidalos built a maze, the famous Labyrinth, in which to conceal this creature, but afterwards fled **Krété** to escape the vengeance of **Minos. Minos** pursued Daidalos to the kingdom of Kokalos in Sikelia (Sicily), and was there killed by treachery, subsequently becoming a judge among the dead.

Minyas, -ans: Minyas is a shadowy figure in mythic tradition (see n. on 1.228–33), with links to both **Iolkos** and **Orchómenos.** Accounts of both his parentage and his wife, or wives, vary wildly. The best-authenticated legend concerning him suggests that he led a colonizing expedition from **Thessalia** into northern **Boiotia** and established **Orchómenos** as his capital: the travel writer Pausanias (9.38.2) saw there what was thought to be his treasury, but in fact was a tholos-type "beehive" tomb of **Mykenaian** provenance and date. He was also regarded as the eponymous ancestor of the "**Minyan**" Argonauts, through the marriages of his various daughters; but evidence for this is largely wanting.

Moon (Seléné): Always rather shadowy as a deity, and more often (e.g., in magical practices) regarded as the moon *tel quel*, **Seléné**'s main anthropomorphic adventure (referred to at 4.54–66, when the goddess is venting her frustration on **Medeia**, whose magic cramped her style, see n. ad loc.) was her passion for **Endymion** (q.v.). She was supposedly the offspring of two **Titans**, Hyperion and Theia, and sister—for obvious reasons—to **Helios** (q.v.) and the personified Dawn, Eos.

*Mopsos: One of two diviners recorded as having lived during the Greek Bronze Age (the other is dated to after the Trojan War: the name recurs in a bilingual eighth-century inscription from Karatépé, which suggests both historicity and either a family or a guild connection). The earlier ***Mopsos,** the one to whom Ap. refers, was son of **Ampykos** or **Ampyx** by the nymph Chloris, and resident seer to the **Argonauts:** for examples of his divination on their behalf see 1.1083–1106, 3.543–55. He was famous for understanding the language of birds. A **Thessalian Lapith,** who is on record as having participated both in the **Kalydonian** boar hunt and in the great battle with the **Kéntauroi** at the wedding of **Peiríthoös,** he escorted **Jason** to his fateful meeting with **Medeia** (3.927–47, 1163–66), once more using his knowledge of bird talk to advise his leader. For his death from snakebite in **Libya,** see 4.1502 ff.

Mossynoikoi, -ians: A primitive and (in every sense) rude tribe on the south shore of the **Black Sea,** located by Ap. between the **Tibarénoi** and the **Philyrians** and **Makrones** (others, however, locate them further w.). The name of their towerlike dwellings, *mossynes,* appears to be Iranian. Xenophon (*Anab.* 5.4, passim) confirms many of the customs described by Ap., including that of public copulation. He also gives an account of the system of royal justice: penalties for corruption or incompetence were severe.

Mount of Myrtles: A famous North African headland in the neighborhood of Kyréné, where the eponymous nymph **Kyréné** strangled a lion (Pind. *Pyth.* 9.25 ff.), and stood with her lover **Apollo** to watch the men of **Thera** dance with the blonde local women (Kallim.

Hymn 2.85–95: he calls it "horned Myrtoussa," Μυρτούσσης κερατώδεος). A temple to "**Apollo** of the Myrtles [μυρτώῳ]" has been excavated there—the **Theraian** colonists made the headland their acropolis–and reportedly myrtles still grow abundantly in the area.

Muses (Mousai): Greek minor deities, traditionally the offspring of **Zeus** and Mnemósyné, and found earliest at sites in **Pieria** and **Boiotia:** hence the regular epithet of "**Pierian**" and the association with Mt. Helikon. They were regarded as the divine source of creative inspiration, more specifically in the spheres (not so differentiated as we tend to conceive them) of poetry, music, art, and dance. The canonical number of nine— **Kallíope** (q.v.), Klio, Euterpé, Terpsíchoré, **Erató** (q.v.), Melpómené, Thalia, Polyhymnia, Ourania—is vouched for by Hesiod, though numerous later variants are found. The notion of specialist functions for each **Muse** (e.g., epic for **Kallíope**) did not fully develop till Roman times. Ap. thus can have fun punning on the supposed erotic associations of **Erató**'s name: she was not yet firmly attached to lyric poetry and hymns. The **Muses** have few myths of their own.

Mygdonia(ns): Name of a tribe, and area, located between the **Sangários** and **Hypios** rivers, i.e., south and west of the **Mariandynians** (q.v.), to whose king, **Daskylos** (1), **Herakles** subjected them. They are not to be confused with the Mygdonians located in Makedonia or Mesopotamia, though the eponymous Mygdon, who raised an army against the **Amazons** at the **Sangários R.** (Hom. *Il.* 3.184 ff.), should probably be regarded as the ancestor of a subsequently widely scattered people.

Mykenai: The great Argolid city best known for its Lion Gate and the events described in Aischylos's *Oresteia.* At the time of the Argonauts' quest, it was ruled over by **Eurystheus** (q.v.: see 1.128).

Myrína: In antiquity as today, the chief city of the island of **Lemnos,** located on a rocky promontory between two excellent anchorages on the west coast.

Myrmidon(s): A son of **Zeus** by Eurymedousa ("Wide-Ruler"), and regarded as the eponymous ancestor of the **Myrmidons** in **Phthia** of **Thessalia.** For the tradition that **Achilles**' father **Peleus** was originally from **Aígina,** and brought the name "**Myrmidons**" with him, see Apollod. 3.12.6, 13.1; Strabo 9.59, c.433.

Myrtilos: The charioteer of **Oinomáos** (q.v.).

Mysia(ns): For Ap., the **Mysians** are found both in the area to the east and south of the **Propontis,** by the **Kios R.,** and further E, well beyond the **Sangários R.,** in the area to the south of the **Mariandynians** (q.v.). It is not clear whether both groups ever formed part of a united **Mysia** or represent, as so often, episodes of tribal migration. In historical times **Mysia** lay far further W, on the **Aigaian,** its south boundary being formed by Mt. Temnos and Lydia.

Naiads: A category of **Nymph** (q.v.) specifically associated with rivers and springs. Ap. presents them as attendants both of **Kirké** (4.710–11) and of the child **Achilles** in **Cheiron**'s home (4.811–13).

Narex: One of the mouths of the **Istros R.,** which, according to Ap., skirted the north side of **Peuké** (Pine Island): 4.311–15. See Delage 1930a, 204–5.

Násamon: A **Libyan,** the eponymous ancestor of the Nasamones tribe: son of **Amphithémis** by a local nymph.

Naubolos (1): An **Argive,** king of Tanagra in Boiotia, son of **Lernos** (1) and father of **Klytónéos.**

Naubolos (2): King of **Phokis,** son of **Ornytos** (1) and father of *Iphitos (2).

Nauplios (1): An **Argive,** son of **Poseidon** by **Amymoné;** father of **Proitos,** and thus grandfather of **Lernos** (1).

***Nauplios** (2): Argonaut, son of **Klytonéos,** and thus descended from **Naubolos** (1). Offers to steer *Argo* after the death of **Tiphys** (2.896–97).

Nausithoös: Father of **Alkínoös** (q.v.) and king of the **Phaiakians** on **Drépané** (Scheria, Corfu). Entertains **Herakles** (4.539–41) after the latter's murder of his children.

Neleus: Twin son, with **Pelias** (q.v.) of **Poseidon;** founder of the **Neleid** dynasty at **Pylos** (we also find a branch at **Kyzikós** [1.959]), and father of, among others, Nestor, **Pero,** and *Periklymenos.

Nepeian Plain: Schol. 1.1116 places this "in the general area of Kyzikós" and makes it fairly clear that it is an alternative name for the plain of **Adrasteia** (q.v.), between the Granikos and **Aísepos** rivers.

Nereus: One Greek version of the Old Man of the Sea (for another see s.v. **Phorkys,** his brother): son of Pontos ("The Deep") and Gaia (Earth), and father by Doris of the fifty Nereids. He possessed the gifts of prophecy and metamorphosis, and was particularly associated with the **Aigaian.**

Nestaian(s): Name of a tribe located on the E. (**Illyrian**) coast of the Adriatic.

Nisaia(ns): The original **Nisaia,** on the Saronic Gulf, was the port of **Megara** (q.v.). Emigrant Megarians in **Kyzikós** (2.747, 847) are thus described by Ap. as **Nisaians.**

Nykteus: By Polyxo (not **Hypsípylé**'s nurse) the father of **Antíopé** (1) (q.v.), who fled his house when he threatened her because of her pregnancy by **Zeus.**

Nymphaía: Ap. mentions this as **Kalypso**'s island, placing it in the eastern Adriatic (4.573–75); but he is the only source to do so, and may well have invented the location.

Nymphs: Local spirits of trees (Dryads, Hamadryads), mountains (Orestiads), springs (Kreneids), rivers (Potameids), water generally (Naiads, Hydriads), etc., and, less often, of specific locations: always represented as young women (νύμφη in Greek = unmarried maiden or bride), fond of music and dancing, and with a penchant for taking human lovers (cf. the story of **Hylas** and the Naiad, 1.1207–39). One kind of frenzied state provoked the epithet νυμφόληπτος, *nympholeptos,* i.e., "possessed by nymphs." Such beliefs still persist in the Greek countryside today.

Nysa, -aian: Traditionally the name of the place where **Dionysos** was born, and thus found at numerous sites in Europe and Asia (Delage 1930a, 36). Ap. however seems to be the only source who locates "Nysa's plain" in Egypt, east of the Nile Delta, and near **L. Serbónis** (q.v.).

Ocean (Okeanos):   The great stream generally believed, at least till Herodotos's day (see Introd., pp. 16, 27) to encircle the flat disk of Earth. **Argos** (2) describes the **Istros R.** as a branch of **Ocean** (4.282); one branch of the **Rhódanos** (Rhône) is similarly said (4.631–32) to discharge into it. But at the same time, with that non-visualizable anthropomorphism so often attributed by Greek tradition to rivers, **Ocean** is also referred to as the husband of **Tethys,** and the father of numerous offspring, including (in addition to the collective **Oceanids**), **Cheiron**'s mother **Phílyra** (2.1238–39), and the **Hespéridés** (4.1414).

Oiágros: King of **Thraké** and father of *Orpheus (q.v.).

Oiaxos, -ian: A town on **Krété** dating back to Minoan times, now known as Axos, and perched on a hill about 12 miles north of **Mt. Ida** (2) (q.v.). Ap. and other writers use it as a synonym for **Krété** as a whole.

Oichalia: Town near Eretria on **Euboia,** and ruled over by **Eúrytos** (q.v. for his dealings with **Herakles** and **Apollo**).

Oileus: Argonaut, king of the **Lokrians,** and father by Eriopis of Aias (Ajax): renowned for his courage in battle (1.74–76).

Oineus: King of Pleuron and **Kalydon** in **Aitolia** (q.v.), and by Althaia the father of Tydeus and *Meleágros.

Oinoíe: Ancient name for one of the the Kykladic islands: so called after the **Naiad** who took in **Thóas** (q.v.) after his escape from **Lemnos,** and became by him the mother of a son, **Síkinos,** who gave his name to the island in historical times.

Oinomáos: King of **Elis** and father of **Hippodameia.** See s.v. **Pelops**, and, for a conspectus of sources, Frazer vol. 2, 157–61.

Olénos: Town in southern **Aitolia,** home of **Lernos** (2).

Olympos, Mt.:   One of the highest (9,754 ft.) and certainly the most impressive of Greek mountains, situated on the east coast of **Thessalia** and extending northward from the Tempe Gorge as far as

	the southern marches of Makedonia. In myth, **Olympos** was regarded as the home of the gods, reaching as it did far above the clouds into the clear vault of heaven.
Onchéstos:	Town in Boiotia, in Haliartian territory, near Lake Kopaïs: traditionally founded by a son of **Poseidon** of that name, and inhabited by **Hyantians** (q.v.). It contained a famous grove and shrine of **Poseidon.**
Ophión:	A **Titan,** sometimes known as **Ophioneus,** married to **Eurynomé** (q.v.), and one-time ruler on **Olympos** before being driven out by **Kronos** (q.v.) and **Rhea.**
Opous, Opountian:	See s.v. **Lokris.**
Orchómenos:	City of northern **Boiotia,** founded by **Minyas** (q.v.), and ruled over later by **Athamas** (q.v.). It was from here that **Phrixos** and **Hellé** fled on the magic ram. The city, as usual, took its name from an eponymous king of that name, according to some the actual founder: thus **Chalkíope**'s assumption (3.265–66) had a basis in tradition.
Oreites:	A **Bebrykian,** squire to **Amykos:** some MSS give his name as **Oreides.** In the melee following **Amykos'** death, he wounds *****Tálaos** (2.110–3).
Oreithyia:	Daughter of **Erechtheus** by Praxithea: carried off by **Boreas** (q.v.) while playing by the **Ilissos** stream in Athens, and bore to him (besides other offspring) the winged brothers *****Zétes** and *****Kalaïs.**
Orikon:	Town on the east coast of the Adriatic, near the outfall of the Aoös River in Epeiros: a party of **Kolchians** settled there (4.1214–15).
Orion:	The famous mythical hunter, after death catasterized as a constellation, which is Ap.'s only reference to him: associated with winter rains (1.1201–2) and regularly used as a steering point by sailors (3.745–46).
Ornytos (1):	A **Phokian,** father of **Naubolos** (2).
Ornytos (2):	A **Bebrykian,** squire to **Amykos;** helps bind the leather strips on his fists for the boxing match against **Polydeukes** (2.65–66).
*****Orpheus:**	Argonaut, picked for the expedition on **Cheiron**'s advice (1.32–34): for Ap., a son of **Oiagros** and the Muse **Kallíope** (q.v.). His early connection with the Argonauts is confirmed by a metope of c. 570 B.C. discovered under the treasure-house of the Sikyonians at **Delphoi.** The founder of Orphism and a magically talented musician, he could charm rocks and trees with his playing (1.26–31) and got his companions safely past the lure of the **Sirens** (4.905–11). Perhaps best known for his failed attempt to bring his dead wife Eurydiké back up from **Hades.**

Ortygia:	Early name ("Quail Island") for **Delos** (q.v.).
Ossa, Mt.:	A high (6,490 ft.) mountain lying immediately south of the Tempé Gorge and **Mt. Olympos** in **Thessalia,** with the long ridge of **Pelion** (q.v.) beyond it. In their battle with the Gods, the Giants attempted to pile **Pelion** on **Ossa** in order to scale the heights of **Olympos.**
Othrys, Mt.:	A long mountain chain in **Thessalia,** extending east from the Pindos range through **Phthiótis** to the sea, and forming the southern boundary of the great **Thessalian** plain.
Otréré:	Daughter or wife of **Ares,** and queen of the **Amazons,** who reputedly built not only (as we might expect) the shrine on the Isle of **Ares** (2.385–87), but also the great temple of **Artemis** at Ephesos.
Ouranos:	The heavens or sky personified: son (and/or husband) of Ge or Gaia (Earth), and father of numerous assorted offspring, including various **Titans,** the **Kyklópés, Iapetos,** and **Kronos.** These he either swallowed or confined in **Tartaros** until castrated by **Kronos** and dethroned. From the bloody drops of this act, nurtured by Ge, sprang the **Giants** (q.v.).
Págasai:	Port of **Iolkos** in **Magnesia,** situated in the northernmost inlet of the landlocked gulf of the same name (today the Gulf of Volos): the traditional departure point and final landfall for the Argonauts at the outset and conclusion of their expedition.
Paktólos R.:	A small river flowing down from Mt. Tmolos in Lydia (Asia Minor), famous in antiquity for two things: the gold dust carried down in its alluvial mud (reputedly the source of Kroisos's wealth), and the swans that frequented it (4.1301–2).
*Palaimónios:	Argonaut from **Aitolia;** by repute a son of **Lernos** (2), but in fact sired by **Hephaistos** and, like him, lame (1.202–6).
Pallas:	See s.v. **Athena.**
Palléné:	The westernmost of the three long promontories of Chalkidike extending SSE into the northern **Aigaian;** once known as **Phlegra** and by tradition the scene of the original conflict between Gods and Giants.
Paphlagonia, -ans:	A people, and extensive territory, lying along the south coast of the **Black Sea,** between the **Billaios** and **Halys** rivers, and covering the whole stretch of the **Long Beach** (q.v.). Ap. places them between the **Mariandynians** to the west and the **Amazons** and **Chálybes** to the east.
Paraibios:	For Ap. a friend, but for other sources (schol. 2.456–57) a faithful slave, of **Phineus.**
Parnassos, Mt.:	A southern spur of the Pindos range, some 8,200 ft. high, looking out on the north side of the Gulf of Corinth and best

known as the setting of **Delphoi,** perched on its south face above the Pleistos Valley.

Parthenia: Ancient name ("Maiden Isle") for **Samos** (q.v.).

Parthenios R.: The most important river of W. **Paphlagonia,** between **Sésamos** and the **Billaios R.,** and traditionally associated with **Artemis,** who was believed to bathe in it and hunt along its banks.

Pasiphaë: A daughter of **Helios** (q.v.) and Perseïs (and thus sister to **Kirké** and **Aiëtés**); married to **Minos** (q.v.), and the mother of (among others) **Ariadné,** Phaidra, and (by somewhat spectacular miscegenation) the Minotaur.

Peirésia(i): Ap. (1.37–39) describes this **Thessalian** hometown of *Asterion as lying at the confluence of two tributaries of the **Peneios R.,** the **Apídanos** and the **Enípeus,** close to Mt. Phylleion (exact site uncertain).

Peiríthoös: One of the **Lapithai** (q.v.), married to **Hippodameia** (2), and a close friend of **Theseus.** The two of them later agreed to wed daughters of **Zeus; Peiríthoös** helped **Theseus** carry off Heléné, and in return **Theseus** descended with his friend to **Hades** in pursuit of Perséphoné. They were, however, caught and bound fast there: **Herakles** managed to rescue **Theseus,** but **Peiríthoös** never escaped. He and **Theseus** became a stock example for Roman poets of devoted male friendship.

Pelasgia, -an: Ap. uses this term to indicate autochthonous **Thessalians,** but the more general usage in historical times was as a blanket label for any **Aigaian** tribe regarded as "aboriginal" rather than "Hellenic" (i.e., immigrant from the north).

***Peleus:** Argonaut from **Aígina,** son of **Aiakos** and brother of *Télamon; both brothers were driven out by their father after conspiring in the murder of their half-brother **Phókos. Peleus** fled to **Phthia,** where he was befriended by *Eurytion (whom long afterwards he accidentally slew during the **Kalydonian** boar hunt). For his marriage to, and relations with, **Thetis** (q.v.), on whom he sired **Achilles** (q.v.), see 4.780–817, 851–79, and Vian 1981, 175–6. For further interesting details of his life, see s.v. *Akastos.

Pelias: Son of **Poseidon** by Tyro, and brother of **Neleus** (q.v.): Tyro was in love with the river god **Enípeus,** in whose likeness **Poseidon** sired both brothers on her— which may explain why, later, when married to her uncle **Krétheus,** the brother of **Athamas** (q.v.), and mother of **Jason**'s father **Aison** (q.v.), she exposed them. Whether **Pelias** denied his stepbrother **Aison** the throne of **Iolkos** after the death of **Krétheus,** or only acceded after **Aison**'s own death (accounts differ: the first version seems more likely), there was (and for good reason) no love lost between them. He clearly dispatched **Jason** to **Kolchis** in the hope that

the expedition would prove fatal; and it seems to have been
on this assumption that he finally did away with **Aison.** His own
death at the hands of his daughters, persuaded by **Medeia** that
by cutting him up and boiling him they could achieve his reju-
venation, thus can be viewed as no more than rough justice. His
son **Akastos** (q.v.) held famous funeral games for him, attended
by heroes from all over Greece, and then exiled both **Medeia**
and **Jason** from **Iolkos** for their part in his father's death.

Pelion, Mt.: A high (5,300 ft.) forest-clad mountain chain immediately south
of **Ossa** (q.v.) on the coast of **Magnesia,** rising steeply from the
sea, and running down as far as C. Sepias. It was traditionally
the home of the **Kéntauroi** (including **Cheiron**), also the scene
of **Akastos**'s attempt to get **Peleus** eaten by wild beasts, and of
Peleus's own first encounter with **Thetis.**

Pelléne: The easternmost of the cities of **Achaia** in the northern Pelo-
ponnesos, close to Sikyon, and one of the oldest cities in
Greece. The **Argives** derived its name from an eponymous
Pellen, the father of **Hyperásios.**

Pelopeia: A daughter, along with Alkestis, of **Pelias,** and sister to **Akastos.**

Pelops: Son of Tantalos by Dione, daughter of **Atlas,** and king of Pisa in
Elis, coming to the throne by way of marriage to **Hippodameia**
(2) (q.v.), daughter of **Oinomáos,** the then king. For the peculiar ordeal, with overtones of incest as well as charioteering,
that won him his future wife's hand, see Frazer, vol. 2, 157–61
(full conspectus of sources). His own childhood was marked by
the peculiar incident of Tantalos killing, cooking, and serving
him up to the gods to see whether they could tell the difference
between animal and human flesh. They could, doomed
Tantalos to eternal punishment for blasphemy, and revivified
the dead boy (all except a bit of his shoulder, snacked on in
error by **Demeter;** this was replaced by an ivory prosthesis).
Pelops gave his name to the Peloponnesos ("Pelops's Isle"),
and for Ap. is also the ancestor of the **Paphlagonians.**

Peneios R.: The chief river of **Thessalia,** rising in the Pindos range and
emerging into the central plain near the Meteóra rock-monas-
teries: from here it flows south as far as **Trikka** (Trikkala), and
then turns E, finally reaching the sea through the Tempe gorge.

*Periklymenos: Argonaut, son of **Neleus** and Chloris, and thus brother to Nestor. He enjoyed the special favor of **Poseidon,** who granted him
superhuman strength and the ability, like Proteus, to change his
form. This did not save him, after the expedition, from being
slain by **Herakles** at the capture of Pylos.

Perkóté, -kosian: Town of **Mysia,** on the **Asiatic** shore of the **Hellespontos,**
between **Abydos** and Lampsakos: the home of **Merops** (q.v.).

Pero: Daughter of **Neleus** and Chloris, and married to **Bias** (q.v.).

Persé: A daughter of **Ocean** (q.v.), and married to the sun god **Helios,** to whom she bore **Aiëtés, Kirké,** and **Pasiphaë**—a group, one might have thought, calculated to give any mother pause. Sometimes known as **Perséïs.**

Perséphoné: Daughter of **Zeus** and **Demeter** (q.v.), and often known simply as Koré ("The Maiden"). Abducted by Plouto to **Hades,** she was sought by her mother, who got **Zeus** to request her return. Forced to comply, Plouto gave **Perséphoné** a pomegranate on departure: by eating it, she committed herself to his realm. Eventually an agreement was reached by which she spent one-third of the year (the winter months) in **Hades** and the rest in the upper world. The story is a classic vegetation myth.

Perses: A **Titan,** son of Krios and Eurybia, and reputed father of **Hékaté** (q.v.). The **Perses** recorded as the son of **Helios** and **Persé,** and thus brother to **Aiëtés** and **Kirké,** may be a doublet of this character.

Perseus: Son of **Danaë** (q.v.) and **Zeus.** When Polydektes, king of the island of Seriphos in the **Aigaian**—where **Danaë** and her child were washed up in the chest to which her father, Akrisios, had consigned them—wanted the grown **Perseus** out of the way, the better to overcome the resistance of the lad's mother, he sent him off to bring back the head of Medousa, the Gorgon who could petrify at a glance. **Perseus** avoided this fate by sighting Medousa in a mirror to decapitate her, and on his return used the Gorgon's head to turn Polydektes and his whole court to stone.

Pétra: As its name suggests, a rocky mountain stronghold on the marches of **Thessalia** and Makedonia, and at various times claimed by both countries.

Peuké: An island, roughly triangular, dividing the two southernmost mouths of the **Istros** (Danube), and thus named (**Peuké** = "Pine Island") from the abundance of pine forest growing on it.

Phaëthon: Son of **Helios,** though sources differ as to his mother. Best known for persuading his father to let him, for one day, drive the chariot of the Sun: unable to control its horses, he came so near the Earth that he was in danger of destroying it by fire. To save the situation, **Zeus** blasted him with a thunderbolt, and his charred corpse fell into the **Erídános** (Po). See also s.v. **Heliádes** and for an extended narrative, Ovid *Met.* 2.1–400.

Phaëthousa: A daughter of **Helios** by Neaira, and joint guardian of the **Thrinákian** cattle of the Sun with her sister **Lampétië** (q.v.).

Phaiakian(s): The population of **Drépané** (Homer's Scheria, later **Kérkyra,** modern Corfu), q.v.

*Pháleros: Argonaut from Athens, son of Alkon and reputed grandson of

	Erechtheus; he is supposed to have given his name to the Athenian roadstead of Phaleron.
Phasis R.:	The main river of **Kolchis,** discharging into the east end of the **Black Sea** somewhat south of the mountains of the **Kaúkasos,** and long regarded in antiquity as the boundary between Europe and **Asia.**
Phérai:	One of the oldest cities in **Thessalia;** ruled over by **Admétos** (q.v.). **Págasai** served as its port.
Phílyra:	A daughter of **Ocean,** and by **Kronos** the mother of **Cheiron** (q.v.).
Philyrians:	A tribe of the SE **Black Sea** region, occupying the coast and an offshore island between the **Mákrones** and the **Mossynoikoi.**
Phineus:	Son of **Agénor,** and formerly king of Salmydessos in **Thraké,** where his first marriage was to **Kleopatra** (q.v. for further details). His second wife, Idaia, accused his sons by **Kleopatra** of making improper advances to her, and either blinded them herself or persuaded **Phineus** to do so. There are several variant accounts of why **Phineus** himself was blinded, exiled to **Thynia,** and persecuted by the **Harpies:** one is that this was the gods' punishment for his cruelty to his sons by **Kleopatra.** The version Ap. follows, however, stresses **Phineus's** role as seer and prophet, and attributes his misfortunes (in the *Arg.* he is very much victim rather than offender) to **Promethean** lèse-majesté, for having revealed to mankind the plans of **Zeus** concerning the future.
Phlegra, -aian:	See s.v. **Palléné.**
***Phleias:**	Argonaut, son of **Dionysos** and Chthonophyle, from **Araithyréa** (q.v.), afterwards known as **Phleious,** on the borders of the **Argolid.**
Phlógios (1):	A **Dolionian** warrior, killed by **Kastor** and **Polydeukes.**
Phlógios (2):	One of the three sons of **Deïmachos** (q.v.).
Phoibos:	See s.v. **Apollo.**
Phokis, -ians:	A small Greek state on the north side of the Gulf of Corinth, tucked in between **Lokris** and **Boiotia,** and centered on **Mt. Parnassos.** Its chief importance was due to the fact that the great oracular shrine of **Delphoi** lay in **Phokian** territory: **Phokis** had originally controlled it (cf. 1.207–10) and continued to dispute this right with the **Delphians,** who administered the shrine (with some intermissions) in historical times.
Phókos:	A son of **Aiakos** and the nymph Psamathé. Because he outdid his legitimate half-brothers ***Peleus** (q.v.) and ***Télamon** as warrior and athlete, they murdered him, and were driven out of **Aígina** as a result.
Phorkys:	An "Old Man of the Sea," son of Pontos ("The Deep") and Ge

or Gaia ("Earth"), brother of **Nereus** (q.v.), and of Kéto ("Sea-Beast"), on whom he incestuously sired the Graiai, Gorgones, and **Hespéridés.** By **Hékaté** (or **Krataïs**) he was the father of the monster **Skylla.**

Phrixos: Son of **Athamas** (q.v.) and Nephélé ("Cloud"), and brother of **Hellé.** As a result of machinations by Ino, **Athamas**'s second wife, **Phrixos** was to be sacrificed to **Zeus;** but with Nephélé's help, and that of **Hermes,** brother and sister escaped by air on the magical golden ram. **Hellé** (q.v.) was drowned en route, but **Phrixos** reached **Kolchis,** sacrificed the ram (its fleece was hung up in a sacred grove and guarded by an unsleeping serpent), and married King **Aiëtés'** daughter **Chalkíope,** by whom he had four sons: **Argos** (2) (q.v.), **Melas, Phrontis,** and **Kytíssoros.** Divergent accounts are given of his later life and death (he returned to **Orchómenos** or was killed by **Aiëtés** in response to an oracle); but Ap. (2.1150–51) follows the version according to which he died peacefully of old age, still in **Kolchis.**

Phrontis: The youngest of the sons of **Phrixos** (q.v.) and **Chalkíope.**

Phrygia,-ans: For Ap., the region adjacent to the southern shore of the **Propontis,** from the **Hellespontos** in the west as far east as the **Rhyndakos R.,** and more commonly known as "Hellespontine Phrygia."

Phthia, -ótis: The southernmost extremity of **Thessalia,** bordered in the east by the Gulf of **Págasai,** in the south by the Maliac Gulf, and to the west by the foothills of the Pindos range.

Phylaké: A town in **Phthia,** home of *Iphiklos (1) (q.v.).

Phyllis R.: A river debouching into the **Black Sea** from **Bebrykian** territory, roughly midway between the **Rhebas** and the **Kalpes:** its name is uncertain (Psyllis?), since in anthropomorphic guise it/he was, as usual, masculine; the father of **Dipsakos** by a local marsh nymph (2.652–57).

Pieria: The region immediately north of **Mt. Olympos** as far as the Haliakmon R. in Makedonia, traditionally the birthplace of the **Muses** (q.v.) and of **Orpheus.** When their cult was introduced into **Boiotia,** a new set of associations developed (e.g., with Helikon).

Pimpleia: A mountain range in **Pieria,** traditional site of the birth of **Orpheus.**

Pityeía (1): A coastal town of **Mysia,** between Parion and Priapos, near the entrance from the **Hellespontos** into the **Propontis.**

Pityeía (2): One of the **Liburnian Isl.** (q.v.) lying along the NE coast of the Adriatic.

Pleiadés: Originally the seven daughters of **Atlas** (q.v.), the **Pleiadés** were metamorphosed into a constellation close to Taurus—either after committing suicide out of grief at the death of their father (or perhaps that of their sisters the Hyadés), or else to escape the unwelcome attentions of **Orion.** Their setting was in late autumn.

Pleistos R.: A river flowing into the valley of that name from **Mt. Parnassos,** below **Delphoi.** Anthropomorphized, **Pleistos** was the putative father of the nymphs associated with the **Korykian** (1) cave on the mountain.

Po, R. See s.v. **Erídános R.**

*Polydeukes: Argonaut, twin brother of ***Kastor** (q.v. for further details).

*Polyphémos: Argonaut, from **Lárisa** in **Thessalia,** son of Elatos ("Pine-Man"), and one of the **Lapithai** (q.v.), with whom in youth he fought against the **Kéntauroi.** A friend of **Herakles,** he married that hero's sister Laónomé. Left behind in **Mysia,** he went on to found the city of **Kios** (q.v.), and died fighting against the **Chálybes.**

Polyxo: The old nurse of Queen **Hypsípylé** on **Lemnos,** and a noted seer.

Pontos: See **Black Sea.**

Poseidon: Son of **Kronos** and **Rhea,** and thus **Zeus**'s brother: the Olympian god of the sea, of horses, and of seismic disturbance. With **Apollo,** he built the walls of Troia for Laomedon. He married the sea nymph **Amphitríté** (q.v.), a powerful lady who controlled a good deal more than his chariot. Nevertheless, his liaisons were as numerous and as varied as those of **Zeus** himself: among his offspring encountered in the *Arg.* are **Amykos,** by **Mélie; Ankaios** (2), by **Astypálaia; Euphémos,** by **Európé** (1); **Nauplios** (1), by **Amymoné; Pelias,** by Tyro; and **Triton** (3), actually by **Amphitríté.** A headland in **Mysia** (1.1279) was named after him.

Priolas: A **Mariandynian,** son of **Daskylos** (1) and brother of **Lykos** (q.v.).; killed in battle against the **Mysians.**

Proitos: An **Argive,** son of **Nauplios** (1) and father of **Lernos** (1).

Prometheus: Son of the **Titan Iapetos** by **Klymené** (2), and father of **Deukálion** and Hellen (mother disputed in each case). Since he not only attempted to deceive the gods (in the matter of sacrificial offerings), but also over various issues—the possession of fire, knowledge of skills and arts, ignorance of (and thus hope for) the future, rescue from mass destruction—benefited and gave knowledge to humankind against the will of **Zeus,** he was punished by being nailed to a rock in the **Kaúkasos,** where an eagle daily gnawed away his liver, which then miraculously regrew itself overnight in preparation for another round of torture next day. See Hes. Theog. 521 ff., Aisch. *PV* 1022 ff., and on the magical herb *prometheion,* supposedly sprung from **Prometheus**'s spilt blood, schol. *Arg.* 854–59 f.

Prómeus: A **Dolionian** warrior killed by **Idas.**

Propontis: The modern Sea of Marmora, a largely landlocked stretch of water connecting the **Aigaian** with the **Black Sea** by way of the **Hellespontos** (Dardanelles) and the **Bosporos;** mentioned by Ap. chiefly in connection with the large near-island of **Kyzikós** (2), situated midway along its southern shore.

Pylos: The seat of the Neleïd dynasty in western Messenia: probably to be identified (the Homeric epithet of "sandy" would seem to confirm this) with the site on the rocky Koryphasion (Palaio-chorti) peninsula at the north end of Navarino Bay, linked by a sandspit to the mainland, and close to the island of Sphakteria.

Pytho: Ancient name for the oracular shrine of **Delphoi,** traditionally (but probably in error) explained as having been occasioned by the rotting (πύθειν) of the monstrous guardian serpent slain by **Apollo.**

Rhea: Daughter of **Ouranos** and Ge (Gaia), and thus sister to **Ocean** and **Iapetos;** wife of **Kronos** (q.v.), to whom she bore, among others, **Zeus, Poseidon, Demeter,** and **Hera.** Identified with the Mother-Goddess **Kybélé** (q.v.) of **Mt. Dindymon,** and thus known in the region as **Dindyméné** (q.v.). In this capacity she remains for Ap. an avatar of the Great Mother, worshipped in a number of guises throughout the Near East.

Rhebas R.: A small river a few miles east of the **Bosporos,** flowing north out of **Bithynia** into the **Black Sea.** Except as a marker for the Argonauts (2.349, 650, 789), it has virtually no history.

Rhipaian Mts.: "Hyperborean" (i.e., unknown and of vaguely northern lo-cation) range of mountains supposed to be where the **Istros** had its headwaters: see further n. on 4.282–93, 3.

Rhódanos R.: Today, the Rhône, which rises in the mountains of Switzerland, at a height of over 12,000 ft., flows west and south through the Alps down to the Lake of Geneva (still some 1,200 ft. above sea level), and thence by way of Lyon and Arles to the Mediter-ranean, an overall distance of more than 500 miles. On Ap.'s beliefs concerning its course and related geography, see Dufner vol. 1, 128–72.

Rhoiteion: A promontory on the coast of the Troad, near the entrance to the **Hellespontos.**

Rhyndakos R.: A large river of eastern **Hellespontine Phrygia,** at one time forming the border between **Phrygia** and **Bithynia,** flowing NW into the **Propontis** by way of Lake Apollonia.

Salamis: The island offshore from **Attika** and **Megara** in the Bay of Eleusis: colonized by *****Télamon** (q.v.), who ruled there after his flight from **Aígina.**

Salángon R.: A river of **Illyria,** mentioned only by Ap., possibly located by Salona in Dalmatia.

Salmónis, C.: The most striking promontory at the north end of the extreme eastern coastline of **Krété,** today known as Cape Sidero.

Samos, Samian: One of the largest islands of the eastern **Aigaian,** lying close offshore between Ephesos and **Miletos. Hera** had a major cult there, and the island, known in early times as **Parthenia,** was the home of **Ankaios** (2) (q.v.).

Samothráké: High (over 5,000 ft.) mountainous island of the northern **Aigaian,** lying NE from **Lemnos** and opposite the estuary of the Hebros R. in **Thraké;** best known for its mystery cult of the Kabeiroi.

Sangários R.: One of the largest rivers of Asia Minor, the **Sangários** in early times formed the eastern frontier of **Bithynia.** It discharged into the **Black Sea** between the territories of the **Bebrykians** and the **Mariandynians.**

Sapeires: A tribe described by Ap. as occupying the area of the eastern Asia Minor littoral between the **Becheirians** and **Byzerians.** Herodotos refers to them as "Saspeirians" and locates them between **Kolchis** and Media.

Sarmatians: A **Skythian** people located to the north of **Kolchis** (and, according to Herodotos, east of the Don R.): sometimes by Greek writers also called Sauromatai. Mentioned by Ap. only on account of their frequent wars with the **Kolchians.**

Sarpedon's Rock: A landmark by the **Ergínos R.** (q.v.), where **Boreas** first possessed **Oreithyia.**

Seléné: See **Moon.**

Sepias, C.: Promontory of **Magnesia,** located at the SE extremity of the long arm of land that closes off the Gulf of **Págasai** from the **Aigaian,** facing the island of **Skiathos.** It was here that *Peleus traditionally lay in wait for the nymph **Thetis** (q.v.).

Serbónis L.: For this lake, on the Syrian-Egyptian border, see Hdt. 3.6, q. Vian 1974, 284.

Sésamos: A coastal town on the southern shore of the **Black Sea,** located in **Paphlagonian** territory E. of the **Parthenios R.,** near the tribe of the **Enétoi.**

Sigynnoi: A trans-Danubian people associated by archaeologists with the Hallstatt culture, and marked by their exploration of the river (Ap.'s **Istros**) for commercial development.

Síkinos: Son of **Thóas** by the nymph **Oinoíe;** the eponymous colonizer of the island of **Síkinos** in the southern Kykládes.

Sindi, -ans: A people located by Ap. along the imagined course of the **Istros** from its source in the **Rhipaian Mts.** before its bifurcation at **Kauliakós,** from where the eastern arm flowed out to the **Black Sea,** while the west one emptied into the **Sea of Kronos** (Adriatic).

Sinopé: The daughter of the river god **Asopos,** and well named (σινώπη = "mustard"), since she contrived (according to the version of her myth used by Ap.) to stand off the sexual advances—always with the same simple trick—of **Apollo,** the **Halys River,** and **Zeus** himself, a formidable trio. However, according to other sources (e.g., Diod. Sic. 4.72.2), **Apollo** not only carried her off to the future site of the city named after her (on the eastern frontier promontory of **Paphlagonia**), but sired a son, Syros, on her, who afterwards became the eponymous founder of **(As)syria** (q.v.), later Kappadokia.

Sintians: A **Thrakian** tribe, supposedly the original inhabitants of **Lemnos.**

Siphai: A coastal village in the NE corner of the Gulf of Corinth, in the territory of **Thespiai,** west of Aigósthena.

Sirens (Seirénes): Accounts of these mythical creatures' names, parentage, nature, number, and dwelling place vary considerably. What is common to all versions (apart from a clear genesis in maritime folktale) seems to be their magical ability to enchant those who heard their song, the earliest (and best-known) account being that of Homer in the *Odyssey,* when Odysseus's crew had their ears stopped with wax while passing them, but Odysseus himself was tied to the ship's mast in order to hear their song and still survive (*Od.* 12.166–200). They are generally located somewhere along the Campanian coast: Ap.'s **Anthemoéssa** (see Strabo 1.2.13, c. 22–3) goes back as far as Hesiod. Ap.also states that their parents were the river god **Acheloös** and the **Muse** Terpsichoré. For the difficulties in reconciling literary and visual versions of the **Sirens** (the latter tended to be anthropomorphized birds, with clear Oriental associations: late poetic explanations of their wings varied), see Frazer vol. 2, 291 n.2. One tradition reports that if anyone got past them unmoved, they would die: both **Orpheus** (4.891–92) and Odysseus supposedly did so, and the story of the **Sirens** throwing themselves into the sea as a result and being turned into rocks is applied to both incidents, leaving one to guess which got into circulation first.

Skiathos: The nearest to the **Magnesian** coast of the Northern **Spórades** island chain, **Skiathos** lies midway between **C. Sepias** and Skopelos: like **Mt. Pelion** on the mainland opposite, it is still heavily forested today, besides possessing some of the finest beaches in the **Aigaian.**

Skylla: Daughter of **Phorkys** by **Hékaté** (or **Krataïs:** whether a separate individual or an epithet of **Hékaté**'s is uncertain). In Homer, she is already a kind of double act with **Charybdis** (q.v.), both being famous mythical hazards for travelers in the Straits of Messina. **Charybdis,** as a maelstrom or whirlpool that sucked down men and boats, defeated the Greek anthropomorphizing urge; but

Skylla (possibly as the result of deadly *pharmaka* surreptitiously dropped in her bathing pool by a sexually jealous **Kirké**) was transformed from an alluring woman into a voracious monster, described by Homer as possessing six long necks and heads, with razor-sharp rows of teeth, a kind of nightmare giant squid. (Another account locates her center of voracity in her groin, all ringed with barking dogs, an early version of that nervous male fantasy the *vagina dentata*). See 4.825–31.

Skythia, Skyths: A people, and area, the definition of which varied throughout ancient history, but used loosely by Ap., as by other Greek writers, to denote the vast region of eastern Europe and western Asia lying north and NE of **Thraké,** roughly between the Karpathians and the Don.

Sparta: Home of the sons of **Tyndáreus:** the ancient kingdom (also known as Lakedaimon) located in the upper part of the fertile **Peloponnesian** valley of the Eurotas R, and protected on either side by the great mountain ranges of Taygetos and Parnon.

Sphódris: A **Dolionian** warrior killed by *****Akastos.**

Spórades: A group of small islands—**Anáphé, Hippouris, Thera**—immediately south of the Kykládés in the **Aigaian.** They should not be confused with the chain today known as the **Spórades:** that is, the **Skiathos**-Skopelos-Halonnesos group, of which the proper title is the *Northern* Sporádés.

Sthénelos: Son of **Aktor** (3); accompanied **Herakles** on his expedition against the **Amazons:** his ghost rises from its barrow (2.911–22) to greet the Argonauts.

Stoichádés: See s.v. **Echelon Isl.**

Stymphalos: A plain and, particularly, a large lake, ringed with mountains, in the NE part of **Arkadia.** The lake is best known for the birds that **Herakles** dislodged from it (2.1052–7).

Styx, R.: A high and inaccessible waterfall in NE **Arkadia,** above the town of Nonakris, the **Styx** descends by a rocky watercourse to join the Krathis R. Its waters were supposed to represent the most sacred oath by which even the gods (e.g., **Hera** in Homer) could swear. Later poets treated the **Styx** as one of the six rivers of **Hades,** and appear to have believed that it actually reached the underworld, an assumption encouraged by the cave-riddled limestone landscape of the Peloponnesos.

Sun: See **Helios.**

Symplegades: See **Clashing Rocks.**

Syrtes: The Greater and Lesser Syrtes in antiquity corresponded to what are today known as the adjacent gulfs of Gabés and Sidra, on the North African coast. They had a bad reputation with sailors (exploited by Ap. to the full) for combining a wild desert coastline, which is true, with sunken reefs, quicksands, and other similar hazards for ships, the dangers of which seem to have been much exaggerated.

Tainaron, C.: The southernmost promontory of Lakonia in the Peloponnesos, today known as C. Matapan. **Tainaron** in antiquity was sacred to **Poseidon,** and also contained a famous cave thought to be one of the descents from the upper world to **Hades** (see **Styx**).

*Tálaos: Argonaut, the son of **Bias** (q.v.) and **Pero,** great-grandson of **Krétheus,** and king of **Argos.** His own children included Adrastos and Eriphyle.

Talos: A man or automaton of bronze, reputedly the work of **Hephaistos,** given to **Minos** (q.v.) either by **Zeus** or by **Hephaistos** himself, and used by **Minos** as a peripatetic guardian of **Krété,** walking three times round the island daily. To discourage strangers, **Talos** would either throw rocks at them, or else heat himself red-hot and then seize and burn them in his metal embrace. Most sources attribute his death to **Medeia,** who (in one way or another—putting him into a magic sleep, promising to make him immortal, or, as in Ap.'s version, hexing him into stumbling) contrived that the ankle-plug holding in his vein of vital fluid should be removed. Other variants have ***Poias** shooting an arrow into his ankle's vulnerable membrane, or the **Boreads** dispatching him.

Taphians: The name of a group of small islands off the west coast of Greece between Leukas and Akarnania: their inhabitants (also known as Taphians) were notorious for piracy.

Tegea: One of the oldest cities of **Arkadia** (q.v.), located in the SE corner of **Arkadian** territory, between the Argolid and Lakonia: home of ***Amphídamas** and ***Képheus** (q.v.).

*Télamon: Argonaut, son of **Aiakos** and Endeïs, and brother of ***Peleus** (q.v. for the circumstances of their exile from **Aígina**). **Télamon** went to **Salamis,** the rule of which was bequeathed to him by Kychreus. Like so many Argonauts, he also took part in the **Kalydonian** boar hunt. A friend of **Herakles,** he accompanied that hero against the **Amazons,** killing **Melanippé.** He was the father (by different women) of both Ajax and Teukros.

Telekles: **Dolionian** warrior killed by **Herakles.**

Téleon (1): A **Lokrian,** father of ***Erybótes** (q.v.).

Téleon (2): An Athenian, son of Ion, and by Zeuxippé father of ***Boútes** (q.v.).

Tenos: A Kykladic island in the **Aigaian,** between Andros and **Delos;** once known as Ophioussa through being snake-infested (**Poseidon** sent storks to keep them down). Ap. commemorates **Tenos** as the site of the **Boreads'** slaying and burial by **Herakles.** Today the island has a miracle-working ikon of the Virgin that draws

thousands of pilgrims on the Feast of the Assumption (15
August).

Terpsíchoré: One of the nine **Muses,** wife of the river god **Acheloös** and
mother of the **Sirens** (q.v.); she presided over choral song
and dancing.

Tethys: Daughter of **Ouranos** and Ge (Gaia), and married to **Ocean**
(q.v.), to whom she bore **Asopos,** Inachos, the **Oceanids,** and
Eidyia, who became the second wife of **Aiëtés.**

Thébé: The nymph who gave her name to Egyptian Thebai: daughter
either of **Triton** (1)—the version followed by Ap.—or the river
god **Asopos,** or of Proteus. Yet another **Thébé,** daughter of
Prometheus, is on record as eponym of **Thebes** in **Boiotia.**

Thebes: Along with **Orchómenos** in the north, the chief city of **Boiotia;**
situated in the southern plain, and divided from **Attika** by the
Kithairon-Pastra range. **Thebes** was one of the oldest cities in
Greece, as its mythic history, extending well back beyond the
Trojan War, makes very clear.

Theiódamas: King of the **Dryopians** (q.v.), and father of **Hylas,** the occasion
of his being killed by **Herakles.** See also n. on 1.1211–20.

Themis: A rather uncomfortably personified abstraction of "the done
thing," "proper order," or "conventional morality." Represented as daughter of **Ouranos** or **Helios** and Ge (Gaia, Earth),
she was at one time married to **Zeus:** their children, too—
e.g., the Hours, Justice, Peace, Good Government—carried
their mother's incurably abstract genes. Alone among **Zeus**'s
other women, she was friendly with **Hera;** abstractions offer
no sexual competition. What interests Ap. is her role as seer
(she is said to have succeeded Ge and preceded **Apollo** as
the prophetic occupant of the **Delphic** oracle), in particular,
her alarming revelation to **Zeus** (when that concupiscent
deity was hot for **Thetis**) that **Thetis** would bear a mightier
son than his father (4.800–2)—another good reason for **Hera**'s
friendship.

Themískyra: The name of a plain, promontory, and town on the southern
shores of the **Black Sea,** between **Paphlagonia** and the territory
of the **Chálybes,** immediately east of the **Thérmodon R.** The
area was identified in myth as belonging to the **Amazons** (q.v.):
in addition to Themískyra they were associated with two other
towns, **Chadésia** and **Lykastia.** In later times the promontory
was known as C. Herakleion.

Thera: Volcanic island, the largest of the **Spóradés** group (q.v.) in the
southern **Aigaian,** today known as Santorini. The name was,
according to mythic tradition, given by **Théras** (q.v.) to replace
the island's earlier appellation of Kallisté, "the most beautiful"
(4.1763–64).

Théras: Son of **Autesion,** former king of **Thebes** (q.v.), and thus great-great-grandson of Polyneikes. From **Sparta** (whither his father had emigrated), he led colonists—including the descendants of those **Lemnian** women impregnated by the **Argonauts,** who had similarly sought refuge in the Peloponnesos—to the island of **Kallisté/Thera** (q.v.).

Thérmodon R.:   A navigable river supposedly having its source in the "**Amazonian** Mountains" and discharging into the **Black Sea** a little to the E of **Themískyra** (q.v.).

Theseus: Son of Aigeus, king of Athens (or, in one version, of **Poseidon**), and of Aithra, daughter of Pittheus, king of Troizen, in the **Argolid, Theseus** was the most important Athenian mythical figure and the subject of innumerable legends, including everything from the slaying of the Minotaur to the unification (συνοικισμός) of **Attika,** two events that, if historical, would be separated by four or five centuries. The two episodes of interest to Ap. (1.101–4, 3.997–1001, 4.433–34) are his marriage to **Ariadné** in **Knossós** and subsequent abandonment of her on the island of **Dia** (Naxos), and his expedition to **Hades** with **Peiríthoös** (q.v.). Abduction seems to have been a habit of his: he had already—long before Paris—carried off the twelve-year-old Heléné, clearly a nymphet who, right from the start, enjoyed being the center of male attention.

Thespiai, -an: An ancient city of **Boiotia,** SE of Askra near the foot of Mt. Helikon, looking south towards the Gulf of Corinth. Home of **Tiphys** (q.v.).

Thessalia, -an: The largest independent territory of northern Greece, its great central plain defined on all sides by mountain ranges: in the W, the great backbone of the Pindos; to the S, the **Othrys** chain; down the east coast, the ramparts of **Pelion, Ossa,** and **Olympos;** and in the N, acting as a frontier between **Thessalia** and Makedonia, the Kambounian range, an extension of the **Keraunian Mts.** (q.v.).

Thestios: An **Aitolian,** son of Agénor grandson of Aitolos (or, by some accounts, of **Ares,** and the father of *****Iphiklos** (2) and—his chief claim to fame—**Leda** (q.v.).

Thetis: A sea nymph, daughter of **Nereus** and Doris, and one of the **Nereids.** She was brought up by **Hera.** When she came of age both **Zeus** and **Poseidon** (despite the fact that he was her grandfather) made a play for her. **Zeus** was put off by the prophecy of **Themis** (q.v.) that **Thetis** would bear a son greater than his father, and combined with **Hera** to marry her off to **Peleus** (q.v. for further details of their relationship), a match she desperately resisted, but in vain. The union produced **Achilles,** thus fulfilling the prophecy.

Thóas:	Son of **Dionysos** and **Ariadné,** and king of **Lemnos.** When the **Lemnian** women killed their husbands in one night, **Thóas** was saved by his daughter **Hypsípylé** (q.v.), cast adrift in a boat or chest, and rescued by a nymph, **Oinoíe** (q.v.), on the island of that name, afterwards known as **Síkinos.**
Thraké, -ia(n):	**Thraké** or **Thrakia** was the name given to an originally some-what loosely defined area of northeastern Greece, between **Makedonia** and the **Black Sea,** and bounded to the north by **Skythia** and the **Istros R.** (Danube): the home of **Boreas** and his sons, of **Oiágros** and **Orpheus,** and of **Phineus,** originally a **Thrakian** king.
Thrakian Harbor:	The eastern port of **Kyzikós** (1) (q.v.).
Thrinákia:	The ancient name for Sikelia (Sicily): sometimes **Trinakria.**
Thunderers, the:	See s.v. **Keraunian Mts.**
Thynia, -an:	The Thynians occupied the area on the European side of the **Bosporos,** in the hinterland of what became the city of Byzantion. **Phineus** lived here in exile from his **Thrakian** kingdom. At some point emigrants crossed into Asia, occupying the area that became **Bithynia.**
Thynias:	A small offshore island located a little beyond the **Kalpes R.** in **Bebrykian** territory; for the Argonaut landing there see 2.672–721.
Tibarénoi:	A tribe on the southern shore of the **Black Sea,** located between the **Chálybes** and the **Mossynoikoi.** Their practice of *couvade* had parallels in other areas, e.g. Corsica (Diod. Sic. 5.14).
*Tiphys:	**Argonaut,** the pilot of *Argo.* Son of **Hagnias,** from **Thespiai.** An expert helmsman, he was sent to **Jason** by **Athena** (1.106–10), but died en route to **Kolchis,** among the **Mariandynians** (2.851–63).
Tisai:	A promontory on the coast of **Magnesia.**
Titans:	The older pre-**Olympian** deities, children of **Ouranos** (Heaven) and Ge or Gaia (Earth): they included **Ocean, Iapetos, Rhea, Themis, Tethys,** and **Kronos.**
Titias (1):	See s.v. **Daktyls.**
Titias (2):	A **Mariandynian** boxer defeated by **Herakles** (2.783–5) during the funeral games for **Priolas.**
Tityos:	A **Giant,** the son of **Zeus** and **Elára,** and father of **Európé** (1). Prodded by **Hera** into making an indecent assault on **Leto,** he was as a result shot by **Apollo,** and hurled down into Tartaros, where his extended body covered nine acres, and a pair of vultures (as in the parallel case of **Prometheus**) devoured his liver.
Trachis:	A city on the Malian Gulf, at the foot of Mt. Oita, and near Thermopylai, where **Herakles** sent his **Mysian** hostages (1.1355–57).

Traukénioi:	A **Skythian** tribe located by Ap. on the **Istros** (Danube).
Trikka:	A town of **Thessalia,** the modern Trikkala, situated near the junction of the Lethaios and **Peneios** rivers, and the home of **Deïmachos.**
Triton (1):	The tutelary river god of the **Neilos** (Nile) in **Egypt,** and father of **Thébé** (q.v.).
Triton (2):	A (possibly mythical) lake not far distant from the coast of **Libya,** sometimes known as **Tritonis** or **Tritonitis,** and according to some sources the birth-place of **Athena;** cf. Aisch. *Eum* 292–3. For a discussion of the geographical problems, see Delage 1930a, 261–70.
Triton (3):	The resident marine deity of **Triton** (2), also known as **Eurypylos.** From Pausanias (9.21.1), we learn that there were a number of **Tritons,** with roughly identical features, in particular a human upper body but the forked tail of a dolphin: this matches Ap.'s description (4.1610–16). The best-known **Triton,** son of **Poseidon** and **Amphitríté,** is mentioned by Homer (*Il.* 13.20): conch and sea horse seem to have been later additions to the iconography.
Tritonian:	See s.v. **Athena.**
Tyndáreus:	A **Spartan,** of uncertain parentage: among his siblings were **Apháreus,** Penélopé's father Ikarios, and **Arété,** who married King **Alkínoös** of the **Phaiakians.** Driven from **Sparta** by the machinations of his stepbrother Hippokoön, he found refuge in **Aitolia** with **Thestios** (q.v.), whose daughter **Leda** he married. One night both he and **Zeus** (as swan) had intercourse with her. The resultant combined impregnation produced **Polydeukes,** Heléné, **Kastor,** and Klytemnestra. Tradition most often credits the first two to **Zeus,** the others to **Tyndáreus,** but sources are by no means unanimous. When Heléné was besieged by suitors, **Tyndáreus** took the advice of Odysseus (in recompense for which he persuaded Ikarios to betroth Penélopé to him) and bound the suitors by oaths to protect Heléné's eventual husband against any wrong done him. Hence the Trojan War. When **Kastor** and **Polydeukes** were translated to heaven, **Tyndáreus** invited that husband, Agamemnon's brother Meneláös, to take over his kingdom of **Sparta.**
Typháon, -onian:	A monster from the earliest stratum of Greek religion (frequently, as in *Arg.*[see 2.38–40, 1209–15], treated as identical to **Typhóeus,** though for Hesiod Typháon is the latter's offspring). Ap. follows the tradition according to which Earth (Ge), enraged at **Zeus**'s blasting the **Titans** down to Tartaros, engendered a motley array of **Giants,** of which **Typháon** was one. Reputed father of Kerberos, the Chimaira, the Lernaian Hydra, and (most relevant for Ap.'s purposes)—after defeat

	by **Zeus,** when banished to the **Kaúkasos**—of the magic serpent that guarded the Fleece.
Typhóeus:	See s.v. **Typháon.**
Tyrrhenia, -ans:	Basically, the Greek name for the Etruscans and Etruria: the **Tyrrhenian Sea** was that part of the Mediterranean that washed the west coast of central Italy. The name is complicated by the fact that early Greek writers (e.g., Hdt. 1.94) assumed that the **Tyrrhenians** (Τυρρηνοί, Τυρσηνοί) colonized Etruria from Lydia (Dionysios of Halikarnassos and modern scholarship tend to believe them indigenous to Italy): this would explain their reported expulsion of **Euphémos**'s descendants from **Lemnos** (4.1760).
Wandering Rocks:	These rocks (in Greek Πλαγκταί), both mobile and volcanic, are located by Ap. in what later came to be known as the Straits of Messina, between Italia and Sikelia, and not to be confused with the **Clashing Rocks** (Συμπληγάδες) at the entrance of the **Bosporos** to the **Black Sea.**
Xanthos R.:	An important and partially navigable river of **Lykia,** which rose in the Tauros Mts.: its name (ξάνθος = "yellow," "tawny") is indicative of the alluvial silt it washed down.
Xynias, L.:	A lake of southern **Thessalia,** near **Ktiméné** in **Dolopia.**
Zelys:	A **Dolionian** warrior, slain by *****Peleus.**
***Zétes:**	Argonaut, brother of *****Kalaïs** (q.v. for further details) and son of **Boreas** and **Oreithyia.** Their sister **Kleopatra,** the wife of **Phineus** (q.v.), was—according to a tradition Ap. does not use— rescued by them from prison, to which she had been consigned at the instigation of **Phineus**'s second wife, Idaia.
Zeus:	The chief **Olympian god,** "father of gods and men": son of **Kronos** and **Rhea,** brother of **Poseidon, Demeter,** and **Hera** (to whom he was married). Ap. mentions his childhood in the cave on **Krété,** and some of his less successful attempted amours (**Sinopé, Thetis**): the homosexual motive for his abduction of **Ganymédés** is emphasized (3.115–16). Though his powers are made clear, he remains very much offstage and out of the action, though he does save **Phrixos** (and nurses a grudge against the **Aiolids** in consequence), gives the **Argonauts** a favoring wind for their voyage, and punishes **Phineus** (though relenting over his pursuit by the **Harpies**). His most notable anger comes after the murder of **Apsyrtos** (4.557–61, cf. 577, 585); we are probably intended by Ap. to assume that this anger was intensified by the secret plotting of **Hera** and **Athena** (3.8–10).

Maps

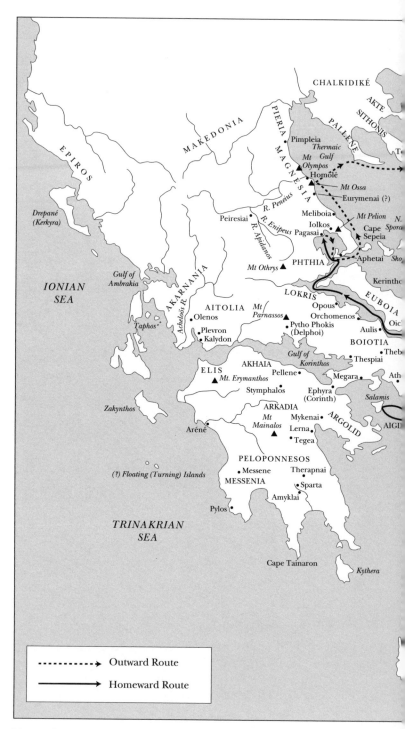

Map 1. The Voyage of *Argo*: The Aigaian

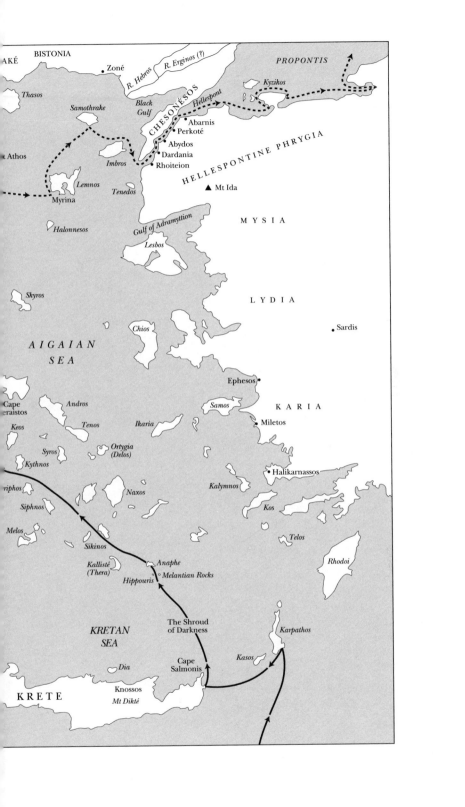

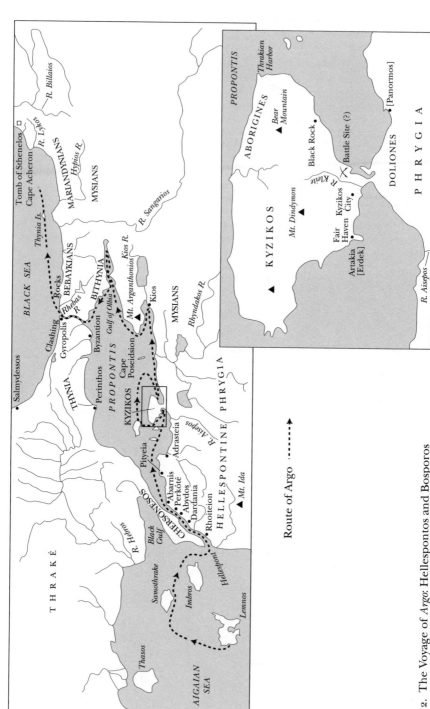

Map 2. The Voyage of *Argo*: Hellespontos and Bosporos

Route of Argo ·······▶

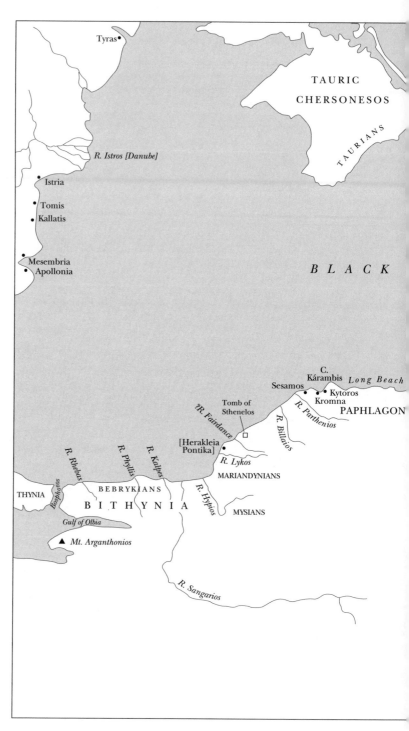

Map 3. The Voyage of *Argo*: The Black Sea

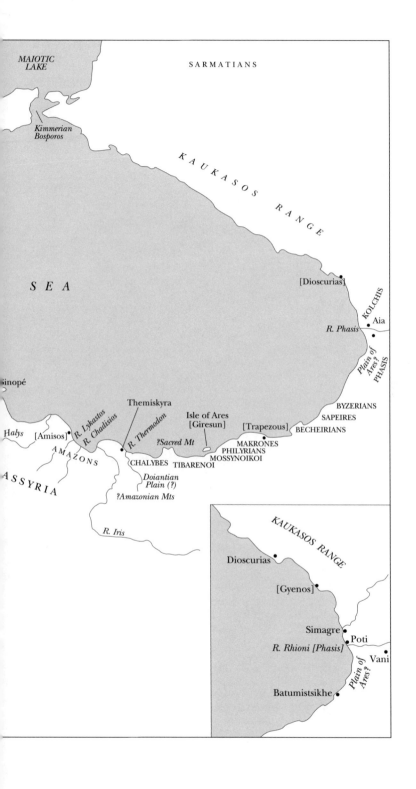

MAIOTIC
LAKE

SARMATIANS

*Kimmerian
Bosporos*

K A U K A S O S   R A N G E

S E A

[Dioscurias]

KOLCHIS

R. Phasis   Aia

*Plain of
Ares?*   PHASIS

Sinopé

BYZERIANS

Themiskyra   SAPEIRES

Isle of Ares   BECHEIRIANS
Halys   [Amisos]   *R. Lykastos*   [Giresun]   [Trapezous]
R. Chadisios
AMAZONS   *R. Thermodon*   MAKRONES
?Sacred Mt   PHILYRIANS
CHALYBES   MOSSYNOIKOI
TIBARENOI

ASSYRIA   *Doiantian
Plain (?)*

?Amazonian Mts

R. Iris

K A U K A S O S   R A N G E

Dioscurias

[Gyenos]

Simagre
Poti
R. Rhioni [Phasis]
Vani

*Plain of
Ares?*
Batumistsikhe

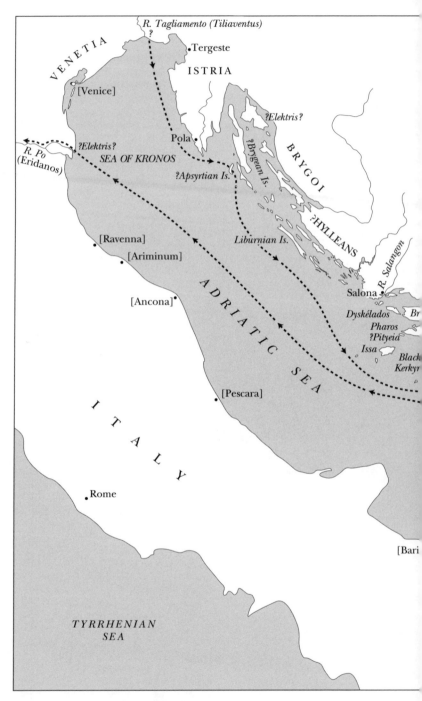

Map 4. The Voyage of *Argo*: The Adriatic

Route of Argo ------▶

ESTAIANS

? Kerossós
[Dubrovnik]

Melité

R. Rhizon   I L L Y R I A

?ENCHELEANS

IONIAN
GULF   Epidamnos

Brundisium [Brindisi]

Tarentum   ?Nymphaia ○   AMANTES
                                  Orikon
GULF OF   Keraunian Mts   EPIROS
TARENTUM   KERAUNIAN
                SEA

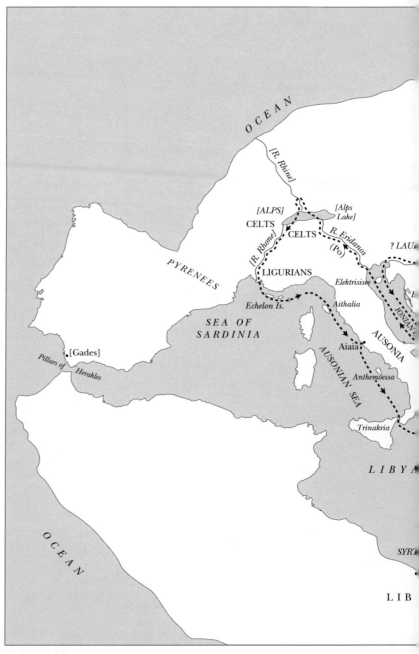

Map 5. *Argo*'s Return Voyage

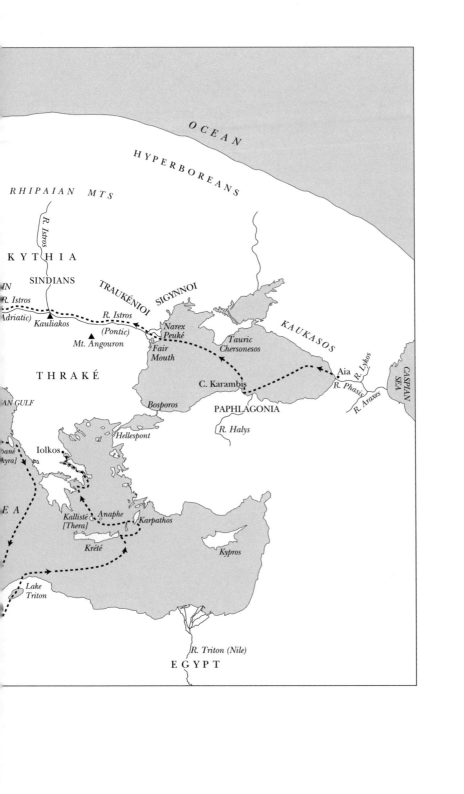

OCEAN

HYPERBOREANS

RHIPAIAN MTS

R. Istros

KYTHIA

SINDIANS

TRAUKÉNIOI SIGYNNOI

IN

R. Istros
(Adriatic)

Kauliakos

R. Istros
(Pontic)

▲
Mt. Angouron

Narex
Peuké

Fair
Mouth

Tauric
Chersonesos

KAUKASOS

Aïa
R. Lykos

R. Phasis

R. Araxes

CASPIAN
SEA

THRAKÉ

C. Karambis

Bosporos

PAPHLAGONIA

R. Halys

AN GULF

Hellespont

bané
kyra]

Iolkos

E A

Kallisté
[Thera]

Anaphe

Karpathos

Krété

Kypros

Lake
Triton

R. Triton (Nile)

EGYPT

INDEX

Compositor:	Integrated Composition Systems, Inc.
Text:	Baskerville
Display:	Baskerville
Printer:	Braun-Brumfield
Binder:	Braun-Brumfield